From Impotence to Authority

FROM IMPOTENCE TO AUTHORITY

The Spanish Crown and the
American Audiencias, 1687–1808

Mark A. Burkholder

D.S. Chandler

University of Missouri Press
Columbia & London

Copyright © 1977 by
The Curators of the University of Missouri
University of Missouri Press, Columbia, Missouri 65201
Library of Congress Catalog Card Number 76-45742
Printed and bound in the United States of America

Library of Congress Cataloging in Publication Data

Burkholder, Mark A.   1943-
    From impotence to authority.

    Bibliography: p.
    Includes index.
    1. Judges—Spain—Colonies. I. Chandler, Dewitt
Samuel, 1938-   joint author. II. Title.
Law   347' .46'014   76-45742
ISBN 0-8262-0219-5

To John Tate Lanning
in memoriam

Preface

In this study, we have endeavored to explain the evolution and suggest effects of the Spanish crown's policy in selecting jurists for the high courts (*audiencias*) of its empire in the Americas and the Philippines. The text rests principally upon examination of the background and objective qualifications of the 693 men named to the royal audiencias between 1687 and 1821, the length of time audiencia ministers served, statements reflecting the crown's intentions and interpretations of its policy, and, to a lesser degree, American reaction to that policy. Emphasis is given to the place of birth of appointees to judicial office and the sale of audiencia appointments and other privileges. On the basis of these materials, we offer new interpretations of both the crown's attitude toward creoles and the participation of these white Americans in colonial government.

We have not attempted to explain the actual functioning of the American courts, nor have we sought to prove behind-the-scenes local influences and networks of patronage. Instead, we have limited the study to defining the pressures that affected appointments to the audiencias, spelling out the changing trends of royal policy toward audiencia membership and showing the results of that policy on the makeup of the courts in America over a period of 134 years. Directly and by implication we raise serious issues that we hope other scholars will investigate. What was the extent of the webs of economic and kinship ties, traceable in notarial and other local records, that connected audiencias with important local families? Were these ties and the conditions we describe responsible for fluctuating standards of justice as revealed in judicial deliberations and decisions? How much did the fact of extended residence in one location influence individual ministers' actions? We regard these and other questions posed for future researchers as being as important as the information and conclusions presented.

Several terms in this study need special explanation. The concept of the "*radicado*," meaning an official of justice rooted in local society by social and economic ties, was central to the crown's concern for control over its audiencia ministers. By anglicizing and employing this word, we feel that we have been faithful to the way Spaniards used it in the eighteenth century—as a term that expressed succinctly the problem the crown saw in "rooted" ministers. We have occasionally expressed the aspirations of creoles as consciously or unconsciously embodying a desire for "home rule." This expression should not be understood in a democratic sense, of course; it was not the "Spanish-American people" who hoped to exercise control over America under royal auspices, but members of the small and aristocratic creole professional and landholding class.

Combining both audiencia judges (*oidores* and *alcaldes del crimen*) and crown attorneys (*fiscales*) in the numerical totals throughout the text posed a difficulty in terminology. The inclusion of fiscales precluded using "judges" or "magistrates" as a comprehensive label. With some misgivings we drew upon the Spanish word *"ministro"* as an umbrella term for any audiencia member, fiscal or judge, and have put it in its English form "minister" to avoid overburdening the text with Spanish terms. We have used "minister" only in reference to members of audiencias or councils, never for officials of cabinet rank. For these officials, such as Julián de Arriaga and José de Gálvez, a term designating their formal rank, such as "secretary" from secretary of state for the Indies, has been employed.

Spanish monetary values pose a problem for this as other studies of the colonial period. Exchange rates and relative values changed over time, and occasionally there was no universal agreement on the worth of a unit of money. Before the second half of the eighteenth century, salaries and other amounts of money were often expressed as, for example, *pesos escudos* of either eight or ten silver *reales*, *doblones* (understood here as four silver *pesos* each), *pesos de oro* or *pesos de minas* of 450 *maravedís* each, and *ducados*, not to mention the *vellón* coinage, money of copper admixture circulating in Spain. We have converted all monetary figures to the *peso fuerte* of eight silver reales each containing thirty-four *maravedís* (a peso of 272 maravedís). When unable to settle upon an accepted conversion to the *peso fuerte*, we have retained the original monetary unit.

Finally, the totals presented in this work, for example, the number of positions sold or Americans appointed to judicial office, are deliberately conservative. Unless otherwise noted, the totals represent the absolute proven minimum rather than the possible or even probable maximum of the category under consideration. We feel that future research will generally enhance these figures and further support the conclusions that we have drawn from them.

Over the course of this study many organizations have provided timely assistance for which we are deeply appreciative. The American Philosophical Society, the National Endowment for the Humanities, Miami University of Ohio, and the University of Missouri—St. Louis provided generous financial support for research. The staffs of various archives and libraries in Spain, Mexico, Peru, and the United States were most helpful. Particularly valuable were our experiences in the Archivo General de Indias (Seville) and the Archivo General de Simancas (Simancas). The Lilly Library graciously filmed Pedro de Bolívar y de la Redonda's *Memorial* for us. The University of Missouri—St. Louis's Computer Center gave invaluable technical assistance in organizing the biographical and appointment information into a usable form, while its History Department provided an excellent typist, Mary Supranowich, who remained cheerful and calm even in the midst of the appendixes.

Many friends and colleagues have encouraged and greatly aided our work over the past years. Individually or jointly we single out for special appreciation Dauril Alden, C. R. Boxer, E. D. Chandler, Steven C. Hause, Charles P. Korr, William S. Maltby, the late John Leddy Phelan, John J. TePaske, and John E. Woodham. Sue Burkholder and Nelda Chandler have given unfailing support from this study's inception in 1969. We thank Sue additionally for commenting on each draft of the manuscript and for making the indexes.

As a growing number of historians are discovering, collaborative research and writing offer many advantages. Not the least of these is enabling each author to shirk the customary avowal of personal responsibility for the text's shortcomings. We jointly claim whatever merit this book contains and blame each other for errors in fact, fallacies in interpretation, and infelicities in style.

M. A. B.
St. Louis, Missouri

D. S. C.
Oxford, Ohio

October 1976

Contents

Figures

From Impotence to Authority

Introduction

The discovery, conquest, and colonization of the New World provided unprecedented financial resources and power for the Spanish crown. Spurred by royal concessions and dreams of riches, individual entrepreneurs rapidly expanded the area of Spanish influence. Proven wealth and a growing Spanish population in America encouraged the crown to press for effective control over its new dependencies. The retraction of privileges granted Christopher Columbus and Charles I's attitude toward the *encomenderos* are early examples of royal intent. The crown's problem, as J. M. Ots y Capdequí has suggested, was to conquer the conquistadores; its solution was to extend the Castillian bureaucracy to the New World.[1]

Roman law and courts to dispense it provided a cutting edge for royal power at the time of the conquests. Ferdinand and Isabella had solidified their authority in Castile in part by their emphasis upon the law. During their reign, judicial bodies became an important part of royal administration. Valladolid became the permanent residence for a chancellery (*chancillería*), and a sister tribunal was established in Granada. Ranking below the Council of Castile, the chancelleries served principally as courts of appeal for inferior jurisdictions. Their ministers included *oidores* (civil judges), *alcaldes del crimen* (criminal judges), and *fiscales* (crown attorneys). These university-trained jurists were an important part of the body of *letrados* who helped to strengthen the crown through the use of law. Precisely at the time when this group was proving its utility in Castile, colonization in America was underway. As part of the effort to establish control over the new lands, Ferdinand and his successors decided to found audiencias in key colonial cities. These tribunals, however, quickly displayed powers that far exceeded the judicial responsibilities of their Castilian progenitors.[2]

Audiencias were established soon after the Spanish Conquest. Tribunals appeared first in Santo Domingo in 1511 and then in Mexico City shortly after Fernando Cortés's defeat of the Aztec Confederation. By the early seventeenth

---

1. J. M. Ots Capdequí, *El estado español en las Indias*, 4th ed. (Mexico, 1965), p. 45.
2. Alfonso García Gallo, *Curso de historia del derecho español*, tomo 1, 5th ed. rev. (Madrid, 1950), pp. 438–39; José Mª Ots y Capdequí, *Historia del derecho español en América y del derecho indiano* (Madrid, 1969), pp. 128–29; J. H. Elliott, *Imperial Spain, 1469–1716* (New York, 1964), p. 165; J. B. Owens, "'Feudal' Monarch and 'Just' Monarch: An Interpretation of Fifteenth-Century Castilian Politics," paper delivered at the 5th annual convention of the Society for Spanish and Portuguese Historical Studies (San Diego, 1974).

century eleven audiencias operated in the Indies, and by 1687 they contained seventy-six authorized positions.[3] Although the size of the tribunals varied, none were as large as the Spanish chancelleries. The audiencias of Mexico and Lima each had eight oidores, four alcaldes del crimen, and two fiscales. Guatemala, Charcas, and Chile had five oidores and one fiscal each, while the remaining tribunals of Manila, Santo Domingo, Guadalajara, Quito, and Panama were each authorized four oidores and one fiscal.

As the ranking civil institutions under the executive, audiencias held prestige and power in judicial, legislative, and executive matters. Among their well-known judicial responsibilities, the courts possessed first-instance jurisdiction for cases that related to the royal exchequer and for certain cases that arose in the seats of the tribunals. As courts of appeal within their districts, audiencias exercised final authority for criminal cases and most civil suits.[4]

The importance of the audiencias, however, rested also on their executive and legislative responsibilities. Whether a district's chief executive was a viceroy or governor, he received the audiencia's advice on all major questions; decisions reached through this consultation (*real acuerdo*) had the force of law unless disallowed by the Council of the Indies. In the executive's absence, the court assumed his duties and governed. Audiencias also were required to enforce royal laws, and to that end judges undertook periodic inspection tours within their districts. Additionally, judges often sat with one or more corporate bodies in a colony, for example, the merchants' guild (*consulado*) or the board of medical examiners (*protomedicato*). The audiencias, then, possessed formidable powers. Their role in judicial affairs and in overseeing the implementation of royal legislation made the decisions of the ministers important to the communities they served. Since appointments were for life or royal pleasure, the audiencia provided an element of continuity at the highest level of government. Incoming executives disregarded their advice only with peril. Armed with far-reaching authority, the audiencias were, always in theory and

---

3 The eleven audiencias and their dates of establishment are: Santo Domingo, 1511; Mexico, 1527; Panama, 1538, reestablished in 1564; Guatemala, 1543; Lima, 1543; Guadalajara (New Galicia), 1548; Santa Fe (New Granada), 1548; Charcas, 1559; Quito, 1563; Chile, 1563, reestablished in 1606; and Manila, 1583. The Audiencia of Buenos Aires was established in 1661 but abolished before the decade ended. The five audiencias north of Panama (Mexico, Guadalajara, Guatemala, Santo Domingo, and Manila) were under the administrative supervision of the Secretariat for New Spain, while the remainder were under the Secretariat for Peru. *Recopilación de leyes de los reynos de las Indias* (Madrid, 1681, reprinted in three volumes in 1943) (hereafter *Recopilación*), libro II, título xv, leyes ii–xii.

4. Aside from relevant portions of the *Recopilación*, information on the organization and responsibilities of the audiencias in America can be found easily in Charles Henry Cunningham, *The Audiencia in the Spanish Colonies as Illustrated by the Audiencia of Manila (1583–1800)* (Berkeley, 1919); C. H. Haring, *The Spanish Empire in America* (New York, 1947); J. H. Parry, *The Audiencia of New Galicia in the Sixteenth Century* (Cambridge, England, 1948); and John Leddy Phelan, *The Kingdom of Quito in the Seventeenth Century* (Madison, 1967). See also Ernesto Schäfer, *El consejo real y supremo de las Indias*, 2 vols. (Seville, 1935–1947), 2:66–157.

often in fact, an important check on other institutions of government. The courts' actual effectiveness in dispensing justice and in fulfilling royal expectations in their other areas of statutory competence during the day-to-day conduct of business, however, depended not just upon legal authorization but ultimately upon the ability, integrity, and respect commanded by the individuals who composed them.

The ministers of American audiencias were part of a specialized bureaucracy with branches in both Spain and the Indies. To enter the ranks of this most professional division of royal administration, a man had to meet both social and educational requirements. Ministers were to be of proven legitimate descent, free from Moorish or Jewish blood. They were trained in the law at one or more of the many universities in the Spanish world and thus held the generic title of "letrados." Following receipt of a bachelor's or higher degree in civil or canon law, a hopeful office-seeker often pursued one or more of several clearly defined routes to the audiencias. Traditionally, either continued attendance at a university in a distinguished major college (*colegio mayor*) or service as a professor afforded the most favorable chance for eventual appointment to an audiencia. Becoming an *abogado* (attorney) and practicing before the royal tribunals, or serving in lesser positions such as legal adviser for a city council or the estate of some grandee or as a district judge, however, were not unusual backgrounds for men who sought audiencia appointments (*pretendientes*). Ministers named directly to the American tribunals with no noteworthy achievement since obtaining legal training were also always in evidence. Whatever a new appointee's background, the chances were good that his first audiencia position would be in one of the nine inferior or pretorial tribunals. Appointment to the more prestigious viceregal courts of Lima and Mexico normally followed a well-defined line of promotion known as the *ascenso*.

The ascenso was a ubiquitous ladder of advancement visible in universities, ecclesiastical chapters (*cabildos eclesiásticos*), and other Spanish institutions as well as in the audiencias. For the courts it provided, in theory, for step-by-step advancement from the lowest position (fiscal) in the lowest-ranking courts to the highest letrado office (oidor) in a viceregal tribunal. In the ascenso's fullest application, for example, a minister might enter the Audiencia of Santo Domingo as a fiscal, become an oidor there, move to the Audiencia of Guadalajara as a fiscal and then advance to oidor. From the New Galician tribunal, promotion would be to Mexico as criminal fiscal and subsequent advancement would be through the ranks of civil fiscal, alcalde del crimen, and at last to civil judge. No minister ever followed this path exactly, but the promotion patterns were well defined and ministers in the tribunals grouped under the Secretariat of New Spain could look forward to promotion to Mexico, while those men in South America, including Panama, could anticipate advancement to Lima or occasionally to Sante Fe.

By law the Council of the Indies recommended ministers of the nine lesser tribunals for the two viceregal courts, and thus a pool of forty-eight men was theoretically available to fill a vacancy in one of the twenty-eight positions in

Mexico and Lima.[5] The frequency of promotion from the lesser tribunals was obviously related directly to promotions, deaths, retirements, and occasional entry into ecclesiastical benefices by ministers in Lima and Mexico. Since few of these men received promotion to a peninsular chancellery or council, openings were created most often by natural causes. Limited in the frequency of its application by relative immobility in the viceregal courts, the ascenso also possessed the drawbacks of a lockstep procedure in which seniority rather than merit was often the criterion for advancement. Still, when working smoothly the ascenso provided an element of fairness, or at least predictability. Many a judge in Manila or Santo Domingo could console himself with the thought that each year in the islands increased his chance to serve someday in the viceregal capital of New Spain.

The first appointments were of letrados born and educated in Spain. The early colonists' desire that their sons be eligible for government office appeared quickly, though, and was an important stimulus to the founding of universities in America. From the second half of the sixteenth century, American-born youths could obtain a higher education in Mexico City or Lima without the rigors of a voyage to Spain, lengthy separation from their families, and the expense of studying in a Castilian university.[6] The appearance of creole lawyers who wanted to serve in the audiencias of their home districts raised questions concerning the nature of justice and the empire.

The crown took seriously the responsibility to provide justice in the colonies. Conflicting "just" demands—to Christianize the Indians and protect them from "unjust" exploitation, to reward persons of Spanish descent who had served faithfully and performed meritorious actions, and to provide for its own strength by forestalling rebellion and collecting taxes—produced a situation in which none of the elements of American society could be wholly satisfied; royal action was necessarily a series of compromises between opposing principles. Colonists believed that their exploits of conquest and settlement deserved royal recognition in the form of rewards such as *encomienda*, land, *repartimiento*, social elevation, and office. Any of these meant, in essence, the right of self-enrichment at the expense of the indigenous population. Since colonists saw royal limitations upon such activity as a threat to their well-being, direct or indirect local influence upon royal officials was one key to American financial success. In spite of stern laws to the contrary, marriage between audiencia ministers and leading local families; ownership of property; and business transactions all provided indirect and often effective leverage for American interests. It was most effective of all for local residents to hold office themselves and thus have direct influence on administration and justice.

To understand colonial concern with audiencia appointments, one must focus upon the audiencia districts and their inhabitants. All Spaniards born in

5. *Recopilación*, libro II, título ii, ley xxxiiii.

6. The University of Mexico operated from 1553 and that of San Marcos de Lima from the 1570s. For the establishment of these and later universities see John Tate Lanning, *Academic Culture in the Spanish Colonies* (London, 1940), chapter 1.

the New World were "creoles." In addition, each creole was a "native son" (*natural*) of the audiencia district of his birth. Thus, for example, a man born in Guatemala was a native son of that province, but simply another creole when traveling outside its boundaries. When examining officeholders in each district, the distinction between native sons and other creoles is critical. Too often discussion of Americans has suffered from homogenizing the two terms.

Failure to refine the term *creole* has obscured the variety of economic, social, and political views that Americans held. Assertions that creoles wanted either equality with peninsulares in appointments to office or a monopoly of the appointments hide an essential point; the desire for office was limited geographically. Native sons wanted positions in their own districts or, at least, in those from which normal promotion would be into their home districts. A man born in Lima (*limeño*), for example, generally had no desire to serve in Mexico; he wanted an appointment to Lima or another South American court from which he could expect promotion to his natal city. The native sons of one audiencia district regarded those of another as outsiders and (except where social ties or economic interest already existed) little more desirable as administrators than peninsulares. Viewing their position within the legal tradition of Spanish regionalism, native sons began to consider their audiencia districts as *patrias*. The argument circulated, moreover, that native sons had a legal right to hold all offices within their patrias. This was a claim for de facto home rule. Americans who sought office had to deal with the crown, whose prerogative of naming audiencia ministers they never questioned before the Wars of Independence. Consequently, royal policy for audiencia appointments was of great significance for them.

The crown's desire to establish and maintain royal authority in the Indies conditioned the evolution of its appointment policy for the audiencias. Administrators in Spain firmly believed that appointees who owed their careers solely to royal pleasure would perform more reliably than men of independent fortune already resident in the Indies. By the time American-born letrados began to seek audiencia positions, the rationale for rejecting their petitions to serve at home was firmly established in Madrid. Conscious that kingship rested heavily on the provision of justice, the crown sought to provide its colonies with ministers who would be, in John L. Phelan's phrase, "Platonic guardians."[7] The appointees were to have no personal, economic, or emotional ties to their district of service. A host of regulations detailed the aloof existence they were to lead.[8] The crown wanted ministers who were isolated from local populations and threatened to suspend its officials for merely suggesting marriage to a local woman. The king also forbade ministers to engage in a variety of social contacts; own land, houses, gardens, or livestock; or invest in any economic enterprise within their jurisdiction. Their families were subject to similar constraints, and royal permission was an indispensable prerequisite for

---

7. Phelan, *Kingdom of Quito*, p. 153.
8. *Recopilación*, libro II, título xvi, numerous laws.

marriage between ministers' children and locally born residents of the district. Aware that government officials were often weak and corruptible, the crown thus sought to prevent the prostitution of justice and administration. The restrictive statutes were double edged. Ministers were forbidden access to local society and its economic resources. Conversely, interested residents were denied social access to the magistrates and the opportunity to influence them.

Prohibited from enjoying indirect entry to the magistracy, local youths were often disqualified from personally serving on their home audiencias by the same restrictions. Although no law explicitly barred native sons from audiencia service, the economic and social background requisite for a university and legal education almost necessarily meant that their appointment would violate one or more of the restrictive statutes.[9] Moreover, many Spaniards believed that birth in the New World adversely affected creoles' physiological makeup and rendered them unfit for high office and that Americans in important positions could pose a threat to imperial security; these beliefs buttressed the case of persons who wanted exclusive appointment of peninsulares. The crown's formal position, however, discounted these general indictments of creoles and maintained the principle that outsiders, whether peninsular or creole, were to staff the audiencias.[10] Although seldom stated, the royal intention to exclude native sons from service in their patrias was clear. Ambitious native sons fought exclusion from service in their home districts. Legalists dredged up ancient commentaries and royal legislation supporting their position. The thrust of their argument was simple: compelling reasons justified, indeed demanded, a complete reversal of policy, a reversal that would mean de facto home rule.

In 1667 a painstakingly detailed publication appeared in Madrid presenting a vigorous case for de facto home rule in the American audiencia districts. Pedro de Bolívar y de la Redonda, a thirty-five-year-old attorney from Cartagena de In-

---

9. As native sons pointed out, the *Recopilación* contained no statute specifically declaring them ineligible for audiencia positions. Ley xxxv, libro II, título ii, however, revealed unmistakable royal concern about native-son appointments to American tribunals. Further ambiguity was apparent when peninsular precedents were employed. Natives of Seville were prohibited explicitly from serving on its audiencia, and Ruth Pike indicates that in the sixteenth century, at least, the prohibition was enforced. A study of the place of birth for the men who served on the various tribunals of the peninsula would clarify the extent and effectiveness of prohibitions against native son service in Spain. *Los códigos españoles concordados y anotados*, 12 vols. (Madrid, 1847-1851), 8:31; Ruth Pike, *Aristocrats and Traders: Sevillian Society in the Sixteenth Century* (Ithaca, N.Y., 1972), p. 75. See also the important article by Richard Konetzke, "La condición legal de los criollos y las causas de la independencia," *Estudios americanos* (Seville) 2:5 (January 1950): 31-54.

10. Juan de Solórzano Pereira warned against the appointment of native sons in America for, unlike in Spain (implicit acknowledgment of their appointment), they were too far from the king and his council to be controlled. While noting legal precedents for not naming native sons, however, he also pointed out that arguments existed for giving them preference in appointments. *Política indiana*, 5 vols. (Madrid, 1647; reprinted 1930), libro V, capitulo IV, points 29 and 30. The crown sold dispensations for birth in the province of appointment as though an explicit prohibition against it existed and seemed to have assumed a connection between native son appointees and corruption.

dias, argued that native sons had a legal right to all offices in their patrias.[11] Personally aspiring to an audiencia appointment (which he received after over a decade of solicitation in 1676), he focused his discussion on the high tribunals. Bolívar wrote to demonstrate the errors in the existing royal policy toward native sons. To do so he had to prove that American birth did not physiologically incapacitate creoles from service, that peninsular ministers did not provide the impartial justice and good administration desired by the crown, and that native sons could serve audiencia positions more effectively. Far from barring audiencia service by native sons, he argued, legislation specified that only natives were to serve in their patrias. As support, the treatise presented references to an imposing array of sacred and secular sources. Church fathers, medieval glossators, histories, and every branch of law—divine, natural, *de gentes*, civil, canon, royal, and municipal—helped to fuel the arguments.

Bolívar briefly dismissed the prejudice that birth in the New World rendered Americans unfit for positions of responsibility. Reputable authorities had witnessed and reported creole capability, and no proof of mental or physical deterioration existed. This question, however, was only peripheral to his case; the crown had never officially contested creole capability, so there was little to gain by dwelling on the matter. Arguments pitting peninsular shortcomings against native-son strengths as a utilitarian justification for the appointment of Americans to their home tribunals were far more important.

Poverty, Bolívar contended, was a principal stimulus for the peninsulares' abuse of office. A well-to-do Spaniard would never leave his family and patria and expose himself to the dangers of a transatlantic voyage to serve on an American audiencia. Expenses of travel were a burden, and consequently these less-than-affluent Spaniards reached their destinations in debt and with no resources other than their moderate salaries. Their struggle to regain solvency opened the door to illegal transactions. The desire for enrichment that had originally motivated them to go to America further stimulated unlawful relationships with local families, and peninsulares quickly established even greater ties (*dependencias*) than many native sons would have had in the district served Locally born magistrates, Bolívar pointed out, did not face the financial strain confronted by their peninsular brethren. The reason for this advantage rested precisely on one of the conditions the crown opposed most vehemently— native sons possessed property within the district. Enjoying a financial base and free from travel expenses, native sons would not enter office obligated to

---

11. Pedro de Bolívar y de la Redonda, *Memorial informe y discurso legal, histórico, y político, al Rey N^{tro} Señor en su real consejo de cámara de las Indias, En favor de los Españoles, que en ellas nacen, estudian, y sirven, para que sean preferidos en todas las provisiones Eclesiásticas, y Seculares, que para aquellas partes se hizieron* (Madrid, 1667). The Lilly Library, Indiana University, kindly provided us with a microfilm copy of this *Memorial*. Bolívar's argument was presented, in part at least, by writers as early as 1620. See Guillermo Lohmann Villena, *Los ministros de la audiencia de Lima en el reinado de los Borbones (1700–1821)* (Sevilla, 1974), p. xxx and J. I. Israel, *Race, Class and Politics in Colonial Mexico 1610–1670* (London, 1975), pp. 83, 195, 197.

creditors. Upright administration of justice and exemplary government would result.[12]

The peninsulares' love of patria also weighed against them. Unlike native sons, they focused their affection back to a Spanish home and lacked the emotional incentive to work toward the well-being of the districts they served. The native son's love of patria was so important and beneficial for sound government, Bolívar maintained, that even if his other qualifications were slightly inferior to those of a competing peninsular, he should be favored for appointment. Bolívar further noted that peninsular appointees lacked detailed knowledge of local customs, problems, and legal traditions. Moreover, if they eventually achieved their desire to return to Spain, their slowly acquired understanding of American conditions would be profitless. Native sons, however, entered office equipped to fulfill their responsibilities from the outset, and, since they had no desire to move, the benefit of their knowledge was not lost.

Bolívar's case did not rest upon negative arguments alone. Although the desire of peninsulares for enrichment and a return to Spain worked to the detriment of the New World and were strong reasons for exclusive appointment of native sons, the very nature of the empire provided important support for de facto home rule. The territorial units attached to the Spanish crown were patrimonial in nature. Their association came only through the person of the monarch. When a ruler had several kingdoms, Bolívar argued, the native sons of each had the right to hold its offices. Thus the American territories were entitled to have locally born officials provide their administration. Local payment of taxes and the performance of services in the region also justified native-son appointments. Since Americans had the requisites for office—in ability, noble birth, and wealth they were equal or superior to peninsular pretendientes— outsiders should be named only in the absence of qualified native sons.

Finally, Bolívar marshaled a variety of legal and historical precedents favoring the appointment of native sons. His strongest direct example was a law previously issued at least six times and later included in the *Recopilación*. As presented in that famous codification, the statute stated that if other factors were equal American-born descendants of the conquistadores and first settlers were to be favored for positions, particularly those in localities where their ancestors had performed their meritorious services.[13] Since Bolívar refused to accept the possibility that Americans were intellectually or physically unqualified for positions, it followed that all posts in each region should be held by native sons.

Despite its inconsistencies and occasional misrepresentations, Bolívar's pamphlet contains the most complete argument yet found for native-son appointments. Some of the same recommendations would appear again in the eighteenth century, but no new arguments would be developed. The ongoing

---

12. Bolívar deliberately overlooked the fact, surely known to him as a pretendiente at court, that nearly all Americans pursuing audiencia appointments had to travel to Spain and the court to secure a position.

13. *Recopilación*, libro III, título ii, ley xiiii. See also ley xvi.

American concern for native-son appointments means that creole success in gaining positions on the high courts of America must be interpreted from the point of view of the native son.

Americans complained about not receiving appointments to their home audiencias, but in implying that their failures were the result of a conscious royal policy they overstated the case. The crown never accepted Bolívar's argument that native sons should hold all audiencia appointments and was in fact reluctant to name them at all. At most times before the late eighteenth century, however, royal advisers lacked information on an aspirant's place of birth and could not have followed an effective policy of exclusion. The lack of information on birthplace is one of the most striking features of the *Cámara* of the Indies's recommendations for appointment (*consultas*) in the late seventeenth and early eighteenth centuries.[14] The most common document submitted by aspiring bureaucrats in these years was a certified statement of academic achievements.[15] Limited to this information, the members of the cámara would have needed personal knowledge of a candidate to consider his place of birth in any recommendation. While such knowledge no doubt existed for some men, the customary absence of any reference to place of origin in the consultas suggests that the king and his advisers did not consider it necessary. Apparently the crown felt the information contained in candidates' university records alone was adequate for reaching a decision. This suggests that discrimination against Americans took place unconsciously or automatically before formal solicitation for office began.

The requirement of formal training in law or canons meant that the route to high letrado positions throughout the empire was through the universities. Although such training was available in various provincial universities and after the 1550s in America, the great medieval institutions of Salamanca and Valladolid and the Isabelline University of Alcalá came to possess a virtual monopoly over the filling of letrado vacancies on councils and chancelleries. The key to their dominance lay in the institution of the colegio mayor. Originally endowed by pious benefactors as residence halls where a few deserving students could be subsidized for a limited number of years, by the late sixteenth century the six colegios mayores (four at Salamanca and one each at Valladolid and Alcalá) had become bastions of privilege.

Richard L. Kagan has recently documented the relatively closed nature of the colegios mayores and demonstrated the relationship between them and the great councils that governed Spain and her empire.[16] By the seventeenth cen-

---

14. The cámara was a select committee of councillors of the Indies specifically charged with making recommendations for offices in the Indies. See Phelan, *Kingdom of Quito*, pp. 129–30 for the origins of the cámara.

15. For example, see Archivo General de Indias (hereafter AGI), Audiencia of Charcas (hereafter Charcas), legajo 196, "Títulos, grados, lecciones, presidencias, y otros exercicios literarios hechos por el Doctor Don Francisco Xavier de Palacios, Opositor que es a las Cáthedras de Canones de esta Universidad," Salamanca, 14 January 1739.

16. *Students and Society in Early Modern Spain* (Baltimore, 1974), particularly pp. 77–158.

tury proof of financial need, the restricted number of scholarships, and the limited period of residence were being ignored. Sons, relatives, or clients of ministers of the high councils enjoyed preferential admission into the colegios and as members (*colegiales*) in turn obtained ready access to high letrado positions. By the time of Philip IV the colegio mayor-council nexus had become self-perpetuating; a majority of serving ministers and councillors in Spain were themselves alumni of the colegios mayores, worked to procure admission to those institutions for their protégés, and saw to it that vacancies on the major tribunals in Spain were filled by colegiales.

Discrimination against Americans occurred at the colegio mayor bottleneck. Officially eligible for scholarships in the colegios on the same basis as peninsulares, creoles suffered increasingly as colegio admissions were determined more and more by the patronage system. The place of their birth meant that most Americans lacked ties of kinship with the more powerful families of Castile. Consequently, the wealthiest and most highborn creole could not expect to fare better in gaining admission to the colegios than the "unconnected" provincial hidalgo born in Spain. Lacking the vital imprimatur of the colegio mayor and without close relatives on the councils, the proud American-born aristocrat understandably felt chagrin at his inability to obtain preferment and rightly complained of "discrimination against Americans." Such discrimination was no less effective for being a largely unconscious by-product of the intimate link between the colegios and the high bureaucracy.

Creoles also faced an additional handicap that increased the largely unintentional discrimination they experienced—the vast distance separating them from that fount of patronage and seat of the councils, the royal court. A system of agents (*agentes de negocios*) and attorneys existed to lobby for distant clients, but prolonged and persistent efforts by an aspirant present at court yielded an obvious advantage. For natives of the New World, pursuit of an audiencia position usually meant a trip to Spain, sometimes to collect additional academic credentials but primarily to forward their candidacy. Such an undertaking involved considerable risks, much time, and heavy expenditures. Only the wealthiest or best-connected creole aristocrat could afford to attend a peninsular university and loiter at court, often for years, in the hope of obtaining an appointment.

Evidence of the "invisibility" of American office-seekers in the eyes of the members of the Cámara of the Indies, and hence of the unconscious nature of the discrimination, exists in the concern voiced by the cámara in 1676 about the difficulty of finding qualified ministers for the American courts.[17] As Bolívar had noted nine years earlier, graduates of the colegios mayores and peninsular pretendientes whose prospects appeared bright were reluctant to take American posts. *Camaristas* bemoaned the fact that only inferior aspirants who lacked

---

17. Richard Konetzke, ed., *Colección de documentos para la historia de la formación social de Hispanoamérica, 1493–1810*, 3 vols. (Madrid, 1953–1962), 2, tomo II, documents 436 and 442.

impressive credentials would go to the New World tribunals. In an effort to make American service more attractive to Spain's elite service families, the cámara decided to reserve chairs on the ranking chancelleries of Granada and Valladolid for qualified senior ministers serving on the audiencias of Lima and Mexico. In its discussion of the proposal, however, the cámara made no comment whatever on the existence of qualified American pretendientes anxious to receive appointments in or near their home districts. The camaristas were not sufficiently aware of the existence of a class of American pretendientes even to bother refuting their claims on this obvious occasion.

In spite of their handicaps, creoles and even a few native sons obtained audiencia appointments as early as 1585.[18] Before 1611 at least six creoles, including one native son, were named to American tribunals. It was the decade following 1611, however, that marked the onset of regular creole entry. From 1611 to 1620 seven Americans were among the forty-three new appointees (16 percent) and in every succeeding decade of that century Americans numbered at least 10 percent of the new men. Indeed, after 1630 Americans accounted for at least 15 percent of the new appointments in every decade. From 1611 to 1687, natives of the New World totaled at least seventy-nine or one out of every five new appointees; however, only fourteen of these were ever named to their home tribunals. While figures to 1687 are far less complete than those for later years, they nonetheless demonstrate early American participation in the high courts.[19]

By 1687 the patterns of appointment and promotion for the American audiencias had been well established for many decades. By this time, too, American pretendientes had developed a tradition of journeying to Spain in pursuit of the coveted *garnacha* (distinctive judicial collar). Americans, particularly limeños, had grown accustomed to receiving at least a few high positions and were prepared to argue for more. With native sons gaining occasional office during the course of the seventeenth century, experience had provided a tantalizing taste of the de facto home rule for which Bolívar y de la Redonda had argued.

---

18. In the following figures, Schäfer, *El consejo,* 2, Appendix 2 was used to obtain the total of men appointed while identification of Americans and native sons came from diverse sources. Those of greatest value were Antonine Tibesar, O.F.M., *Franciscan Beginnings in Colonial Peru* (Washington, D.C., 1953), Appendix IV; Luis Antonio Eguiguren, *Diccionario histórico cronológico de la Real y Pontificia Universidad de San Marcos y sus colegios. Crónica e investigación,* 3 vols. (Lima, 1940–1951), 1:523–30 and 2:135–205; Manuel de Mendiburu, *Diccionario histórico-biográfico del Perú,* 8 vols. (Lima, 1874–1890); Guillermo Lohmann Villena, *Los americanos en las órdenes nobiliarias (1529-1900),* 2 vols. (Madrid, 1947); Juan Luis Espejo, *Nobiliario de la capitanía general de Chile* (Santiago, Chile, 1967); José María Restrepo Sáenz, *Biografías de los mandatarios y ministros de la real audiencia– (1671 a 1819)* (Bogotá, 1952); and Abraham de Silva i Molina, *Oidores de la real audiencia de Santiago de Chile durante el siglo XVII* (Santiago, Chile, 1903). The number of Americans indicated is undoubtedly low.

19. See p. 79 on the dominant position of Peruvians among American appointees to the audiencias.

Part One
The Age of Impotence
(1687–1750)

Overview

Spain reached its political and economic nadir during the final third of the seventeenth century.[1] The collapse of royal authority, hastened by the revolts of Portugal and Catalonia in the 1640s, was apparent on every side two decades later. A political resurgence of the high nobility highlighted the crown's loss of control, and the succession of titled favorites who wielded power during the reign of the hapless Charles II (1665-1700) vividly revealed Spain's political bankruptcy. Indeed, the crown's raison d'être seemed little more than to encumber its treasury further by providing relief for nobles anxious to dine at the state's expense. In this environment, occasional efforts at reinvigoration of royal authority were doomed to failure.

Economic and fiscal chaos mirrored the political prostration. The inflation produced by the importation of American silver in the sixteenth century had priced many of Spain's exports out of the European market, and further decline followed in the seventeenth century. Depopulation, a depleted tax base, and currency devaluations added to Spain's economic woes. Currency stabilization did occur in the late 1680s, but its beneficial effects were not obvious for decades. Despite its exhaustion, the monarchy prolonged fitful efforts to reconquer Portugal and struggled to defend its remaining possessions in northern Europe from the growing power of France. Beginning in 1667, the Bourbon Louis XIV proved that he could despoil Hapsburg Spain of its possessions in the north at will. He was restrained only by his long-range plans for the Spanish sucession, not by successful troops in the pay of Castile. To finance its defense, the crumbling Spanish state sent northward revenue collected not only by "normal" taxation but also by irregular and sometimes disruptive devices; for example, sequestration of merchants' capital, the debasement of currency (until 1685), and the sale of office. The consequences of such actions extended beyond the immediate conflict. By hampering the economy and administration, they prevented the recovery that intervals of peace might have provided and thus forced reintroduction of similar measures during the next

---

1. This section is based upon numerous secondary works, the most important of which were: J. H. Elliott, *Imperial Spain, 1469–1716* (New York, 1964); John Lynch, *Spain under the Habsburgs,* 2 vols. (New York, 1964-1969), 2; Henry Kamen, *The War of Succession in Spain, 1700–1715* (Bloomington, Ind., 1969); Richard Herr, *The Eighteenth-Century Revolution in Spain* (Princeton, 1958); Pedro Aguado Bleye and Cayetano Alcázar Molina, *Manual de historia de España,* 10th ed., 3 vols. (Madrid, 1967), 3; and Modesto Lafuente, *Historia general de España, desde los tiempos más remotos hasta nuestros días,* 30 vols. (Madrid, 1850-1867), 17-19.

crisis. The endless conflicts of the late seventeenth century not only continued to sap Castile, the heart of the monarchy, of its strength but also to entrap the crown further in an administrative mire of its own making.

Royal economic and political control over the American empire also weakened during the reign of Charles II. Poor communications and the incursions of other European nations and pirates were partly responsible, but the state of the Spanish economy was even more important. As America began its slow recovery from the demographic catastrophe initiated by the Spanish Conquest and as its economy diversified, less reliance on the metropolis was necessary. Fueled by internal growth, the economy of Spanish America had become healthier than that of the mother country and increasingly less complementary. With Spanish producers in the late seventeenth century unable to provide even a quarter of the goods the colonists wanted and the Spanish market often unable to absorb colonial products other than precious metals, American traders increasingly sought to engage in commerce with merchants outside the monopolistic trading system. Contraband trade increased, and in 1700, the year that Charles died, the largest share of Spanish-American trade flowed into the hands of Spain's enemies. The commercial difficulties, frequent wars, government by favorites, and the colonies' own economic development weakened the crown's political control over America. Officials from viceroys down to lowly provincial administrators profited from lax supervision, and government in America, as in Spain, reflected local and regional rather than imperial interests. The monarchy never surrendered in principle to centrifugal pressures, but by the late seventeenth century it was unable to control distant officials and powerful subjects. As the seventeenth century ended, the position of the monarchy within Spain and the empire was unenviable. Awareness of its weakness and efforts to curb the most flagrant abuses in administration had failed. Spain was moribund in 1700, without resources even to reap many benefits from America's slow ascent from depression. The problems of the last Hapsburg monarch passed intact to his Bourbon heir.

The accession of Philip of Anjou to the Spanish throne in 1700 changed the political spectrum of Europe. Contemporaries understood that war probably would result from such a major increase in the power and influence of the Bourbons; in spite of the peninsular monarchy's decrepit condition, control over Spain and especially its transatlantic possessions was considered a major asset. Military operations commenced as early as 1702, but Philip V's position became desperate only with the invasion of Spain launched by the Archduke Charles in 1705. The struggle for mastery of the peninsula continued until 1709, and the Bourbon cause was not secure until the Battle of Villaviciosa in 1711.

The desperate struggle to avoid dismemberment of the Spanish crown's patrimony wiped out financial and administrative reforms inaugurated between 1701 and 1704. Thrust back into the Hapsburg quagmire of fighting a war without adequate financial reserves, Philip's secretaries returned to the extraordinary measures bequeathed by their predecessors in order to raise revenue. At the same time, the traditional bureaucratic machinery with which the Hapsburgs had governed ceased to function. Royal secretaries shelved considerations of justice and normal standards of administration as all principles yielded to the imperative of self-preservation. Only the end of conflict allowed the crown to return to the important task of expanding its authority.

The new dynasty made determined efforts to correct some of the long-standing problems plaguing the state. Fortunes of war made possible the abrogation of Catalan and Aragonese liberties, and the central government achieved the political unification of Spain at last (excluding Navarre and the Basque provinces). From this step came a new and more productive tax and administrative system for the crown of Aragon. To improve further central administration, in 1714 Philip created four offices of secretary of state to absorb many of the responsibilities formerly vested in the lethargic councils. A new secretary of state for the Indies, for example, reduced the Council of the Indies to primarily judicial duties. Centralization was also the goal of an unsuccessful effort to establish the French-inspired intendant system throughout Spain. Determined to rejuvenate the Spanish monarchy, the Bourbons increased tax revenues and rebuilt the military power of the state. Philip made strong efforts to sponsor industrial growth and development and, under several energetic ministers, emphasized the redevelopment of the Spanish navy and merchant marine in hopes of reestablishing effective control over Spanish America. Throughout the period between the War of the Spanish Succession and the general conflict of the 1740s, however, a frenetic foreign policy derived from the ambitions in Italy of Elizabeth Farnese, second queen of the melancholy Philip, prevented more than short-term improvement in Spain's financial condition. A sequence of small but expensive wars marked these years, and, even though a significant beginning toward economic recovery took place, financial crises were frequent.

In late 1739 a maritime conflict erupted between Spain and England, and within a short time the War of Jenkins' Ear had merged with the general struggle growing out of dynastic aspirations in central Europe. Since Spain's prime enemy was England, defense of ports and coastal fortifications in America became a major consideration. The need for funds to defend the Indies once again led to the use of extraordinary devices for revenue. Even under conditions of war, however, the effort to revive the Spanish economy continued. Administrative and economic reforms remained a matter of royal concern, and in the late 1740s the new monarch Ferdinand VI extended the intendant system throughout the peninsula at last. Awareness of the need for basic changes in the empire stimulated projects for reform of administration and commerce. Execution of these schemes, however, awaited peace, able ministers, and adequate financial resources.

Spain's inability to stay clear of foreign involvement and the consequent heavy demands on the royal treasury profoundly affected the American audiencias. For the courts, the systematic sale of appointments that commenced in 1687 and was not definitively ended until 1750 heralded an age of royal impotence. The sales both illustrated and increased the crown's weakness. By making cash more important than professional qualifications for office, the monarchy obtained the services of numerous native sons, precisely the men it considered least desirable as ministers. In addition to providing this direct representation, sales impaired the ascenso. This prevented normal advancement and opened the way for local families to enjoy increased indirect access to the ministers who remained in one location for a prolonged period of time.

In examining the audiencias, one can profitably consider the years 1687–1750 in three subdivisions: 1687–1712, a time highlighted by sales; 1713–1729, a period characterized by efforts to return to traditional standards for appointments and to erase the impact of sales; and 1730–1750, a period again marked by sales and the crown's inability to insist upon professional over financial services. From the royal perspective, the sales that ended in 1750 had devastated the control of the king over the courts and created problems in direct and indirect representation that would not be completely resolved until the late 1770s. From the perspective of local interests, on the other hand, the crown's impotence ushered in the golden age of their political power.

The Advent of Sales

By the late seventeenth century the penurious Spanish monarchy had tried a wide range of extraordinary means to raise revenue for financing its conflicts with Louis XIV's France. To augment royal income further, the hard-pressed Charles II broke with tradition in 1687 and inaugurated the frequent sale of appointments to American audiencias. Once begun during times of particular fiscal strain, this expedient proved irresistible until the mid-eighteenth century. The Age of Impotence for the crown and the American audiencias spanned the years of sales from 1687 to 1750.

The Hapsburg dynasty initiated the sale of offices in Spain on a massive scale. Philip II (1556–1598) began the practice of selling certain hereditary and transferable offices through public auction (*oficios vendibles y renunciables*).[2] These included notarial, "miscellaneous fee-earning," and municipal posts. Only during the seventeenth century did the list expand to include salaried positions. Burdened by mounting expenses in the effort to meet the challenge of empire, Philip IV (1621–1665) overrode the opposition of the Council of the Indies and began the sale of treasury offices. By the mid-seventeenth century their sale was common; unlike the oficios vendibles y renunciables, these offices were sold by private transaction rather than auction. The sale of provincial governorships followed soon afterward, also proceeding through private contract between purchaser and crown. Continuing fiscal need pressed the government into making an even larger number of offices available for purchase, and by the end of the seventeenth century it had sold appointments not only to

---

2. For general information on the sale of office within Spain and the empire, see J. H. Parry, *The Sale of Public Office in the Spanish Indies under the Hapsburgs* (Berkeley, 1953).

the audiencias but also for the prestigious office of viceroy for both Peru and New Spain.[3]

Sales of appointments to the highest positions on the audiencias—those of oidor, alcalde del crimen, and fiscal—did not fall under the classification of oficios vendibles y renunciables. Rather, they were individual transactions made without provision for inheritance or resale. Technically, the crown sold the appointments but not the offices, although for convenience we will refer to the transactions as the sale of positions. Unlike members of the sovereign courts in France during the Old Regime, purchasers of audiencia positions did not enjoy any special proprietary rights. Moreover, if a purchaser died soon after taking office, his heirs received nothing. The purchaser's transaction involved a gamble on longevity, for once in office he would serve for life or royal pleasure. Unless removed for cause, he would receive the purchase price plus 5 percent annual interest should the king elect to dispense with his services.[4]

The cost of appointments varied according to the desirability of the position—the post of oidor in Mexico or Lima generally sold for substantially more than one in Guatemala or Chile—and the dispensations the purchaser wanted. Men often paid sums equal to several years' salary for the post obtained.

From 1687 to 1712 the amounts varied from the two thousand pesos peninsular Gregorio Manuel de Villa Barreda paid to become fiscal in Manila to the twenty thousand pesos delivered by native son Bartolomé de Munárriz for a regular (*numero*) appointment as a criminal judge in Lima.[5] Whatever the sum paid, purchasers in these years customarily delivered a down payment of 60 percent or more of the price to the royal treasury in Spain and the balance in the Indies before taking office.[6] The frequent division of payments between branches of the treasury probably reflected a compromise between the crown's desire for cash available for immediate disposition in Spain and the difficulty Americans experienced in raising large sums in the peninsula. Few creoles could match the ability of Juan Antonio de Mena Caballero, son of a merchant of the consulado of Lima, to pay sixteen thousand pesos at court.[7] Aspiring

3. Antonio Domínguez Ortiz, "Un virreinato en venta," *Mercurio peruano* (Lima), año xxxix, vol. xlix, uúm. 453 (enero-febrero de 1965), 46–51.

4. See p. 91.

5. Archivo General de Simancas (hereafter AGS), Sección XXIII, Dirección General del Tesoro, Inventario 2, legajo 8, documento 42 (title [título] of Gregorio Manuel de Villa Barreda, Madrid, 8 July 1710); legajo 4, documento 31 (title of Bartolomé de Munárriz, Buen Retiro, 20 July 1708). All of the materials from the AGS employed in this study are located in Sección XXIII, Dirección General del Tesoro (hereafter XXIII) and carry inventory, legajo, and document numbers. Future references will be limited to these numbers (2–4–31) with a short form of the name of the person receiving the title and the place and date of its issue in parentheses (e.g. Munárriz, Buen Retiro, 20 July 1708).

6. See Appendix III.

7. AGI, Indiferente General, legajo 525, "Relación de los empleos de Justicia, Políticos y de Real Hacienda de los Dominios de el Perú, que se han concedido por servizio pecuniario desde el año de 1700 al de 1746." Mena paid 4,000 doblones, a sum equal to 16,000 pesos.

ministers went into debt to meet the considerable costs of travel and residence in Spain, and the purchase of a position added to their financial burdens and thus susceptibility to influence.[8] The possibility that a network of financiers similar to that behind *corregidores* existed for the ministers calls for investigation.

Critics of the sale of audiencia appointments could not impugn six hundred thousand pesos for appointments between 1687 and 1712, nearly a fourth of this amount during the peak years of 1710 and 1711.[9] Moreover, appointments sold produced tax revenue (*media anata* or *anata entera*) just as appointments granted for merit did. Nonetheless, the expansion of sales to include audiencia positions never sat well with jurists at court. Within the philosophical framework of the Spanish monarchy, the dispensation of justice had a theological significance that outweighed its political aspects. For Spaniards the essence of kingship was justice, and the monarch was first and always the highest magistrate. That modern kings had delegated this responsibility to legists did not detract from the sacredness of the undertaking. Armed with theological support, Spanish legal theorists argued against the sale of positions of justice. Only in emergencies such as imminent peril to the crown could sales take place without transgression of human or divine law and then only if certain standards were upheld.[10]

Authorities agreed that the crown could sell judicial positions only to persons so qualified that under normal conditions they would deserve appointment on their merits and prior service alone.[11] Moreover, the price of these offices should be moderate in order that qualified applicants could buy them even if their purses were thin. Doing otherwise would limit the magistracy to the wealthy, whatever their qualifications. A cynic might well regard these standards as impossible to maintain; the crown sold positions only to raise money, and to the extent that it attempted to limit prices the practice was self-defeating. Nonetheless, seventeenth- and eighteenth-century legal theorists took these principles seriously and labored to measure up to them.

The systematic sale of audiencia appointments began in 1687. In late November of that year, Miguel Núñez de Sanabria received an appointment as alcalde del crimen in Lima with a dispensation for being a native of the district.[12] Núñez de Sanabria's appointment revealed two features that characterized many subsequent sales. The appointment of a native son, although it

---

8. For instance, Juan del Corral Calvo de la Banda commented that his journey to Spain for additional education and lobbying for preferment at court cost him 27,000 pesos, most of this sum borrowed from unnamed sources. José Toribio Medina, *Biblioteca hispano-chilena (1523–1817)*, 3 vols. (Santiago, Chile, 1963), 2: 466.

9. See Appendix III.

10. AGI, Audiencia of Mexico (hereafter Mexico), legajo 1970, Consulta of the Council of the Indies, 21 August 1737 provides a full explication of the argument.

11. Ibid.

12. AGS, XXIII, 24–171–211 (Núñez de Sanabria, Buen Retiro, 21 November 1687); AGI, Contaduría, legajo 149, ramo 1. Figures in this study begin with this crucial appointment, the last made in 1687.

became common with sales, was a novelty in 1687. In the years after Americans first began to receive audiencia appointments, only fourteen native sons had been involved, and eight of these reached their home tribunal only after service elsewhere.[13] In addition, Núñez de Sanabria's appointment violated the ascenso; direct appointments to a viceregal tribunal were exceedingly rare prior to 1687. The single confirmed sale of an initial appointment before 1687 had involved neither of these features.[14]

Frequent vending of these high judicial posts was unprecedented, a fact demonstrated by the storm of protest from persons in both Spain and America evoked by rumor of sales as well as by an examination of appointments made from the establishment of the audiencias until 1687.[15] During periods of heavy sales after 1687 the majority of purchasers had to settle for either the promise of a future appointment (*futura*) or a post in excess of the authorized number (supernumerary). Prior to the onset of sales, only in 1643, 1661–1664, and 1672 did more than one such appointment occur in a single year. In the years from 1651 to 1686, less than 5 percent of the new appointments were irregular (non-numero).[16] By contrast, between 1687 and 1700, almost one-third of the

---

13. Moreover, several of these native sons reached their home courts by purchase or other special dispensation. See note 15, below.

14. Limeño Antonio Martínez Luján purchased an appointment as oidor in Charcas in 1683 for 18,000 pesos. In addition, peninsula-born Domingo de la Rocha Ferrer purchased an appointment as oidor in Santa Fe for 8,000 pesos, but the documents are unclear as to whether this was his original appointment in 1685 or reappointment in 1693. AGI, Contaduría, legajo 235, ramo 6.

15. In addition to the definite earlier sale to Martínez Luján in 1683, several earlier appointments perhaps were purchased. The appointments of Luis de Loma Puertocarrero as supernumerary oidor and Agustín de Medina y Vega as alcalde del crimen futurario in 1643 to their home tribunal of Lima are certainly suspicious. Similarly suspect is the appointment of Alonso del Castillo y Herrera to his home tribunal of Quito in 1660. Ernesto Schäfer, *El consejo real y supremo de las Indias*, 2 vols. (Seville, 1935–1947), 2:483, 488, 514. No direct evidence that these appointments were sold has yet appeared. If they were, they represent individual exceptions to the crown's policy before the 1680s. The cases that do come to light are not sales of initial appointments to new men. For instance, in 1627 Juan de Padilla, a native of Lima, was named oidor in Santa Fe. A few years later the crown suspended him for some infraction. In 1637 Padilla paid 14,000 ducats to have the suspension lifted and for promotion to his home tribunal as alcalde del crimen. Richard Konetzke, ed., *Colección de documentos para la historia de la formación social de Hispanoamérica, 1493–1810,* 3 vols. (Madrid, 1953–1962), 2, tomo 1, document 234. In 1668 Gonzalo Suárez de San Martín was named fiscal del crimen in Mexico. Twenty-six years earlier, in 1642, he had purchased the important letrado post of protector of the Indians for Santa Fe for 4,000 pesos. AGI, Indiferente General, legajo 128.

The crown assigned audiencia posts for more exotic reasons, of course, as it did for the Council of the Indies. Andrés Sánchez de Ocampo was named oidor supernumerary in Mexico in 1653 for marrying the queen's handmaiden. Similarly, Alonso de Zárate de Verdugo, a limeño, received a post in the criminal sala in Lima as part of a dowry in 1660, and limeño José Tello de Meneses received appointment to the Audiencia of Guadalajara for the same reason in 1664. Schäfer, *El consejo*, 2: 127, 456, 496n.

16. Figures taken from ibid., 2.

new appointments were irregular, and for six of these fourteen years the proportion was at least half.[17]

Opponents in Spain excoriated Manuel García de Bustamante for his unrestrained venality in the sale of high posts, especially those of justice, in the late 1680s.[18] Outraged protest against the innovation also came from Mexico. In June 1690 the viceroy and audiencia ministers of Mexico commented in shocked terms on a report that a position of oidor on the tribunal had been granted in return for cash.[19] The audiencia mentioned no names, and it appears the judges were reacting to rumors from Spain.[20] In high dudgeon they spoke of their "grief" upon learning that the king had promoted a letrado to their number "only because he served your Majesty with money." In a final expression of pique the tribunal vowed that it would not admit the unnamed individual to his place until the king had reconfirmed the appointment. Such vigorous reaction reflected resentment and disapproval toward a fundamental change of policy.

Even though the Council of the Indies denied the Mexican audiencia's accusation and treated the issue as hypothetical, it reacted with some heat to the threatened rebuff to a royal appointee.[21] Yet the councillors' denial had a hollow ring, for in addition to the sales already negotiated, they were in that same month discussing the appointment of José de Miranda Villayzán, another purchaser.

The frequent sale of audiencia positions that began in 1687 and the protests such transactions aroused inaugurated recurring themes of the Age of Impotence. From 1687 to 1750 the crown alternated between bowing to financial demands by selling audiencia offices and upholding traditional standards by appointing men on the strength of their social, educational, and administrative qualifications. The subdivisions of this age largely reflect the shifting balance between these two positions.

The Appointment of Native Sons

Native sons and especially Peruvians vied successfully for appointments each time the crown sold audiencia positions. Nonetheless, the sales that began in 1687 and continued through the War of the Spanish Succession fell

---

17. See Appendix IX.

18. Lafuente, *Historia general*, 18: 212–13. The Marqués de los Vélez, at the time superintendent of the treasury, had placed García de Bustamante in effective control of his office.

19. AGI, Mexico, legajo 10, Viceroy and Audiencia of Mexico to the king, Mexico, 30 June 1690.

20. The judges were almost certainly reacting to reports of the secret sale of an oidorship in Mexico to the Spaniard Miguel Calderón de la Barca in 1689. Calderón paid 12,000 pesos for the regular appointment. AGI, Contaduría, legajo 235, ramo 6.

21. AGI, Mexico, legajo 10, consulta of the Cámara de Indias, 28 March 1691. The cámara voted to fine the Audiencia of Mexico 6,000 ducats for its impertinence.

into three distinct periods. The first group of sales, twenty-four in number, occurred during the years 1687–1695. Eighteen of the sales were to audiencias of the Secretariat of Peru, and limeños purchased nine of the posts and accounted for four of the five native sons.[22] These sales were accompanied by uneasiness and intimations of reform, however. In 1691 Charles II issued a decree stating that supernumerary ministers should be removed from office and the American tribunals returned to their authorized strength.[23]

The 1691 decree removed at least one purchaser from his office. Mexican José Miranda Villayzán secretly purchased an appointment as supernumerary oidor in New Galicia in the spring of 1691.[24] Having not yet advanced into a numero position when the order appeared, Miranda lost his office. The law guaranteed that, until a vacancy occurred, reformed ministers would receive half salary, unless the appointment had been by purchase. Purchasers were entitled to full pay even while awaiting a vacancy in the numero positions. Early in 1692 Miranda petitioned for his entire salary, citing his servicio as justification. A check of the records of the *Contaduría de Indias* for 1691 revealed that he had delivered eight thousand pesos escudos to the crown for unspecified reasons, and the president of the Council of the Indies conceded that Miranda was a purchaser although his title of office had not recorded the fact. The defensive, almost apologetic tone permeating the discussion of the transaction underscores the departure that the sale of letrado posts represented. Perhaps motivated by his demand for full payment, Charles II quickly designated the Mexican to be fiscal futurario in New Galicia and empowered him to serve in the illnesses and absences of the incumbent. Within a year or two, Miranda achieved numero status and served in Guadalajara for over a quarter of a century.[25]

The intentions of 1691 were, in any case, firmly reversed by another decree of October 1693, in which Charles II resolved to continue the sale of audiencia appointments.[26] The arguments advanced to support his position were almost identical to those Philip V would employ a half-century later; while opposition to sales was correct from a legal and moral perspective, it was irrelevant before raison d'état. The Cámara of the Indies, perhaps bowing before the inevitable, responded with a proposal in December 1694 that in addition to the traditional

---

22. For the names of the individuals involved, see Appendix III. Full names of all men referred to in this and subsequent sections can be found in the Index of Audiencia Ministers.

23. AGI, Indiferente General, legajo 826, copy of the royal decree of reform of 17 July 1691, Madrid, 23 July 1691.

24. Ibid.

25. AGI, Audiencia of Guadalajara (hereafter Guadalajara), legajo 128, consulta of 31 May 1692. The reform also affected Fernando de Prado y Plaza. Fiscal in Santa Fe for nearly twenty years, Prado was appointed a supernumerary oidor of the tribunal in May 1691, possibly by purchase. Removed by the reform, he was retired at full pay in 1693. AGS, XXIII, 24–170–83 (Prado, Madrid, 13 February 1671); 24–172–135 (Prado, Madrid, 31 December 1693).

26. Konetzke, *Colección*, 3, tomo I, document 18.

concern for academic records and accomplishments, candidates for American audiencias should be investigated for signs of "the judgment, capacity, and endowments that cannot be discovered in the writings of a *relación*."[27] This comment clearly implies that the era of sales brought forth a new and, from the cámara's perspective, undesirable class of pretendiente. The early 1690s ended then with a victory for continued sales but uneasiness about the qualifications of the candidates the sales produced.

No sales of first appointments occurred for four years after 1695, perhaps reflecting the winding down of the War of the League of Augsburg that terminated in 1697.[28] A new flurry of sales began in 1699 and 1700, and at least seven appointments were granted for payment. A marked change from the sales of the early 1690s was apparent, for now native sons predominated. Five of the seven proven purchasers gained appointment to their home tribunals—four limeños and one Mexican, the Mexican being the first American to purchase an initial appointment to the northern tribunal.[29] Interestingly, all of the old judges in Mexico who had protested sales in 1690 had now passed from the scene. Continued reliance upon supernumerary appointments was again evident; only one of the native sons gained an immediate numero position. The seventh sale placed a limeño as oidor in Charcas, a position directly below Lima in the ascenso.[30] The sales of these two years suggest an erosion of the crown's reluctance to sell direct appointments on the major audiencias to native sons, a shift from the attitude apparent in the early 1690s.

The reform decree of 6 March 1701 temporarily halted the sale of audiencia positions.[31] This celebrated document restated with little modification Charles II's decree of a decade earlier. Philip ordered that the tribunals of America be reduced to their authorized strength and all ministers serving as supernumeraries be excluded from participation on the courts. He softened the blow by declaring that those men affected would receive special consideration in filling future vacancies and that those known to have purchased their appointments would receive refunds. The language of the decree reveals explicitly the secrecy attached to some of the sales. Some men "had not wanted what they gave to be expressed in their titles of appointment." Given the purchasers' desire for anonymity, the secretariats of the council had little information about them. Unless the title recorded the fact of sale, royal officials had no way of

---

27. Ibid., document 25.

28. In 1697 a judge already serving in a minor audiencia purchased a promotion to the viceregal audiencia of Mexico, but as he had already been appointed to an audiencia position on merit, his case lacks the significance of an initial appointment. See AGI, Mexico, legajo 1121, consulta on the appointment of José Osorio Espinosa de los Monteros as oidor supernumerario to Mexico; also Indiferente General, legajo 131.

29. Listed chronologically, the men are: Vásquez de Velasco, Aranburu, Núñez de Rojas, Rojas y Acevedo, Villavicencio, Anguita Sandoval, and Ayala Marín. Anguita was the Mexican.

30. This was Gregorio Núñez de Rojas.

31. Manuel Moreyra y Paz-Soldán and Guillermo Céspedes del Castillo, *Virreinato peruano: documentos para su historia. Colección de cartas de virreyes–Conde de la Monclova,* 3 vols. (Lima, 1954–1955), 3: document 287.

identifying purchasers. Consequently, the burden of proof was upon the secret purchasers themselves. Far from representing economic savings, this reform, as other efforts to return to traditional norms, implied a heavy cost to the crown. Not only did the king undertake to return all *servicios,* but he also agreed to pay salaries to ministers who did not serve but only awaited a vacancy. Nothing else testifies so clearly to the depth of opposition to the innovation of selling audiencia positions.

As a consequence of the reform of 1701, eleven persons, all Americans, lost their positions. Only one served in the audiencias of New Spain, a reflection of the geographical dispersion of sales; the other ten were in the tribunals of Lima, Chile, and Charcas.[32] Limeños accounted for nine of the eleven men and four of the five native sons. Although only nine of the men affected were proven purchasers, the other two had almost surely entered *"por vía de beneficio."* [33]

Few men who lost their posts by reform sat back complacently. The ultimately successful effort of charqueño Juan del Corral Calvo de la Banda to regain his seat on the Audiencia of Chile illustrates the kind of pleading and petitioning to which the crown was subjected in consequence of this effort to restore the audiencias to traditional standards.[34] Corral's plea also sheds light on the vicissitudes of placeseeking in the 1690s. After recounting at great length his personal merits, Corral noted that his trip to Spain in search of preferment had cost him over two years and twenty-seven thousand pesos, much of this sum borrowed from unnamed sources. After a brief stay at the University of Salamanca, he had spent fourteen months at court in 1694 and 1695 trying to gain a position before coming to the conclusion that the one he sought had been filled by sale. Faced with the unpalatable prospect of returning to America emptyhanded as well as penniless, Corral borrowed more money and for eight thousand pesos obtained his título as oidor futurario in Chile. The unhappy creole painted a moving scene of his dismay on learning, after returning home at great expense with the inevitable *"dilatada familia,"* that his appointment had been nullified. The return of his eight thousand pesos was small consolation in the face of the total expenses of his trip.

The reform of 1701 originally provided that supernumeraries affected would be removed and left without salary while awaiting a vacancy. In the months following, however, Philip V relented and allowed the decree to be interpreted more leniently. Supernumeraries would lose their right to serve and the honors due a minister, but would continue to draw salary until a vacancy occurred. Calling himself a supernumerary, Corral wheedled some months of salary out of viceregal officials before the crown discovered that his appointment was only a futura or promise of a regular appointment and carried no automatic right to enter a vacant numero position. The council halted the pay-

32. The eleven were: Santiago de Céspedes, Corral Calvo de la Banda, Vásquez de Velasco, Aranburu, Núñez de Rojas, Rojas y Acevedo, Ignacio Antonio de Castillo, Valverde Contreras, Villavicencio, Anguita, and Ayala Marín.
33. Castillo and Valverde Contreras.
34. Medina, *Biblioteca Hispano-chilena,* 2: 463–69.

ment of his salary and may have demanded restitution. Corral's persistence eventually paid off and, after another interval of service from 1708 to 1714, he rejoined the Chilean tribunal definitively in 1723 and served until his death in 1737.[35] The return on his investment was no doubt far less than he had antici- pated.

Persistence such as Corral's and continuing crises eroded the royal will al- most from the day the reform decree appeared. Only three of the eleven men removed failed to regain an audiencia position, and one of these three became a canon in the Cathedral of Lima, perhaps the best bargain of all.[36] The other two men were already in their fifties and perhaps lacked the much younger Corral's incentive to protest vigorously.[37] Six of the eight men who regained appointments were still in Spain in 1701 or returned there immediately to pur- sue their appeals. Within three years they held new but rarely the same ap- pointments. Only one of the four who had held direct appointments to Lima or Mexico managed to retain his prestigious position.[38] The other three settled for demotion to lesser audiencias. The reappointments might reflect Philip's inabil- ity to refund the servicios to all the men in the deteriorating international situa- tion of the next few years. And one may speculate freely on how many of these reconfirmed American ministers did as limeño Gregorio Núñez de Rojas and simply paid again for their office in a manner reminiscent of the way in which land titles were periodically revalidated. The second purchase of Núñez de Rojas in 1708, a year of heavy sales, illustrates how easily reform decrees failed in the hard-pressed empire.[39]

The appearance of reform decrees in 1691 and 1701 apparently threatened to dissuade potential purchasers from investment in positions. Consequently, during the last hectic years of sales before 1712, purchasers often obtained, along with routine dispensations for nativity, marriage, or economic activity, the assurance that they were safe against a future reform. In a situation ap- proaching the ridiculous, men bought exemptions in advance against laws that denied the possibility of such exemptions. No guarantee could be more explicit than the king's assurance to Mexican native-son purchaser Agustín Franco Vel- ásquez de Toledo that "if any reform should occur before you enter a regular seat, you will not be affected, even though you might be expressly men- tioned."[40]

The crown's temporary abdication of its prerogative to rescind previous commitments occurred during the last period of sales. Harried by the growing war, Philip V again had retreated from traditional appointment practices and turned to the sale of audiencia posts. This third period opened hesitantly in

35. José Toribio Medina, *Diccionario biográfico colonial de Chile* (Santiago, Chile, 1906), p. 215.
36. Villavicencio became a canon.
37. Santiago de Céspedes and Valverde Contreras.
38. Anguita, who died before reclaiming his seat.
39. AGS, XXIII, 2–4–97 (Núñez de Rojas, Madrid, 13 December 1708).
40. AGI, Indiferente General, legajo 1847, "Razón de los Empleos Beneficados de Nueva España."

1704 with only two transactions, both involving limeños who purchased supernumerary appointments to their home tribunal.[41] This initial restraint reveals that there was some intention to avoid a complete relapse, but the conflict over the renewal of *beneficio* reveals that by 1704 the power of patronage had passed from the hands of the staunchest opponents of sales, the letrados on the Council of the Indies. When the council got word in 1704 of the sale of an appointment to the limeño Pedro Gregorio de la Canal, it protested vigorously that the action represented "exceptional favoritism" as it undercut the promise to give first consideration to those purchasers removed from office in 1701.[42] The failure of the protest underlines the council's weakness in patronage during times of sales.

Philip's hesitancy to sell audiencia positions yielded in 1706, and purchasers multiplied until 1712.[43] One of the two sales in 1706 was to a native son in Quito, and both appointees were supernumeraries. In the following year sales accelerated, and Mexicans in particular entered the market. Of the eight new men who purchased appointments in 1707, three were native sons, two Mexicans and one limeño. In 1708 eight more men purchased posts. Five of the new purchasers were native sons, three from Lima and one each from Santa Fe and Mexico. Although the crown sold five new appointments and a promotion in 1709, none went to a native son.[44] The high point of sales came in 1710 and 1711 when twenty-three men, including four Mexicans among the six native sons, purchased positions.[45] The deluge ended with the termination of major fighting in Spain; in 1712 only one of the two new appointments was by sale, and the crown turned down at least two would-be purchasers.[46] Fittingly, the final purchaser of the period was a native son.

The number of native sons serving as ministers escalated with sales. Figure 1 presents their appointments by both year and region. Peruvians and Mexicans were especially successful in obtaining appointments both to their home and other tribunals. Every purchaser going to Lima and eight of fourteen to Mexico were native sons. Moreover, Peruvians and Mexicans who could not purchase appointments at home invariably did so for tribunals within the ascenso that led to their natal courts. Thus limeños went to Charcas, Chile, Panama, and Quito, while Mexicans stayed in Guadalajara and Guatemala.

---

41. Pedro Gregorio de la Canal and Peralta.
42. Paz-Soldán and Céspedes, *Virreinato peruano,* 3: 193*n.*
43. For the purchasers of these years see Appendix III.
44. Alvaro Navia Bolaños purchased a promotion from oidor in Charcas to supernumerary oidor in Lima for 500 doblones. AGS, XXIII, 2-6-9 (Navia, Madrid, 16 June 1709).
45. Also Nicolás Chirino Vandeval purchased a promotion from oidor of Santo Domingo to alcalde del crimen in Mexico, and Juan Fernando Calderón de la Barca paid 6,000 pesos to stay in Lima as oidor rather than move to the Chancellery of Valladolid. AGS, XXIII, 2–8–133 (Chirino, Madrid, 28 February 1710); 2–10–11 (Calderón, Zaragoza, 20 May 1711).
46. Quiteño Sánchez de Orellana was the sole purchaser; those turned down were Campo y Zárate (appointed years later) and a son of alcalde del crimen in Mexico Juan de Ozaeta y Oro.

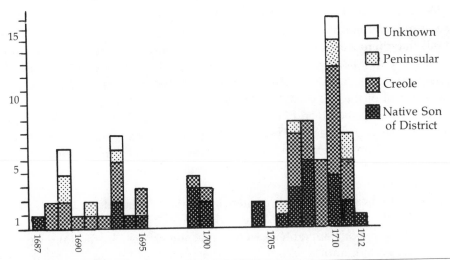

Figure 1. Purchasers' Place of Birth, 1687–1712

Place of Birth	Number of Purchasers	Number of Native Sons
Lima	34	16
Mexico	17	8
Santa Fe	3	1
Santo Domingo	3	
Quito	2	2
Charcas	2	
Guadalajara	1	
Panama	1	1
Chile	1	
Spanish America, district of birth unknown	1	
Spain	10	
Unknown	5	
	80	28

Considering that the point of sales was to raise money, the crown seemed particularly willing to accommodate native sons, for they required dispensations that enabled raising the price of the office. The four peninsular purchasers to Mexico paid an average of 6,750 pesos for their posts, while eight native sons paid an average of 9,300 pesos.[47]

The origins of the purchasers reflected the material and educational advantages available in the viceregal capitals. Almost two-thirds of the purchasers and all but four of the native sons came from Lima and Mexico. In contrast, peninsulares accounted for only one-seventh of the total number of appointees. For Peruvians, dominance in native son and total creole appointments continued a tradition of audiencia service that dated back to the late sixteenth century. Mexicans, on the other hand, entered the audiencias in significant numbers only with sales.

The relative absence of Mexicans among appointees from 1687 to 1706 seems to have reflected, in part at least, a difference in royal policy toward the

47. Barbadillo Victoria, Francisco de Casa Alvarado, Robles, and Calderón.

two viceregal tribunals. Before the group of sales that began in 1704, aside from Francisco de Anguita Sandoval, no native son bought an appointment to the Mexican tribunal, while eight gained posts in Lima. The disastrous state of affairs in Spain in 1706, however, marked a change, and Mexicans became native-son ministers in unprecedented numbers: three from 1707 to 1709 and four in 1710 and 1711 bought positions. At the same time the pool of financially and educationally qualified limeño aspirants must have been nearly drained. By the end of 1709 twenty-four limeños had already purchased appointments, and the Lima tribunal was saturated, as fourteen native sons had bought posts there. From 1709 to 1712 only two more would do so; three other limeño purchasers went to already-full tribunals in the Lima ascenso pattern. At the same time, Mexico was still able to absorb native sons. Four purchasers of 1710 and 1711 entered the viceregal court, and five other Mexicans gained entry into its principal feeder tribunals of Guatemala and Guadalajara.[48] Perhaps in Mexico the lingering disapproval of the old judges who had protested the sale in 1690 had served as a deterrent in that decade. In addition, the example of the only native-son purchaser named before 1707 promptly losing his post in the reform of 1701 was apt to restrain all but the most ardent pretendientes until the chances of survival had improved.

While the sale of appointments was the most important development for the audiencias in the Age of Impotence, it accounted for under half of the new men named from 1687 to 1712. Comparison of Figures 1 and 4 reveals the origins of the other appointees. Americans obtained over half (seventy-seven) of the 150 new appointments between 1687 and 1712, but only one-sixth (thirteen) of these creoles joined the audiencias without purchasing their positions.[49] In contrast, the majority of the Spaniards obtained positions without payment. Indeed, the crown named most of the peninsulares in the years of few sales. Although forty-nine men were named during the years of heaviest sales, 1707–1711, only nine were Spaniards, three of them purchasers. From the renewal of sales in 1699 until 1712, peninsulares received only thirty-seven appointments (six by purchase), while Americans gained fifty-five with a maximum of only five and perhaps none appointed for merit rather than pecuniary service.[50]

Appointments reveal the crown's policy toward staffing the audiencias but provide only a crude idea of who was actually serving, since a few men never reached their posts, some were removed, and others died shortly after taking possession. Examination of the assigned composition of each tribunal over time

---

48. The four Mexican native sons were Oyanguren, Franco Velásquez de Toledo, Sánchez de Alcázar, and Vequenilla. The five going into feeder audiencias were Fernando de Urrutia, Rodezno, Lugo, Real y Quesada, and Arana.

49. This figure is doubtless high, as circumstantial evidence strongly suggests that at least seven and possibly more of the thirteen American nonpurchasers were actually secret buyers. The seven highly probable purchasers were: Calvo Domonte, Laya Bolívar, Ignacio Antonio de Castillo, Valverde Contreras, Soria Velásquez, Díez de Bracamonte, and Terreros Ochoa.

50. See Appendix III.

better indicates the long-term results of the appointments made. Appendix V illustrates the presence of a constant minority of Americans after 1687 and the expansion in the number of both native sons and other creoles with continued sales. The presence of supernumeraries in 1690, 1695, and 1700 is apparent, as is the impact of the reform decree of 1701 in 1705 when the number of positions was only one over that authorized by the *Recopilación,* and both native sons and other creoles were fewer than in 1700. The burgeoning sales that began in 1706 had, by 1710, pushed the tribunals to twenty-six men above authorized numero strength as well as giving native sons a significant minority and all creoles an absolute majority of the posts. A further slight deterioration of Spanish strength was apparent by 1712, the year sales ended.

Overall composition figures show that native-son strength tripled and total American strength more than doubled as percentages of total positions held from 1695 to 1712. The geographical location of these ministers, however, meant that creoles were never a majority in all audiencias and, despite the presence of twenty-five native sons in 1712, seven of the eleven tribunals had no direct representation. Appendix V demonstrates the variations among the courts. Mexico, Santa Fe, Santo Domingo, Guatemala, Guadalajara, and Manila had none or only one American serving in 1687, but creoles were dominant numerically in the audiencias of Chile, Quito, and Panama. Lima and Charcas had a minority of Americans. The picture had changed noticeably by 1712, largely reflecting the pattern of sales. Again Americans were absent in Manila and Santo Domingo and dominant numerically in Chile, Quito, and Panama, but here the similarity ends. In all other audiencias creoles were highly visible. Both Charcas and Chile had only one peninsular. Lima, Santa Fe, Mexico, Guadalajara, and Guatemala had American majorities. Native sons were clustered in four audiencias: Mexico (twelve), Lima (ten), Santa Fe (one), and Quito (two). At some point during the intervening years after 1687, however, Santo Domingo, Panama, and Charcas had also had native sons named. Awareness that local men had made good either at home or, more frequently, by gaining appointment to tribunals outside their place of birth, doubtless stimulated the hopes of budding letrados in the colonies.

The most psychologically satisfying representation of the interests of local families was to have a native son from their midst join the home audiencia. But even in the most propitious times, only a minority of tribunals enjoyed this direct representation. Far more frequently local merchants or *hacendados* had to rely upon indirect access to the audiencia's power. The entire purpose of the multiple restrictions on the ministers, as on viceroys and the lesser judicial officers, was to prevent ministers and local families from using each other for personal benefit at the expense of the crown or the general population. Ministers who sought enrichment and residents who hoped to benefit in influence through association with them in effect conspired to advance their respective interests.

Illegal participation in economic ventures and the formation of ritual kin-ship ties (*compadrazgo*) were two ways in which ministers could align them-selves with local residents. Marriage to the daughter of a prominent local fam-ily was an even stronger bond and one from which the first two could flow as well. Audiencia ministers automatically joined the elite by virtue of their posi-tions, and their brides also came from the upper reaches of society. It is neces-sary to stress the mutual advantages present in ties between ministers and their constituents. Both parties expected to profit from these relationships, the minister from the establishment of family life and the improvement of his for-tunes and his in-laws from the benefits that they anticipated would evolve from association with a powerful official.

The crown's need for funds led it to sell exemptions from the laws that prohibited marriage between ministers and women of their district of service. Unlike the sale of positions, relaxation of the marriage restrictions was not an innovation initiated in 1687; an official in Madrid wrote in the 1680s that in the previous two decades the king had never denied any minister in Lima a permit to marry a native.[51] In several instances the crown sold blanket permits to creole women that authorized them to marry any minister who could be in-terested.[52] After 1687 the sale of such privileges became much more common and the prices escalated. During the period of sales from 1687 to 1712, almost every tribunal at all times had at least one and frequently several ministers who had taken advantage of the crown's financial travail to establish local ties and thus compound the difficulties that sales had caused for the king.

The sales from 1687 to 1712 set the tone for over half a century. From them native sons gained unprecedented access to their home tribunals. The sales diminished the crown's control over the powerful American courts; they marked a formalization of the local strength that had been growing in what John Lynch has termed the "age of inertia."[53] While the succeeding seventeen years to 1730 would display a renewed royal effort to master the situation, the fact of extensive sales during the time of war conditioned Americans to seek appointments for cash whenever Spain faced financial crisis.

Ironically, at the same time that native sons enjoyed unprecedented ap-pointments, the discrimination they faced became more explicit and calculated. In "normal times" before heavy sales, native sons, as all Americans, would frequently suffer in their pretensions for lack of membership in one of the six colegios mayores, influential relatives, and friends at court. Their handicaps, however, were by circumstance more than design. Through sales the crown regularly subjected native sons as well as other creoles to heavy payments, in effect a deliberate discriminatory tax. Few peninsulares paid such a price.

---

51. AGI, Indiferente General, legajo 819, "Rⁿ de las licencias que de veinte años a esta parte se han concedido para casarse a diferentes Ministros del Perú."

52. Ibid.; Konetzke, *Colección*, 2, tomo II, document 553.

53. John Lynch, *The Spanish American Revolutions, 1808–1826* (London, 1973), p. 7.

The Reckoning

The financial prostration that made the sale of audiencia positions attractive and the expanded crisis provided by the War of the Spanish Succession gave the crown neither inclination nor time to consider dispassionately the effects on the American audiencias of its revenue-raising policies. The efforts at reform put forward in 1691 and 1701 testified to a continuing concern in some agencies of the imperial government to retain traditional standards of appointment, but Philip's desire to preserve his throne meant that he would employ any action that promised to produce funds and thus strengthen his position. The monarchy sold offices and dispensations with no thought for the morrow; inevitably the gray and cheerless morning that arrived after 1712 revealed the results of twenty-five years of abuse.

The letrados of the Council of the Indies opposed on principle the sale of posts of justice. They saw themselves as keepers of the flame of integrity for the judicial bureaucracy. During the seventeenth century their predecessors had developed a body of concepts to enhance the professional nature of the judiciary. Among these were proper social and educational background as guaranteed by the colegios mayores, enshrinement of seniority in the ascenso principle, and a well-defined code of ethics and law governing behavior in office. By emphasizing financial above traditional considerations for office-holding, the sale of positions prostituted these standards. To the jurists sales meant lower, not just different, standards. Moreover, the ministers of the cámara rightly viewed sales as a threat to their most jealously guarded prerogative, the patronage they exercised for the Indies.

Whenever the crown decided to sell audiencia positions, it created a special committee (junta) or named a specific individual to oversee the transactions. In 1693 Charles II entrusted the sale of offices in the Indies to the superintendent of the treasury, the Marqués de los Vélez, and during the War of Succession special secretaries such as José de Grimaldo controlled patronage.[54] Camaristas, therefore, had ample reason to oppose the sale of audiencia posts beyond their traditional concern for standards. When patronage remained safely in their hands they had no compunctions about bestowing favors or appointments based on nonprofessional grounds.[55] Initiated by com-

---

54. Konetzke, Colección, 3, tomo I, document 18; Kamen, War of Succession, p. 113.

55. For example, in 1751 Diego Fernández de Madrid received a direct appointment as alcalde del crimen in Mexico, although aged twenty-five and thus barely old enough to serve without a dispensation; his title of appointment specified that his naming was due to the merits of his father, Luis Fernández de Madrid, oidor of Mexico who had died in the previous year. AGS, XXIII, 2–38–32 (Diego Fernández de Madrid, Buen Retiro, 17 November 1751). Félix Suárez de Figueroa was given a direct appointment as supernumerary oidor in Mexico with full salary in 1716 because of the extensive services of his father and brother in the wars. AGS, XXIII, 2–16–88 (Suárez, Madrid, 3 February 1716). In 1741 the council recommended membership in a military order for the son of Lima fiscal Francisco Ortiz de Foronda; the boy was not yet in his teens. AGI, Indiferente General, legajo 1628.

petitors, such actions constituted abuse. Massive sales always reflected the temporary downgrading of the council and its cámara.

The relaxation of standards that the council feared often did accompany the sale of appointments. This was especially true in the flood of sales from 1706 to 1712. The crown's experience with Nicolás de Ulloa Calleja illustrates the dangers of a cursory investigation of purchasers. Ulloa, a native of Oaxaca, purchased an appointment as supernumerary oidor in Guatemala for 1500 doblones in April 1709.[56] A perfunctory inquiry revealed that he possessed acceptable credentials—a law degree from the University of Mexico, membership in the prestigious Colegio de San Ildefonso there, and standing as an abogado in New Spain. Only after Ulloa had been granted the post and paid his servicio did the shocked councillors learn that the Mexican was an unreconstructed drunkard with a long record of scandalous conduct. Covert efforts to admonish him failed, for Ulloa had already left Madrid for America. Then, when the council received news that the appointee was continuing his binges in Seville, it could no longer avoid informing the king. In December 1709 the ministers graphically portrayed the probable consequences of Ulloa's service and advised revocation of his appointment and refund of his payment. When the king expressed no concern and merely acknowledged the protest, the council repeated its advice in stronger terms. Writing of Ulloa's suitability for the position, it declared that his chief qualification for high office had been the 1500 doblones paid. Happily for the people of Guatemala, the crown grudgingly agreed, and Ulloa received his money back.[57] In analogous cases the king was even less attentive to the council's nagging voice of conscience, and gross violations of professional standards occurred.

The deterioration of standards that sales brought to the judiciary is further visible in the appointment of both young and inexperienced men. While one might argue that youths could provide idealism and energy, contemporaries regarded their appearance on the audiencias as an abuse. Men under twenty-five years of age were minors; regardless of other qualifications, their appointments violated the law and required a special dispensation.[58] During the period 1687–1712, the crown named at least fourteen men who were aged twenty-four or younger; thirteen definitely purchased their appointments. Most (twelve) appointments of minors and twelve sales to minors occurred during the peak years 1707–1712. Most glaring of all, three purchasers were in their teens; two were nineteen and one may have been as young as seventeen.[59] The lack of administrative experience possessed by many men named

56. AGS, XXIII, 2–7–93 (Ulloa Calleja, Buen Retiro, 13 April 1709); AGI, Guatemala, legajo 274, consultas of the Council of the Indies, 3 and 13 December 1709.
57. AGI, Guatemala, legajo 274, consultas of the Council of the Indies, 3 and 13 December 1709.
58. This statement is based upon an examination of exemptions that the crown granted for minority status.
59. AGS, XXIII, 2–3–3 (Solís Vango, Buen Retiro, 24 May 1707); the other two were Mirones and Sagardia. At least five additional men were just twenty-five years old when named; two of them definitely purchased their appointments.

directly to the senior audiencias again illustrates the decline of standards. While age carried the presumption of wisdom and experience in colonial society, only half of the men whose age is known and who at forty or over purchased appointments had judicial or governmental service important enough to note among their accomplishments.[60]

The breakdown of the ascenso was the most serious and long-lasting effect of the sale of audiencia appointments. The nature of colonial society meant that Mexico and Lima contained most of America's wealthy and aspiring young letrados as well as the prestigious viceregal tribunals whose posts purchasers sought most keenly. Faced with a lack of vacancies at times when it desperately wanted revenue, the crown often appointed supernumeraries during years of sales and thus burdened the senior tribunals and those nearest them in the ascenso with many extra ministers. In 1712 the Audiencia of Mexico, authorized fourteen ministers, had twenty-six; and the court in Guatemala counted nine, three beyond its quota. Not only did young men or those with little experience join senior tribunals, sometimes with sad results, but also morale declined noticeably throughout the system as deserving judges in lesser positions lost their anticipated promotions. The ascenso never worked perfectly, but in tranquil periods ministers could reasonably expect advancement every several years until they became oidores in Lima or Mexico. Sales disrupted the ascenso for a generation.

Judges of lesser tribunals were quick to observe the loss of anticipated advancement. Oidores serving in Santo Domingo and Panama complained to the council in 1689 that they were being denied their due because of direct appointments to Mexico and Lima.[61] The injured parties claimed that "some colegiales and others who took advantage of illicit favors" were preventing their merited promotions. In addition to noting the harmful effects of such practices on the caliber of the magistracy, the judges craftily reminded the crown that ignoring the ascenso cost the treasury money. A direct appointment to one of the senior audiencias touched only one person, but the proper functioning of the ascenso meant that a vacancy of oidor in Mexico or Lima would set off a "ripple effect" that could involve several men; since the crown collected a tax of at least one-half of a year's salary for each initial appointment and promotion, the money lost through direct appointment was considerable. The king took no action and the oidores' charge may have been exaggerated, since very few appointments before 1687 had violated the ascenso. The growth of sales, however, gave weight to such complaints. Sales benefited a few men serving on lesser tribunals, but many junior magistrates lacked the financial resources to purchase advancement and consequently languished without promotion. The appointment of men without experience to senior tribunals was particularly offensive to them.

---

60. The men were Santiago de Céspedes, Oyanguren, Lastero, Zúñiga, and Aranburu.
61. Konetzke, *Colección*, 2, tomo II, document 555.

The problem of stalled advancement appeared in Peru at the turn of the eighteenth century. Pablo Vásquez de Velasco, fiscal in Lima since 1690, sought promotion to alcalde del crimen or oidor. He claimed that he was "delayed in his ascenso because of the many places that had been sold." Sympathetic, the cámara voted in January 1700 to give him the first vacancy, without regard to the prior rights of the ranking supernumerary then serving. The king acquiesced, and Vásquez served as oidor until his death in 1720.[62]

A disrupted ascenso also affected the northern audiencias in the Secretariat of New Spain. Around 1706 Juan de Ozaeta, alcalde del crimen in Mexico, printed a formal memorial and distributed it to the Councillors of the Indies.[63] In Ozaeta's view, his turn for promotion to oidor passed in 1705, when a native son (and probable purchaser) received a direct appointment as oidor. Ozaeta recounted some twenty years of service and his considerable accomplishments and complained that the crown no longer rewarded loyal servants. Unfortunately for him his protest failed, and, after at least another decade of labors, Ozaeta died without promotion to the civil chamber, the senior criminal judge in Mexico. Francisco de Feijóo Centellas faced a problem similar to that of Ozaeta.[64] Oidor of Guadalajara since 1687, Feijóo had served over two decades without promotion. Responding to his protest, the council praised his accomplishments and noted that sales had deprived him, as they had other long-serving ministers, of the promotions they deserved; always opposed to the sale of office, the consejeros were quick to champion such appeals. The backlog that sales had placed in Mexico, however, meant that the best they could do was to provide a futura to that tribunal. When Americans, sometimes of dubious qualifications, bought directly into the highest tribunals in the Indies and deprived more experienced judges sitting on the lesser courts of timely promotions, the cost in bitterness and loss of morale was high.

The abuse that sale of audiencia positions represented was often compounded by the sale of exemptions to various restrictive laws governing the conduct and local involvement of judges.[65] Aspirants purchased such dispensations both separately and as part of the total appointment "package." Indeed, purchasers of audiencia positions often had no choice but to purchase additional dispensations. A native son who owned a nearby hacienda and whose wife was locally born automatically violated laws designed to isolate ministers from the families and economic activities of the region served. The chief exemption he required concerned his nativity. While no law unequivocally prohibited a native son from serving, the crown granted dispensations as though one existed. Both native sons and outsiders were often anxious to obtain one or more of the other dispensations available. The right to marry a local woman, the right to hold property within the audiencia district, and a guaran-

62. AGI, Lima, legajo 344, consulta of cámara, 18 January 1700.
63. AGI, Mexico, legajo 523.
64. AGI, Mexico, legajo 452, consulta of council, 22 June 1709; AGS, XXIII, 2–6–71 (Feixóo Zentellas, Madrid, 9 August 1709).
65. See Appendix III for the dispensations granted with purchased appointments.

tee that the purchaser would be exempted from the operations of a future re-form decree were three common dispensations.[66] Many judges purchased marriage permits for themselves or their children for fees ranging from two to as much as six thousand pesos.[67] The usual range during the period under consideration was from twenty-five hundred to four thousand pesos.

The saga of Salvador Sánchez de la Barreda exemplifies the conditions attached to sales. A limeño who purchased an appointment as oidor *supernumerario* to the audiencia in Santiago for twenty-five hundred doblones in 1708, Sánchez received dispensation to marry a native and assurance that, should he die before serving, the crown would restore the two thousand doblones he had already delivered.[68] In addition, the crown assuaged his fears that he might later be deprived of his post with a promise that no reform could depose him. Prepared to serve, the young letrado set sail for America. Then disaster struck; the Dutch captured his ship, and he perished. Immediately his father petitioned the crown to keep the money already paid plus that due and an additional five hundred pesos in exchange for naming another and still younger son, Francisco, to the post.[69] The king agreed but on the condition that should Francisco also die the treasury would keep not only the two thousand doblones already paid but also the additional five hundred pesos that had been offered. Francisco's luck was better than his brother's and he died at his post after over twenty-five years of service.[70]

The quarter-century of abuses to traditional standards fulfilled the prophecies of the opponents of such practices. By 1712 the crown's quest for revenue had left the major audiencias of America largely in the control of native sons, while the wholesale approval of dispensations from restrictive statutes meant that local families enjoyed extensive access to the jurists. Failure to observe traditional concern for appointees' qualifications allowed the entrance of ministers of questionable character and professional conduct. Direct sales to the viceregal audiencias gave rise to young or otherwise inexperienced men in the highest positions. Beyond these immediate concerns, the appointment of many extra ministers led to the breakdown of the ascenso and thus prolonged the other problems for years. When the councillors of Philip V found their voices after 1712, their dominant theme was to end the abuses of impotence and return to traditional standards.

---

66. Other dispensations included permission to remain absent from one's post for a period of time, dispensation for being of minority status, and a money-back guarantee if one were unable to assume the purchased position.

67. See AGI, Indiferente General, legajo 525, "Relación de los empleos" for examples of the varying prices.

68. AGS, XXIII, 2–5–142 (Salvador Sánchez de la Barreda, Buen Retiro, 8 July 1708).

69. Ibid., 2–8–30 (Francisco Sánchez de la Barreda, Madrid, 7 August 1710).

70. Juan Luis Espejo, *Nobiliario de la capitanía general de Chile* (Santiago, Chile, 1967), p. 738.

Readjustment

By 1712 the Bourbons controlled all of Spain except for Gibraltar and Catalonia, and the monarchy's need for ready cash became less desperate. General as well as domestic peace descended in 1715, and for the next decade traditional attitudes of administration reappeared to guide royal policy toward the audiencias. Under a newly created Secretariat of the Indies, a revitalized council took harsh actions to restore royal control over the ultramarine tribunals. Chief among the crown's problems was that many ministers serving in the New World lacked the professional and personal qualifications called for in law and custom. Among these ministers were incompetents, many purchasers, and men with extensive direct and indirect local connections.

The actions taken by the crown and the Council of the Indies reflected not only traditional professional concerns but also the struggle at court between opposing factions. The arrival at the palace of the forceful Elizabeth Farnese and the reaction of elements of the bureaucracy and high nobility to excessive French influence created disputes in the organs of government as well as court intrigues. The housecleaning zeal that appeared in the new secretariats and the Council of the Indies in 1715 and 1716 probably arose from a desire to embarrass previous officials and political opponents as well as from a sincere concern for the welfare of the realms.

On 17 April 1716 the Council of the Indies debated the state of the American audiencias.[71] The Conde de Frigiliana, recently named secretary of the Indies, revealed the depth of official concern in his proposal that "only peninsulares be named to the American audiencias." This extraordinary suggestion went beyond not only statutory provisions but also the spirit of long-standing policies that included rewarding deserving subjects of American origin. In response to such concern, in 1717 the council established a special junta to deal with "the deplorable state of all [the audiencias]."[72] The junta identified sales as the origin of difficulties and delineated the abuses they had brought: unnecessary supernumeraries and futurarios, ministers without the needed preparation for high office, and young men who displayed other *vicios* for which they had obtained dispensations. To prevent a recurrence of such scandalous conditions, the junta urged that the king never again sell audiencia positions.

The consideration of a candidate's birthplace became an issue during the years of sales through the frequent dispensations issued to native sons, and beginning in 1717 Frigiliana's concern over place of origin was reflected in the appointment process. Lists of pretendientes for vacancies in American audiencias routinely began to carry notations giving the audiencia district of birth for Americans and indicating Spaniards as such.[73] This practice conspicuously de-

---

71. AGI, Indiferente, legajo 1293, consulta of council, 17 April 1716.

72. Ibid., report of the special junta, 1717. In January 1717 the council itself underwent a purge. See Gildas Bernard, *Le secrétariat d'état et le conseil espagnol des Indes (1700–1808)* (Geneva, 1972), pp. 12–15.

73. AGI, Audiencia of Santa Fe (hereafter Santa Fe), legajos 283 and 284.

parted from that of earlier decades, when colegio and university affiliation alone were generally listed. Place of birth continued to be noted regularly throughout most of the 1720s. Although the council often spoke of sales and their abuses and rarely of native sons, the sudden appearance of place of origin on consultas in addition to comments such as that by Frigiliana suggests that the ministers considered sale of office synonymous with heavy American and especially native-son infestation of the audiencias.

The government did more than reprehend the state of the American courts. Between 1717 and 1720 a flurry of punishments, *visitas*, and other investigations removed at least twenty-six ministers from office for sundry crimes and abuses. Certainly sixteen and probably eighteen of these men were American purchasers, and at least twelve of them were native sons.[74]

In Quito, Juan Larrea Zurbano and native sons Juan Bautista Sánchez de Orellana and Lorenzo Lastero de Salazar were among those affected.[75] With some exaggeration, other judges on the court charged that Larrea, a New Granadan who had purchased his appointment in 1711, was not a licenciado as he claimed but "only a captain of cavalry." The viceroy of Peru similarly impugned Larrea's "incapacity and utter lack of learning." The hapless judge departed in 1717 and recovered his post only in 1738. His colleague Sánchez de Orellana, the final purchaser during the War of the Spanish Succession, was more justly accused of lacking letrado status, that most basic professional requirement for audiencia judges. Philip V had granted Sánchez the position in 1712 with a perfunctory admonition that he must finish his legal education within one year. In response to an inquiry by the council, the viceroy of Peru reported in 1717 that Sánchez was not yet a letrado and, furthermore, exhibited "total incapacity" and "bad habits." According to common report, the judge and his wife were related to everyone of note in the province of Quito, and he voted according to his relatives' needs. Convinced of the mistake, the king removed Sánchez and returned his money.[76]

In 1718 Philip abolished the Audiencia of Panama, dominated by purchasers, as corrupt and harmful to sound administration in the area. The five ministers serving were charged with unnamed crimes, and one, Peruvian purchaser Pedro Gómez de Andrade, was actually sent to Spain a prisoner.[77]

---

74. The twenty-six were Torralva, Aranburu, Díez de Bracamonte, Llorente, Lastero, Peña y Flores, Robles y Lorenzana, Castañeda, Zapata, Oyanguren, Franco, Terreros, Sánchez de Alcázar, Sánchez de Orellana, Ypes, Suárez de Figueroa, Larrea, Gómez de Andrade, Pérez Buelta, Alzamora, Clavijo, Mirones, Echavarría, Echave, Valenzuela, and González de Agüero. Seven men (Gómez de Andrade, Gaspar Pérez Buelta, Alzamora, Clavijo, Mirones, Echavarría, and Echave) later regained their posts.

75. AGI, Lima, legajo 983, consulta of council, 16 December 1716; Viceroy of Peru to Señor, Lima, 7 November 1717.

76. AGS, XXIII, 2–20–62 (title to refund money to Juan Sánchez de Orellana, Aranjuez, 18 May 1722).

77. Ibid., 2–21–132 (absolution from charges, Pedro Gómez de Andrade, Balsain, 9 August 1723). The other judges removed were Gaspar Pérez Buelta, Alzamora, Clavijo, and Mirones.

Three men lost their posts simultaneously in the Audiencia of Santa Fe. The king charged the trio, which included two purchasers (one of whom was a native son), with scandalous and rebellious conduct growing out of an effort to remove by force the captain-general.[78]

From Lima in 1720 the crown removed oidores Juan Bautista de Echavarría Zuloaga and Pedro Echave and protector of the Indians Isidro López de Ezeyza, all native sons and purchasers, and ordered their money refunded.[79] The councillors suggested that replacements for the two oidores be sought among the excessive supernumeraries serving on the Audiencia of Mexico, nearly all of whom were Mexicans. Doubtless the letrados of the council thought it fitting to attack two problem audiencias at once by transferring Mexicans south to replace limeño native sons. Three years later, in 1723, the council still worried about the Peruvian tribunal. It observed that four of the five members of the recently reestablished Audiencia of Panama had originally purchased and should never be considered for promotion to the viceregal tribunal.[80] Although the fact was not mentioned, after a five-year investigation of the judges of Panama, the council must have known that all four were limeños. It was much easier to attack the clear-cut violation that purchase represented, however, than the legally ambiguous abuse of native-son service.[81]

The drive to regain control and punish corruption in the judiciary extended to New Spain as well as to the south. In 1720 a newly appointed visitor-general focused his attention on the letrados of the Audiencia of Mexico, most important of the high courts of New Spain and the one most heavily affected by sales. On 3 August Visitor-General Francisco de Garzarón reported to the king that he had suspended from office eleven of the eighteen

---

78. The three men were Aranburu, Ypes, and Zapata. José María Restrepo Sáenz, *Biografías de los mandatarios y ministros de la real audiencia—(1671 a 1819)* (Bogatá, 1952), pp. 332, 334, 453.

79. AGI, Lima, legajo 348, consulta of council, 22 April 1720.

80. Ibid., legajo 475, consulta of cámara, April 1723. Similarly, in 1720 the papers of the natives of Lima serving in Charcas were not even considered when the cámara filled a vacancy of oidor in Lima. Ibid., list of the Audiencia of Lima in 1720.

81. A shakeup similar to that of Panama occurred in Quito, although much less is known about it. The audiencia was suppressed from 1718 to 1720; see, for example, José Mª Ots y Capdequí, *Historia del derecho español en América y el derecho indiano* (Madrid, 1969), p. 133. In that same period a number of the judges of the Audiencia of Manila were jailed for wrongdoing, and the tribunal almost ceased to function; see Emma Helen Blair and James Alexander Robertson, eds., *The Philippine Islands, 1493–1898*, 55 vols. (Cleveland, 1903–1909), 44: 152–55. Further evidence of the crown's zeal to improve administration and correct deficiencies can be seen in the decision taken in 1725 to create a "permanent supernumerary" position on the Audiencia of Manila. Authorized four oidores and a fiscal, the tribunal repeatedly suffered from a shortage of ministers. Often two or even three years might elapse before Madrid would learn of a death on the tribunal and more time would pass before a replacement would take his seat. During war the time-lag might be five or six years, and at times Manila was staffed by only one or two judges. From 1725 until the extra position was regularized in 1776, the king filled vacancies in the fifth and supernumerary oidorship as with the other four. See AGS, XXIII, 2–58–215 (title of Cacho Calderón de la Barca, Aranjuez, 12 June 1774) for an explanation of the decision reached in a consulta of 28 February 1725.

ministers.[82] He gave the stunned magistrates fifteen days to leave the city and ordered them to remain at least twenty leagues outside its environs. The charges against them apparently did not arise from weighty issues of principle but rather from routine peculation and influence peddling. The eleven appealed to the Council of the Indies, which later upheld their deposition. The suspensions left the tribunal with only six of its authorized fourteen judges present, three oidores and three alcaldes del crimen.[83]

The coincidence between the charges and the majority of native sons and purchasers that had existed in Mexico for a decade underlined the council's conviction that the sale of judicial offices inevitably meant poorly qualified judges and contamination by local interests. The eleven ministers affected did not include an outsized share of the proven or suspected purchasers and accounted for only slightly more than an equivalent proportion of native sons. Nevertheless, the fate of some of those not removed and the character of the ministers selected to replace the dismissed men revealed the crown's attitude. The evidence collected by Garzarón would not support the removal of two other purchasers (one a native son) serving in the criminal chamber, but it apparently destroyed their hopes for advancement to the more prestigious civil sala. Although first in the ascenso to oidor in Mexico, both were bypassed repeatedly by new oidores promoted from lesser courts or named directly from universities.[84] The appointment of four new ministers to Mexico by the end of 1721, three and probably all four of whom were peninsulares, changed the Mexican tribunal from one controlled by purchasers and native sons to one in which Spaniards and other outsiders, primarily nonpurchasers, exercised a narrow majority.[85] The audiencia received eight more replacements before the end of 1725; five were Spaniards, two were creoles born outside the district, and one was a native son who had proven himself in a lesser tribunal.[86] In five years the crown obliterated the effects of the heavy sales period in Mexico. By 1725 control of that audiencia had passed to Spaniards, most of whom merited their appointments by years of prior service.

---

82. AGI, Mexico, legajo 670A, Garzarón to Señor, Mexico, 3 August 1720. Those removed were Valenzuela Venegas, Díez de Bracamonte, González de Agüero, Terreros Ochoa, Franco, Suárez de Figueroa, Peña y Flores, Robles, Castañeda, Sánchez de Alcázar, and Oyanguren.

83. Those on hand were Uribe Castejón, Soria Velásquez, Oliván Rebolledo, Chirino Vandeval, Vequenilla, and Barbadillo Victoria. Oviedo y Baños was assigned but never arrived to serve because of illness and eventual death.

84. Affected were Vequenilla and Barbadillo. The latter died in 1727 and the former in 1736. Between 1720 and 1727 six new oidores were assigned to Mexico. From 1720 to 1736, nine oidores had been named. Therefore, one might say that the true effects of the visita meant that nine of the eleven proven or probable native sons and eleven of the fourteen proven or probable purchasers lost office or had their careers blighted.

85. The four appointed at the end of 1721 were González Pimentel, Carrillo Escudero, Gutiérrez de la Peña, and Picado.

86. The eight were Pedro de Malo de Villavicencio, Fernández Pérez, Lugo Coronado, Osilia, Prudencio Antonio de Palacios, Ambrosio Tomás de Santaella y Melgarejo, Aguirre Negro, and Julián de Velasco.

The pattern of the removals in Quito, Panama, Lima, and Mexico is suggestive. Although there is no explicit statement that the crown removed any of the men because of purchase or place of birth, the ubiquity of native sons and purchasers in these fiascos cannot be coincidence. It matters little whether purchase or nativity meant that these ministers were morally or intellectually unfit for office, or whether their local ties, preexisting or soon established through purchase of dispensations, gave them a propensity for abuse of office. From the viewpoint of the crown, purchase and native birth were by definition abuses. The heart of the royal attitude during these years is revealed in a decree issued on 31 March 1720. Philip V indirectly condemned sales by ruling that the laws which prevented natives of a province from obtaining posts of justice in that province should be observed rigorously in the future.[87]

A toughened attitude toward the marriage of ministers into local elite families provides another indication of royal efforts to regain control of the audiencias. The crown issued a permit authorizing marriage to a local woman in 1713 and another in 1716, antedating the council's investigation of the audiencias.[88] Policy changed, however, after the revelation that the indirect local influence created by marriage threatened royal control nearly as much as direct local connections. In 1720 the crown denied the newly named fiscal of the Audiencia of Lima a permit to marry locally, apparently the first such refusal to a member of that tribunal since the time of Philip IV.[89] In the same decree in which he attacked service by native sons, Philip V commented on the *"graves perjuicios"* that failure to observe the marriage laws had occasioned and restated the traditional ban against local marriage.[90]

Not long afterward, however, the Spanish crown's determination to root out abuses and regain control over American tribunals seemed to weaken. In a remarkable about-face in 1722 and 1723, the king reestablished the Audiencia of Panama with the same five ministers who had been removed under charges in 1718.[91] Purchaser and native-son protector of the Indians Isidro López de Ezeyza, removed from office in Lima in 1720, was named fiscal of the Audiencia of Guatemala in the following year.[92] His promotion after the removal points to the centrality of native-son status in the crown's judgment of suitability for office and suggests the inability of the treasury to reimburse him. Oidor Echavar-

87. Antonio Muro Orejón, ed., *Cedulario americano del siglo XVIII*, 2 vols., (Sevilla, 1956–1969), 2, document 375. This decree strengthened the interpretation that taken together the restrictive statutes on local involvement by ministers prohibited native-son appointments. There was, however, no single law explicitly prohibiting native-son appointments. See p. 6, notes 9 and 10.

88. Pedro Gregorio de la Canal (Lima) received a permit to marry locally in 1713 and Francisco de Barbadillo Victoria (Mexico) received one in 1716. No more such permits appeared until 1726.

89. AGI, Lima, legajo 348; Indiferente General, legajo 819, "Rⁿ de las licencias que de veinte años a esta parte se han concedido para casarse a diferentes ministros del Perú."

90. Muro Orejón, *Cedulario*, 2, document 365.

91. See p. 38, note 77.

92. AGS, XXIII, 2–19–83 (López de Ezeyza, Aranjuez, 2 May 1721).

ría of the Audiencia of Lima, removed along with López in 1720 and promised a refund of his purchase price, regained his post in 1725 because Philip V could not fulfill his promise of restitution.[93] Nor could the royal treasury meet Echavarría's claim for the backpay due him. It eventually liquidated the debt by granting him a title of nobility.[94] His colleague, Pedro de Echave, also continued to serve and probably for the same reason. The financial strain of Spain's aggressive foreign policy in the 1720s took its toll on administrative priorities.

The exemption from future reforms bought by purchasers of audiencia posts underlay the connection between royal finances and the drive to regain control of the tribunals. The anxiety generated by the reform of 1701 prompted many pretendientes, including all those Mexican purchasers serving in 1720, to purchase assurances of immunity from future reforms. Legally, then, the crown could not remove purchasers because they were supernumeraries or futurarios, as before, but only for misconduct, a charge that had the added attraction of relieving the king of any obligation to refund their money. Philip's restoration of the ministers in Lima and Panama suggests his government's inability either to prove misconduct or to refund their servicios. The sale in 1726 of the first marriage permit in a decade underscored the growing financial pinch.[95] Only in Santa Fe and Mexico was the crown able to establish "cause" and enforce its removals. Spain's apparent inability to spare the money necessary to dismiss undesirable ministers prolonged royal impotence before local interests.

The changing balance of outsider and native-son strength on the American audiencias reveals the successes and failures of the royal policy. During the period 1713–1729 sixty men, of whom at least forty-nine were peninsulares, received their first appointments to an American audiencia (see Figure 4). Of the eight confirmed Americans named, seven were limeños, and the eighth had been educated at the University of San Marcos in Lima.[96] Unlike the preceding period, however, none of the Americans were direct appointees to viceregal audiencias, and only four of them, including the Panamanian educated in Lima, were directly in the Lima ascenso. Moreover, no American appointee was a native son.

The efforts to rehabilitate the ascenso can be seen in the appointments to Mexico and Lima. While the crown named twenty men to the Audiencia of

---

93. AGI, Lima, legajo 596, "De Parte," Council of the Indies, 10 July 1726.

94. Rubén Vargas Ugarte, *Títulos nobiliarios en el Perú*, 4th ed. (Lima, 1965), p. 63.

95. This permit to Francisco Xavier de Salazar y Castejón was ex post facto authorization in return for two thousand pesos. AGI, Indiferente General, legajo 525, "Relación de los empleos."

96. The seven limeños were Miguel de Gomendio Urrutia, Castilla y Lisperguer, Tomás de Salazar, Zárate y Alarcon, Arviza y Ugarte, Villalta y Núñez, López de Ezeyza; the non-limeño was Gómez García. Three of the sixty men were of unknown origin. One, Félix Suárez de Figueroa, may have been of Guatemalan or Mexican origin, while the other two, Julián de Velasco and Juan Pérez García, were probably peninsulares.

Mexico, only six went by direct appointment. One of these was Félix Suárez de Figueroa, specifically named in recompense for the services of his father and brother.[97] Another was Julián de Velasco, promised an appointment in Mexico in return for six-years' service as a professor of law in the Philippines.[98] To Lima the king named sixteen men, including eight direct appointees. Half of the direct appointments occurred between 1718 and 1721, the period of the most intensive effort to regain control. That three appointees were graduates of the elite colegios mayores suggests the care the crown was taking in its appointments.[99] Of the fourteen named directly to the viceregal tribunals, all but one were numero appointees, further ratification of the difference between these direct namings and those of the sales period.

Reduction by attrition of American and native-son strength present at the end of 1712 began almost immediately (see Appendixes V and VI). A slow decline continued into the early part of 1720 when Americans still claimed half (51 percent) of all positions, and native sons remained in sixteen audiencia seats (20 percent), all in Lima and Mexico. Even though the crown had appointed almost exclusively Spaniards to the tribunals since 1713, the lingering effect of the sales continued. The year 1720 brought a drastic reduction in the number of Americans and native sons serving on the courts. As a result of the visita in Mexico and less dramatic reductions elsewhere, in 1725 only seventy-seven men were serving, a number only one above the legal strength of the tribunals. Thirty-one (40 percent) of these were Americans, ten of them (13 percent) native sons. By the end of 1725 only Chile and Charcas retained American majorities, and native sons no longer dominated any audiencia, although Lima still had a strong minority of seven Peruvians.

The reduction in native-son strength was patent even to casual observers. Bitter disappointment descended on American letrados whose hopes to serve at home had been nurtured in the heyday of sales. The influx and subsequent removal of native sons was most apparent in Mexico, where Juan Antonio de Ahumada viewed the purge from the Colegio of Todos Santos. Influenced too by rumors that Philip had ordered the Cámara of the Indies not to propose Americans for political or military positions, Ahumada protested.[100] Although his text contained no reference to Bolívar y de la Redonda's tract, the sources employed and arguments advanced often closely followed those of the earlier

---

97. AGS, XXIII, 2–16–88 (Suárez de Figueroa, Madrid, February 1716).

98. Ibid., 2–22–98 (Julián de Velasco, Aranjuez, 1 June 1724).

99. The colegiales were Rodríguez de Castañón, Ceballos Guerra, and Salazar y Castejón.

100. Juan Antonio de Ahumada, *Representación político=legal Que hace a nuestro Señor Soberano Don Felipe Quinto, [que Dios guarde] Rey poderoso de las Españas, y Emperador siempre augusto de las Indias: para que se sirva declarar, no tienen los Aspañoles* (sic) *Indianos óbice para obtener los empleos políticos y militares de la América; y que deben ser preferidos en todos, así eclesiásticos como seculares* (1725; reprint ed., Mexico, 1820). Other writers have noted Ahumada's protest and used it for various purposes. See, for example, Francisco López Cámara, *La génesis de la conciencia liberal en México* (Mexico, 1969) and Mauro Olmeda, *El desarrollo de la sociedad mexicana,* vol. 2 (Madrid, 1969).

writer. The major point was identical: native sons should hold all positions. Despite canards maligning their talents and dependability, Americans were capable and trustworthy. Moreover, specific laws favored them in their pretension to hold the offices within their home districts. With misplaced hopes, Ahumada sought an explicit declaration acknowledging that Americans were not prohibited by law from holding office and requested that they be given all posts.

The Mexican attorney's pretension was no more successful than Bolívar's had been. And, unlike the New Granadan, Ahumada's journey to Spain brought not the robes of high judicial office, but only a purchased appointment as corregidor in Zacatecas.[101] Nonetheless, at about the time he wrote, the crown's drive to regain control over the American audiencias faltered. No more purges occurred and, although native sons did not enter the courts in number until the sale of appointments began again, the renewed sale of marriage permits in 1726 marked success for the silent advocates of indirect influence.

The composition of the tribunals changed little from 1725 to 1730 and, while native-son representation was lower than it had been a decade earlier, extensive indirect influence remained as a result of previous marriage and property dispensations and the lingering effects of the disruption of the ascenso for most of the lesser audiencias. In sum, although the crown had effected remarkable changes temporarily, by 1730 it had not firmly reestablished its control. The resurgence of traditional seventeenth-century attitudes toward appointments evident during most of the decade after 1715 weakened because of growing royal preoccupation with affairs in Italy during the 1720s. After 1730 both direct and indirect local influence began to grow once again, prolonging and indeed expanding royal impotence with regard to the audiencias of the New World.

Relapse and a Resurgence of Standards

War and attendant financial emergencies monopolized the crown's attention from 1730 to 1750. Having just emerged in 1729 from a small but unsuccessful conflict over its Italian pretensions, in the mid-1730s Spain plunged into the War of the Polish Succession. The financial pressure from these conflicts had barely eased when general war broke out in 1739, lasting almost a decade. The intermittent character of these conflicts precluded a consistent policy toward audiencia appointments and prolonged the state of impotence that had existed for two generations. Nonetheless, during the temporary lull between wars in the late 1730s, traditional concern for professional standards again surfaced in the Council of the Indies. Until the expenses of the War of Jenkins' Ear swept

101. AGI, Indiferente General, legajo 1847. "Relación que se ha formado de orden de S.M. comunicada por el Exmo Sor Marqués de la Ensenada . . ."

aside debate over legalities, the council protested relaxation of standards and particularly the sale of audiencia positions. Financial weakness and obsession with dynastic goals, however, overshadowed its concern.

Salary arrears to officials in Spain provide unmistakable evidence of the crown's increasing financial plight. In the mid-1720s, councillors of the Indies complained that their salaries were fourteen months behind schedule and noted that ministers of the councils of Castile and War were suffering similarly.[102] The councillors' quandary increased in the following years, and in 1731 they begged the king to note that they had gone unpaid for over two and a half years and that most of them subsisted only by borrowing from private sources.[103] Councillor José de Valdevieso later bemoaned his lack of compensation for two years of service in the House of Trade from 1730 to 1732.[104] Such shabby treatment of high officials suggests an accompanying deterioration of professional standards at the highest level; presumably such developments opened the Council of the Indies to the same external pressures that affected audiencias during time of financial crisis.

Despite its difficulties, the crown successfully avoided selling audiencia positions for nearly twenty years after the War of the Spanish Succession. The circumstances of some appointments in 1730, however, strongly suggest secret sales in that year. The ministers named had much more in common with proven purchasers than with men chosen for their merits alone. In contrast to the low percentage of American and non-ascenso appointees in the years since 1712, three of the four new men in 1730 were creoles and two of them went directly to viceregal tribunals. Charqueño Clemente del Campo y Zárate, a would-be purchaser of 1712, joined the Audiencia of Mexico with a dispensation for being married to a *mexicana*.[105] Even more striking, Francisco Ortiz de Foronda, new fiscal to Lima, escaped being a minor by only two months and was the first native son appointed in America since 1712.[106]

The first proven purchases in two decades occurred in 1733 and 1736, when limeños Pedro Bravo de Rivero and Manuel Antonio de Borda y Echevarría bought direct supernumerary appointments to their home court.[107] The Council of the Indies apparently did not participate in the selection of either candidate. Bravo's purchase was unrecorded and thus unknown to contemporaries. The title of appointment for Borda, however, proclaimed the twenty-one thousand pesos paid. The public sale to Borda may have given the

---

102. AGI, Indiferente General, legajo 1697, Council of the Indies to the king, 22 February, 18 August 1723.

103. Ibid., 19 July 1731.

104. Ibid., Valdevieso to the king, undated.

105. AGS, XXIII, 2–26–108 (Campo y Zárate, Cazalla, 25 June 1730).

106. AGI, Lima, legajo 596; AGS, XXIII, 24–179–149 (Ortiz de Foronda, 14 June 1730). The other two appointments for 1730 were to José Ignacio de Ortiz Avilés y Guzmán and Francisco Xavier de la Fuente y Santa Cruz.

107. AGS, XXIII, 2–29–151 (Bravo de Rivero, San Ildefonso, 2 October 1733); AGI, Lima, legajo 1082, testimony number seven, duplicate (Pedro Bravo de Rivero to José Antonio de Areche, Lima, 3 November 1777); AGS, XXIII, 2–30–351 (Borda, San Ildefonso, 11 July 1736).

council its first solid proof that the king was again prostituting justice, for not long after the transaction the cámara vented its anger over the renewal of sales. In a lengthy memorial of 21 August 1737, the camaristas protested the recent violations of professional standards for all categories of appointments to America.[108] After stressing the legal and theological arguments from earlier centuries, they asked Philip V to sell no more posts of justice. The easing of the military situation during the brief interval between the wars of the Polish Succession and Jenkins' Ear perhaps led to a temporary improvement in the crown's finances. In any case, after carefully pointing out that the decision antedated the cámara's protest, the king informed the cámara that he had agreed to withhold letrado posts from the market. New appointments bear out the royal declaration. From the sale to Borda in mid-1736 to the naming of a Mexican to Manila at the end of 1739, twelve men, at least eleven of them definitely peninsulares, took their places on the audiencias without payment. The only two of these to go directly to a viceregal court, both to numero assignments, were patently qualified.[109]

The council's victory over the threat of sales was part of a vigorous although short-lived drive to improve the judicial bureaucracy. From 1737 to 1739 the crown, at the urging of the council, moved against a broad array of abuses and weaknesses. One feature of this effort was the refusal to grant marriage dispensations. After a decade of reluctance, between 1729 and 1736 the crown had sold eight and granted two more dispensations for ministers or their children to marry locally, while turning down only one such request. In the renewed toughness from 1737 to 1739, though, only one minister, Ortiz de Foronda, received a dispensation for marriage and this was for his children to marry locally.[110] During the same years the king refused permission to two judges who wanted to marry local woman, in one case citing the royal decision of 1720 that expressly prohibited exemptions from the laws.[111]

The spirit of the late 1730s is nowhere more visible than in the crown's decisions to expand the Audiencia of Mexico and to increase the salary of its members. With some eleven thousand cases awaiting consideration, the Mexican court was not only several years behind in its workload but steadily losing ground. A large part of the problem was that the number of ill and otherwise absent oidores often prevented those who remained at the bench from operating two civil chambers as the laws prescribed.[112] To overcome this hindrance,

---

108. AGI, Mexico, legajo 1970, consulta of council, 21 August 1737.

109. The twelve, chronologically, were Sotillo, Calderón Enríquez, Chinchilla, Trespalacios, Verdugo y Oquendo, Alvarez de Castro, Jiménez Caro, Campuzano, Padilla, Balmaseda, Francisco Xavier de Palacios, and Aróstegui. Chinchilla and Padilla went directly to a viceregal court.

110. AGI, Lima, legajo 596.

111. The refusals were to Francisco Antonio de Echávarri y Ugarte (1739) and to Manuel Chinchilla y Henestrosa (1737); the crown made specific reference to the order of 1720 in its reply to Chinchilla.

112. AGI, Mexico, legajo 452, Viceroy of New Spain to the king, Mexico, 24 May 1736.

Philip V took the extraordinary step of increasing the number of oidores and alcaldes del crimen from twelve to eighteen.[113] With the additional magistrates, three civil chambers could simultaneously dispatch cases and thus erase the backlog. The crown assumed that this expansion would end the problem and consequently ordered that until attrition had returned the court to its normal complement, no new appointments were to take place.

The decision to add six judges occurred shortly before the crown learned of three vacancies by death among the superannuated ministers in the Mexican capital.[114] The combined circumstances of the additions and the deaths gave the king an opportunity to reshape the Audiencia of Mexico unmatched since the early 1720s. The new appointees in 1738 and 1739 epitomize the royal concern to reinvigorate the tribunal and strengthen control over its personnel. All the men selected were energetic, experienced in the American judiciary, and without attachments in Mexico.[115] Antonio Andréu y Ferraz exemplified the qualities the crown sought.[116] An Aragonese educated at the University of Huesca, Andréu had been the most junior oidor on the Audiencia of Guatemala. Probably in his forties, he had proven his abilities during his three years in Guatemala and had no known connections in Mexico. Andréu's advancement was one of several moves that violated the principle of the ascenso. In bypassing senior judges on the lesser tribunals, however, the crown rejected men who were aged, had personal ties in Mexico, or were, indeed, natives of the viceregal capital. Largely as a result of the appointments of the late 1730s, the Audiencia of Mexico in 1740 and 1741 was virtually free of compromising ties between ministers and local families.

Final confirmation of the crown's effort to improve justice in Mexico was the decision in 1738 to raise the salaries for the court's ministers and thus decrease their necessity to engage in illicit activities.[117] The letrados had repeatedly complained that their annual salaries of eight hundred thousand maravedís de plata, a trifle less than three thousand pesos, were inadequate and, moreover, disturbingly lower than what their counterparts in Lima received. By raising the salaries to an even four thousand pesos, Philip V provided the first pay increase for an audiencia since the early days of the empire. In spite of continued financial straits, the crown elected in the late 1730s to increase its financial support for the courts, a decision that reflected serious commitment to professionalism and determination to tighten its control.

The percentages of native sons and Americans serving during the 1730s il-

---

113. Ibid., consulta of the council, 2 February 1737.

114. The three were Uribe Castejón, Soria, and Oliván Rebolledo.

115. The appointments to Mexico in 1738 and 1739 included Rodríguez de Albuerne, Andréu y Ferraz, Fernando Dávila Madrid, Fernández Toribio, and Luis Manuel Fernández de Madrid.

116. AGI, Mexico, legajo 452, Relación de méritos . . . Andréu y Ferraz, 1731; AGS, XXIII, 2–30–13 (Andréu, Aranjuez, 11 June 1735) and 2–31–152 (Andréu, Buen Retiro, 30 March 1738).

117. AGI, Mexico, legajo 1640, king to the Audiencia of Mexico, San Ildefonso, 3 October 1738.

lustrate the changing royal policy (see Appendix VI). In 1730 the number of native sons had declined to nine, a little more than 10 percent of the ministers serving; this percentage was the smallest for native sons since 1705, and it would not be lower until the 1770s. The increase in native sons to ten (13 percent) by 1735 was not reflected in the overall percentage for Americans serving; this remained at about 40 percent, approximately the same as in 1730. A similar proportion of representation existed in 1739, when 36 percent of the men serving were Americans and about 11 percent were native sons. The pressures of the 1730s had halted the decline in American fortunes seen in the 1720s, but sales did not occur with sufficient frequency to reverse it noticeably. Nevertheless, although they dominated no single tribunal throughout the 1730s, native sons and other American ministers maintained a solid base upon which the sales of the 1740s would build.

The Renewal of Sales

The brief efforts to provide better government that were begun in 1737 crumbled under the outbreak of war with Great Britain late in 1739. Financial crisis provoked immediate resort to the sale of audiencia positions, now a proven source of revenue. The sales from 1740 to 1750 expanded the number and altered the character of appointments. As from 1687 to 1712, the increased number of appointments, especially after 1744, reflected purchased supernumerary positions. Again native sons and other Americans opened their purses and obtained preferment with ease. A simultaneous reversal of policy on marriage dispensations further aided local families' penetration of the chambers of justice. In consequence, although the crown had displayed greater concern for traditional standards than during the War of the Spanish Succession, at midcentury the audiencias in America once again were overstaffed and locally compromised.

In December 1739, a highly placed writer noted that the reappearance of war made it imperative to increase revenues, particularly in the Indies where defense costs would be great.[118] He asked the Marqués de Villadarias, chief minister and favorite, to convince the king at once to allow unrestrained sale of all letrado positions in America.[119] Evidently Villadarias either experienced dif-

---

118. AGI, Mexico, legajo 1970, Unknown writer to the Marqués de Villadarias, Buen Retiro, December 1739. Villadarias is also referred to as Villarias, which Julio de Atienza indicates is the correct title. *Nobiliario español: Diccionario heráldico de apellidos españoles y de títulos nobiliarios*, 2d ed. (Madrid, 1954), pp. 1000 and 1007.

119. The probable author of the letter was Fernando de Verdes Montenegro, a nonletrado member of the Council of the Indies since 1728 who a few days after this letter was written became secretary of state for the Treasury. As a councillor, Verdes would have been familiar with earlier sales and his rapid rise to power in 1740 coincided with the change of policy on sales. See Bernard, *Le secrétariat*, p. 216. The Marqués de Vil-

ficulty in overcoming Philip V's scruples or encountered opposition from other sources, for the king determined some four months later that judicial positions were not to be included in the reopened sale of posts in Spain and the Indies.[120] This decision disappointed officials charged with raising revenue; headed by Secretary of the Treasury Fernando de Verdes Montenegro, they lobbied for reconsideration. Success followed, and within weeks Verdes informed Secretary of the Indies José de la Quintana that the king had added letrado posts in America to the list of salable offices.[121]

Following precedent, Philip V bypassed the Council of the Indies and vested management of sales in a committee, the Junta de Hacienda, which Verdes headed. Even before announcing the decision to sell letrado posts, Verdes had advised Quintana that the Junta awaited offers from persons seeking preferment in non-letrado posts.[122] He requested the council to provide him with lists of all posts previously sold, adding that he was particularly interested in the most recent prices offered. Quintana, like Verdes a former *capa y espada* (non-letrado) member of the Council of the Indies, voiced no opposition to the sale of judgeships at this time and obligingly passed the request to the council.

In July 1740 letrados in the council reacted to this invasion of their traditional authority in patronage.[123] Faced with a fait accompli, the cámara grudgingly acknowledged the decision to sell judicial posts and promised to send the requested information to the Junta de Hacienda. Evidently fearing that confusion and delay would result from their loss of control over personnel, however, the camaristas asked that the junta speedily notify purchasers of their success and not allow paperwork to bog down. In developing their argument against sales, they noted some current critical vacancies in audiencias and governerships, particularly those in areas exposed to potential enemy attack. The cámara begged the king to withhold at least these positions from sale so that it could select suitable men. Having delicately raised the specter of dissolute judges and unsoldierly governors facing a British invasion, the cámara asked for guidance in filling the key vacancies of the governorship of Santa Marta and an oidorship on the Audiencia of Mexico. The ministers had placed the crucial issue squarely on the table—did the decision to raise revenue by selling positions in America override concern for security and reliability in war zones?

Months passed without action on the cámara's query. Early in October 1740 Quintana stressed to Villadarias the danger of delay in resolving the sales issue.[124] Now sharing the cámara's concern for security, he reported that the

---

larias was Sebastián de la Quadra, a Biscayan who became royal favorite after the death of José de Patiño in 1736. He was, in effect, prime minister. Aguado Bleye and Alcázar Molina, *Manual*, 3: 116.

120. AGI, Mexico, legajo 1970, Verdes Montenegro to José de la Quintana, Buen Retiro, 13 May 1740.

121. Ibid.

122. Ibid., 5 May 1740.

123. Ibid., consulta of the cámara, 18 July 1740.

124. Ibid., Quintana to Villadarias, Madrid, 5 October 1740.

viceroy of New Granada was pressing for the prompt selection of an able soldier to fill the vacant governorship of Cartagena. The reason for the untimely delay became obvious when Villadarias had to request another copy of the cámara's complaint of July 1740 because a fire at the Palace of San Ildefonso had destroyed the document.[125] Finally, in March 1741 Philip responded with an order to continue the traditional method of filling audiencia vacancies in America. He had changed his mind and there would be no sales.[126]

Any elation felt by the council's letrados was misplaced for, despite the king's assurance, the sale of audiencia posts had begun in mid-1740 and continued sporadically until mid-1742, when they ceased until 1744. Considering that a limeño had heralded sales in 1687, it was fitting that another, José Clemente de Traslaviña, headed the line of purchasers during this era with a promise in July 1740 to pay seventeen thousand pesos for a futura as oidor of Chile.[127] Six more sales occurred before the end of the year.[128] In 1741 two of the three new appointees purchased, and another sale took place in mid-1742.[129] Philip's disavowal of audiencia sales in March 1741 was, in fact, bracketed by sales in February and May.

Although anxious to raise revenue, the royal government was determined to prevent the abuses caused by earlier sales. Excesses in the Tribunal of Accounts in Lima led the cámara in December 1741 to consider a royal resolution recommending the return of all "tribunals" to their statutory strength.[130] The plan expressed preference for men named on merit alone and suggested that excess purchasers receive annual interest of 5 percent on their servicios while awaiting a vacancy. The short-lived royal order appearing on 26 April 1742 that embodied these proposals was reminiscent of the rulings of 1691 and 1701.[131] Unlike earlier, however, apparently no purchaser lost his position solely as a result of the reform decree. Most of the nine purchasers in 1740 and 1741 had gained numero appointments, and nearly all the supernumeraries had quickly moved into regular positions, since no backlog of excess judges had yet developed. No more than one purchaser could blame his temporary removal even in part on the operations of the order.[132]

Uncertainty marked royal decisions during the early 1740s, and the destruc-

---

125. Ibid., Villadarias to Quintana, El Pardo, 25 February 1741; Quintana to Villadarias, Buen Retiro, March 1741.

126. Ibid., resolution of the king recorded on copy of 18 July 1740 consulta, remitted to cámara on 28 March 1741.

127. AGS, XXIII, 2–32–264 (Traslaviña, Buen Retiro, 1 July 1740).

128. The purchasers were Martínez Patiño, José de Tagle Bracho, Calvo de la Puerta, Carfanger, Urquizu Ibáñez, and Bahamonde.

129. The two purchasers in 1741 were Ambrosio Eugenio de Santaella y Melgarejo and Rodríguez de Toro; the 1742 purchaser was Aparicio del Manzano. As in the earlier period of sales, there are several men for whom strong grounds exist for suspicion of secret sales; for example, Giráldes y Pino, Félix Malo, and Querejazu.

130. AGI, Indiferente General, legajo 800, consulta of cámara, 11 December 1741.

131. The cédula is referred to in AGS, XXIII, 2–41–178 (title restoring audiencia post to Sebastián Calvo de la Puerta, Buen Retiro, 22 March 1755).

132. Ibid.

tion of key documents by fire added to the confusion. Several of the secretaries of state were new to their offices—Verdes became secretary of the treasury at the beginning of 1740, and Quintana assumed the comparable post for the Indies in July 1739.[133] The chief adviser and favorite, Villadarias, had emerged since 1736, and his title of nobility dated only from 1739; furthermore, he was notoriously timid and anxious to please his sovereign.[134] The years between the death of the powerful royal secretary José de Patiño in 1736 and the rise of Campillo in late 1741 were, in fact, a transition period that lacked strong leaders. Under the pressure of fast-changing conditions and receiving advice from weak advisers, Philip V changed his mind more than once about selling letrado positions in America. The nature of the sales that took place from 1740 to 1742 illuminates this vacillation. The titles of appointment openly proclaimed the eight sales during 1740 and early 1741 (the decision to sell the latter post had been reached in mid-1740).[135] In contrast, secrecy surrounded the two sales of mid-1741 and mid-1742. The titles of appointment do not reflect the transactions, and proof of sale can be found only in later admissions or the working papers of the financial committees that handled the arrangements.

The appointment of José Rodríguez de Toro as oidor of Mexico in May 1741 exemplified the secret purchase.[136] A native of Caracas, where his peninsula-born father was the first Marqués del Toro, Rodríguez did not lack qualifications for appointment on merit alone. Educated at least in part in Spain, he had competed for academic chairs at the University of Salamanca. Rodríguez apparently had no connections in Mexico and, though quite young, had reached the minimum legal age for an appointment. After secretly paying fifteen thousand pesos for his post, Rodríguez served honorably for many years.[137] In an annotated roster of the judges serving in Mexico in 1759, information currently available to the council appeared beside each name.[138] By that date several men who had bought posts elsewhere in the 1740s had advanced by promotion to Mexico and the circumstances of their initial nominations were properly recorded in the margin. Beside the name of Rodríguez de Toro appeared only the information that he had been a resident of Salamanca when appointed. The purchaser's secret was safe.

Dire financial necessity alone induced the crown to sell posts of justice, for loss of control and abuse of standards were implicit in the expedient. Failure to pay close attention to the preparation and background of purchasers in the War of the Spanish Succession had not only yielded tribunals rife with scandal and the influence of local families, but also, as the fates of Larrea Zurbano and Sánchez de Orellana had illustrated, the need for subsequent embar-

---

133. Bernard, *Le secrétariat,* p. 217.
134. Aguado Bleye and Alcázar Molina, *Manual,* 2: 116.
135. Titles of appointment have been found for only seven of the eight sales involved.
136. AGS, XXIII, 2–33–99 (Rodríguez de Toro, Aranjuez, 7 May 1741).
137. AGI, Mexico, legajos 240 and 385.
138. Ibid., legajo 1640, Estado . . . of Audiencia of Mexico, 6 October 1759.

rassing and expensive remedies. Under the sudden press of war in early 1740, however, the crown temporarily ignored earlier lessons and opened the doors with little restraint. Beginning with Traslaviña, eight successive appointees purchased. Among them was Ambrosio Eugenio de Santaella, an American who bought admission to the Mexican tribunal in which his father was serving.[139] These sales were open, and the dispensations often accompanying them appeared in the titles of office. Protest about this latest debasement of the judiciary forced the king's new ministers to retreat, and subsequent sales until 1745 were few in number, cloaked in secrecy, and involved more carefully selected purchasers. Unlike in 1740, the king even refused an offered servicio simply because the aspirant was a native son.[140] Steeled by the protests and perhaps aided by a temporary improvement in its finances, the crown displayed greater concern for traditional qualifications from 1742 to 1744 than in the preceding two years.

Evidence of purchase again appeared in títulos in 1745 and the ministers involved did not blush about their payments.[141] With the new openness, sales soon approached the volume reached during the War of the Spanish Succession. A partial victory for proponents of traditional standards was evident, however, in a royal order designed to prevent a recurrence of previous mistakes.[142] Knowing that native sons would be the men most anxious to purchase, the king sought better information about the qualifications and origin of pretendientes. Officials responsible for allowing appointments of nominees lacking full qualifications would be subject to punishment. As additional insurance, the presidents of America's audiencias were to confirm purchasers' qualifications through personal examination before allowing them to assume their seats.[143] Such concern successfully barred men with gross deficiencies from

---

139. AGS, XXIII, 2–33–6 (Santaella, El Pardo, 12 February 1741). See Appendixes III and IX for the other appointees.

140. AGI, Indiferente General, legajo 1628. The case is that of Félix Malo de Villavicencio who offered to purchase a position on the Audiencia of Guadalajara in 1742 for 12,000 pesos. The king refused the offer, citing the fact that Malo had been born in New Galicia while his father was oidor there. Instead, Félix was given a futura to succeed his aged father as oidor in Mexico; possibly a servicio was involved here also, but no proof has been found. The crown's position is unusual, for despite Malo's birth in New Galicia he had grown up in Mexico and had all his contacts there. Still, the episode reveals royal concern for native-son status.

141. As Marcelin Defourneaux has pointed out, the celebrated Pablo de Olavide purchased his position on the Audiencia of Lima in 1744, but his título does not reveal the fact. Pablo Olavide ou l'afrancesado (1725–1803) (Paris, 1959), pp. 36–37 and AGS, XXIII, 2–34–238 (Olavide, San Ildefonso, 14 August 1744). The same decree provisions that governed the sale of a position to Rodríguez de Toro still applied in 1744. Less than a year later, however, the title of appointment of Zurbarán proclaimed his purchase; see AGS, XXIII, 2–35–95 (Zurbarán, Buen Retiro, 8 July 1745).

142. AGI, Mexico, legajo 384, Royal Order, Buen Retiro, 18 July 1745.

143. One case of an examination has been found, that of Manuel de la Vega y Bárcena before he received his appointment as supernumerary oidor in Quito. AGI, Audiencia of Quito (hereafter Quito), legajo 224, undated note ordering the fiscal of the House of Trade, José de Alsedo, to examine Vega.

gaining office, and no Ulloa Calleja appeared to vex the Council of the Indies. Although several purchasers were later suspended or removed, the wholesale purge of the period 1717–1720 was not repeated. When Visitor-General and later Secretary of the Indies José de Gálvez arrived in Mexico during the mid-1760s, he found no fault with the personal conduct or qualifications of the audiencia judges, although four purchasers from the 1740s were then serving.[144] Similarly, while Visitor-General José de Areche brought many charges against ministers of the Audiencia of Lima in the 1770s, he uncovered no grounds to move against them either for laxity in their personal life or for inadequate professional preparation. The crown had prevented a recurrence of the massive scandals of an earlier age.

Emphasis upon maintaining professional standards and the distinct geographical distribution of the positions sold suggest a conscious effort to control sales in the late 1740s. Aware of the problems that overstaffing the senior tribunals had created earlier, the crown seemed intentionally to channel some purchasers to the lesser audiencias. Improved control also appears in Alvaro Navia Bolaños's failure to place his son on the Audiencia of Lima.[145] The rejection of his offered servicio of 240,000 reales de vellón strikingly reveals how much tighter the crown's standards were in 1748 than in 1741, when it had blithely sold a similar appointment in Mexico to the younger Santaella. Finally, the absence of heavy sales to audiencias within the major theater of war after the early 1740s testifies to the crown's retention of some direction over appointment even when it desperately needed revenue.

The crown's overriding concern for defense best explains the noticeable differences in the number and location of sales made within the secretariats of New Spain and Peru between 1740 and 1750 (see Figure 2). When the cámara searched for a telling argument to forestall sales in July 1740, it singled out the military danger of vending posts in areas "continually exposed to invasions." The point was buttressed by Villadarias's subsequent acknowledgment that since 1717 the crown had withheld from sale because of their military importance a number of American governorships, mostly located in the Caribbean, Gulf of Mexico, and coastal cities of the mainland.[146] It was not fortuitous, then, that purchases varied greatly from region to region. Manila, Santo Domingo, the Gulf Coast of Mexico, Guatemala, and Santa Fe with Cartagena and the Spanish Main were all choice areas for English attack, and the audiencias within them had few sales, only one of which occurred in the more stringent atmosphere that followed the initial flurry of 1740–1741. Guadalajara, on the other hand, was inland and relatively safe from threats on its northern Pacific coasts. Although somewhat more exposed than New Galicia, the audiencia seats of Pacific South America also received protection from distance

144. AGI, Mexico, legajo 1509, report of visitor-general to viceroy of New Spain, Mexico, 31 December 1771.
145. AGI, Lima, legajo 983.
146. AGI, Mexico, legajo 1970, Villadarias to Quintana, El Pardo, 12 May 1741.

Figure 2. Geographical Distribution of Sales by Secretariat

Peru			New Spain		
Lima	10	$(12)^2$	Guadalajara	6	
Charcas	7	(8)	Mexico	2	(3)
Chile	5		Guatemala	1	
Quito	5		Santo Domingo	0	
Panama	3		Manila	0	
Santa Fe	1				
TOTALS	31	(34)		9	(10)

1. The two confirmed sales before 1740 went to limeños Pedro Bravo de Rivero and Borda.
2. Numbers in parentheses include probable but unconfirmed purchasers.

and topography.[147] Defensive considerations thus helped to spare the Secretariat of New Spain from the subsequent paralysis of the ascenso that plagued the Secretariat of Peru.

Purchases enabled thirty-nine of the sixty-six new men named from 1740 to 1750 to don the judicial robe (see Figure 3). Fourteen native sons, twenty-two other Americans, and three Spaniards provided the crown with over 750,000 pesos, most of this amount from 1745 to 1750.[148] Associated with the purchases were the same dispensations available during the War of the Spanish Succession. In 1749 limeño Domingo Orrantia paid the highest price of the decade, 47,500 pesos, for an appointment as supernumerary oidor in Lima and a full package of dispensations: native birth, ownership of property, permission to marry a native, and assurance that he would be exempt from any reform.[149] The frequent granting of marriage licenses signaled the crown's abandonment of its commitment to the enforcement of the marriage laws that had characterized the early 1720s and the late 1730s. In the eleven years ending at midcentury, it sold twenty-one dispensations with audiencia appointments and eight separately while granting only three freely. During this time, the crown punished only one judge for neglecting to secure approval before marrying; this man had received his first audiencia appointment in 1700 and should have known better.[150]

The consequences of the crown's decision to sell audiencia positions were apparent when sales closed in 1750 (see Appendix V). Limeños dominated their home audiencia as well as the ascenso tribunals of Chile, Charcas, and Quito. The wholesale vending of permits for ministers to marry locally born women presaged a generation of extensive indirect local influence on the tribunals. Despite the crown's concern for purchasers' qualifications and avoidance

147. The Audiencia of Panama, opening on the Caribbean but with several sales during the 1740s, is an obvious exception. In the preceding half-century, however, the tribunal had declined considerably in importance, and it would again be abolished in 1751.
148. See Appendix III.
149. AGS, XXIII, 2–37–101 (Orrantia, Buen Retiro, 14 March 1749).
150. The aged satyr was Ignacio Antonio de Castillo.

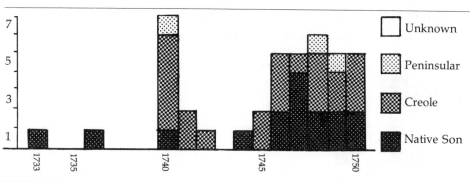

Figure 3. Purchasers' Place of Birth, 1733–1750

Place of Birth	Number of Purchasers	Number of Native Sons
Lima	22	9
Chile	4	2
Santo Domingo	3	
Panama	3	2
Guadalajara	2	2
Mexico	1	
Quito	1	1
Charcas	1	
Guatemala	1	
Spain	3	
	41	16

of the worst abuses accompanying the sales of the War of the Spanish Succession, it had lost much of the control regained at great expense in the 1720s and 1730s. The alienation of royal authority implicit in sales and marriage exemptions had created a problem, particularly in the south, that would plague the king's advisers for over a quarter of a century.

A Disrupted Ascenso and Radicados

The sale of positions highlighted the crown's inability to exert its traditional authority over the audiencias and influenced the high letrado bureaucracy in America more than any other factor from 1687 to 1750. Direct and indirect local influence on the tribunals mushroomed with sales; large numbers of native sons entered the courts, and extensive relaxation of marriage restrictions occurred. The appointment of supernumerary purchasers to the viceregal courts also produced overstrength audiencias for many years. With little mobility possible, judges sometimes remained for decades in one location, thus compounding the effects of marriage and economic dispensations. Not until the return of authority after 1750 was the principle of orderly career advancement effectively restored.

Figure 4. New Appointments to the American Audiencias, 1687–1750

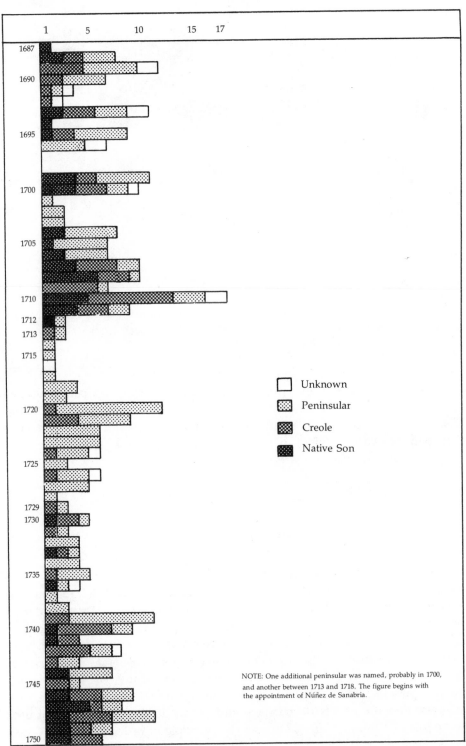

NOTE: One additional peninsular was named, probably in 1700, and another between 1713 and 1718. The figure begins with the appointment of Núñez de Sanabria.

The longer a minister served in a district, the more likely he was to sink deep roots. Marriage was often followed by the acquisition of property and increasing participation in economic ventures, typically in association with male members of the wife's family. In 1757 the viceroy of New Spain described such individuals as *radicado en el país* despite their birth elsewhere.[151] In varying degrees all the American audiencias had "radicado" ministers for much of the Age of Impotence. The crown had long recognized that the formation of local ties hampered upright administration. Viceroy Francisco de Toledo recommended in the sixteenth century that ministers of the Lima tribunal be transferred after five years' service to prevent the establishment of bonds that would affect their performance.[152] In the 1620s the Conde Duque de Olivares made a similar proposal, echoing sentiments written into legislation restricting the terms of office for various other offices in the time of Philip III.[153] Ministers who served lengthy periods of time on one audiencia frequently became "radicado," even in times when royal authority was strong. Weakened control over the audiencias, a consequence of sales, magnified the problem.

In the absence of research in local archives for each of the audiencias, one can hypothesize that ministers who served five or more years in a district were apt, much as native sons, to reflect a local perspective toward a specific problem. Prior residence, attendance at the local university, an expressed intention to marry locally, or preexisting kinship or economic ties with natives meant that even judges with less than five years' service in a locality can similarly be regarded as "radicado." Determination of the number and location of outsiders who served a quinquennium or more in a district added to those with less service but local ties, then, can provide an imperfect but suggestive indication of

151. Archivo General de la Nación, Mexico (hereafter AGN), Correspondencia de Virreyes, Vol. 2, folio 133, Viceroy of New Spain to Julián de Arriaga, Mexico, 27 May 1757.

152. Arthur Franklin Zimmerman, *Francisco de Toledo, Fifth Viceroy of Peru, 1569–1581* (Caldwell, Idaho, 1938; reprint ed., N.Y., 1968), p. 119. For a recent study of the impact of long tenure on judges' performance in the mid-sixteenth century see Constance Ann Crowder Carter, "Law and Society in Colonial Mexico: Audiencia judges in Mexican society from the Tello de Sandoval visita general, 1543–1547" (Ph.D. dissertation, Columbia University, 1971). The four judges examined in this study had all served over five years before Tello arrived (p. 39).

153. John Leddy Phelan, *The Kingdom of Quito in the Seventeenth Century* (Madison, 1967), p. 224; *Recopilación*, libro V, título II, ley x. Solórzano also pointed out that the question of naming audiencia ministers for specific terms had been raised many times, but that in 1629 Philip IV had settled for limiting the term of capa y espada presidents of the tribunals to eight years; Juan de Solórzano, *Política indiana*, 5 vols. (Madrid, 1647, reprint ed., 1930), libro V, capítulo IV, para. 33. Professor Phelan has been one of the few historians to emphasize the importance of long tenure among audiencia ministers. In his most systematic development of the idea, he uses ten years as a cutoff for what he calls *"españoles simpatizantes."* John L. Phelan, "El auge y la caida de los criollos en la audiencia de Nueva Granada, 1700–1781," *Boletín de historia y antigüedades* (Bogotá) 59: 697, 698 (November and December 1972): 603–4. More recently but less systematically, Guillermo Lohmann Villena has pointed out the importance of long service on ministers' creation of local ties in Lima in *Los Ministros de la audiencia de Lima en el reinado de los Borbones (1700–1821)* (Sevilla, 1974), pp. xciii–xcv.

indirect local influence on each court. Adding the number of native sons serving gives a rough indication of total local influence on each tribunal. The combined totals for each audiencia during the period 1687–1750 presented in Appendix VII suggest that most of the audiencias of America were often heavily compromised by local interests.

The breakdown of the ascenso and the consequent multiplication of ministers' local ties resulted directly from the sale of appointments. From 1667 to 1687 the ascenso worked smoothly.[154] Together the two viceregal tribunals received nearly three times as many ministers by promotion as by direct appointment, and few supernumeraries appeared. The logic of sales forced disruption of this promotion system. The crown sold appointments solely to obtain immediate revenue, and given the small number of numero positions it could expect only five or six vacancies a year. Since filling these alone would produce little cash, the crown sold many supernumerary appointments and futuras, most of them directly to the two viceregal tribunals. In contrast to the preceding two decades, direct appointments (most of them supernumerary) outnumbered regular promotions to Mexico and Lima from 1687 to 1712 and later during the 1740s. Each direct appointment probably delayed the advancement of two or three ministers. With direct appointments to the two senior courts numbering forty-one from 1687 to 1712 and twenty-three from 1730 to 1750, the breakdown of the path of promotion is clear.[155]

The direct appointment of supernumeraries and futurarios (often purchasers and thus frequently native sons) was most responsible for the disruption of the ascenso, particularly in the south. Twelve of eighteen and twelve of fourteen direct appointees to Lima in the two major periods of sales were excess ministers. For Mexico the corresponding figures were fifteen of twenty-three and three of nine. The latter low figure reflects the crown's decision not to sell posts in Mexico during the heavy years of sales from 1745 to 1750. The breakdown in the ascenso had the immediate effect of turning most of the lesser tribunals into bastions of radicado ministers. Left with little hope of promotion, these men settled down to make the best of their situation. Appendixes VII and VIII show the increase in radicado ministers growing out of the first period of sales, the decline in the early 1720s, and the expansion of indirect influence in the final period of sales.

The effect of sales on the advancement and consequently the tenure of judges in the audiencias of the Secretariat of New Spain is clear from a com-

---

154. The year 1667 was selected arbitrarily as providing a full twenty-years' experience before the appointment of Núñez de Sanabria. The information on appointments during this period comes from Schäfer, *El consejo*, 2, Appendix 2.

155. A caveat is in order. While direct appointments to Lima or Mexico slowed promotion from the ascenso tribunals, they were not all equally harmful when viewed from the royal perspective. When the crown made direct numero apppointments, it was often to place a hand-picked "king's man" in a troubled tribunal. For this type of assignment a colegial was often considered a perfect choice; in the eyes of ex-colegiales in the cámara, his membership alone marked him as a man of good judgment, ability, and requisite social background.

parison of promotion patterns during the two decades preceding 1687 with those for the subsequent years to 1750. From 1667 to 1687 letrados advancing up the ladder of promotion to Mexico outnumbered direct appointments by nearly three to one. Chiefly Guadalajara and Guatemala provided replacements for the viceregal court, as most men from Santo Domingo went first to one of the two intermediate mainland tribunals and thus formed part of a three-tiered system of ascenso.[156] That none of the three subordinate courts had a majority of long-tenured ministers and that Santo Domingo had none at all in 1687 is additional proof that the chain of promotion was working as the crown had envisioned. In contrast, from 1687 to 1712 direct appointments to Mexico outnumbered indirect, and at the end of sales the audiencia was swollen with twelve supernumerary ministers, most of them native sons. For men serving in the lesser tribunals, the undesirable effect was a lack of vacancies in the viceregal court that prevented the normal promotions they expected.

Unlike Mexico, the audiencias of Santo Domingo and Guadalajara did not acquire a backlog of supernumeraries. Both of these lesser courts, however, had majorities of radicado ministers in 1712. An unattractive location, Santo Domingo received no purchasers during the sales years. Timely deaths and departures and a purchased promotion by one of its judges to Mexico left it only one above strength.[157] Three of its judges, though, had served over five years and two others for over a decade.[158] Guadalajara had only its five authorized men in 1712 because several old ministers had recently died and three had advanced to Mexico as supernumeraries in 1710 and 1711 (two by purchase and one by special favor).[159] Most of the judges serving, however, were radicado; three had more than five years' experience (one with twenty) and another had asked for a license to marry a native.[160] Although the crown had sold positions to both Guadalajara and Guatemala, the southern tribunal experienced neither the deaths nor the purchased promotions to Mexico that had

---

156. The Audiencia of Manila figured only slightly in the movement of ministers during this period. The conditions of service and especially of travel meant that few ministers survived a tour in Manila and the arduous voyage across the Pacific to attain promotion to the mainland.

157. The purchasing judge was Chirino Vandeval. Santo Domingo would have been at authorized strength had it not had an extra oidor "en depósito." Tomás Fernández Pérez spent over fourteen years "deposited" there as the result of a dispute that originated in his rising from the meeting of an acuerdo in Quito before the proceedings had been properly adjourned.

158. The three who had been there for five years or more were Laysequilla y Palacios, Fernández de Barco, and Lozano y Peralta. The ministers with over ten years' service were Torre y Angulo and Cereceda.

159. The three who had advanced to Mexico were Oliván Rebolledo (one of the few two-time purchasers), Castañeda, and Feijóo Centellas. Feijóo Centellas was promoted on merit. Castañeda was granted the unique privilege of retaining his Guadalajara appointment for as long as he remained a supernumerary in Mexico; he still held the dual appointment when removed in 1720. See AGS, XXIII, 2–9–34 (Castañeda, Zaragoza, 21 March 1711).

160. The long-tenured judge was Miranda Villayzán, purchaser of 1691. Newly-arrived purchaser Real y Quesada had a permit to marry locally.

occurred in the New Galician court. As a result, in 1712 Guatemala had a surplus of ministers, and, by length of tenure or local involvement, five of its nine members posed a threat to royal control.[161]

For the audiencias of the north, the dominant event during the twenty-five years following sales was Visitor-General Garzarón's dismissal in 1720 of eleven of the eighteen judges assigned to the Audiencia of Mexico.[162] Having removed most of Mexico's native sons, purchasers, and long-tenured men, the crown filled the resultant vacancies largely from the ascenso tribunals, which except for Santo Domingo had changed little in composition since 1712.[163] Promotions to fill the void in Mexico created two vacancies in Santo Domingo and three each in Guatemala and Guadalajara. The dramatic restoration of royal control in Mexico broke the logjam that had existed since the days of heavy sales and provided the only upward movement for the mainland feeder tribunals before the 1730s.

The recovery of balance within the Secretariat of New Spain did not reinstate completely the patterns of the seventeenth century. Reduction to authorized strength did not obviate the radicado problem in the lesser audiencias. Guadalajara retained one and Guatemala three old purchasers from the sales period and, since the crown repeatedly passed over these men, three of them Mexicans, for advancement to their home tribunal, they remained in the smaller courts for decades and established extensive local ties.[164] Also, the ascenso pattern that emerged from the 1720s and continued until 1808 was no longer three-tiered. Although Guadalajara and Guatemala continued as the main sources of replacements for Mexico, the Audiencia of Santo Domingo now sent far more men directly to Mexico than to the two intermediate tribunals, and ministers serving on the island could expect to reach the viceregal capital with their first rather than second promotion.

The condition of the five tribunals of the Secretariat of New Spain in 1750 illustrates how difficult it was for the crown to keep the courts under tight control. During the preceding two decades, direct appointees to Mexico about equaled the number of men promoted there. Since most of the direct appointees assumed numero positions, the accumulation of excess ministers evident in the 1710s in Mexico did not reappear. Moreover, the expansion of the court in 1738 and the timely deaths of several long-tenured men soon afterward produced a tribunal relatively free from local influence by 1740. Even the crown's limitation on sales and refusal to name any native sons in the succeeding decade, however, could not maintain this purity. Extensive marriage exemptions

---

161. These five were Duardo (another 1691 purchaser), Gutiérrez de la Peña, Carrillo Escudero, Oviedo y Baños, and Rodezno.

162. For details on these removals, see pp. 39-40.

163. Santo Domingo had benefited from deaths and its old connection as a sometime feeder audiencia to Santa Fe as well as Mexico. Between 1712 and 1720 two judges, Laysequilla y Palacios and Lozano, had gone from the islands to New Granada. By 1720 Santo Domingo was at numero strength and had only two judges with more than five-years' tenure—Fernández Pérez and Cereceda.

164. The four old purchasers were Arana, Rodezno, and Domingo de Gomendio Urrutia in Guatemala, and Fernando de Urrutia in Guadalajara.

and the presence of new men who had quickly established local ties meant that radicado ministers again dominated the court in 1750.

Conditions in the lower-ranking tribunals were mixed at midcentury. This status was the creation of sales in Guadalajara, the crown's responses to local conditions in the 1740s in Guatemala and Santo Domingo, and the high death rate of ministers in Manila. Although both Guadalajara and Guatemala had majorities of radicado ministers in the 1730s, in the following decade they exhibited substantial differences. Guadalajara was the only northern tribunal to experience heavy sales during the 1740s. The purchase of supernumerary positions, coupled with the absence of many ascenso vacancies in Mexico (the result of its augmentation rather than the few sales), meant that the New Galician tribunal was overstaffed by 1750. In contrast, the king sold only one Guatemala position and, five years later in 1745, forcibly removed and replaced the purchaser as well as the three ministers of longest tenure because of local problems.[165] Consequently, in 1750 the audiencia was at normal strength and contained no one who had served there before 1742. Similarly, in Santo Domingo the effects of a specific royal action at rehabilitation were still evident in 1750. Several old judges with many years in the islands had staffed the audiencia in 1740. The crown was anxious to maintain tight control on this theater of war, however, and replaced them with younger men, most of whom were still serving in 1750.[166] Manila, as earlier, did not contribute heavily to the mainland tribunals because of deaths. Only two men received regular promotions to Mexico (and only one of them lived to serve) while a third received a special supernumerary appointment in 1736.[167] Often ignored until premature death overcame them, ministers in the Asian tribunal remained heavily involved with local society throughout the 1730s and 1740s.

The impact of sales and the consequent disruption to the ascenso was even more apparent in the Secretariat of Peru than in New Spain. In the twenty years before Núñez de Sanabria's direct appointment in 1687, only one in three ministers assigned to Lima had not previously served in a lower tribunal. Nearly all the promoted letrados came from the Audiencia of Charcas, a court fed chiefly by direct appointments. Primarily because of deaths, Chile at this time fulfilled an ascenso role no more effectively than did Manila, although

165. Those removed were Arana, Orozco Manrique de Lara, Alvarez de Castro, and Martínez Patiño. See AGS, XXIII, 2–35–115 (Aguirre y Celaa, San Lorenzo, 27 November 1745) and 2–35–245 (Velarde y Cienfuegos, El Pardo, 31 March 1746); see also AGI, Guatemala, legajo 274.

166. Three oidores and the fiscal in Santo Domingo either retired, died, or were transferred to "safe" mainland audiencias (e.g. Guadalajara) during the early 1740s. They were Rey Villar de Franco, Blancas y Espeleta, García Chicano, and Fuente y Santa Cruz. In the cases of García, Fuente, and Rey, explicit reference was made to the appointment of younger men. See AGS, XXIII, 2–33–40 (Velarde, Aranjuez, 31 May 1743); document 370 (Correa Vigil, San Ildefonso, 26 September 1742); document 313 (José Pablo de Agüero, San Ildefonso, 4 October 1742); and 24–181–21 (Villaurrutia y Salcedo, San Ildefonso, 18 September 1742).

167. The two receiving regular appointments were Francisco Fernández Toribio (who never served in Mexico) and Pedro de Bedoya y Osorio. Francisco de López de Adán received an unusual supernumerary appointment to Mexico in 1736.

normally it also provided some judges to Lima as well as Charcas. The Audiencia of Santa Fe functioned as an intermediate tribunal, drawing men from Panama and Santo Domingo as well as from direct appointments and serving as the apex of its own small promotion ladder while occasionally sending men to Lima.

The sale of appointments to Lima destroyed the ascenso as anything more than an ideal in the south. Direct supernumerary purchases by limeños so distorted the promotion chain that, lacking a purge like that which struck Mexico in 1720, no effective pattern of advancement can be discerned during the 1720s and 1730s. In the absence of timely promotions, the smaller audiencias, themselves often oversized from sales, had majorities with long tenure and local ties. Abortive reforms occurred in 1701 and 1720 with some effects in the few years following, but in the general trend these effects were lost. Men died, a few malefactors lost posts, and occasional movement occurred in one or another audiencia, but the dominant trends were direct appointment to Lima, stagnation in the lesser courts, and consequent local ties for ministers. The new influx of purchasers to Lima, Chile, Charcas, and Quito during the 1740s ensured that the old problems would continue for decades.

The hypothesis that native sons and radicado ministers provided roughly equal local influence on the courts needs to be tested by detailed examination of decisions made by audiencias dominated by each group. In the absence of such investigation, a comparison of the two viceregal tribunals in 1745 suggests the underlying similarity between a court dominated by native sons and one staffed wholly by outsiders of long tenure and with local connections by marriage. The ties growing out of long tenure in Mexico probably provided such extensive indirect influence for prominent families of the region that "total local influence" in the northern court nearly equaled that present in the Audiencia of Lima, dominated by native sons.

Mexico had no native son serving in 1745; twelve of its eighteen ministers had been present five years or more, however, and several newcomers had joined or planned to join prominent families through marriage. The senior oidor, Domingo Valcárcel y Formento, had lost no time in making a place for himself in Mexico. Assigned in 1727, four years later he purchased a license to marry a local woman and the following year wed a daughter of the Condes de Santiago de Calimaya, one of the most prominent noble families in Mexico. Valcárcel's daughter María Josefa would later marry the son of José Uribe, long-time dean of the audiencia who had established extensive social and economic ties before his death in 1738.[168] Subdecano oidor Francisco Antonio de Echávarri and oidor Juan Rodríguez de Albuerne also married Mexican

168. See AGS, XXIII, 2–24–26 (Valcárcel, San Lorenzo, 13 November 1727); AGI, Mexico, legajo 385 for license to marry, 1731. Unless otherwise cited, the biographical information in the remainder of this section derives from Manuel de Mendiburu, *Diccionario histórico-biográfico del Perú*, 8 vols., Lima, 1874–1890); Guillermo Lohmann Villena, *Los americanos en las órdenes nobiliarias (1529–1900)*, 2 vols. (Madrid, 1947); Restrepo Sáenz, *Biografías*; Espejo, *Nobiliario*; Vargas Ugarte, *Títulos*.

women.[169] Rodríquez, moreover, later obtained permission for his children to marry and hold property within the district.[170] His wife, of the influential Pérez de Tagle and Sánchez de Tagle families, brought her husband the title of Marqués de Altamira. Although Fernando Dávila Madrid is not known to have married within the district, his two sons were reared there during his years of service from 1738 to 1754.[171] The first, Fernando, probably attended the University of Mexico and in 1748 became an oidor in Manila. The other son graduated from the university and became a legal adviser in the Contaduría General de Tributos in Mexico. Luis Fernández de Madrid, also appointed in 1738, served until 1750. He had married a quiteña while serving in Guatemala earlier, but raised and educated his sons in Mexico City.[172] One of them would succeed him on the audiencia in the year of his death, and the other became an attorney and practiced before that tribunal.

José Rodríguez de Toro represented a new generation on the court. He had purchased his post in 1741 and was still in his twenties in 1745. Soon after arriving in Mexico he married a daughter of the late decano Uribe; thus Domingo Valcárcel's daughter later became the sister-in-law of Rodríguez, whose daughter later married Domingo Ignacio de Lardizábal, treasurer of the Audiencia of Mexico.[173] Rodríguez had another in-law on the Audiencia of Guadalajara, since its oidor Martín de Blancas y Espeleta had married another of Uribe's daughters. Oidor Domingo de Trespalacios y Escandón, named in 1741, also quickly established local connections by marrying the daughter of fellow oidor Rodríguez de Albuerne and the Marquesa de Altamira.[174] Trespalacios' nephew, Cosme de Mier, would later follow his uncle on the audiencia.[175] Clemente del Campo y Zárate, a *charqueño* who had recently advanced from the criminal chamber, was a long-time resident of the city and had married a Mexican woman several years before his initial appointment in 1730.[176] The junior oidor, Félix Malo, was probably not yet twenty-six years old in 1745. Successor to his father's position, young Malo had been reared and educated in Mexico.[177] His brother Enrique later received a doctorate in theology from the University of Mexico while Félix was serving.

169. For Echávarri, AGI, Mexico, legajo 1697, Dª Bárbara Rita de Tamayo to Señor, Mexico, 17 August 1763.

170. Ibid., legajo 385.

171. AGS, XXIII, 2–36–180 (Fernando Dávila, Buen Retiro, 15 October 1748); AGI, Indiferente General, legajo 159, Relación de méritos of his son Ignacio.

172. AGI, Indiferente General, legajo 159, Relaciones de méritos of sons Diego and Luis; AGS, XXIII, 2–38–32 (Diego Fernández de Madrid, Buen Retiro, 17 November 1751).

173. AGS, XXIII, 2–33–99 (Rodríguez de Toro, Aranjuez, 7 May 1741); AGI, Mexico, legajos 240, 385, 1859 and Indiferente General, legajo 1313.

174. AGS, XXIII, 2–33–44 (Trespalacios, San Ildefonso, 2 August 1741); AGI, Mexico, legajo 385.

175. AGS, XXIII, 2–60–168 (Mier y Trespalacios, San Ildefonso, 26 July 1776).

176. Ibid., 2–26–108 (Campo, Cazalla, 25 June 1730); dispensation for marriage to a native was written into the title. AGI, Indiferente General, legajo 144 contains Campo's relación de méritos, 1730.

177. AGS, XXIII, 2–33–270 (Félix Malo, San Ildefonso, 4 October 1742).

The dean of the criminal chamber was José de la Mesía de la Cerda, who had married the Mexican sister of a fellow oidor while serving in Guadalajara years earlier.[178] While in New Galicia Mesía had also sheltered the young orphan Francisco Gamboa, future oidor and regent of the Mexican tribunal.[179] The young peninsular alcalde del crimen, Manuel Chinchilla y Henestrosa, had no known ties in Mexico; nonetheless, his intentions to establish them were clear at the time of his appointment in 1737, when Philip V refused his request to marry a local woman.[180] Antonio de Rojas y Abréu, a criminal judge since 1739, would ask permission for his locally reared children to marry natives in 1764.[181] The most junior criminal judge was Ambrosio Eugenio de Santaella, son of a former oidor in Mexico.[182] Young Santaella, like Malo, represented the child of the bureaucracy who, although born elsewhere, was reared and educated in Mexico. Santaella married a Mexican and eventually got a license for his children to marry locally. Both of his sons attended the University of Mexico as had their father.

Of the eighteen ministers serving in 1745, at least seven and probably ten had married into prominent local families. The University of Mexico had provided education for two of the eighteen, and several judges had seen their children graduate from it. Four men received dispensations for their children to marry within the district, one unsuccessfully asked for a license to marry a native, and one obtained permission for his children to hold property in the district. Ties of kinship through marriage bound Valcárcel and Rodríguez de Toro. Although none of the men had been born locally, the Audiencia of Mexico in the mid-years of the eighteenth century showed a majority of judges with proven ties to the district. Indirect influence was at work.

Unlike the Audiencia of Mexico, which had no native sons in 1745, the Audiencia of Lima had little else. Eight sat in the civil chamber, three in the criminal chamber, and one was a fiscal. At least seven of the oidores and one of the alcaldes had purchased their appointments. The decano and only peninsular in the civil chamber in 1745 was Alvaro Navia Bolaños. Navia had married two limeñas over the course of his career in the City of Kings from 1709 to 1757.[183] His first wife was the daughter of the rich peninsular merchant Bernardo González de Solís, who in 1707 not only obtained an oidor as a son-in-law but also purchased appointments as oidor supernumerary of Chile for his

178. AGI, Mexico, legajo 1640, Estado . . . de la Audiencia de Mexico, 6 October 1759.

179. AGI, Indiferente General, legajo 159; AGS, XXIII, 2–71–263 (title of Gamboa as regent, San Lorenzo, 17 November 1787).

180. AGS, XXIII, 2–31–104 (Chinchilla, Aranjuez, 21 May 1737); AGI, Mexico, 385.

181. AGS, XXIII, 2–32–17 (Rojas, San Ildefonso, 23 August 1739); AGI, Mexico, legajo 1699, consulta on marriage of daughters, 29 May 1764.

182. AGS, XXIII, 2–33–6 (Santaella, El Pardo, 12 February 1741); AGI, Indiferente General, legajo 166, relación de méritos of Santaella, 1734; legajo 158, relación de méritos of Santaella's son of the same name.

183. AGS, XXIII, 2–9–9 (Navia y Bolaños, Madrid, 16 June 1709); AGI, Lima, legajo 596, extract, Cámara of the Indies, 8 June 1736.

son and the presidency of Guadalajara for himself.[184] Almost immediately after his marriage, Navia had paid five hundred doblones for a promotion to Lima, pleading ill health and asking a dispensation for his marriage to a native. In 1748 he attempted unsuccessfully to purchase an appointment for a son on the Audiencia of Lima.[185] Sixteen years later another of his sons joined the Audiencia of Santo Domingo.[186] A daughter of Navia's first marriage married the future Conde de Villa Miranda, while a son by his second wife became the Conde de Bolaños in 1768. The old colegial from Oviedo had firmly established himself and his family among the prominent houses of Lima.

The only man serving in 1745 whose father had previously held a post in Lima was the sub-decano, limeño Gregorio Núñez de Rojas, an oidor since 1729.[187] Gregorio's paternal line in Peru stretched back to 1631, and his mother's family had been in America even longer. Maternal grandfather Gregorio de Rojas y Acevedo, born in Buenos Aires in 1622, had been the first professor (*prima*) of laws at the University of San Marcos and died in 1680 *electo* fiscal of Charcas.[188] Although Gregorio Núñez de Rojas apparently left no heirs, despite using the permission to marry he had purchased in 1708 along with reinstatement as oidor of Charcas, he nonetheless was related to other important families of Lima. His nephew José Antonio Villalta y Núñez, an alcalde del crimen, was married to Juana Rosa de Santiago Concha, daughter of the first Marqués de Casa Concha, himself a judge in Lima from 1693 to 1741.[189] Villalta would serve in Lima for nearly four decades. Three years after his death, his brother-in-law, Melchore de Santiago Concha, another limeño who had purchased his initial appointment, would join the Lima tribunal.[190] Melchor's retirement in 1794 ended a century of Santiago Concha family ties to the court.

Another long-serving native son in 1745 was Pedro Bravo de Rivero, a first-generation creole and brother of a former oidor of Charcas who in 1745 was bishop of Arequipa.[191] Shortly after purchasing his appointment, Bravo gave another three thousand pesos for a license to marry a native. His wife's father was *contador mayor* of the tribunal of the Santa Cruzada in Lima. Through her maternal line she was descended from one of the conquistadores

---

184. AGS, XXIII, 2–3–3 (Solís Vango, Buen Retiro, 24 May 1707). González de Solís is also referred to as Rodríguez de Solís.

185. See note 145, p. 53.

186. AGS, 2–48–173 (Núño de Navia Bolaños, Buen Retiro, 18 June 1764).

187. Ibid., 2–25–273 (Núñez, Seville, 6 November 1729); Núñez was a son of the aforementioned Miguel Núñez de Sanabria, who was appointed in 1687.

188. AGI, Lima, legajo 103.

189. AGS, XXIII, 2–31–336 (Villalta, San Lorenzo, 30 November 1738); AGI, Lima, legajo 596; AGS, XXIII, 24–172–176 (José de Santiago Concha, Madrid, 22 March 1693); see AGS, XXIII, 2–4–97 (Núñez de Rojas, Madrid, 13 December 1708) for permit to marry native, and Lohmann Villena, *Los ministros*, p. 82, for his wife.

190. AGS, XXIII, 2–61–4 (Melchor de Santiago Concha, El Pardo, 26 January 1777).

191. Ibid., 2–29–151 (Bravo de Rivero, San Ildefonso, 2 October 1733); AGI, Lima, legajos 615, 791; for his brother Juan, see AGS, XXIII, 2–5–48 (Juan Bravo, Buen Retiro, 20 June 1708).

of Peru.[192] In 1775 Bravo would obtain permission for his children to marry in the district and own property, thus further widening his already extensive ties with local families. His son Diego Miguel, a future oidor in Lima, would later marry into another conquistador family, the Aliagas, and take the hand of the third Marquesa de Fuente Hermosa de Miranda.[193]

Similar portraits could be drawn of the other native sons on the tribunal. Moreover, the connections expanded with more sales in 1740s. Let one example suffice. Juan José de la Puente y Ibáñez, a limeño, purchased an appointment as alcalde del crimen supernumerario in 1747.[194] Almost simultaneously his brother Gaspar purchased the position of *contador mayor de bienes de difuntos*. Juan José married the daughter of the peninsular fiscal from 1727 to 1748, Lorenzo de la Puente Larrea. Through marriage he was also related to oidor Querejazu and the future minister Melchor de Santiago Concha.[195] Through Santiago Concha he was distantly related through marriage to Villalta. Since Santiago Concha married a daughter of the president of Charcas and was then, as a rebuke, transferred to Chile, the links of the judges extended not only throughout the families of Lima but into the capitals of the feeder audiencias of Chile and Charcas as well. With limeños also serving in Quito, the City of Kings had prominent sons in each of its usual sources of future judges. In 1750, Quito had five limeños holding appointments, Charcas had four, and Chile had two.[196]

Of the three peninsulares serving in the criminal chamber and the one peninsular fiscal, three were married to limeñas. Criminal judge Alfonso Carrión's wife was a daughter of the prominent and wealthy Marqués de Torre Tagle.[197] The fiscal Lorenzo de la Puente had married the Marquesa de Villafuerte y Sotomayor and alcalde del crimen Francisco Xavier de Salazar y Castejón had married a limeña niece of the Marqués de Montemira.[198] Of the peninsular ministers, only the criminal judge Juan Gutiérrez de Arce, a colegial of San Ildefonso and *caballero* of Santiago, did not marry locally.[199] Having

---

192. Lohmann Villena, *Los americanos*, 1: 63.

193. AGS, XXIII, 2–95–17 (Diego Miguel Bravo de Rivero, Palacio, 14 March 1814).

194. Ibid., 2–36–95 (Puente Ibáñez, Buen Retiro, 20 January 1747).

195. AGS, XXIII, 2–24–76 (Puente Larrea, San Lorenzo, 19 November 1727).

196. In Quito the limeños were Gómez de Andrade, Juan de Luján y Bedia, Santa Cruz y Centeno, Manuel de la Vega y Bárcena, and Hurtado de Mendoza; in Charcas were Melchor de Santiago Concha, Pedro de Tagle Bracho, Pablo de la Vega y Bárcena, and Llano y Valdés; the Peruvians in Chile were Traslaviña and Juan José de la Fuente y Villalta.

197. AGS, XXIII, 2–25–328 (Carrión, Seville, 29 April 1729); Carrión received his license to marry in 1733 for a payment of 3,000 pesos. AGI, Indiferente General, legajo 525, "Relación de los empleos."

198. AGS, XXIII, 2–24–76 (Puente, San Lorenzo, 19 November 1727); for Salazar, see 2–19–54 (24 January 1721); also AGI, Indiferente General, legajo 525, "Relación de los empleos."

199. AGS, XXIII, 2–21–96 (Gutiérrez, San Ildefonso, 22 November 1723).

served in Lima twenty years already, however, he was probably involved in campadrazgo and financial relationships.[200]

The native-son purchaser in Lima and the radicado minister in Mexico during the 1740s graphically illustrate the effects of the Age of Impotence on the audiencias. The sale of positions and marriage dispensations that occurred during most of the period placed many native sons on tribunals and permitted the formation of ties between "outsiders" and leading families in their districts. Moreover, sales broke down the ascenso, especially in the south; tribunals filled with long-tenured ministers, and local involvement expanded. When the crown sought to reassert its authority over the courts after 1750, it discovered local influence everywhere. Nearly three decades would pass before it reduced to acceptable amounts local direct and indirect influence on the audiencias.

Ministers By Default

There were always far more ambitious letrados than positions in the Spanish Empire. The first sign of a vacancy often sent dozens of aspirants scurrying for their dossiers. An opening of oidor in Panama in 1664 produced seventy-six applicants, while twenty-two years later nearly forty men sought a similar post in Chile, and even in the war-disrupted year 1705 thirty-three men pursued an opening of fiscal in Panama.[201] Intense pressure prevailed, particularly when posts were filled on the basis of nonmonetary qualifications, as the ninety-two men seeking the post of criminal fiscal in Chile in 1776 attest.[202] Numbers give no indication of the quality of the applicants, however, and during the Age of Impotence few displayed the credentials the crown preferred. From the royal perspective, the best candidates came from the six colegios mayores and thus were likely heirs to a tradition of family service in government or had proved their worth by obtaining a professorial chair, preferably at Salamanca, Valladolid, or Alcalá. Men with these backgrounds were a known quantity, and the crown presumed they were capable of holding high positions without prior administrative experience. Conversely, the crown opposed the appointment of native sons on principle and often seemed unaware of the existence of American pretendientes. Spanish colegiales and professors, the most desirable candidates, together numbered only sixty, 19 percent of the total new appointees during the Age of Impotence; Americans, including native sons,

---

200. For a detailed analysis of the family ties in Peruvian society at mid-eighteenth century approached through an examination of members of the cathedral chapter of Lima, see Paul Bentley Ganster, "A Social History of the Secular Clergy of Lima During the Middle Decades of the Eighteenth Century" (unpublished Ph.D. dissertation, University of California, Los Angeles, 1974).

201. AGI, Audiencia of Panama (hereafter Panama), legajo 124; Chile, legajo 84.

202. Ibid., Chile, legajo 258.

provided 44 percent. These figures highlight the crown's inability to staff the courts as it wished. An examination of first the peninsulares and then the creoles named will demonstrate this weakness and also will reveal the distinctive characteristics of each group.

Great family networks dominated Spain's councils of state in 1687.[203] Sons of ministers benefited from their fathers' influence and frequently followed them into high office, usually after residence in one of the six colegios mayores attached to the universities of Salamanca, Valladolid, and Alcalá. These highborn letrados did not have to serve in America. Consequently, except for four men from 1687 to 1750, they remained at home.[204] The fathers of two of the four, Baltazar de Lerma and Nicolás Fajardo, served on the Council of Hacienda and the House of Trade, bodies well below the Council of Castile in prestige.[205] Their sons, moreover, initially received low-ranking appointments in Quito and Chile.[206] Despite eventual promotions to Lima (which only Fajardo served), neither man returned to Spain to serve a letrado position. Such lack of preferment suggests personal weaknesses that outweighed the considerations commonly given men of their background. The career of José de Pineda y Tabares was more what one would expect from a man whose father held a high position. Son of a councillor of the Indies, Pineda spent a decade as a judge in Guatemala before advancing to the Chancellery of Granada in the early 1750s.[207] The fourth scion of Spain's high letrado families to go to America was Domingo Valcárcel y Formento, representative of the pinnacle of the service elite. A colegial of San Ildefonso at the University of Alcalá, Valcárcel's father and both grandfathers had served on the Council of Castile.[208] He was appointed directly to the Audiencia of Mexico at the unusually young age of twenty-seven years, an example of the advantage available to the highborn. On the other hand, the fact that he spent his entire career in Mexico suggests

---

203. See Richard L. Kagan, *Students and Society in Early Modern Spain* (Baltimore, 1974), chapter 6.

204. The unhappiness of Spanish letrados at the thought of having to serve in America permeates Diego Antonio de Rivas's tearful statement. "Y obligando la cortedad de sus medios, por no desamparar su familia, se determinó apretender en Indias (aunque con el dolor de desterrarse voluntariamente de su Patria). . . ." This rendering of his grief is in AGI, Lima, legajo 344, consulta of council, 20 April 1703. Although he received an appointment as oidor in Lima in 1703, Rivas never served. In 1706 he took the Hapsburg side in the War of the Spanish Succession and his post was later declared vacant. AGI, Lima, legajo 346.

205. On Lerma's father see AGI, Indiferente General, legajo 135. The services of Fajardo's father are noted in AGS, XXIII, 2–6–64 (Felipe Nicolás Fajardo, Madrid, 4 August 1709).

206. For Fajardo, see note 205. For Lerma, see AGS, XXIII, 24–173–49 (Lerma y Salamanca, Madrid, 11 October 1703).

207. Ibid., 2–34–170 (Pineda, Buen Retiro, 4 July 1744); also, 2–39–176 (title of Manuel Díaz, Buen Retiro, 20 December 1752) provides Pineda's new assignment.

208. Ibid., 2–24–26 (Valcárcel, San Lorenzo, 13 November 1727); AGI, Indiferente General, legajo 169, relación de méritos of his son Antonio.

either personal preference (he married a native) or that his original appointment was a gilded exile masking some secret failing.[209]

Since most sons of ministers on Spanish tribunals shunned service on American audiencias, colegiales who lacked such intimate connections became the favored candidates. These men also generally disdained serving in the Indies, however, and the few who went were probably on the fringes of the colegio-council patronage circle and thus unable to obtain immediate high office in the peninsula. The aura attached to the colegios mayores meant that for most of the period 1687–1750 even alumni who had failed in the web of peninsular patronage frequently received the best American posts. The small number who accepted appointment in the Indies, however, reveals the crown's inability to recruit members of the acknowledged service elite for service in America.

The forty-two colegiales named to New World tribunals from 1687 to 1750 accounted for no more than one-third of the appointees with peninsular educations and only 13 percent of the total. The attitudes that had surrounded the royal effort to attract them to American service in earlier years continued into the Age of Impotence, and the offices colegiales received from 1687 to 1712 underlined their favored status.[210] Over half of them went directly to the two viceregal audiencias or to the middle-ranking tribunals of Santa Fe and Charcas. Nor was the absence of colegiales from the lesser tribunals accidental. While filling a vacancy in Panama in 1690, the camaristas remarked that normally colegiales were not even considered for this minor audiencia.[211] The crown's decision to sell appointments undermined its efforts to recruit colegiales, however, for, since they had far less incentive to purchase in America than native sons, none did.[212] With 80 posts sold of the 150 granted between 1687 and 1712, the sixteen colegiales named were even fewer than usual (11 percent).

The return to traditional means of appointment after 1712 brought colegiales again into the American courts. From 1713 to 1729 they accounted for almost 40 percent of all peninsular university graduates going to America and nearly 30 percent of the total appointees. The seventeen colegiales received

209. See AGI, Mexico, legajo 385 for the license to marry, and Lohmann Villena, *Los americanos,* 2: 141 for his wife.

210. See Konetzke, *Colección,* 2, tomo II, document 436 for the effort of the Council of the Indies to lure more colegiales to America in 1676.

211. AGI, Panama, legajo 124, Proposición de personas para una plaza de oidor de Panamá, 1690.

212. Positions on Spanish audiencias and perhaps chancelleries were being sold during this period, and colegiales were undoubtedly more interested in them than in posts in the Indies. For one sale, that to Francisco de los Ríos who purchased a supernumerary appointment as oidor on the Audiencia of Seville for two thousand pesos escudos in 1712, see AGI, Mexico, legajo 1970, consulta of the Council of the Indies, 28 April 1712. Also, a supernumerary oidorship on the House of Trade was sold for 8,000 pesos in 1740 to Francisco Xavier del Arco; Relación de los empleos, 19 August 1740. The extent of such sales in Spain requires additional research.

customary advantage; ten went to Lima, Mexico, or Santa Fe.[213] Appointment practices had returned to the pattern existing before sales began, and once more the crown was anxious to recruit colegiales for American service.

Preferential treatment of colegiales diminished in the years from 1730 to 1750, and the percentage and number of appointments they received declined markedly. Sales were only partly responsible for this drop; in relation to total peninsular appointments, colegiales did even more poorly in the 1730s than in the 1740s. More importantly, the colegios' place within Spain itself was deteriorating, a consequence perhaps of Philip V's unsuccessful effort to reform them in the 1720s.[214] The belief that colegiales made the best ministers was fitfully coming under attack, and during 1730–1750 the nine colegiales named accounted for but one-fifth of the graduates of Spanish universities assigned to American audiencias and only 9 percent of the total appointees. The changed nature of their appointments confirms that the status of colegiales was deteriorating. During these two decades more went to the four lowest-ranking tribunals than to the viceregal courts. Also, for the first time in at least three generations and probably ever, a colegial accepted an initial appointment to the least desirable audiencia of the Indies—Manila.[215] Colegiales no longer received the deference of earlier years.

Although the benefits of colegio affiliation were declining from the 1730s, for another half century colegio alumni still held the most prestigious credential a pretendiente could present. Colegiales were frequently appointed directly to the most desirable courts, and the crown was willing to name them even when they had neither held an academic chair nor served a previous position—these facts manifest their elite status. Only five colegiales named from 1687 to 1750 held permanent academic appointments, and but one other had an American appointment before joining an audiencia.[216] Thus, thirty-six colegiales went directly from their privileged preserve to a high court in America.

For Spaniards who had not belonged to a colegio mayor, a university professorship or service in a civil post either in Spain or America was beneficial.

213. The ten going to major audiencias are: Ypes, Rodríguez de Castañón, Enríquez de Iriarte, Ceballos Guerra, Martínez Malo, Salazar y Castejón, Quintana y Acevedo, Bárcena y Mier, Valcárcel y Formento, and Puente Larrea. The seven going elsewhere are: Flores y Guzmán, Rivera Aguado, Fernando Dávila Madrid, García Catalán, Fernández Toribio, Granado Catalán, and Blancas y Espeleta.

214. Luis Sala Balust, *Reales reformas de los antiguos colegios de Salamanca anteriores a las del reinado de Carlos III (1623–1770)* Valladolid, 1956), pp. 60–62.

215. AGS, XXIII, 2–34–187 (Merino y Rivera, Buen Retiro, 10 December 1744). The four lowest-ranking tribunals, by general agreement, were Santo Domingo, Manila, Panama, and Quito.

216. The six who had been proprietary professors were Sierra Osorio, Rodríguez de Castañón, Uribe Castejón, Martínez Malo, Fernández Toribio, and Alas Cienfuegos. Juan de Gutiérrez de Arce had been a *teniente de gobernador* and *auditor de guerra* in Cartagena de Indias before becoming an oidor in Santa Fe. Since he was named to the tribunal in Santa Fe barely three months after his teniente appointment, however, he had probably not left Spain before gaining the more desirable position. Nonetheless, he served in Cartagena and did not assume his post in Santa Fe until 1719. Restrepo Sáenz, *Biografías*, p. 339.

The crown considered any law professor in a Spanish university particularly well qualified for a judicial post, and the rapidity with which such men advanced to the audiencias, chancelleries, and councils in Spain testified to the importance of the *cátedra* (chair) as a means to enter the high letrado bureaucracy. On many early lists of candidates for audiencia vacancies in America, law professors at specified institutions received *ex officio* consideration before other categories of pretendientes.[217] Small wonder contemporaries lamented that men sought professorial chairs with the sole intention of using them as a base for seeking preferment.[218]

Advancement from an academic chair to the bench was so routine that on occasion the crown promised an audiencia appointment to successful competitors for a professorship. The difficulty of luring men with peninsular degrees to teach in the smaller American universities was such that in 1687 Charles II bribed two letrados to teach law for five years at the new University of San Carlos de Guatemala with futuras as oidores on the audiencia there.[219] Bartolomé de Amezquita, doctor of laws from the University of Oñate, took the prima chair of laws, and Pedro de Ozaeta y Oro, a limeño educated in Spain, became prima professor of canons. Early in 1693 both men took possession of their audiencia seats. In 1714–1715 a similar arrangement was made to assist the University of Manila. Francisco Fernández Toribio, a Spaniard from the colegio mayor of San Ildefonso, became prima professor of *Institutes*, and Julián de Velasco took the corresponding chair of laws.[220] Both men received honors of oidor at Manila that entitled them to the same privileges and public recognition as the serving judges, and the promise that after six years as professors they would be promoted to the first vacancies on mainland tribunals. Appointments were conferred to both professors in 1724.[221]

Given the crown's willingness (indeed, anxiety) to appoint peninsular professors, the small number who joined American audiencias reveals again the royal inability to enlist the men most preferred for service in the Indies. Most of the professors who went to America represented the less fortunate members of the scholarly world. Prima professors of laws or canons at Salamanca or Valladolid realistically expected to join a Spanish chancellery or council and scorned American service as worthy only of men from less prestigious

217. AGI, Chile, legajo 84, list of pretendientes, 1686; Panama, legajo 124, list of pretendientes without date, but from the 1680s.

218. Vicente Palacio Atard, *Los españoles de la ilustración* (Madrid, 1964), pp. 132–34.

219. John Tate Lanning, *The University in the Kingdom of Guatemala* (Ithaca, 1955), pp. 75–78; Schäfer, *El consejo*, 2: 477; see AGS, XXIII, 2–14–176 and 188 (order for pension to the sister of Amezquita, listing his services; pension to be paid from *indios vacos*, El Pardo, 6 July 1714).

220. AGS, XXIII, 2–22–54 (Fernández Toribio, Aranjuez, 1 June 1724); 2–22–98 (Velasco, Aranjuez, 1 June 1724).

221. Only Velasco made good his promise immediately; he became an alcalde del crimen in Mexico. Fernández did not take up his post in Guatemala, but was later assigned to the Audiencia of Manila. He refused later efforts to promote him, citing problems of health.

schools.[222] Ten of the eighteen professors named from 1687 to 1750 had taught in such institutions, Seville and Huesca being the most common.[223] As with the colegiales, the small number of peninsular professors indicates that those who enjoyed or hoped to enjoy preference in Spain viewed service in America with a distinct lack of enthusiasm.

Most other peninsular letrados shared the aversion of the colegiales and professors to accepting any American post below audiencia rank. Their reasoning was sound; none of the other letrado positions—asesor general, protector of the Indians, teniente asesor, and auditor de guerra—provided either a decent salary or a reasonable prospect for promotion. From 1687 to 1750 only fourteen Spaniards, 9 percent of the total, reached an audiencia after holding a lesser letrado position and one, Francisco de Barbadillo Victoria, had to purchase his advancement.[224] Only three more peninsulares ascended to an audiencia from other posts in the Indies.[225] Although fifteen went directly to American tribunals after minor service in Spain, their previous positions were diverse and no pattern emerges from their backgrounds.[226]

There was widespread reluctance among Spanish letrados to go to the New World without audiencia rank, which forced the crown to draw from a small pool of the least-favored colegiales and professors. Nearly half (70) of the 157 Spaniards appointed from 1687 to 1750 boasted neither affiliation with a colegio mayor, nor a professorship, nor previous regular government employment. These men had few if any professional qualifications beyond law degrees, the privilege to practice law before the royal councils, or, in some cases, fleeting appearance in competitions (*oposiciones*) for academic chairs or brief substitution in a professor's classroom. Although most had degrees or at least incorporation at the major universities of Salamanca, Valladolid, or Alcalá, the majority of these men were the dregs left by the colegial-dominated system of patronage.[227]

Failure to obtain preferment in Spain need not imply that the letrados who

---

222. This is clear from Kagan, *Students and Society;* see particularly tables 4 and 11, pp. 93, 151.

223. Alarón y Vargas, Jáuregui y Ollo, Ortiz Avilés, and Lugo y Arrieta were at Seville; Brun, Andréu y Ferraz, and Aróstegui were at Huesca. Only four Spaniards had been catedráticos at Valladolid, Salamanca, or Alcallá (Torralva, Verdugo, Gómez de la Torre, and Becerra); three of these were named in the period 1730–1750.

224. Barbadillo, García Chicano, García de Quesada, Manuel Bernardo de Alvarez, López de Urrelo, Pablo Cavero, and Prudencio de Palacios were teniente asesores; Alcedo y Sotomayor was an asesor to a teniente general in Popayán; Zárate was asesor to a viceroy and Antonio de Casa Alvarado was a teniente/auditor in Yucatan; Gutiérrez de Arce was a colegial in addition to being a teniente asesor; and Aguirre Negro (teniente asesor) and Brun (protector of the Indians) were also previously professors. Tineo was a protector of the Indians in Mexico and received an appointment as alcalde del crimen supernumerario when his previous position was abolished.

225. Antonio de Casa Alvarado was previously an alcalde mayor, Manuel de Zárate a corregidor, and Fernández de Villanueva Veitia Linaje (who was educated in Mexico), administrator general for the mercury of New Spain.

226. These men are indicated in Appendix IX.

227. See Appendix IV for a summary of university attendance.

went to America were inferior in intellect or ability to their more fortunate brethren. Connections, more than talent or brilliance, determined one's fortunes in the letrado bureaucracy. Nonetheless, in a patronage network largely run by great letrado families whose social rank had been secured through generations of service, those persons left aside were often of less elevated descent. Fragmentary material presently available on the fathers of peninsular-born ministers supports this contention. Only 6 of the fathers of 157 peninsular appointees were themselves ministers in Spain or America; 9 more held notable rank in the Spanish bureaucracy; and 14 others held local office or low-ranking military positions.[228] Unfortunately, the sources available contain little information about fathers who were not bureaucrats or did not hold a military or local office. Without more information, one can only speculate that most of the remaining fathers were at best either self-sacrificing petty hidalgos, businessmen (*comerciantes*), or investors. The crown's willingness to grant military habits (*hábitos*) to newly appointed ministers to America suggests its awareness not only that this honorific might attract some otherwise uninterested letrados to American service but also that the social standing of most of its appointees needed enhancement.

Membership in a military order provided public testimony of a man's elevated social position. Knights of Santiago, Calatrava, and Alcántara proudly wore distinctive uniforms testifying to their nobility, legitimacy, and freedom from the taint of "New Christian" ancestry.[229] As the number and influence of letrados expanded in the sixteenth and early seventeenth centuries, they began to enter orders as one way of confirming both their nobility and their growing power. By the mid-seventeenth century letrados were regularly gaining hábitos, and protests by the Council of Orders that only men with extensive military service should be admitted were without lasting impact. Indeed, the Council of the Indies, when it considered ways of making American service more appealing to colegiales in 1676, recommended that the king dispense membership in the orders more generously.[230] A royal refusal to relax the standards for admission soon yielded to the persistence of honors-hungry letrados.

By the end of the seventeenth century, ministers expected to join a military order as a matter of course. Miguel Calderón de la Barca, for example, petitioned for admission immediately after his appointment as oidor in Mexico in 1689. Perhaps exaggerating only slightly, he stressed the routine nature of his request and emphasized the king's customary willingness to enhance judges' status by granting them hábitos. The cámara warmly seconded his request and the king approved.[231] Citing reasons similar to those of Calderón,

---

228. See Appendix IX.

229. Information on the military orders is from L. P. Wright, "The Military Orders in Sixteenth- and Seventeenth-Century Spanish Society," *Past and Present* 43 (May 1969): 34–70.

230. Konetzke, *Colección*, 2, tomo II, document 436.

231. AGI, Mexico, legajo 10, consulta of the cámara, Madrid, 28 June 1690.

José Uribe Castejón, a colegial assigned to the Audiencia of Mexico in 1702, requested entrance in a military order "not excluding that of Santiago," and the crown again acceded.[232] By 1750 thirty-four of the peninsula-born ministers named after 1687 had donned the tunic.[233]

The prominence of colegiales among the ministers who gained admission into the military orders is final evidence for their favored status.[234] Not only did colegiales garner almost half the hábitos of Santiago, the most prestigious order, but also they seemed to gain their honors earlier in their careers than most of their colleagues. Those going directly to the ranking tribunals of Lima, Mexico, and Santa Fe were particularly favored, accounting for nine of the fourteen colegiales serving in America who entered orders.[235] Peninsular colegiales were the undisputed elite in a bureaucracy dominated from 1687 to 1750 by ministers whom, had it been able to attract the kind of men it wanted, the crown would not have appointed.

The crown's financial weakness and inability to attract the colegiales and professors it wanted for service in the Indies opened the door for fifty-three native sons and eighty-five other Americans from 1687 to 1750. From the crown's perspective, the least desirable appointee was a native son, for his ties to the district would threaten administration and justice. Although this overt antipathy did not extend to creoles willing to serve away from their home districts, all Americans found it difficult to gain appointment by means other than purchase. They labored under several handicaps: lack of membership in one of the six colegios mayores; university training in America that was only rarely complemented by later attendance at Salamanca, Valladolid, or Alcalá, the universities attended by three-quarters of all Spanish appointees; a disadvantage in the number of friends and relatives at court; and the need for an expensive trip to Spain to ensure proper handling of their solicitations.[236] These handicaps served to render Americans invisible. Aside from a few favored professors, "other Americans" were often lumped together at the bottom of a list of candidates, evidence of the perfunctory way in which their petitions were received.

To the colegiales prominent on the Council of the Indies, the backgrounds of most American-born appointees must have seemed appalling. None were

---

232. Ibid., legajo 11, consulta of the cámara, Madrid, 6 April 1699; legajo 522, Uribe Castejón to Señor, with recommendation of cámara appended (no date, approximately 1702).

233. This is a minimum figure. Seven other men were referred to as being in an order but how many actually obtained hábitos and for which orders is unknown.

234. 44 percent (15 of 34) of the colegiales going to America entered a military order; for Spaniards as a whole, the figure was 22 percent (34 of 157).

235. The nine who were colegiales, members of orders, and ministers in Lima, Mexico, or Santa Fe on first appointment were: Bernardo Angel Izunza y Eguiluz, Juan Fernando Calderón de la Barca, Uribe Castejón, Gutiérrez de Arce, Ypes, Rodríguez de Castañón, Valcárcel, Echávarri, and Chinchilla y Henestrosa. The six who were in orders and served elsewhere initially are Ron, Zúñiga y Tovar, Picado Pacheco, Alvaro Navia Bolaños, and Pineda y Tabares; Velarde y Cienfuegos, an Aragonese, was a member of Montesa.

236. See Appendix IV for university attendance.

colegiales or sons of ministers serving on Spanish tribunals. While fifteen sons of audiencia ministers in America followed their fathers into the tribunals, at least ten paid for their appointments, thus indicating again the gap between men who served in America and their counterparts in Spain.[237] Seven of these men (including six purchasers) received posts from 1687 to 1712 and eight from 1730 to 1750. The closest American parallel to Domingo Valcárcel dramatizes the gulf between the letrado elites in America and Spain. Clemente del Campo y Zárate received his education at the University of San Marcos in Lima and was an abogado of the viceregal tribunal from 1708. Son and grandson of judges in Charcas and Lima, he represented the elite of American-born letrados. Following the path of many American hopefuls, he sought his post through personal solicitation at court. Not even an offer to purchase in 1712 brought him a robe. Only in 1730, after a second costly trip to Spain, did he gain a post and under circumstances that suggest that cash and not his *méritos* had swayed the balance.[238]

Paradoxically, during years of sales native sons became the most favored aspirants, for they were anxious to serve at home and would pay high prices in order to obtain the necessary dispensations. Particularly noticeable in this regard were Peruvians and other Americans educated in Lima. Peruvians had early established their claim to audiencia positions. In 1642 the representative at court for the University of San Marcos had secured publication of a memorial briefly setting forth alumni and professors considered qualified for secular and ecclesiastical preferment.[239] During the following decades, such lobbying, as well as a tradition of Peruvians traveling to court to solicit employment, paid dividends. In the late seventeenth century, professors at the University of San Marcos were regularly grouped separately near the tops of lists of pretendientes for audiencias of first entrance in South America, tribunals from which advancement would generally lead back to Lima.[240] Peruvians as a group continued to win appointments, and a tradition of royal service seems to have developed. Moreover, since Lima was the center of the commercial system of the Viceroyalty of Peru, it housed a group of wealthy merchants who not only could afford to educate their sons but also could perceive the advantages that

---

237. The ten men who purchased are Paredes, Luna, Corral Calvo de la Banda, Núñez de Rojas, Rojas y Acevedo, Larrea Zurbano, Urquizu Ibáñez, Ambrosio Eugenio de Santaella y Melgarejo, Melchor de Santiago Concha, and Pérez Buelta. The nonpurchasers are: Oviedo y Baños, Campo y Zárate, Feijóo Centellas, Félix Malo de Villavicencio, and Fernando Dávila.

238. AGS, XXIII, 2–26–108 (Campo, Cazalla, 25 June 1730); AGI, Indiferente General, legajo 144, relación de méritos of Campo, 1730; and legajos 1120, 1861, and 1970 and Santa Fe, legajo 284.

239. AGI, Lima, legajo 337, memorial (printed) by Doctor don Nicolás Polanco de Santillana, 1642. We thank Professor Charles J. Fleener of Saint Louis University for obtaining a microfilm copy of this document for us.

On the desire of Peruvians for ecclesiastical appointments in the seventeenth century, see Antonine Tibesar, "The *Alternativa*: A Study in Spanish-Creole Relations in Seventeenth-century Peru," *The Americas* 11:3 (January 1955): 229–83.

240. For examples, see AGI, Chile, legajo 84 and Panama, legajo 124.

family representation on the Lima tribunal or one of its feeder courts, particularly Čharcas, could provide. A son's appointment to a high court added prestige to the family name and aided in a family's transition from commerce to more traditionally "noble" pursuits. Certainly each time the sale of audiencia appointments commenced, limeños hurried to extend their offers.

Purchase, indeed, was by far the most important single route by which native sons and other Americans entered the audiencias. During the Age of Impotence, 44 native sons and 57 other Americans bought appointments.[241] Combined, the two groups accounted for almost three-quarters of the 138 American appointees and 32 percent of the 311 total appointees. Cash had been added to a record of university or public service by 35 of the 101 American purchasers to gain appointment. The other purchasers had legal training alone to accompany their money.[242]

Only about half (nineteen) of the nonpurchasing Americans gained office after other service. Five were professors, three were protectors of the Indians, two were teniente asesores, five claimed other preappointment service, and four boasted a combination of these employments. Eighteen of the Americans who assumed audiencia positions exhibited little beyond standard legal training and a willingness to serve.[243] In their lack of notable credentials, these eighteen creoles joined the large group of equally undistinguished peninsulares whom the crown sent to America. Colegiales serving on the Cámara of the Indies must have felt that their patronage responsibility had degenerated to a process of selecting merely acceptable men from an inferior lot.

Further evidence that American appointees often came from backgrounds undistinguished in traditional terms can be seen through an examination of their fathers. Few fathers were ministers, and many could claim no noteworthy government or military service. Incomplete evidence suggests that a majority of the creoles named were the sons of recent immigrants. The American-born son of a newly arrived peninsular was by common definition as much a "creole" as a man descended in both lines from conquistador families. Audiencia appointments, however, reveal a significant division between the first-generation creole and his more rooted brethren. Although a small minority among the white population, first-generation sons entered the tribunals more frequently than other creoles.

Knowledge of the birthplace of fathers is too scanty to permit analysis for the years 1687–1712. However, of the forty-one men for whom this information is available, twenty-six were first-generation creoles. From 1713 to 1750 a minimum of thirty-two of the sixty-one Americans named were the sons of immigrants (only four of whom were audiencia ministers) and the fathers of at least thirteen were definitely creoles (four were audiencia ministers).[244] Fathers

---

241. See Appendix III.
242. See Appendix IX.
243. Several of these eighteen were probably secret purchasers.
244. In addition to archival sources, Lohmann Villena, *Los americanos* has been the most useful work in obtaining these figures.

of the remaining nineteen men are of unknown origins. These figures, although incomplete, force the conclusion that well over half of the American appointees were first-generation creoles. The implication is clear. The further a creole was from ancestors and close relatives born in Spain, the smaller his chance to obtain an audiencia appointment.

At the same time, the small number of first-generation creoles whose fathers were audiencia ministers or held any government office suggests that many appointees' fathers were merchants whose success had enabled them to provide sons with the requisite education (and often the cash) to obtain an audiencia position and thus add prestige to the family name. To give but one example, Martín de Echavarría y Zuloaga, a Basque born in 1649, went to Peru as a young man, entered into commerce, and over the years prospered. He reached the pinnacle of recognition in Lima's commercial community in 1711, when he became prior of its merchant guild.[245] Juan Bautista, son of Martín and his limeña wife, entered the colegio of San Martín in Lima and later received his doctorate from the University of San Marcos. While in his twenties, he journeyed to Spain, purchased an appointment as supernumerary oidor in his home tribunal in 1708, and in the following year joined his father in the military Order of Santiago.[246] Painstaking research in local records would undoubtedly reveal numerous merchant families connected with the audiencias. Unfortunately, although reference to a father's "unquestioned nobility" is commonplace in *relaciones de méritos*, pretendientes whose fathers were in commerce but not prior or consul in a merchant guild would rarely mention the fact. Instead, where possible, they would refer to any civil or military appointments or honorifics that their fathers had held or any monetary services they had provided to the crown.

Examination of American appointees who entered military orders further emphasizes the prominence of Peruvians, first-generation creoles, and sons of merchants among the ministers. Sixteen of the twenty American ministers admitted from 1687 to 1750 were Peruvians.[247] This disproportionate number reflects perhaps the famed hauteur of the limeño aristocracy and the desire to legitimize financial success with appropriate noble accoutrements. Sixteen of the twenty ministers, including thirteen of the limeños, were first-generation creoles, while at least six were sons of merchants, a low figure that future research will undoubtedly raise.[248] Fathers of only eight of the American minis-

245. Lohmann Villena, *Los americanos*, 1:138; Manuel Moreyra y Paz Soldán, ed., *El tribunal del consulado de Lima*, 2 vols. (Lima, 1956–1959), 1:266*n*. 111.

246. AGS, XXIII, 2–5–46 (Chavarría Zuloaga, Buen Retiro, 3 July 1708); AGI, Indiferente General, legajo 525, "Relación de los empleos"; Lohmann Villena, *Los americanos*, 1:138.

247. These twenty men were identifiably in a specific order; as with peninsulares, there were attributions that have not been substantiated. Most importantly, in AGI, Indiferente, legajo 1628 are many documents admitting men to orders, without specifying which one. Why most of these transactions were not completed remains unknown.

248. The six sons of merchants were: Solís Vango, Echavarría, Ortiz de Foronda, Querejazu, Tagle Bracho, and Puente y Ibáñez.

ters admitted to orders themselves had hábitos. The marriage of wealth and office implicit in the purchasers of the Age of Impotence is made public in the backgrounds of these fathers. Five were merchants, two were audiencia ministers, and one was the wealthy Conde de San Juan de Lurigancho, treasurer of the mint in Lima. The recent prominence of the paternal line is apparent in the fact that six of the eight sons were first-generation creoles.[249]

Circumstantial evidence indicates strongly that cash opened the door for creoles to enter orders much as it enabled them to enter audiencias. Philip IV had sold hábitos throughout his reign (1621–1665), and, since the crown had resorted to the sale of previously sacrosanct audiencia positions in the 1680s, there is little reason to believe it then withheld entry into the military orders from the market.[250] As late as 1743, Secretary of the Indies José Carvajal y Lancaster advocated selling hábitos to Americans.[251] Certainly there was an uncommon coincidence between Americans who bought appointments and who donned the tunic. All ten between 1687 and 1712 and six from 1740 to 1750 joined an order almost immediately after buying their appointments. Moreover, an examination of the years in which audiencia appointments were sold to Americans reveals heavy entrance in the orders for creoles in general.[252] The frequent close relationship between appointments and entry into an order for Americans contrasts with the situation for Spaniards. Date of entrance into an order for peninsulares often bore no relationship to the date of their appointment to an audiencia.[253]

Entry into orders confirmed the unique place of Peruvians among American appointees much as it did for colegiales among peninsulares. Moreover, the hábitos exemplified the nature of limeño participation in government. All but two of the sixteen Peruvian knights had purchased their audiencia appointments.[254] The sustained ability and willingness to pay for office and honor, coupled with the crown's greater concern for defense around the Caribbean, enabled limeños to continue to set themselves apart from other Americans. The seventy-three Peruvians were not only an absolute majority of American appointees, but their confirmed purchasers alone (fifty-four) outnumbered Spanish colegiales (forty-two). More importantly, thirty-five limeños named from 1687 to 1750 went to their home tribunal, twenty-seven by direct purchase and three others by purchased advancement from Charcas. A major-

---

249. The six sons were: Solís Vango, Echavarría, Malo de Villavicencio, Querejazu, Santa Cruz, and Puente y Ibáñez.

250. Wright, "The Military Orders," p. 57; Antonio Domínguez Oritz, *La sociedad española en el siglo XVII* Madrid, 1964), p. 203; *XVIII* (Madrid, 1955), 1:82n.5.

251. AGI, Indiferente General, legajo 1628B, José Carvajal y Lancaster to the Marqués de la Ensenada, Madrid, 13 July 1743.

252. Lohmann Villena, *Los americanos*, 1:lxxv.

253. For example, Pedro de Bedoya y Osorio had served on American audiencias over fifteen years before being admitted to the Order of Santiago; Pedro Calderón Enríquez served over a decade before being admitted to the Order of Calatrava.

254. The two exceptions were Ortiz de Foronda and Querejazu. It is probable that both of these men had purchased as well, although proof is lacking.

ity of the sixty-three men named to the City of Kings, limeños were also a pervasive influence in the feeder tribunals of Charcas, Quito, and Chile, where they joined other American ministers who had been educated in Lima. The Age of Impotence was the age of Peruvian political influence almost everywhere in Spanish South America.

The prominence of Peruvians among the American appointees is particularly striking when compared to the paucity of Mexicans. The contrast—73 (53 percent) Peruvians to only 26 (19 percent) Mexicans of the 138 appointees—raises questions about the nature of the two viceregal societies that at the present time can be approached only speculatively. Although both regions had universities operating by the 1570s and, thus, trained letrados eligible for audiencia appointments, only Peru sent its sons into the tribunals. Before the introduction of sales in 1687, Peruvians were the majority of the Americans named, and they outnumbered Mexicans 48 to 6.[255] Perhaps Peru's early economic importance had enabled a large number of Peruvians, many of whom were probably first-generation sons of merchants, to travel to court in pursuit of appointments. From such beginnings a tradition of employment in the audiencias and an awareness of the material and social benefits that such service yielded could have been established.

When sales commenced, Peruvian letrados were predisposed to seek appointments. In addition, by the late seventeenth century they faced less favorable economic opportunities than those available in New Spain.[256] Although fortunes could still be made in trade and mining, the security of a prestigious position that paid a regular, although modest, salary attracted letrados anxious either to obtain or confirm an enviable place in local society. Moreover, in contrast to the purge of native-son ministers that Mexico suffered during the Garzarón visita, few Peruvians had been removed, and these men had often obtained reinstatement. Finally, in the last period of sales, most of the courts within the ascenso to Lima were outside the perimeter of defense that influenced the crown's aversion to selling posts in Mexico, Guatemala, and Santo Domingo. Only detailed analysis of the other forms of employment available to both Peruvians and Mexicans and the social and economic rewards they carried will allow an adequate understanding of the presently puzzling prominence of Peruvians among the audiencia ministers named prior to 1750.

The crown's impotence toward the American audiencias from 1687 to 1750 grew out of its financial weakness. By seizing upon the sale of audiencia positions, royal advisers opened the way for over seventy-five years of travail. Never able to recruit adequate numbers of the peninsular colegiales and law professors it preferred as ministers, the crown abdicated its traditional standards of appointment in favor of cash and thus lost mastery over the tribunals. Always anxious to serve, native sons flocked to Spain with purses open. Since

255. See note 18, p. 20 for the sources employed to obtain these figures.

256. D. A. Brading and Harry E. Cross, "Colonial Silver Mining: Mexico and Peru," *Hispanic American Historical Review* (hereafter *HAHR*) 52:4 (November 1972): 576.

their legal disabilities required them to pay higher prices, the crown welcomed their offers and, although they represented interests inimical to its own, granted them offices in unprecedented numbers. This forced generosity joined with the vending of marriage and property dispensations that provided legally authorized ties between ministers and their constituents, and thus further weakened royal authority.

The disruption of the ascenso that sales caused exacerbated the problem of local influence in government. Yet for a financially prostrate crown, no options were attractive. Unless "cause" could be found, it could remove purchasers only by repayment, a costly expedient. Alternately, allowing them to remain jeopardized justice, the traditional essence of kingship. In the end, the crown took no decisive action to resolve this dilemma. After the War of the Spanish Succession, it removed the worst appointees and purged the Audiencia of Mexico but allowed many purchasers to remain in office, particularly in the tribunals of South America. Subsequently it sought to discriminate among prospective purchasers and retain at least minimal professional standards. Far more careful selection than the crown employed, however, would not have prevented ministers forced to remain for five, ten, or even twenty years in one location from establishing close personal relationships and engaging in economic activities that by their nature threatened royal control over the colonies. A major legacy of impotence was the radicado minister, as much a bane to royal authority as his native-son colleague.

Ironically, the crown's volte-face toward native-son appointments underscored the discrimination that all Americans faced. One hundred three of the 138 Americans named had to pay for their appointments in contrast to only 13 of 157 Spaniards. In other words, while almost 75 percent of the creoles paid to serve, only 8 percent of the peninsulares did. The disparity reveals the extent to which discrimination against Americans had changed from more or less unconscious disadvantages, often present before actual solicitation began, to calculated exploitation. At the same time, although initially exploited, native sons and other Americans had gained a substantial number of audiencia posts, and in 1750 some courts nearly provided the de facto home rule that Bolívar y de la Redonda had advocated. The problem of eradicating the direct and indirect influence in government that these creoles, along with radicado peninsulares, represented challenged the crown into the 1770s.

Part Two
The Age of Authority
(1751–1808)

Overview

Beginning in the 1750s, the balance of empire again began to favor the metropolis. From midcentury to 1808 the keynote was "authority"—the reestablishment and expansion of royal authority at the expense of long-entrenched colonial establishments.[1] Comparing the empire in 1808 with that of 1750 indicates the reinvigoration of royal authority and the extent of change that had occurred. At midcentury, Spanish America had three viceroyalties, eleven audiencias, and over two hundred *corregimientos* and *alcaldías mayores*. Although in economic decline, Peru still legally dominated trade with the mining regions of the central Andes. New Spain's silver production, although generally rising, was but a fraction of its later yield. Commerce existed in a nether world of contraband and ships of register; the fleet for Peru was moribund and that for New Spain nearly so. The House of Trade still oversaw legal trade, while other colonial affairs rested in the hands of a secretary and the Council of the Indies. While traces of modern thought now reached the colonies, universities were dominated by requirements and chairs often dating back to their founding.

By 1808, institutions, commerce, mining, intellectual life, and even the map exhibited some markedly different features, and the population was steadily expanding. The establishment of the Viceroyalty of the Río de la Plata in 1776 and the elevation of Venezuela and Chile to the rank of captaincy-general displayed the crown's concern for tighter control over burgeoning regions previously on the periphery of administration. The later institution of audiencias in Buenos Aires, Caracas, and Cuzco further testified to royal desire for expeditious administration of justice and stronger representation of the king's will. The presence of intendants in every region but Santa Fe and Manila in place of the notoriously corrupt corregidores illustrated the effort to centralize and hence tighten authority. The House of Trade and the fleet system were but memories, and commerce, when free from British harassment, was "free" within the empire. Legal trade had increased several fold since 1778. Since the

---

1. See John Lynch's works for the thesis of the colonies' "first emancipation" by the end of the seventeenth century and the subsequent "new imperialism" that sought to reverse it in the late eighteenth century. *Spain under the Habsburgs*, 2 vols. (New York, 1964–1969), 2, chapter 8, and *The Spanish American Revolutions, 1808–1826* (London, 1973), pp. 1–7.

establishment of regular postal service in 1764, communications in time of peace had never been better, and royal knowledge of American affairs was more comprehensive than ever before. Even the Secretariat of the Indies, itself a child of the eighteenth century, had disappeared, its responsibilities divided since 1790 among five secretaries organized on a functional rather than a geographical basis. In many spheres of knowledge the intellectual lag present in 1750 had effectively disappeared by 1808, and formal education had benefited from modernization. The Jesuits, of course, had been expelled four decades earlier, victims of the crown's desire for unchallenged authority. Similarly, a substantial militia and regular colonial army existed where neither had been considered necessary at midcentury.

The transformation after midcentury had a coherent goal: the crown sought to increase the power, prestige, and prosperity of Spain and to restore her as a leading state in Europe. The key to success lay in the integration of its dominions, a concept denoting carefully supervised exploitation of the Americas for the benefit of Spain. Any necessary justification for this rather routine goal of eighteenth-century statecraft can be found in José del Campillo's famous "Nuevo sistema de gobierno para la América" (c. 1743), which lay bare the core of this program of reinvigoration.[2] Although not circulated widely at the time of its composition, this document faithfully reflected the spirit of the age. His premise, as followed by successors after midcentury, was that proper exploitation of the colonies would yield the benefits the crown sought. Specifically, the possessions in the New World were to be "classic" colonies—producers of raw materials, purchasers of finished goods, and noncompetitive with Spain. Changes were necessary, however, before this system could work properly. Spain must implement both administrative and commercial reforms after detailed examinations (*visitas generales)* had provided exact knowledge of the colonies' resources. Among Campillo's proposals were improvement of communications, establishment of the intendant system in America, and institution of so-called "comercio libre" by opening major Spanish and American ports to each other's trade and permitting all products made in Spain to be exported. The secretary's scheme was not unique in scope; ambitious proposals were a part of the national heritage of *arbitrismo*. But after 1750 circumstances proved propitious for the trial and then more general implementation of the main lines of Campillo's solution.

Integrating Spain and the colonies into a profitable economic unit demanded both creation of the conditions for effective exploitation in America through administrative and commercial changes and an increase in Spanish production to supply the growing market. Consequently, emphasis upon production at home marked many royal efforts to aid the imperial economy. The government invested in new textile factories, sought to elevate the status of artisans, encouraged "useful" knowledge and the economic societies that

---

2. For the following synopsis see Miguel Artola, "Campillo y las reformas de Carlos III," *Revista de Indias* 12:50 (October–December 1952): 685–714.

helped to spread it, and attacked "unproductive" and hence "useless" groups in Spanish society. Groups that seemed to be obstacles to efforts at reinvigoration or the growth of royal authority that the crown perceived as necessary to stimulate improvement, such as colegiales and Jesuits, fell by the wayside.

The sweeping proposals of Campillo might have foundered on the shoals of expensive wars had Ferdinand VI not been committed to peace. The Treaty of Aquisgran (Aix-la-Chapelle) in 1748 terminated Spain's involvement in the War of Jenkins' Ear, while a treaty with Portugal in 1750 brought a temporary halt to a vexing boundary dispute in the New World. A decade of peace and financial recovery followed. During these years Ferdinand made important advances, including the permanent establishment of intendants in Spain (1749) and the famed Concordat of 1753, which gave the crown greater authority over the Church than it had ever previously enjoyed. Other administrative improvements in Spain and an increased silver flow from Mexico helped to strengthen royal finances. When Ferdinand died in 1759, he left his half-brother a surplus in the treasury, an unprecedented boon for the more martial-minded Charles.[3]

It was during this decade of peace that the "modern" approach to knowledge and problem-solving that was making notable inroads among the literate minority received official sanction. Ferdinand's decree in 1750, which prohibited criticism of the writings of the great eclectic Father Benito Feijóo, demonstrated the growing strength of those who advocated the use of observation, experience, and critical reason.[4] A further illustration that linked modernity with reinvigoration dates from 1751, when the powerful Marqués de la Ensenada, secretary of the Indies, Marine, War, and Treasury, called for the appointment of new men to high office to balance traditionalists with innovators. He recommended that *manteistas* be given half of the seats on the Cámara of Castile,[5] posts that would then enable further appointments of non-colegiales and thus putative innovators to lesser tribunals and administrative positions. The seed was planted for the overt attack on the colegios that came a generation later.

War erupted soon after Charles III's accession. Quickly breaking with Ferdinand's policy of neutrality, the new king again tied Spain to France in the Third Family Compact (1761) and thus committed her to share defeat in the Seven Years' War. Spain recovered Havana and Manila from the British by treaty but only at the cost of Florida. Louisiana, ceded to Spain by France, was questionable recompense. The shock of defeat and the desire for vengeance as well as a concern for the future led the king to focus his attention more closely on the empire. The Marqués de la Ensenada's scheme of holding American

---

3. Modesto Lafuente, *Historia general de España, desde los tiempos más remotos hasta nuestros días*, 30 vols. (Madrid, 1850–1867) 19: 384.

4. Richard Herr, *The Eighteenth-Century Revolution in Spain* (Princeton, 1958), p. 39.

5. Vicente Rodríguez Casado, *La política y los políticos en el reinado de Carlos III* (Madrid, 1962), pp. 82–83. *Manteistas* were university students not associated with a colegio mayor.

revenues in reserve for emergencies gave way to a more positive program of expanded exploitation of the American possessions that followed many of the lines suggested two decades earlier by Campillo.[6]

The new focus was expressed in revitalization and expansion of the colonial militia and an increase of troops of the line in America.[7] Military preparedness on such a scale demanded great increases in revenues, and Charles sought to boost Spain's resources through improved administration and tax collection, increased trade, and a growth in mining. The success of Visitor-General José de Gálvez in raising revenues in New Spain through tighter administration, abolition of certain tax farms, and the establishment of the profitable tobacco monopoly confirmed the value of the general visitation as a means of furthering royal interests.[8] Within days of Gálvez's own promotion to secretary for the Indies in 1776, he designated José Antonio de Areche and Juan Francisco Gutiérrez de Piñeres as visitor-generals for Peru and Santa Fe de Bogotá. Everywhere the crown's efforts at reinvigoration expanded the bureaucracy. The "new men" in new posts that D. A. Brading has noted in Mexico were particularly obvious in the office of intendant, a powerful position almost invariably filled by peninsulares.[9] These new officials exercised supervisory powers taken of necessity from the existing treasury agents, viceroys, and audiencias.

The financial success of the new royal pressure on America was immediately evident. Revenues from New Spain, the principal source, soared as silver production reached new peaks, the tobacco monopoly yielded large amounts, and general revenue responded to the growth of population and prosperity.[10] Even the bedraggled Viceroyalty of Peru responded, and the increase in revenues visible after 1760 generally continued into the 1790s.[11] The

---

6. Lafuente, *Historia general*, 19: 383 refers to Ensenada's view toward American revenue.

7. See Lyle N. McAlister, *The "Fuero Militar" in New Spain 1764–1800* (Gainesville, 1957).

8. Herbert Ingram Priestley, *José de Gálvez, Visitor-General of New Spain (1765–71)* (Berkeley, 1916).

9. D. A. Brading, *Miners and Merchants in Bourbon Mexico 1763–1810* (Cambridge, England, 1971), part one. For peninsular intendants see John Lynch, *Spanish Colonial Administration, 1782–1810: The Intendant System in the Viceroyalty of the Río de la Plata* (New York, 1969), appendix I and J. R. Fisher, *Government and Society in Colonial Peru: The Intendant System, 1784–1814* (London, 1970), appendix I; Brading, *Miners and Merchants*, p. 64.

10. Alejandro de Humboldt, *Ensayo político sobre el reino de la Nueva España*, ed. Juan A. Ortega y Medina (Mexico, 1966), pp. 386–89; Brading, *Miners and Merchants*, p. 131; Bernard E. Bobb, *The Viceregency of Antonio María Bucareli in New Spain, 1771–1779* (Austin, 1962), p. 258; Hugh M. Hamill, Jr., *The Hidalgo Revolt: Prelude to Mexican Independence* (Gainesville, 1966), p. 1.

11. Fisher, *Government and Society*, pp. 119–20; John J. TePaske, review of Fisher in *HAHR* 52:1 (February 1972): 137. After peaking in 1799, registered silver production in Peru dropped but still remained respectable until 1812. See "Silver mining and silver miners in the viceroyalty of Peru, 1776-1824," a 1974 seminar paper by J. R. Fisher that will appear in a collection of papers on Peru in the Monograph Series of the University of Liverpool Centre for Latin American Studies. We thank Dr. Fisher for sending us an

Viceroyalty of the Río de la Plata had little surplus to remit but was self-sufficient and, like the captaincy-general of Caracas, able to maintain expanded military forces and a larger bureaucracy.[12]

Legal and hence taxable trade jumped dramatically as Charles reduced restrictions and allowed increased competition under the concept of "free trade within the empire." Despite its loss of monopolistic privileges, Cádiz remained the principal port and after 1778 witnessed nearly two decades of "spectacular expansion" ended only by the conflict with England that begain in 1796.[13] Not only did trade increase, but the percentage of transactions involving Spanish-manufactured goods increased. By the end of the eighteenth century, goods from Spain accounted for perhaps four times the percentage of a hundred years earlier.[14]

The expansion in mining and trade and more effective collection of taxes strengthened the fiscal condition of the crown. When temporarily deprived of American revenue, Charles III could finance activities during the English colonies' war for independence with the interest-bearing bonds known as *vales reales*. Although discounted over 20 percent at one point, they regained strength after hostilities ended and circulated above par from 1786 to 1792.[15] Only after war with England began in 1796 and colonial resources and trade were no longer regularly available did a permanent breakdown of royal credit take place.[16]

From the crown's vantage point in 1808, the Age of Authority was a success. Spain and most of the colonies had enjoyed unprecedented prosperity until conflict with England began in 1796. After that date it was Spain, not the colonies, that suffered the most. The strain of war, although severe, had not seriously weakened administration within the colonies.[17] While commerce was at the mercy of the British, Charles IV could anticipate realistically that peace and the regular flow of Mexico's still-rising silver production would restore prosperity.

It was precisely the crown's strength during the Age of Authority that frustrated some Americans. Growing prosperity had whetted American appetites for continued, indeed, increased responsibility and power at the time when the crown consciously began to limit the direct and indirect influence of local families in government. While the stresses of war from the 1790s opened a brief era of opportunity for reinvigorated city councils to purchase conces-

advance draft of this paper. See also John Fisher, "Silver Production in the Viceroyalty of Peru, 1776–1824," *HAHR* 55:1 (February 1975): 25–43.

12. Herbert S. Klein, "Structure and Profitability of Royal Finance in the Viceroyalty of the Río de la Plata in 1970," *HAHR* 53:3 (August 1973): 450–55.

13. Antonio García-Baquero González, *Comercio colonial y guerras revolucionarias: la decadencia económica de Cádiz a raíz de la emancipación americana* (Seville, 1972), pp. 127–57.

14. Herr, *Eighteenth-Century Revolution*, p. 147.

15. Ibid., p. 146.

16. Ibid., pp. 393–96, 400.

17. The argument that a crisis of administration occurred before 1808 appears in R. A. Humphreys and John Lynch, eds., *The Origins of the Latin American Revolutions, 1808–1826* (New York, 1966), pp. 14–15.

sions, the wholesale disposal of keys to power that had occurred during the Age of Impotence was not repeated.[18] Although the crown demanded and obtained substantial financial support from the colonists, after midcentury it granted few of them personal benefits in return for their aid.

For the audiencias, the Age of Authority displayed a continuity absent in the preceding period. From midcentury until she entered the Wars of the French Revolution, Spain enjoyed more years of peace than in the preceding century. The freedom that peace provided and, from the 1770s, the greater flexibility made possible by rising American revenues allowed the crown to pursue consistently the traditional policy of naming outsiders to the American audiencias. Once it had reasserted its authority, the crown generally maintained a firm grip over personnel. The accession of Charles III and Charles IV, José de Gálvez's tenure as secretary for the Indies, and the ascendancy of Manuel Godoy were more notable for continuity than change of policy toward the judicial tribunals. Even while the Wars of the French Revolution devastated both trade and the celebrated effort (1803) to revitalize the intendant system, control over the audiencias and selection of personnel were affected only slightly. In sum, while the crown took a series of notable actions to improve its fiscal position and military strength, most of these from the 1760s to 1780s, clear concern and specific actions directed toward reestablishing control over the audiencias predated the better known reforms and continued beyond them. The consequence was that many antagonists to Spanish rule after 1808 rightly focused on the tribunals as bulwarks of loyalist sentiment.

Royal innovations during the post-1750 era did, however, constitute a limited redefinition of the scope of activities associated with the audiencias. Establishment of new offices and institutions such as *asesores generales* to provide legal guidance to executives, expansion of the network of treasury officers, and the imposition of the intendant system left the audiencias with more narrowly defined and purely judicial responsibilities than had been customary during the Hapsburg period. Encouragement of specialized agencies such as the *Acordada* had a similar effect.[19]

An examination of the audiencias from 1751 to 1808 reveals two major periods separated by the expansion of the courts in 1776 and 1777. In the first, the crown sought to regain control lost as a result of sales. By 1775 both direct and indirect local influence was in full decline. The expansion of the tribunals from seventy-two to ninety-eight men and the attendant stimulation of the as-

---

18. John Fisher, "The Intendant System and the Cabildos of Peru, 1784–1810," *HAHR* 49:3 (August 1969): 445–47; John Preston Moore, *The Cabildo in Peru under the Bourbons: A Study in the Decline and Resurgence of Local Government in the Audiencia of Lima, 1700–1824* (Durham, 1966), p. 179. In at least one case the crown refused a proffered donation. See Lynch, *Spanish Colonial Administration*, p. 229.

19. See Colin M. MacLachlan, *Criminal Justice in Eighteenth Century Mexico: A Study of the Tribunal of the Acordada* (Berkeley, 1974). Some incursions into traditional areas of audiencia interest may have been offset by the crown's more aggressive attitude toward the Church, expressed in some cases through the audiencias; see N. M. Farriss, *Crown and Clergy in Colonial Mexico 1759–1821: The Crisis of Ecclesiastical Privilege* (London, 1968).

censo was the coup de grace. From 1778 to 1808 the crown continued the momentum of the earlier years in audiencia appointments and focused on the expansion of revenue through nonjudicial means. During these years native-son strength averaged about seven men, only a third the number of 1750. At its peak in the mid-1790s, renewed local influence was still less than it had been from 1751 to 1770.[20]

The audiencia appointees in the Age of Authority constituted part of a new bureaucracy. As part of a far-reaching reform of the universities and an effort to break the hold of the old bureaucracy on the tribunals in Spain, the colegios mayores lost their privileged place. Consequently, after the 1770s, colegiales, the elite in the old bureaucracy, were absent from the ranks of the new men. Universities of the periphery replaced the traditional Castilian schools as the principal suppliers of Spanish-born ministers for America. With the end of sales in 1750 the Americans named to New World tribunals declined in number and were often more mature and experienced men than their predecessors; native sons rarely appeared. The changed background of appointees was not the only difference between the Ages of Impotence and Authority. With native sons largely excluded from high posts, local protests against the reinvigorated policy began to appear in the 1770s. The crown's success in regaining and then maintaining control of the American audiencias came at the cost of additional creole resentment.

Toward Control

Peace and a consequent improvement of royal finances enabled the crown to stop the recognized abuse of selling audiencia positions in 1750. Although the return to appointments based on merit paralleled the course followed after the War of the Spanish Succession, by the end of 1750 an additional impetus for the immediate end of sales was circulating at court. The *Noticias secretas* of Jorge Juan and Antonio de Ulloa vividly dwelled on corruption in government in Panama, Quito, and Lima. "The practice of sales," they avowed, was "the origin of all the excesses." For the future they recommended that the king sell no appointments and name only men of proven ability and integrity for American positions, be they on audiencias or in local government (corregidores).[21] Although no royal order halting sales has been found, the use of beneficio for gaining appointment to either an audiencia or a more humble corregimiento apparently ended in 1750, as the two travelers had suggested.[22]

---

20. See Appendix VIII.

21. Jorge Juan and Antonio de Ulloa, *Noticias secretas de América* (London, 1826), 1: 483.

22. John J. TePaske, "The Collapse of the Spanish Empire," *Lex et Scientia: The International Journal of Law and Science* 10: 1–2 (January–June 1974): 39 *n.* 10. Our research has revealed no sales of corregimientos after 1750, either.

The close of sales terminated heavy native-son and other creole entry into the audiencias. The legacy of this influx marked the following twenty-five years and triggered royal efforts to reduce direct and indirect local influence. A survey of the audiencias at the end of 1750 reveals that only Manila, Guatemala, and Santo Domingo were at normal strength. In the other tribunals, supernumeraries and futurarios swelled the total rolls to ninety-three instead of the seventy-seven ministers authorized by statute.[23] Surplus ministers after the War of the Spanish Succession had limited opportunities for new appointments; similarly, after 1750 appointments of new men were low for years. Unlike in the earlier sales period, however, the purchasers of the 1740s did not include extreme examples of incompetence and unfitness. The crown found it easier to let death and routine retirement reduce the number of ministers than to embark on wholesale trimming. Fewer new men were named from 1751 to 1775 than in any other twenty-five year period after 1687.

The number of Americans in the audiencias peaked in 1750; fifty-one of the ninety-three ministers were from the New World (see Appendixes V and VI). With only Guatemala lacking a creole minister, aspiring American lawyers could see the possibility of reaching the apex of letrado success in the Indies. Of greater importance, native sons held appointments on six tribunals, and everywhere outsiders had taken advantage of the crisis years to gain permission to establish local ties.[24] Lima provided the best example of direct representation with thirteen native-son appointees. Never again would a colonial tribunal come so close to the ideal of native-son monopolization that Pedro de Bolívar y de la Redonda had outlined in 1667.

Not only were native son and American representation at their apogee, but the surplus of ministers and consequent paucity of new appointments meant that the length of tenure grew. Just over half of the seventy-five men for whom approximate ages are known were aged forty or younger in 1750, and only fifteen men were fifty-one or older.[25] Nearly two-thirds of the Americans still held appointments in 1763. The continued importance of sales was evident in 1775 when seventeen purchasers still served. In that year, a quarter of the men (twenty-six) holding appointment at midcentury remained on the bench, at least one in every tribunal but Manila and Guatemala. The laxness of the war years had provided a surplus of often long-lived ministers, widespread direct participation, radicados in every tribunal, and a particularly clogged ascenso in the Secretariat of Peru.

Ferdinand VI opened the attack on the audiencias in 1751 by suppressing the tribunal of Panama as an unnecessary source of disruption in its region.[26]

---

23. In addition to the seventy-six positions authorized in the *Recopilación*, a permanent supernumerary post was attached to the Audiencia of Manila by consulta of 28 February 1725. See note 81, p. 39.

24. Native sons were in Charcas, Chile, Guadalajara, Lima, Panama, and Quito.

25. The ages are calculated on the basis of figures presented in Appendix IX.

26. Archivo Histórico Nacional (Madrid), Sección de Códices y Cartularios, legajo 727B, A—vol. II, entry 120.

The action eliminated two native-son purchasers from the high bureaucracy, Rather than keep Gaspar Francisco Pérez Buelta in an overstocked magistracy, the crown returned his servicio with 5 percent interest in 1753.[27] It granted the other Panamanian purchaser, Antonio Sanz Merino, an oidorship in Charcas only after he had spent nearly a decade off the bench.[28] Peninsular Luis de Carrillo de Mendoza was the sole minister immediately named to another tribunal.[29] Outside of Panama only one purchaser lost his post, and, as royal officials had established "cause" for his dismissal, the monarch felt no obligation to provide a refund.[30] This restraint contrasted markedly with the massive removal of purchasers that followed the War of the Spanish Succession.

Being allowed to remain in office did not mean that purchasers always enjoyed normal careers. While generally sharing the same benefits as their fellows, purchasers occasionally suffered discrimination from a monarch that in the last analysis regarded them as slightly inferior to outsiders named for merit and experience alone. An appointment made to the Audiencia of Guadalajara in 1754 exemplifies the treatment purchasers sometimes received. The secretariat ordered the Cámara of the Indies to propose candidates for the vacant positions of *decano* and *subdecano* on the New Galician tribunal. Since the court had been overstaffed, however, the cámara advised filling only the place of decano and thus restoring the audiencia to authorized strength. Moreover, the secretary recommended bypassing the three purchasers on the tribunal for the decano appointment, although naming one of them would have been a normal ascenso.[31] Accordingly, Francisco de Galindo Quiñones, a Spaniard serving as oidor in Santo Domingo, advanced to the senior chair in Guadalajara.[32] The concern expressed in this appointment can be interpreted both as anxiety over the quality of specific purchasers and an awareness that purchase regularly included dispensations that enabled ministers to establish close ties with the local population. The latter was probably the case here, for two of the three purchasers were native sons, and the third was married to a New Galician.[33]

While limited efforts to deal with the audiencias appeared immediately after midcentury, the long tenure of Baylio Frey Julián de Arriaga as secretary of Marine and the Indies from July 1754 until his death in early 1776 enabled him to make significant changes during the period that ended in 1775. Arriaga inaugurated a policy of reducing native-son and creole influence in the tribu-

27. AGI, Indiferente General, legajo 1308.

28. AGS, XXIII, 2–44–3 (Sanz, Buen Retiro, 16 November 1760).

29. He took possession of his position of oidor in Santa Fe in mid-1752. José María Restrepo Sáenz, *Biografías de los mandatorios y ministros de la real audiencia—(1671 a 1819)* (Bogotá, 1952), p. 365.

30. Juan Aparicio del Manzano was deprived of his post as fiscal in Guadalajara in 1752.

31. AGI, Guadalajara, legajo 128, Nota de la Secretaría para la Cámara, 5 October 1754.

32. AGS, XXIII, 2–41–62 (Galindo Quiñones, Buen Retiro, 22 November 1755).

33. López Portilla and Garza Falcón were native sons, and Gómez Algarín was married to a native.

nals and limiting indirect access through marriage. Arriaga regarded this policy not as a revolutionary innovation but rather as renewed respect for the law and a return to traditional attitudes formulated during Hapsburg rule. The secretary's perspective was clear; native sons and indirect ties were incompatible with upright administration of justice.

Reports from America indicated the problems that sales and native-son appointments had created. Men who purchased an audiencia appointment expected to gain both prestige and tangible profit. Added to the usual expenses of travel and attendance at court in pursuit of an office, the cost of an appointment meant that the recipient was often, perhaps almost always, in debt when he assumed his post. Spanish-born Andrés de Pueyo y Urríes was still in debt a decade after gaining his unpurchased appointment as oidor in Santo Domingo for the expense of moving his family from Spain.[34] If such obligations afflicted a peninsular appointed on merit, one cannot wonder that American purchasers sought to liquidate their obligations and accumulate a profit through exploitation of their offices. Salaries alone were inadequate to provide a style of life that the magistrates considered appropriate, and, given a burden of debt, ministers must often have felt they had little choice but to favor the highest bidder in their decisions.[35]

Diego de Orbea's experience reveals the importance of credit in procuring an appointment and also suggests that a quick return on the investment was expected. In 1749 limeño Orbea offered 41,400 pesos for appointment as a supernumerary alcalde del crimen in Lima. Required to pay a down payment of 3,000 pesos, he borrowed 2,942 1/2 pesos in Madrid. A decade later he had neither paid the balance due for his appointment, nor taken office, nor repaid his creditor.[36] One can surmise that Orbea reached Lima only to discover that no one would loan him the remaining 38,400 pesos. The Lima tribunal was already glutted with native-son supernumeraries and, with only a criminal judgeship involved, potential creditors probably doubted that they could recoup their investment.

For men who paid their full servicio and swore the oath of office, an immediate return on their investment was essential. One of the last limeño purchasers, Domingo de Orrantia, had secured an appointment as supernumerary oidor in Lima in 1749 for the extraordinarily high price of 47,500 pesos.[37] Still without a numero position and thus receiving only half-salary in 1764, Orrantia protested that he was not receiving even 5 percent interest on the purchase price.[38] For some purchasers, even full salary was inadequate interest. Corrup-

---

34. See AGI, Santo Domingo, legajos 921 and 922.
35. The crown was always reluctant to increase salaries but did so in Mexico in 1738 and as part of the expansion in 1776. See John Leddy Phelan, *The Kingdom of Quito in the Seventeenth Century* (Madison, 1967), pp. 147–50 for a forceful discussion of the impact of inadequate salaries throughout the bureaucracy.
36. AGI, Lima, legajo 811, expediente 9.
37. AGS, XXIII, 2–37–101 (Orrantia, Buen Retiro, 14 March 1749).
38. See AGI, Lima, legajo 615.

tion in the audiencia was widespread in Lima, the largest center of purchasers. Juan and Ulloa found little evidence of integrity in the 1740s, and Viceroy Manuel de Amat later reported that several ministers were among the largest merchants in the realm.[39] Gifts and bribes were the best arguments a suitor could present when his case reached the court.[40]

The presence of native sons was undesirable enough even in the absence of venality. The Council of the Indies observed in accepting a case appealed from Lima in 1752 that the claimant's son sat on the tribunal, all but one of the civil judges were fellow limeños, and impartial justice was thus impossible. Moreover, similar difficulties existed in the other courts.[41] Five years later the viceroy of Mexico, an Arriaga appointee, expressed concern not only about native sons but also long-term residents serving on the tribunal. He pointed out that if Antonio Andréu y Ferraz received a post in Spain the fiscal civil, Luis Mosquera y Pimentel, would advance routinely to the civil chamber as an oidor, and then the native-son junior fiscal Antonio Joaquín de Rivadeneira would automatically become the new fiscal civil. The viceroy recommended that the ascenso be overridden and the civil post be given to a peninsular, adding that it was poor policy to have it in the hands of "native sons or those already rooted [*radicado*] in the country."[42] The point was clear. The fiscal civil wielded too much power to be compromised by local interests.

The perspective the viceroy expressed coincided perfectly with the view of Arriaga. When the fiscal civil gave up his post to return to Spain, Ferdinand VI implemented the viceroy's proposal in substance but adhered to the letter of the law and respected the ascenso. The native son Rivadeneira did succeed as fiscal civil but within fourteen months was promoted into the civil chamber as oidor. A peninsular, Juan Antonio Velarde, had entered as criminal fiscal replacing Rivadeneira and succeeded to the civil *fiscalía* when the native son was "kicked upstairs." Velarde was replaced by another peninsular in the criminal post.[43] The viceroy's protest was resolved, but, in the Arriaga manner, neither law nor custom was violated.

Other sources from the late 1750s and early 1760s further reveal the crown's concern over ministers' place of birth and marital status. These sources also inadvertently display the crown's abysmal lack of ready, accurate information. In an annotated list of the ministers serving on the Audiencia of Mexico in 1759, names and dates of appointment of the fourteen judges appeared. Mar-

---

39. Juan and Ulloa, *Noticias secretas, passim.*; AGI, Lima, legajo 639, Manuel de Amat to Julián de Arriaga, Lima, 24 March 1762.

40. TePaske, "Collapse," p. 37.

41. AGI, Lima, legajo 596, Consejo de Yndias en sala de Just[a], 23 March 1752.

42. AGN, Correspondencia de Virreyes, Vol. 2, VRNE to Arriaga, Mexico, 27 May 1757, folio 133, letter 141. The *Recopilación*, libro II, título XVIII, ley i provided for automatic advancement from the criminal to the civil fiscalía.

43. AGS, XXIII, 2–44–18 (Rivadeneira, Buen Retiro, 21 June 1760); 2–45–137 (Rivadeneira, San Ildefonso, 15 August 1761); 2–44–156 (Velarde, Buen Retiro, 23 December 1760); 2–45–141 (Velarde, San Ildefonso, 19 August 1761); 2–47–272 (Rojas, San Lorenzo, 4 November 1763).

ginalia erroneously stated that Félix Malo was a Mexican. While Ambrosio Eugenio de Santaella's purchase and his father's service as oidor of Mexico were duly noted, Ambrosio was described as "probably Mexican." In fact both he and a similarly misidentified Diego Fernández de Madrid had been born in Guatemala. His birth in Santo Domingo apparently unknown, purchaser Sebastián Calvo de la Puerta was simply described as resident in Spain when appointed.[44] The information given suggests that the official compiling the list had little but copies of the titles of appointment available as sources. A similar lack of material is evident in a comparable list for the Audiencia of Charcas. The writer knew that the fiscal was from Guadix, Spain, the protector of the Indians from Tenerife, two oidores were creoles, and another a native son, but would not even guess as to place of birth for two other civil judges. For the final oidor, Pablo de la Vega y Bárcena, he reserved only the laconic comment: "He does not have a relación de méritos and there are unofficial reports that he has died." If the information about place of birth was fair, the knowledge displayed about marriage was hopelessly inadequate. Marital status was known for only José Giráldes y Pino, "married to a native of the Indies."[45] Similar lists for Manila and Santa Fe further confirm the crown's concern over place of birth and local marriages.[46]

Two additional specific examples of Arriaga's intention to prevent the entry of native sons into audiencias and the establishment of new local ties date from the early 1760s. When the creole attorney Domingo de la Rocha y Landeche sought an appointment as fiscal in his home city of Santo Domingo, Arriaga squelched his chances with the cryptic comment "it is not suitable for the service of the country."[47] The man named was a peninsular from the colegio mayor of San Bartolomé.[48] Almost simultaneously Arriaga instructed the cámara that the king wanted the replacement for the recently removed native-son decano of the Audiencia of Lima to be a Spaniard who, if possible, had no personal relationships in the Indies.[49] After the peninsular appointee begged off serving in order to remain in Santa Fe, the cámara's officials enumerated the peninsulares serving in the minor audiencias of the Secretariat of Peru who could be considered for promotion to the senior chair in Lima.[50] The short list

---

44. AGI, Mexico, legajo 1640.

45. AGI, Charcas, legajo 196, Lista de los Ministros de que se compone la Real Audiencia de Charcas, con expresión de sus méritos, y de donde son naturales y si son o no casados (no date). Internal evidence indicates that this was compiled in the early 1760s.

46. AGI, Manila, legajo 273, "estado" for 1756, *borrador;* Santa Fe, legajo 283, R1 Aud^a que reside en la Ciud^d de Sta F^e Año de 1756; legajo 285, Lista de los Ministros de que se compone la Audiencia de Santa Fe (c. 1765); and lista de los Ministros de q^e se compone la audiencia de Sta F^e, 1770.

47. AGI, Indiferente General, legajo 1308, note of 8 November 1763.

48. AGS, XXIII, 2–48–174 (Herrera y Rivero, Buen Retiro, 18 June 1764).

49. AGI, Lima, legajo 825, expediente 38, Para la Cámara, Año de 1765.

50. Peninsular Casal y Montenegro had recently married María Antonia Alvarez y Casal, a native of Santa Fe and daughter of the fiscal of the audiencia there, Manuel Bernardo de Alvarez. Restrepo Sáenz, *Biografías,* p. 360.

that resulted showed only eight Spaniards among the four tribunals of Charcas, Santa Fe, Quito, and Chile. Since the Secretariat of New Spain was compiling an analogous document, the Secretary of the Indies and the cámara knew the composition of the audiencias in detail by the mid-1760s and thus the number of peninsulares in each.[51]

The royal concern with native-son strength and the limited number of peninsulares serving on the audiencias can be further seen by an examination of the new appointments made from 1751 to 1775. Appointments during these years differed markedly from those of the preceding two decades. They demonstrated explicitly the crown's return to its traditional policy of naming far more peninsulares than creoles and exercising great restraint toward native sons. Also, the surplus of ministers at midcentury meant few new appointments. In the first twelve years of this period the crown named only twenty new men, including but one native son among the four Americans. In the following thirteen years it named over twice as many new men, but not a single native son appeared among the five creoles (see Figure 6).[52] Native sons and other Americans received a smaller percentage of appointments only during the decade and a half after 1712. The inevitable consequence was an increasingly obvious decline in native sons and other American ministers as those named before midcentury died or retired.

With the end of sales and the direct appointments they brought, the ascenso began to recover from its eclipse. Only two of seven appointees to Lima from 1751 to 1775 joined the court directly. Chilean Cristóbal Mesía y Munive owed his appointment to royal gratitude for the services of his cousin, the Marqués de Valdelirios, a minister of the Council of the Indies and the Spanish representative in the boundary dispute with Portugal over the colony of Sacramento.[53] The other direct appointee, peninsular Gerónimo de Ruedas, had a distinguished career at the colegio of San Clemente at the University of Bologna.[54] In the same period, only three of the twenty-one men named to the Audiencia of Mexico were direct appointees. The creole Diego Fernández de Madrid received his post as an expression of royal appreciation for the services of his father on the audiencias of Guatemala and Mexico.[55] Bartolomé de Bruna y Ahumada, colegial of Santa Cruz in Valladolid, specifically benefited from his father's service on the Council of Castile and was the last representative of the

51. AGI, Lima, legajo 825, expediente 38, Para la Cámara, Año de 1765. The research for the Peruvian list was better than for the earlier enumeration for Charcas. Palacios, whose place of birth was unknown in the previous compilation, is now correctly recorded as a peninsular.

52. Limeño Mansilla was appointed oidor for Lima in 1770, his first effective appointment. He had been originally named a supernumerary alcalde del crimen there in 1750, however, and had not served because he was unable to pay the balance due on his servicio. AGS, XXIII, 2–38–422 (Mansilla, San Lorenzo, 7 October 1750); 2-54-45 (Mansilla, El Pardo, 18 March 1770).

53. Ibid., 2–41–32 (Mesía y Munive, Buen Retiro, 21 December 1755); Dauril Alden, *Royal Government in Colonial Brazil* (Berkeley and Los Angeles, 1968), p. 90.

54. AGS, XXIII, 2–51–234 (Ruedas, Madrid, 16 May 1767).

55. Ibid., 2–38–32 (Diego Fernández de Madrid, Buen Retiro, 17 November 1751).

colegio-council network to go directly to Mexico.[56] The third appointment went to a native from Guadalajara, Francisco Xavier Gamboa, a protégé of long-time alcalde del crimen José de la Mesía de la Cerda (1733–1760). In Spain as an agent for the merchant guild of Mexico City from the mid-1750s, Gamboa had recently published an important work on mining in Mexico.[57] Strikingly, the first three of these five direct appointments occurred within the initial five years of the period and reflected royal gratitude for services by relatives rather than the recipients. Similar appointments occurred rarely afterwards, as personal achievement and experience became the honored criteria.

Restraint in appointments erased the excess of supernumeraries present at midcentury, and by 1775 the total membership of the audiencias was at its lowest since before 1687. Significant regional variations among the tribunals remained, however, and the seventeen purchasers still serving were prominent in several (see Appendix V). Lima continued to be a center for native-son strength, while Quito had as many creoles as peninsulares serving. Chile displayed the extreme of American representation with two native sons among its five creole ministers, all of whom had been present over fifteen years. With eight native sons among its twenty-one Americans, the Southern Secretariat had undergone significant change since midcentury but yet awaited transformation.[58] Creoles numbered half or more of the members in four of these five tribunals; in the fifth, Santa Fe, two Americans sat among the six ministers. For the five audiencias of the Secretariat of New Spain, 1775 was the nadir of both native-son and creole participation. One native son sat among the five Americans spread among Mexico and its ascenso tribunals of Guadalajara and Guatemala.[59] The effects of a quarter century of systematic appointment of peninsulares were apparent in each of the northern courts. From an imperial perspective, the policy of returning the audencias to peninsular control was well established and had already born fruit in the north. The appointments that accompanied the expansion of the tribunals in 1776 would seal peninsular control everywhere but in Lima, and the tribunal there succumbed soon afterward as well.

The crown's effort to reestablish royal authority over the courts through the appointment of peninsulares was seconded by a new attitude toward marriage dispensations after 1750, a return to the traditionalism last seen in the late 1730s. The crown sold no marriage permits after 1750 and granted licenses only with reluctance and with the clear implication that they were special marks of the king's compassion. An innovation of the 1760s further indicates tighter control. From that time the crown increasingly began to grant marriage dispensations only on condition that the newly married minister accept an immediate

56. Ibid., 2–41–24 (Bruna, Aranjuez, 22 June 1755).

57. Toribio Esquivel Obregón, *Biografía de Don Francisco Javier Gamboa* (Mexico, 1941), p. 26; Brading, *Miners and Merchants*, pp. 160–62.

58. The native sons were: (Lima) Urquizu, Querejazu, Mansilla, Villalta, Borda, Puente y Ibáñez; (Chile) Verdugo, Martínez de Aldunate.

59. Antonio de Villaurrutia y Salcedo (Mexico) was the native son.

transfer.[60] In this manner it could harmonize respect for the laws with recognition of the realities of American service and satisfy the magistrates' physical desires without compromising the independence of the judiciary.

Americans soon grasped the significance for future native-son appointments of the crown's return to traditional policy. Not unexpectedly, an interested party voiced dismay. Francisco Antonio de Moreno y Escandón, protector of the Indians for the Audiencia of Santa Fe from 1765, had routinely filled in as fiscal of the court during the absences and illnesses of the incumbent. By cédula of 12 November 1770, however, Charles III ordered that the cases the old fiscal could not handle were to be assumed by the most recently named oidor rather than by the protector, who was "a native of that Kingdom." Upon receiving word of this decision Moreno promptly protested that his services to the crown deserved better treatment. The protector requested the king to retract the offending cédula and issue a statement that would affirm his right to promotion in Santa Fe, notwithstanding his origin. Part of the justification of the prohibition on naming native sons rested on the presumption of relatives, friends, and clients in the district; noting that he had few local connections, Moreno avowed he was as much a "foreigner" in Santa Fe as if he were a peninsular.[61]

When the old fiscal requested retirement, Moreno at once repetitioned and asked for the position, claiming that he had been omitted from consideration solely because of his origin.[62] The immediate consequence of Moreno's protest was mixed. A former colegial of San Ildefonso serving in Santo Domingo received the appointment as fiscal; however, a decree of 1773 allowed Moreno to fill in as fiscal in the absences and infirmities of the incumbent.[63] Moreno's travail thus reveals that the monarch in 1770 consciously rejected the appointment of new native sons, regardless of qualifications, even for interim service. An affected party who protested and cogently argued for his right to serve, nonetheless, could sometimes persuade the crown to retreat from a strict interpretation and allow a native son to join his home court.

The City Council of Mexico City submitted the best known statement of native son pretensions in 1771. Incensed by a letter that insulted American abilities and contended that creoles should not hold high positions, and undoubtedly aware of recent appointment trends, the City Council argued that "Americans" should receive nearly all civil and ecclesiastical positions in the Indies. The thrust of this protest leaves no doubt that when it came to positions

60. In 1768 Andrés de Pueyo y Urríes, oidor of Santo Domingo, received a license allowing his four daughters to marry within that audiencia district but with the provision, added by Julián de Arriaga, that Pueyo should move in that eventuality. See AGI, Santo Domingo, legajos 921 and 922.

61. AGI, Santa Fe, legajo 547, Tomás Pérez de Arroyo (in name of Francisco Antonio Moreno y Escandón) to Señor (no date).

62. Ibid., Tomás Pérez de Arroyo (in name of Francisco Antonio Moreno y Escandón) to Señor, Madrid, 21 December 1771.

63. Ibid., Decree of 29 April 1773; AGS, XXIII, 2–54–122 (Ríos y Velasco, San Ildefonso, 5 August 1770); 2–56–20 (Ríos y Velasco, El Pardo, 22 February 1772).

in Mexico, native sons should be the favored contenders. The arguments advanced followed much the same line as those of Bolívar y de la Redonda a century earlier, although mercifully without the morass of Latin examples. The city fathers concluded by requesting an explicit statement in favor of Americans for all but a handful of senior positions.[64] It does not appear that the king replied directly to this petition but subsequent appointments reveal that its content had been rejected. Comparing the composition of the audiencias of New Spain in 1770 and 1775 shows that both native-son and creole membership declined in the five-year interval. In 1770 the five tribunals contained ten Americans, twenty-five Spaniards, and one person of unknown origin; five years later they had only five Americans and thirty-one Spaniards. Although two native sons were serving in Mexico in 1770, only one remained in 1775. No other tribunal had any native sons at either date. This definitive response revealed the chasm between native-son hopes and expanding royal pretensions.

In the quarter-century preceding the death of Secretary Arriaga in early 1776, the crown regained control of a majority of the American audiencias as native sons and radicados slowly declined in number. A traditionalist policy of adherence to statutes and the utilization of opportunities caused by attrition had accomplished more than the root-and-branch removals of several decades earlier. Peace and slowly improving finances made possible the continuity of policy essential to the patient and unspectacular administration of Julián de Arriaga. His successor would maintain the momentum and place the capstone on the program. By the end of the 1777 the difference in total direct and indirect representation still visible between the tribunals of the secretariats of New Spain and Peru in 1775 would be largely eliminated and, except for Lima, the audiencias throughout the empire would be subject to unprecedented royal authority.

Transition

Administrative expansion in 1776 emphasized the crown's determination to bring the audiencias and colonial establishments under tighter control and to improve treasury receipts as well as the quality of justice and administration. New high-ranking officials soon appeared everywhere. Visitor-generals

---

64. "Representación que hizó la ciudad de México al rey D. Carlos III en 1771 sobre que los criollos deben ser preferidos a los europeos en la distribución de empleos y beneficios de estos reinos," in J. E. Hernández y Dávalos, ed., *Colección de documentos para la historia de independencia de México de 1808 a 1821* (Mexico, 1877; Kraus reprint, 1968), 1: 427–64. Native son oidor Rivadeneira was the major if not sole author of this representación. "Memorial no concluido copia del que se p.ntto al Rey por la N.C. de México formado por el Senor dn Antonio Joquín de Rivadeneira Oidor que fue de aquella cortte a favor de los Americanos," n.d., Centro de Estudios de Historia de México, Condumex, S.A., Fondo Independencia XLI-1, Carpeta 1–24, documento 75.

traversed the viceroyalties of Peru and New Granada; four new letrados joined the Council of the Indies; and each American audiencia received a regent and at least one other minister.[65] Adding these men to the growing batallions of new treasury officials, Americans must have felt that a plague of peninsulares had descended upon them. By the end of 1777, when the necessary audiencia appointments were completed, only the court in Lima retained an American and, temporarily, native-son majority. Two years later this tribunal too had fallen to the wave of Spaniards, and royal control over the courts was complete. For the audiencias, 1776 and 1777 were years of transition, at once a fitting climax to the policy carefully pursued by Arriaga and the beginning of three decades largely marked by maintenance of the gains won. Added to the new office of regent, the expansion of letrado positions on the council opened the way for unprecedented advancement in the American magistracy. The rule of experience was at hand.

For the Council of the Indies the addition of four new letrado councillors by decree of 26 February 1776 raised the number of robed ministers to its peak.[66] Joined to the creation of regents in America, this expansion concluded the restructuring of promotion channels to the council that had begun in 1773. Until that year, the Council of the Indies had ranked below its Castilian counterpart. A royal decree of 13 September altered the old relationship by declaring the two tribunals equal in rank and granting the councillors of the Indies the same salaries and prerogatives enjoyed by their former superiors. This decision transformed the Council of the Indies by making it the end of an ascenso and removing it from the avenue of promotion to the Council of Castile.[67] Ambitious ministers serving on other Spanish tribunals henceforth seldom looked to the Council of the Indies as a doorway to greater things, and men with experience in America soon monopolized it. At the same time, the council's elevation in rank and subsequent increase in positions enabled young peninsular letrados to view American service as something more than exile.

The traditional near-monopolization of letrado positions on the Council of the Indies by men without service in America and the importance of the coun-

65. The expansion of the audiencias raised the number of authorized positions to one hundred. Although the audiencias of Buenos Aires (1783), Caracas (1786), and Cuzco (1787) were soon established, they obtained ministers principally from existing tribunals and the situation as clarified in a *reglamento* of 1788 revealed that the total of authorized ministers had declined to ninety-eight. Actually, the number of men holding appointments did not drop that low because the audiencias of Mexico and Guadalajara were maintained at their previous strength, a reflection of the prosperity of mining in New Spain. For example, the office of *fiscal de hacienda* was created for the tribunal of Mexico in 1779 and, although the reglamento of 1788 reduced the number of fiscal positions to the traditional two, the first incumbent was duly replaced in 1794. See note 66 below, for the 1776 changes and AGI, Audiencia of Cuzco, legajo 4, "Nuevo reglamento de las audas de Indias; aprobado por S.M. en 27 de marzo de 1788" for the 1788 reordering.

66. AGI, Indiferente General, legajo 405, royal decree to the Duque de Alva, Aranjuez, 6 June 1776.

67. *Los códigos españoles concordados y anotados*, 12 vols. (Madrid, 1847–1851), 7:426 *n.* 10; Jose Mª Ots y Capdequí, *Historia del derecho español en América y del derecho indiano* (Madrid, 1969), p. 120.

cil's place in the ascenso to the Council of Castile can be easily demonstrated. From 1687 to 1750 only six of seventy-seven appointees reached the chief tribunal for America directly from service in the New World, and only seven of those promoted from peninsular posts had previous American experience.[68] In sum, scarcely one-sixth of the appointees had any American experience. This figure clearly indicates that service in America was not a favored route to the pinnacle of the bureaucracy. At the same time, sixteen of those named to the Council of the Indies proceeded to that of Castile, confirming the lower tribunal's place in the peninsular ascenso. Some change was apparent after midcentury, although the general pattern persisted until 1773. Of twenty-two appointees to the Council of the Indies during these years, four came directly from service in America. Since another three had held posts in the Indies prior to assuming their new positions, nearly a third of the new men had personal American experience. While still not large, the percentage was nearly double that for the earlier period. Frequent advancement to the Council of Castile continued, with nine men benefiting.[69]

After the 1773 decree only seven Spanish letrados without American service received appointments to the council. The other thirty-nine appointees to 1808 had personal experience in the Indies: twenty-five came directly from American audiencias; two returned after service as visitor-generals; six advanced from the House of Trade; five proceeded from Spanish tribunals, and one's earlier appointment had been as intendant in Cuba. That none of these forty-six men received subsequent appointment to the Council of Castile confirms the separation of the ascensos for letrados in American and Spanish offices.

---

68. These and the subsequent figures on the councillors derive from titles of office found in the AGS; Ernesto Schäfer, *El consejo real y supremo de las Indias,* 2 vols. (Seville, 1935–1947), 1, appendix I; Gildas Bernard, *Le secrétariat d'état et le conseil espagnol des Indes (1700–1808)* (Geneva, 1972), appendix II.

69. The place of the Council of the Indies in the ascenso to the Council of Castile during the Hapsburg period can be seen best in Richard L. Kagan, "Education and the State in Habsburg Spain" (Ph. D. thesis, Cambridge University, 1968), Table 8, "Promotions to the Royal Council of Castile." The provenance of the seventy-seven new men named fiscal or oidor of the Council of the Indies from 1687 to 1750 was:

Sala de alcaldes de casa y corte	20
Council of Hacienda	9
Council of Orders	5
Council of Aragon	1
Chancellery of Valladolid	5
Chancellery of Granada	4
Other Spanish courts	10
House of Trade	4
Other letrado backgrounds	2
American service	6
audiencia president	1
audiencia ministers	4
visitor-general	1
Unknown	11
Total	77

While tracing the appointments of letrados named to the Council of the Indies clarifies movement into and out of that tribunal, knowledge of the number with American experience serving at any one time better indicates the expertise available. From 1687 to the declaration of equality in 1773, this number never exceeded five and more frequently was only two or three of the eight generally serving. By the end of 1775 the situation had already changed greatly, as eight letrados with American experience were serving. Examinations at succeeding five-year intervals until 1808 reveal no less than eight and as many as twelve veterans serving. The corpus of personal knowledge of America available on the council was probably never greater than from the mid-1770s until 1808.[70]

The expansions of 1776 not only increased the number of letrados on the council but also provided in the office of regent a new step in the American ascenso. Modeled after its counterpart in Spanish tribunals, the regent of each American audiencia was the ranking magistrate. He was empowered, among other things, to determine the composition of the chambers and the assignment of cases. His salary was originally twice that of an oidor, an indication of the prestige and importance the crown attached to the post.[71] In a broad perspective the new office represented one of several efforts after 1750 to curtail the authority of the executives in America.[72]

Both the place of the new office in the ascenso and the crown's concern to improve further peninsular strength in the audiencias is visible in the selection of the ten original regents. Two came from the Spanish Chancellery of Val-

---

70. Letrados fresh from American positions were not the council's only source of personal expertise. The growing concern for firsthand knowledge on the council affected appointments for capa y espada ministers also. Sometimes these men were as well or even more qualified in American affairs than letrados and their lack of legal training prevented them only from voting in judicial matters. In 1750, a year in which the council had only two letrados with American experience serving, Ferdinand VI named the Peruvian-born Marqués de Valdelirios specifically for his "knowledge of America." Valdelirios drew upon his New World expertise until his death as a member of the cámara in 1793. The powerful *contadores* Tomás Ortiz de Landazuri and Francisco Javier Machado, who together provided thirty-five years of continuity on the council from 1767 to 1802, were other examples of non-letrado ministers with firsthand knowledge of the Indies. Such men, however, served more to flesh out the composition of the council than to provide its backbone. For a fuller discussion of personnel changes in the council, see Mark A. Burkholder, "The Council of the Indies in the Late Eighteenth Century: A New Perspective," *HAHR* 56:3 (August 1976), 404–23.

71. AGI, Mexico, legajo 1641, Royal decree to the Conde de Valdellano, El Pardo, 11 March 1776; Indiferente General, legajo 379, "Instrucción de lo que deben observar los regentes de las reales audiencias de América: sus funciones, regalías, como se han de haber con los virreyes, y presidentes, y éstos con aquellos," Aranjuez, 20 June 1776. Most of the regents' salaries were reduced in 1788 as part of a general effort to trim the cost of the audiencias, but they still exceeded those of the other ministers. AGI, Cuzco, legajo 4, "Nuevo Reglamento de las Aud.ᵃˢ de Indias: aprobado por S.M. en 27 de marzo de 1788."

72. See Brading, *Miners and Merchants*, part one, pp. 33–92 for what he terms "The Revolution in Government," the Bourbon attack on Hapsburg institutions.

ladolid, one from the House of Trade, and one from the Audiencia of Seville.[73] Such movement from a Spanish to an American tribunal was without precedent, at least since the late seventeenth century, and emphasized again the importance of the new office. The other six men were experienced in the Indies, and only one, the former professor and member of the colegio of San Clemente at Bologna, Gerónimo de Ruedas, had less than a decade of prior service on an American court. Five of these original appointees later advanced to the Council of the Indies, early travelers on what became the most important road to that distinguished body.

The selection of the first regents illustrates the concern of the secretary of the Indies to have peninsulares inaugurate the office. For the two highest tribunals, Mexico and Lima, the king named oidores from the Chancellery of Valladolid. The peninsular decano of Mexico was passed over as too old and too intimately connected within his district.[74] For the position in Lima, the cámara had a divided opinion, but the majority's three ranking choices were native sons, including two purchasers.[75] In another consulta of the same date for the regency of Chile, the cámara again selected three Americans as its first choices, one a native son.[76] Charles III, however, appointed an Asturian with ten years' experience as fiscal in Charcas and Lima.[77] Similarly, for Charcas the king rejected the recommendations of the cámara, which included two Americans and a peninsular purchaser, to name a Spaniard who had served in Lima for nearly a decade.[78] For Santa Fe, too, the monarch ignored the cámara's nominees to name Juan Francisco Gutiérrez de Piñeres, an oidor of the House of Trade, as regent and visitor-general for the viceroyalty.[79] For the remaining five audiencias, the king also named peninsulares.[80] The rejection of the cámara's candidates, men routinely proposed from serving ministers in America, suggests that the new secretary of the Indies, José de Gálvez, personally intervened in ·

73. Francisco Roma Rossell and Melchor Jacot Ortiz Rojano were from Valladolid, Juan Francisco Gutiérrez y Piñeres from the House of Trade, and José García León y Pizarro from the Audiencia of Sevilla.

74. AGI, Mexico, legajo 1643, "Proposición de los ministros de la cámara de Indias Dⁿ Ignacio Omulrian y Dⁿ José Pablo Valiente . . . ," Madrid, 18 September 1819: AGS, XXIII, 2–60–273 (Roma Rossell, San Lorenzo, 1 November 1776); Juan Sempere y Guarinos, *Ensayo de una biblioteca española de los mejores escritores del reynado de Carlos III* (edición facsímil, Madrid, 1969), tomo V, 48–51.

75. AGI, Lima, legajo 881, expediente 36, consulta of the cámara, 23 September 1776. The three men were Pedro Bravo de Rivero, Urquizu, and Querejazu.

76. Ibid., Chile, legajo 172, consulta of the cámara, 23 September 1776. The choices were Puente y Ibáñez, Mesía y Munive (native), and Melchor de Santiago Concha.

77. AGS, XXIII, 2–60–286 (Tomás Alvarez de Acevedo, San Lorenzo, 14 November 1776).

78. AGI, Charcas, legajo 423, extract of consulta of 23 September 1776. Among the men recommended were Santa Cruz y Centeno, Echeverz, and Pey y Ruis. Named was Gerónimo de Ruedas y Morales. AGS, XXIII, 2–60–285 (Ruedas, 14 November 1776).

79. AGI, Santa Fe, legajo 547, consulta of 23 September 1776; AGS, XXIII, 2–60–316 (Gutiérrez de Piñeres, Madrid, 18 December 1776).

80. Sánchez Pareja (Guadalajara), Herrera y Rivero (Guatemala), Pueyo y Urríes (Santo Domingo), Martínez Sánchez de Araque (Manila), and García León y Pizarro (Quito).

the selection of the appointees. A former visitor-general to New Spain (1765–1771), Gálvez had become familiar with the Audiencia of Mexico and returned to Spain confirmed in his belief that peninsulares should dominate the tribunals.[81] In this regard he was a worthy successor to Arriaga. The appointments for regent clearly continued the policy his predecessor had followed.

The appointments to the other seventeen new audiencia positions similarly displayed continuance of the post-1750 policy.[82] Six of the posts were filled by the advancement of three Spaniards and three creoles already serving; each of the Americans had purchased his initial appointment before 1750.[83] To fill three additional seats the crown appointed the protectors of the Indians whose positions the decree of expansion abolished.[84] One of these, and the only other American named to a new post, was Francisco Antonio de Moreno y Escandón who had been a protector in his home district of Santa Fe for over a decade. Charles named Spaniards to the eight remaining posts.[85]

Appointments to fill the new positions and the vacancies that resulted from promotions and disciplinary actions in 1776 and 1777 involved thirty-four new men, including but one native son and two other creoles (see Figure 6). The expansion had offered an unprecedented opportunity, and the results appropriately climaxed a quarter-century of efforts to reduce direct and indirect local influence in the audiencias. The number of Americans holding appointments at the end of 1777 was smaller than in 1775 (twenty-one as opposed to twenty-six), and, in spite of promotions of Moreno and a limeño previously in Chile, the number of native sons declined from nine to eight (see Appendix V). The great increase in the number of positions, moreover, meant that American influence of all kinds had diminished. Accompanying the deterioration in American strength was a decline in the number of long-tenured ministers. The consequence was greater royal control than had been present since the Hapsburgs began selling audiencia appointments.

---

81. In a manuscript written before his *visita* to Mexico, Gálvez condemned the appointment of native sons to the audiencias. Nonetheless he recognized that it would be unjust to deprive them of their positions and that, in fact, there were capable, qualified men among them. Ramón Ezquerra, "La crítica española de la situación de América en el siglo XVIII," in *Estudios sobre la emancipación de hispanoamérica* (Madrid, 1963), pp. 337–38.

As expected, upon reaching Mexico City Gálvez discovered native sons on the audiencia "despite the express prohibition of the laws." (In fact only two were serving.) He reported, however, that they were upright men and that the relationships (*parentescos y alianzas*) they had with important families of Mexico did not affect their actions. Indeed, they voluntarily withdrew from judging cases that involved their relatives. AGI, Mexico, legajo 1509, "Informe, que el Sor Visitador ha dado a S. E. con fecha de 31 de Diz^e de 1771."

82. These positions were created by the decree of 11 March 1776. See note 65, p. 99.

83. Spaniards: Gómez Algarín, Cistué, Mier y Trespalacios. Americans: Traslaviña, Borda, Juan Antonio Verdugo.

84. Fernando Márquez de la Plata, Villalengua, Francisco Antonio de Moreno y Escandón.

85. In order: Jover, Andino, Irisarri, Martín Merino, Gacitúa, Revenga, Cerdán, and Tosta.

The appointments of 1776 and 1777 continued the trend established under Arriaga, but four factors gave them added significance: the paucity of creoles among the new appointees underlined the traditional discrimination Americans faced; the lack of creole regents pointed to an effort to prevent native sons or other creoles from enjoying the pinnacle of success in the American judiciary; the exceedingly heavy number of appointments, particularly in the south, made peninsular predominance much more noticeable than had been the case in 1775; and, finally, the appointments confirmed to Americans that the crown was inaugurating explicit, legal discrimination as suggested in a royal order of 21 February 1776.

The crown never formally stated that Americans would be deliberately excluded from audiencia positions in the New World, but this royal order implied such a stance. The order suggested that creoles enjoyed an undesirably strong position in cathedral chapters and audiencias of the Indies. To rectify this situation and better integrate the colonies with Spain, more peninsulares were to be named canons, prebendaries, and audiencia ministers in America. Specifically the order called for consideration of Americans for vacancies in Spanish cathedrals and audiencias, and peninsulares for the corresponding posts in America. It stated that creoles were to be assured one-third of the prebends and canonries in American cathedrals, but did not extend this reservation to audiencia positions.[86] Americans felt that the order's implication was ominously transparent; the crown would systematically favor peninsulares for American positions and discrimination against creoles would be explicit rather than merely circumstantial as in the past. The appointments of 1776 and 1777 could only confirm Americans' worst fears.

The 21 February order brought an immediate call for its revocation from the City Council of Mexico.[87] The cloister of the University of Mexico was also alarmed by the crown's determination in implementing the order and even more concerned by a subsequent order that Spaniards were to be considered for the vacant deanship in the Cathedral of Mexico City. It protested that the "fundamental laws of the realm" called for preference in appointments for the descendants of the conquistadores and first settlers.[88] Although not specifically cited, this was an obvious reference to Book III, Title II, Law xiiii of the *Recopilación,* the traditional bedrock for native-son pretensions. In a novel advance on this position, the cloister further avowed that the American-born children of later immigrants, descendants of administrators of illustrious ancestry and others who had chosen to migrate to the established colonies, deserved

---

86. AGI, Lima, legajo 620, *mesa* report to 19 February 1794. The royal order is printed in Richard Konetzke, ed., *Colección de documentos para la historia de la formación social de Hispanoamérica, 1493–1810,* 3 vols. (Madrid, 1953–1962), 3, tomo I, document 234. See also Konetzke, "La condición legal de los criollos y las causas de la independencia," *Estudios americanos* (Seville) 2:5 (January 1950): 31–50.

87. Royal order of 2 January 1778, printed in Konetzke, *Colección,* 3, tomo I, document 244.

88. Alberto María Carreño, *Efemérides de la real y pontificia universidad de México según sus libros de claustros* (Mexico, 1963), 2: 676–80.

appointments as well. In other words, all creoles by virtue of their birth shared in the preference customarily assigned to those who counted *beneméritos* as forebears. The cloister pointed out that Americans had always enjoyed substantial representation in the Church and in fact held over a third of the positions in 1776. Creoles had traditionally attained less influence in secular posts, however, and the direction of policy in 1776 did not appear encouraging. If a quota upon employment in the American Church were implemented without additional guarantees in the secular sphere, well-qualified alumni and professors of the university would be even worse off than before. In consequence, the cloister asked that the two royal orders be disregarded and Americans (i.e. native sons) be considered for American posts without restriction. José de Gálvez's irritated reply to such arguments in 1778, however, made it clear that the king was determined to favor Spaniards for American positions.[89]

As part of its efforts to regulate the appointment of Americans and ascertain which candidates were applying for posts in their home districts, in 1776 the secretary of the Indies sought to standardize the relaciones de méritos that pretendientes submitted when soliciting appointment. While in the late seventeenth and early eighteenth centuries many hopefuls had merely presented formal statements from a university secretary that testified to their activities and accomplishments in the academic world, now the secretary demanded that the vitas note unequivocally place of birth. The phrase *"natural de"* not *"oriundo de"* was to be employed. The order itself spelled out the reason for this innovation: "in order to distinguish by these means those [men] properly Europeans [from] the Spanish Americans, that they call creoles. . . ."[90] Implementation of this order obviated the unintentional appointment of native sons. Lists of pretendientes from the 1780s often included place of birth as the first item following the aspirants' names.[91] The standardization of the relaciones de méritos reflected the concern during the Age of Authority over place of birth and the decline of identifiably "elite" education as a candidate's guarantee of background and suitability.

The expansions of 1776 provided the final shape for the high letrado bureaucracy for America. Changes in the audiencias in the 1780s did not alter

---

89. Konetzke, *Colección*, 3, tomo I, document 244. Americans interested in serving in Spain, of course, could and did invoke this order in their favor. One such creole was Tomás Pérez de Arroyo, son of a former minister in Panama. On 1 March 1776 Pérez solicited an appointment in Spain on the strength of this order. It would take a study of the appointees to Spanish tribunals to determine how often Americans sought and received preferment on the peninsula. A few cases, however, are known. For examples, see Jaime Eyzaguirre, *Ideario y ruta de la emancipación chilena* (Santiago, 1957), p. 56, *n.* 47.

90. AGI, Indiferente General, legajo 10, "Para govierno de la Secretaría," Madrid, 24 May 1776.

91. For examples see AGI, Charcas, legajo 423, consulta of 6 November 1780; Lima, legajo 926, expediente 66, "Para la Cámara, Año de 1789"; Chile, legajo 172, consulta of 24 September 1792; and Lima, legajo 959, expediente 28, "Cámara. Año de 1796."

The same format and notations for ecclesiastical appointments also appeared during these years. See AGI, Lima, legajo 959, "Cámara año de 1796, num. 7, expediente para consultar la Dignidad de tesorero de la Yglesia Metropolitana de Lima."

the regular path of advancement from America to Spain that the augmentations had provided. Experience in the colonies had become the critical determinant in appointments to the Council of the Indies. The decree establishing equality between the councils of the Indies and Castile coupled with the increment of letrado ministers exemplified America's increased importance among the king's possessions, and the appointments of 1776 and 1777 on the heels of the decree of 21 February 1776 illustrated Charles's determination to hold Spain's colonies on a tight leash. The actions of these two years climaxed a quarter-century of efforts to assert royal authority over the audiencias. The overall success permitted the crown subsequently to emphasize other areas of colonial administration and concern itself more with maintenance than expansion of authority over the courts.

The order of 21 February and the American response to it add to the pivotal quality of this two-year period. Charles's directive to integrate the empire through appointment of Spaniards to American offices and creoles to positions in Spain introduced a concept of "equality" unknown to previous generations of Americans. While the crown offered "equality" in appointments on an imperial basis, Americans wanted "equality" at the local level. They wanted appointments in their home districts. If honorably employed at home, they often looked upon transfer to Spain as involuntary exile. Americans wanted de facto home rule, albeit within an imperial framework. They harked back to the patrimonial concept of justice ("equality" in the modern perspective) that called for native sons to hold the posts in their districts. It did not bother them that this argument would give peninsulares all of the posts in Spain. "Equality" for them meant the right to determine local affairs.

By the end of 1777 the crown's attitude toward the place of native sons and other creoles on the audiencias had hardened. Similarly, local frustration over the 21 February 1776 order and the deluge of peninsulares appointed was evident. For the next thirty years an uneasy balance existed. Overall native son and other American participation on the tribunals remained approximately what it was in 1777, and the crown's attitude toward native-son pretensions also remained constant. It took Napoleon's invasion of Spain to shatter the spell.

The Golden Age of Authority

War dominated the last three decades of Spanish rule in America. In 1779 Spain declared war against England. Within the following two years Túpac Amaru II in Peru and the *comuneros* in New Granada initiated revolts. Only in 1783 were both the international and colonial conflicts ended. A decade of peace and general prosperity ensued, but Spain's support of the royalist cause in France initiated a new period of foreign war that continued intermittently to

1808. It is axiomatic that the economic and commercial disruption that resulted weakened Spain's hold over her American possessions. On the other hand, it is a measure of the crown's continuing administrative strength that neither this conflict nor the almost simultaneous advent of the powerful royal favorite Manuel Godoy seriously threatened its hard-won control over the American audiencias. Indeed, from 1778 to 1808 the crown consolidated its mastery over the tribunals. Starting from a position of strength, it successfully maintained its grip through regular observance of traditional attitudes and procedúres strengthened since midcentury for the selection, promotion, supervision, and marriage of ministers. Other branches of administration were faltering even though, in a few cases, they expanded at the expense of the nonjudicial functions of the audiencias. As far as the crown was concerned, however, this was the golden age of authority over the high courts.

Having secured control in every audiencia but Lima by the end of 1777, the crown could afford to name more native sons and other Americans and still not jeopardize peninsular dominance. In consequence, ten native sons received appointments from 1778 to 1808, over twice the number so honored from 1751 to 1777. The first one became an oidor in Mexico in 1786 after sixteen years of service in the lower tribunals of Manila and Guadalajara.[92] In the next six years two more joined their home tribunals, both in Santa Fe.[93] Subsequently, seven others were named before 1808.[94] Of these ten men, three began as supernumerary appointees, two enjoyed normal ascensos to their home tribunals, and two others obtained well-justified appointments on the basis of previous service to the crown.[95] The remaining three benefited from merits contracted, extensive lobbying at court, and, in one case, a father's services.[96] The increase in the number of native sons named over that from 1751 to 1777, however, did not significantly alter their total on the tribunals. After the reduction in Lima, the number fluctuated between six and eight, far below the twenty-one serving in 1750 (see Appendix VI). Nowhere, moreover, did native sons dominate a tribunal; direct local representation in the courts had disappeared as a problem. That any native sons received appointments suggests that the crown felt enough confidence in its control to allow a few gestures to mollify local irritation. Such tokenism was slight solace to creole lawyers who wanted to remain at home.

For American attorneys willing to serve outside their patrias the years from 1778 to 1808 provided significant opportunities. Four times as many creoles entered the courts during this period as from 1751 to 1777, and the percentage of

92. González Maldonado.

93. Mosquera y Figueroa and José Antonio Berrio y Guzmán.

94. Foncerrada, Aldunate, González Calderón, Baquíjano, Arias de Villafañe, José Santiago Concha Jiménez Lobatón, and José de Alvarez de Acevedo.

95. Supernumeraries: Aldunate, Arias de Villafañe, and González Calderón. The latter's appointment was after prior service in Guatemala and Lima. Ascensos: González Maldonado and Foncerrada. Previous service: Berrio and Mosquera.

96. Merits and lobbying: Baquíjano and Arias de Villafañe. Father's services: Alvarez de Acevedo.

new appointments going to Americans more than doubled. Nevertheless, although 49 creoles were among the 162 new men named, overall American representation remained generally stable at about 25 to 30 percent of the total (see Figure 6 and Appendixes V and VI). Aside from Lima briefly in the 1780s, and in the minor tribunal of Chile from 1780, nowhere did Americans comprise half or more of a tribunal's members. Having recovered mastery over the courts the crown seemed content to let Americans hold about a quarter of the total positions as long as they were reasonably dispersed.

An unmistakable mark of regularity in the high judiciary from 1778 to 1808 was the paucity of direct appointments to Mexico and Lima. Legal advisers to the viceroy (*asesores generales*) accounted for the only three "direct" appointments to Mexico during these years, but the changed nature of their office made the advancement notably different from earlier direct appointments.[97] For Lima, as usual, the story was less tidy. Of the eight direct appointees, two were previously asesores generales, one had accumulated his credits as part of the visita in Peru, and two, both peninsulares, left no sign of their education or any previous career.[98] The final three men defy classification. Native son José Baquíjano y Carrillo obtained his appointment through shrewd and persistent petitioning, personal presence at court, and a willingness to serve initially without salary.[99] Miguel de Eyzaguirre, member of a prominent family in Chile and a professor at the University of San Felipe in Santiago, was also at court when he received his appointment and probably benefited from personal solicitation and persistence as Baquíjano had earlier.[100] The last direct appointee in these years was Gaspar Antonio de Osma y Tricio, a thirty-year-old peninsular attorney who had attended the universities of Valladolid and Alcalá.[101] Apparently of undistinguished ancestry, he had no known credentials to qualify him for direct appointment to Lima; other men of similar background satisfied themselves with a beginning post as teniente asesor to an intendant, a position that by the 1790s had become a common point of entry into the audiencias. Osma's lack of notable credentials give credence to the scurrilous writer who implied that the lawyer owed his appointment to the patronage of the powerful Manuel Godoy, Príncipe de la Paz.[102]

While bringing the number of native sons to an acceptable level and avoiding the pitfall of making numerous direct appointments to Mexico and Lima,

---

97. Miguel Antonio Bataller y Vasco, Valenzuela y Aguilar, and Rafael Bachiller de Mena.

98. Asesores generales: Valle del Postigo, Portilla y Gálvez. Visita: Antonio Boeto. Undetermined merits: Pardo and Viderique.

99. See Mark Alan Burkholder, "José Baquíjano and the Audiencia of Lima" (Ph.D. dissertation, Duke University, 1970), chapter 9.

100. AGS, XXIII, 2–89–148 (Eyzaguirre, San Lorenzo, 22 October 1805). See Jaime Eyzaguirre, ed., *Archivo epistolar de la familia Eyzaguirre, 1747–1854* (Buenos Aires, 1960) for information on the Eyzaguirre family and Miguel's activities in Spain before his appointment.

101. AGI, Lima, legajo 624, relación de méritos y servicios, 17 January 1800.

102. Ibid., legajo 770, Letter by Juan Ygno Collantes to Señor, Lima, 25 February and 15 March 1809.

the monarch also sought to curb indirect local representation in government. One innovation was to appoint salaried legal advisers (asesores generales) for viceroys and other executives, ending their traditional prerogative of seeking legal opinions and advice from whomever pleased them. Previously, favorites, clients, and sometimes the senior oidor had provided these services, and on occasion the private asesor was a lawyer with extensive ties to local society.[103] Starting with New Spain in 1777, the king converted the previously semiprivate office into a royal appointment subject to the same standards and controls as audiencia posts. Within two years the other viceroyalties received similar positions.[104] The men selected as asesores generales were living confirmation of the crown's intention to circumscribe the viceroys and further limit indirect local representation in government. The first two sent to Mexico, for example, were mature and experienced lawyers who had practiced at court for years and whose judgment the crown trusted.[105] Moreover, no asesor was a native son or radicado in the district when appointed.

Spaniards serving in America shared the crown's view that the asesor general was another means of protecting royal interests. In 1803 the captain-general of Guatemala had no official adviser and reportedly relied heavily upon the creole oidor Jacobo de Villaurrutia, an ardent defender of local interests. Two other oidores, both peninsulares, protested to Charles IV and suggested that he name an official asesor. They specifically requested that the man selected be European. The peninsular regent had expresssed such sentiments earlier, and the appointment of Joaquín Ibáñez Ramos in 1805 conformed exactly to the proposal.[106]

Soon after inaugurating the use of royally appointed asesores to limit local influence on the viceroys, the king turned to the centuries-old problem of controlling marital ties between audiencia ministers and women from important local families. While the crown had been gathering information on existing marriages and quietly tightening its control since midcentury, the visitas of Areche in Peru and Gutiérrez de Piñeres in New Granada provided detailed information of such relationships and moved the crown to an open attack on the problem of local access to the chambers of justice.[107] This action was only a

---

103. For example, Baltazar Ladrón de Guevara had been educated in Mexico and served for many years as a *relator* before being named interim asesor by Viceroy Bucareli. Although the crown approved this appointment in 1775, in the future it, not the viceroy, selected the advisers.

104. 1778: Moreno Avendaño (New Granada); 1778: Manuel de Ortega y Espinosa (Río de la Plata); 1779: Portilla (Peru).

105. Bataller y Vasco (1777) and Valenzuela (1784).

106. AGI, Guatemala, legajo 617, unsigned opinion of a fiscal of the council paraphrasing a letter from Juan Collado and Francisco Camacho Cánovas dated 3 August 1803; AGS, XXIII, 2-89-208 (Ibáñez Ramos, Aranjeuz, 1 May 1805).

107. AGI, Lima, legajo 1082, Testimony number seven, duplicate. "Respuestas de los Ministros de la R¹ Audiencia de Lima," and Santa Fe, legajo 556, letter 26 "reservada" from Juan Gutiérrez de Piñeres to Jph. de Gálvez, Santa Fe de Bogotá, 30 March 1778. See also, John L. Phelan, "El auge y la caida de los criollos en la audiencia de Nueva Granada, 1700–1781," *Boletín de historia y antigüedades* (Bogotá), 9:697, 698 (November

partial expression of a broader concern to regulate the marriages between bureaucratic families and between bureaucrats and the general populace.

Although the crown sold no marriage exemptions for judges or their children after 1750, it had continued to grant them. Then, reflecting his desire for fiscal improvement, in 1779 Charles III signed an order declaring his intention to enforce marriage legislation to the letter for all the bureaucracy, especially treasury officials.[108] From that date progressively tighter interpretations of the laws appeared and correspondingly fewer exemptions were authorized. A strong statement issued in 1791 explicitly placed the audiencias under the renewed enforcement.[109]

Between 1778 and 1808, eighteen ministers obtained licenses for themselves or their children to marry locally. By contrast, there was a combined total of twenty-two refusals, licenses granted only on condition of an immediate transfer, or punishments for infractions of the laws. Furthermore, royal policy became less lenient over time. During the 1780s licenses granted outnumbered refusals and punishments by almost two to one; in the following decade, reflecting the royal statement of 1791, observances of the law outweighed permissions by seven to five; and between 1801 and 1808 refusals or punishments outnumbered permissions by three to one (see Figure 5). At the same time, the crown displayed flexibility when circumstances dictated; it treated judges in the hardship post of Manila with marked leniency, for instance, while exacting more compliance to the statutes in the viceregal centers. Respect for the legislation on marriage was never greater than during the last years of normal administration.

Indications of the invigorated attitude in Madrid can be traced in several cases that came before the Council of the Indies. Vicente de Herrera y Rivera, regent of the Audiencia of Mexico, wrote the king in 1782 asking not only permission to marry a Mexican woman but also the outright repeal of the marriage laws for the two major tribunals of Mexico and Lima. He protested the injustice that full enforcement of these laws would work on the judiciary and cogently argued that the restrictions were less necessary in his time than they had been a century earlier, when cities were smaller and judges had exercised more power and influence over local and governmental affairs. Although still neces-

---

and December 1972): 606–13; Leon G. Campbell, "A Colonial Establishment: Creole Domination of the Audiencia of Lima During the Late Eighteenth Century," *HAHR*, 52:1 (February 1972): 1–25; and Mark A. Burkholder, "From Creole to *Peninsular:* The Transformation of the Audiencia of Lima," *HAHR*, 52:3 (August 1972):395–415.

108. AGI, Ultramar, legajo 855, Royal order to viceroys, presidents, and audiencias of America, San Ildefonso, 9 August 1779. This emphasized the effort to prevent relatives from serving within the same office of the financial bureaucracy that had been stated in a cédula of 20 January 1775. Phelan, "El auge y la caida," p. 608.

109. The circular royal order of 24 March 1791 was issued to enforce the restrictive laws of libro II, título XVI of the *Recopilación* with special reference to ley lxxxiiii (prohibition against even discussing or contracting marriage with a local woman). It was cited in the royal decision of 29 May 1802 in response to a letter of Regent of Lima Manuel Arredondo to the Ministry of Grace and Justice (undated). See AGI, Indiferente General, legajo 1818.

Figure 5. Marriage Licenses, Refusals, and Punishments

	Relaxation of Restrictions		Observance of Restrictions					
	Permit to Marry Locally	Permit to Child, Locally	Refusal for Local Marriage	Refusal for Child, Locally	Permit Granted, Move Required	Child's Permit, Move Required	Illegal Marriage, Transfer Required	Illegal Marriage, Removed
1778-1790	9	1	3	0	3	0	0	0
1791-1800	4	1	4	1	0	1	1	0
1801-1808	0	3	6	0	1	0	0	2

*These figures are of course incomplete; there are undoubtedly other examples of permissions and refusals which have not yet come to light.

sary for tribunals in small cities, such restraints surely were superfluous for courts in the major metropolises.[110] The council tersely rejected his argument without comment but granted Herrera the individual exemption he wanted.[111]

Over fifteen years later royal officials in the secretariat learned indirectly that the Spaniard Cosme de Mier y Trespalacios, oidor in Mexico, had married a local woman with the blessing of the viceroy. José Antonio Caballero, secretary of grace and justice, immediately chastized the viceroy for his conduct and threatened action, possibly removal, if a similar case arose. The offended official wrote to tender his resignation, pointing out that he had done no more than recognize a cédula dating from the 1780s that had granted Mier the right to marry whomever he chose. While Caballero responded to this new information with a graceful apology, the strong language of his original message had unmistakably conveyed how seriously he viewed the marriage laws.[112]

The full force of this stringent attitude became even more evident after the turn of the century. Perhaps the brief return of peace in 1802 allowed Charles IV greater freedom of action, for attention to marriage laws seems to have reached a peak between 1802 and 1806. Only three marriage dispensations have been identified for those years (allowing local marriage for the children of two audiencia judges in Lima and one in Buenos Aires) as opposed to six refusals for permits and two removals from office.[113] In Lima, Lucas Muñoz y

110. Ibid., legajo 1814. Vicente de Herrera y Rivera to the king, Guatemala, 6 July 1782.
111. Ibid., Royal order to Vicente de Herrera y Rivera, Madrid, 8 July 1783.
112. Ibid., legajo 1817. Caballero to Viceroy Azanza, Aranjuez, 30 March 1799.
113. The three who received permits for their children to marry locally were Pino, Rodríguez Ballesteros, and Juan Bazo y Berri. The six who were denied permits to marry locally were Arredondo, Muñoz y Cubero, Pardo, Campuzano y Salazar, Fernando Antonio Gutiérrez de Piñeres, and Castaño. Removed from office for marrying locally (although restored a few years later) were Bodega and Díaz de Rivera. Another judge, Esterripa, was allowed to marry a local woman only if he accepted an immediate transfer.

Cabero, although already replaced as oidor on the audiencia, was refused permission to marry a limeña until he had assumed his new post as regent in Buenos Aires. Officials in Madrid and Lima feared that if allowed to marry first, Muñoz would then refuse the promotion and attempt to remain in Lima as a supernumerary judge.[114] In another case, Manuel Arredondo, regent of the Audiencia of Lima, repeatedly asked for a license to marry a local woman during the years 1802–1805. The council summed up its denial with the observation that while in the past the king had granted licenses to some ministers, it was always with great reluctance. As final confirmation of its attitude the council sent the viceroy a copy of the marriage order of 1791 and ordered him to determine if Arredondo had dared to marry secretly.[115]

Helping the crown to pay greater attention to the marriage restrictions were the *montepíos de ministros y de oficinas*. These pension funds, operated by the crown for the survivors of government servants, provided a means of channeling marriage requests and ensuring a consistent scrutiny of the process.[116] Furthermore, in the power to withhold pensions from widows and orphans in case of irregularities, the montepíos provided the teeth for the marriage restrictions. The montepíos, established in America in the 1760s and 1770s in imitation of the peninsular agencies, were intended to professionalize and depersonalize welfare services for the survivors of government officials. Inevitably, in the spirit of paternalism and heavy-handed controls that permeated the old monarchy, the institutions extended their attentions to morality as well as legality and to the social standing and good name of the prospective bride.

By the 1780s all high-ranking letrados belonged with senior treasury officers to the montepío de ministros, the agency that administered to the small number of high-ranking royal agents in the centers of government. Each member paid regular salary deductions to the agency, and the crown also provided support. Each class of officials enrolled had a representative on the governing junta. An audiencia judge who desired to marry would apply through his representative on the junta for acceptance of his betrothed; without montepío approval and registration the wife could draw no pension later. The examination was indeed just that—the montepío sought testimony that would establish that the lady was of proper social standing and of a family into which an audiencia judge might marry.[117] If all went well, the woman was listed as a legal dependant of the official, entitled to a pension for life upon his death. Children were added as necessary.

The montepío could not exempt a member from the laws forbidding marriage to a native. In those special cases the minister still had to petition the king

114. AGI, Indiferente General, legajo 1818, Ministry of Grace and Justice to Viceroy of Peru, San Lorenzo, 26 November 1804.

115. Ibid., order to the viceroy of Peru, 15 April 1804, refusing Arredondo's latest request.

116. For a discussion of the montepíos, see Dewitt Samuel Chandler, "Pensions and the Bureaucracy of New Spain in the Later Eighteenth Century," (Ph.D. dissertation, Duke University, 1970).

117. See ibid.

and then, if successful, present his license to the junta. The role of the montepío was important but passive. A judge who married locally without permission in the old days might have escaped exposure for years or even permanently; but through its formal investigation the montepío closed such loopholes. The agency was charged with enforcing the laws and obliged to report any irregularity. With a widow's pension at stake, only the very wealthy could afford to indulge in secret marriage with impunity. The montepío's regularization of procedure thus enhanced the rigor with which the government enforced the marriage laws at the close of the colonial period.

The men and local families affected by the crown's vigorous attack on indirect representation in government correctly perceived it as inimical to their interests. Traditionally audiencia ministers had sought marriage to perpetuate their names and houses and to benefit materially as well. As the cases of Herrera and Arredondo make clear, those serving in the last decades of Spanish rule opposed general enforcement of the prohibitions. Moreover, they wanted to see their children and grandchildren assume prominent places in society and thus secure the family name. Most ministers had witnessed a colleague's family left impoverished by his untimely death, and the possibility of a similar fate for their wives and children was never far from their minds. For Sebastián Calvo de la Puerta, supernumerary alcalde del crimen of the Audiencia of Mexico during the 1760s, the problem was simple. For judges who were not independently wealthy—and most were not—bureaucratic, ecclesiastical, or military posts for sons, and a convent or marriage for daughters, were their only hopes for the conservation of their families.[118] Like Calvo, the typical minister of the late eighteenth century was anxious to make successful marriages for his daughters at the first opportunity and felt the strict laws were unnecessarily harsh.

It is quite possible that ministers serving in most tribunals from 1778 to 1808 benefited more from marrying locally than did the families into which they married. Quite apart from royal policy, economic conditions seem to have influenced the attractiveness of ministers to the leading families of a region. Thus, in the case of Guatemala, from the 1550s to the 1570s oidores and other high officials sought to join the elite of "entrepreneurial encomenderos," while for most of the seventeenth century the ministers themselves were the ones pursued by families seeking betterment.[119] The advantage that a cash salary (as well as patronage) had provided in the seventeenth century in regions short on capital, however, certainly eroded in districts benefiting from the rapid economic expansion of the late eighteenth century. This situation might help to explain the continuing high number of local marriages contracted by ministers in Lima, a region somewhat left aside in the general growth. Perceptive local

---

118. AGI, Mexico, legajo 1697, Sebastián Calvo de la Puerta to the king, Mexico, 9 August 1761.

119. Murdo J. MacLeod, *Spanish Central America: A Socioeconomic History, 1520–1720* (Berkeley and Los Angeles, 1973), pp. 312–13.

families recognized also that the improved communications and the introduction of new officials, particularly the intendants, had diminished the power of the audiencias. As a consequence, although ministers were desirable sons-in-law, they were no longer as avidly sought as their predecessors had been.[120] Nonetheless, the crown's enforcement of the marriage laws disturbed prominent families.

While the unlawful nature of most advantages that local families gained from marriages to ministers meant that their protests over the restrictions were not couched in political or economic terms, one can safely assume that the arbitrary limitation of access to power and possible material gain angered them. Awareness of local unhappiness with the recent rigorous enforcement doubtless colored Arredondo's assertion that three or four ministers of the audiencia should be married into "the first families" of Lima to improve local morale and reliability.[121] The traditional policy of routine acquiesence to ministers' requests to marry locally, moreover, caused touchy aristocrats to view refusal of a permit as a personal insult. When Charles IV rejected the 1801 request of Lima oidor Manuel Pardo to marry the daughter of the Marqués de Fuente Hermosa and ordered the viceroy to second no more such illegal petitions, the offended noble himself wrote to the king, attested to his descent from *pobladores* and conquistadores, and expressed his surprise and shame that the proposed marriage had not found official approval. He noted that the news of the refusal had brought the entire family anguish and dismay and would cause the local populace to view the woman and her father's house as in some way unworthy of the match.[122] Implicit in this claim was the assumption that marriage alliances between the local *gente decente* and officialdom were a long-standing tradition and that only something extraordinary could account for royal disapproval. Unmoved, the ministers in Madrid resolutely rejected the plea.[123]

During the years from 1778 to 1808 the bureaucracy of experience ruled. Promotion-minded ministers could realistically expect that competent service would provide eventual advancement to the Council of the Indies. The smooth working of the ascenso after 1778 exemplified the regularity lauded in much of eighteenth-century thought. Within this reign of order both direct and indirect local representation on the audiencias were kept within bounds. The crown appointed some deserving native sons and other Americans but not enough to threaten peninsular dominance on any major tribunal. Moreover, vigorous enforcement of marriage regulations, in part through the newly instituted montepío de ministros, markedly restrained the co-optation of ministers by prominent families in their district. Dismay among Americans correspondingly

---

120. Brading, *Miners and Merchants*, p. 44.
121. AGI, Indiferente General, legajo 1818, consulta of the Council of the Indies, undated, summarizing Arredondo's letter of 8 October 1801.
122. Ibid., Marqués de Fuente Hermosa to the king, Lima, 30 April 1804.
123. Ibid., marginal note, dated 29 November 1804, appended to a consulta of Pardo's case summarizing the correspondence to that date.

increased at the ongoing disregard of local pretensions, and the conflict between modern "equality" and patrimonial "justice" expanded.

Pressure for Office

Americans' irritation over the limiting of indirect access to the audiencias complements the better-known anger they displayed over the lack of direct representation. While more native sons and other Americans gained appointments from 1778 to 1808 than had from 1751 to 1777, the number was still a small minority of the total. Such discrimination had provoked protests in the past; in the midst of demographic expansion and an increased number of graduates from American law schools there was greater pressure on creole aspirants than ever before, and resentment again surfaced.

The population of Spanish America grew dramatically in the second half of the eighteenth century. Among the urban centers that exhibited marked increases were Buenos Aires, which rose from about ten thousand inhabitants in 1744 to roughly forty thousand by the end of the century, and Caracas, which increased by perhaps a third from 1778 to 1800.[124] The traditionally populous capital of Mexico City also showed impressive growth. While the percentage of growth that arose from the creole population is unknown, there can be no doubt that whites participated in the expansion. Their number in New Spain expanded from 565,000 in 1742 to nearly 800,000 in 1772 and to over a million in 1793.[125]

The growing creole population created rising pressure for government employment, and mounting frustration over the inadequate number of positions going to native sons was visible. While the total number of positions increased from the 1760s to the 1790s, the appointment of peninsulares to a majority of the most desirable ones bred resentment among native sons. The creation of forty-two positions of intendant from 1764 to 1790 highlighted their problem.[126] Powerful and prestigious, these new posts also paid well, a not unimportant consideration.[127] But by 1808 no American, let alone a native son, had obtained a confirmed royal appointment as intendant in Perú or the Río de la Plata, and few if any had appeared elsewhere.[128] The steady appearance of

---

124. Bailey W. Diffie, *Latin American Civilizations: Colonial Period* (New York, 1967), p. 449; Angel Rosenblatt, *La población indígena y el mestizaje en América,* 2 vols. (Buenos Aires, 1954), 1:195.

125. Woodrow Borah, *New Spain's Century of Depression* (Berkeley, 1951), p. 18.

126. For an imperial perspective toward the intendant system see Luis Navarro García, *Intendencias en Indias* (Seville, 1959).

127. The salaries varied between four and seven thousand pesos. Lynch, *Spanish Colonial Administration,* p. 69.

128. Ibid., 290–301; Fisher, *Government and Society,* 239–250; Brading, *Miners and Merchants,* p. 64.

peninsulares in new offices provoked native sons to a new awareness of the discrimination they faced.

The number of native sons eligible for appointment to the audiencias was also rising in the late eighteenth century. Protest by and in behalf of this limited group formed part of the more widespread unhappiness over appointments that was visible during the closing decades of the Age of Authority. In any region eligibility for a *plaza* was limited to a small part of white society. Not only were legitimacy and social requirements considered; an aspirant needed university training in the law, preferably training that culminated in an advanced degree of licentiate or doctor in laws or canons. Fragmentary evidence suggests that the number of men with legal training rose after 1750 and expanded greatly in the final quarter of the eighteenth century. These numbers reflect both the establishment of new universities and the consequent increase in opportunity and a general resurgence of university enrollment in the Spanish world. Previously, Chileans had needed to travel abroad, usually to Lima, for legal education. After 1758 those unable to afford such expenses could study at the University of San Felipe in Santiago.[129] In Caracas the impact of the university founded in 1725 on the legal profession was profound. For the first time a substantial group of locally born lawyers became prominent. The establishment of an audiencia in 1783 was the crowning step in this region, for it obviated the need for any travel to become an abogado.[130] In Guatemala the University of San Carlos graduated more men with legal degrees from 1775 to 1799 than during the preceding fifty years.[131] That the increased numbers reflected the overall growth of enrollments at the institution as a result of a reinvigorated intellectual climate does not detract from the implications of a growing group of letrados within the region.

The rising number of men with degrees in law produced an expansion of the number of attorneys authorized to practice before the audiencias (abogados). By 1808 the total number of abogados in America was probably around a thousand. New Spain had the most, with roughly four hundred, but scarcely half of them (210) were practicing.[132] The city of Lima counted 91 in 1790, but the remainder of Peru did not seem to be proportionately as well represented.[133] The Audiencia of Buenos Aires had admitted fewer than 100 abogados to practice by 1802, while the captaincy general of Caracas boasted 105

129. José Toribio Medina, *Historia de la real universidad de San Felipe de Santiago de Chile*, 2 vols. (Santiago, 1928), 1:541–51 shows the rising number of law degrees beginning in the early 1760s.

130. Hector García Chuecos, *Estudios de historia colonial venezolana*, 2 vols. (Caracas, 1937–1938), 1:292.

131. John Tate Lanning, *The University in the Kingdom of Guatemala* (Ithaca, N.Y., 1955), p. 203.

132. Konetzke, *Colección*, 3, tomo II, document 374.

133. "Plan demostrativo de la población comprehendida en la ciudad de Lima . . . ," *Mercurio peruano* 1:10 (3 February 1791); Luis Antonio Eguiguren, *Diccionario historico cronológico de la Real y Pontificia Universidad de San Marcos y sus colegios: Crónica e investigacion*, 3 vols. (Lima, 1940–1951), 3:348–55.

by 1805.[134] Whatever the precise total, the crown suspected that the Indies harbored an excess. Its conviction produced a cédula in 1784 that ordered the Audiencia of Cuba not to examine aspirants for abogado, since Havana had too many attorneys already.[135] Five years later the regent of the audiencia recommended the continuation of this order in full vigor and, moreover, tightening of the requirements for entry into the legal profession.[136]

Concern over the number of lawyers surfaced again in 1802 when Charles IV ordered an investigation to determine if surpluses of attorneys required the establishment of quotas.[137] The lawyers' guild (colegio) in Mexico City reported that although the region had over 200 practicing attorneys, some areas of the viceroyalty lacked any, and certainly (as the audiencia later agreed) there was no excess.[138] In contrast, by 1796 the lawyers' guild in Caracas had already decided to take steps to prevent a surplus and moved to establish a limit of fifty in the capital. Looking ahead, it proposed not to limit entry into the profession, but rather to place a ceiling on the number allowed to practice in the capital (thereby securing its members' livelihoods) and thus force newcomers to establish offices in less favorable locations.[139]

Upon examination, then, the "abogado problem" was not excessive numbers but imbalanced distribution. Most of these well-educated men preferred the amenities of urban life in the capitals to the humdrum existence of the provinces. They probably believed that the possibility of notable economic and professional success was greater in the capitals than elsewhere. While awaiting fortune, however, the lot of most was unenviable. The solution to the problem, from the attorneys' perspective, was simple: appointment to office. The lawyers' guild in Mexico City proposed that one answer to the dearth of abogados in the countryside and the poverty of those in the city was for the crown to select men from its number to hold half or at least one-third of the corregimientos and alcaldías mayores of New Spain. In addition, the guild advocated that men who served in these posts for fifteen years should then be given preference by the crown for one-third of the *togado* posts in America and Spain. While Charles was apparently convinced that the total number of attorneys did not call for reduction or even mandatory stabilization in 1804, he refused to accede to the plea for, in essence, guaranteeing American advocates a fixed proportion of the positions.[140] The king's refusal faithfully mirrored the

134. Vicente Osvaldo Cútolo, "Los abogados en la revolución de mayo," in *Tercer congreso internacional de historia de América* (Buenos Aires, 1961), 5:202; García Chuecos, *Estudios*, 1:296.

135. Konetzke, *Colección*, 3, tomo II, document 317.

136. Ibid.

137. Ibid., document 374. This reflected a parallel concern in Spain. See *Los códigos*, 8:98–99 *n*. 9–10.

138. Konetzke, *Colección*, 3, tomo II, document 374.

139. García Chuecos, *Estudios*, 1:292–94.

140. Konetzke, *Colección*, 3, tomo II, document 363. The crown continued to try to prevent an enlargement of the excess in Havana. For example, it authorized Francisco Marcos Santaella as "abogado de Indias" except in Cuba. AGS, XXIII, 2–88–201 (Santaella, San Ildefonso, 9 September 1804).

royal attitude for the entire period. Earlier calls for native-son appointments had already revealed Americans' resentment at the intensified discrimination they faced. Uniformly, however, the crown responded negatively to creole protests.

In the course of the comunero revolt in New Granada in 1781, the rebels enumerated their grievances. Although opposition to an increase in taxation had been the immediate stimulus for the rising, one of the complaints focused on offices. Responding to the diminution of local influence that took place in the late 1770s as a result of the visita of Gutiérrez de Piñeres, the comuneros called for preference for creoles in filling posts in New Granada. With both direct and indirect representation on the Audiencia of Santa Fe de Bogotá and in other important offices largely excised, this article can best be interpreted as a call for the immediate return of native sons to office.[141] The failing revolt did not elicit sympathy for this demand, and but two native sons entered the audiencia before 1808.[142]

In New Spain the dilution of local strength that had accompanied the Gálvez visita had already drawn cries of anguish in the 1770s. Failure to obtain redress, however, prompted yet another effort in 1792 when the City Council of Mexico resubmitted its 1771 petition almost verbatim. This repeated call for almost total native-son appointments brought a promise that creoles would receive half of the positions in the choirs (*coros*) in the cathedrals of New Spain but no similar assurance for civil posts.[143]

At almost the same time the City Council of Lima composed a set of instructions for its agent to follow at court. While the Audiencia of Mexico had no more than one native son serving from the early 1770s and had enjoyed only a brief overlap of nine years when two had served simultaneously since the late 1730s, Lima had grown accustomed to extensive direct representation from the late seventeenth century. Never less than five native sons served in Lima from the mid-1690s, and this number had peaked at midcentury when thirteen native sons held appointments. It had declined to six in 1780 and to only four at the end of 1792. The trend was obvious; no Peruvian had been appointed since Melchor de Santiago Concha gained promotion from Santiago in 1777. Moreover, the remaining native sons were old and appeared to be close to the grave. In the face of this deterioration the city council asked its agent to request that Peruvians be given one-third of the positions in both Lima and Cuzco. In addition he was to seek explicit assurance that no objection would be made to ministers serving in their home districts.[144] Unlike the Mexico city council, which had requested a condition never previously enjoyed, the Lima cabildo sought, in effect, a return to the "good old days."[145] Its protest, like that from Mexico, brought no satisfaction.

The Lima instructions represented a retreat from previous creole claims

141. See Phelan, "El auge y la caida."
142. Mosquera y Figueroa and José Berrio y Guzmán.
143. Hamill, *Hidalgo Revolt*, p. 31.
144. Archivo Municipal (Lima), Libro de Cabildo 39, fols. 139–146b.
145. For a fuller discussion see Burkholder, "From Creole to *Peninsular*."

that only native sons should govern; nonetheless they requested an augmenta-tion of local representation. The specific demand for Peruvian rather than "American" ministers reflected limeño recognition of the nature of appoint-ments since royal control had triumphed. Evidently realizing that the crown would consider even their plaintive call an extreme demand, however, six years later the cabildo advised a new agent to use discretion in even mention-ing the request.[146] Not until 1809 would it again press the issue, and then it joined a widespread clamor for more native-son appointments.

The New Bureaucracy: Men

Peninsular as well as creole ministers named after 1750 were distinct from their predecessors in professional and family backgrounds, a reflection of the crown's reassertion of control over appointments. Unlike during the Age of Impotence, after 1750 the crown displayed success in keeping native sons off the courts; the few named represented royal beneficence. Conversely, the crown was able to attract more of the kind of peninsulares that it wanted to serve in America. The preferred peninsulares now, however, were from a dif-ferent background than earlier. In the 1770s, "reform" of the colegios termi-nated their grip on patronage and brought an end to vestiges of deference given their members. Although sons of ministers still enjoyed an advantage, henceforth the crown gave preference to men who had proven their abilities in lower office, most often as an asesor general or a teniente asesor.

Emphasis upon experience, the termination of the colegio-council patron-age circle, and the end of sales opened letrado posts in unprecedented num-bers to men from families previously excluded from the highest ranks of gov-ernment. Limeños shared loss of favor with peninsular colegiales. Americans born and educated outside of Peru were the new creole bureaucrats. Simul-taneously, peninsulares educated at schools other than Salamanca, Valladolid, and Alcalá obtained the majority of posts going to Spaniards. The end of minis-ters' membership in military orders and a decline in the number of appointees whose fathers held government positions joined the changes in place of birth and education to confirm the appearance of ministers from "new" families.

Scarcely one of each eight peninsular appointees from 1751 to 1808 had fathers in government service of any kind (twenty-six of two hundred), a figure even lower than that for the previous period. Although fourteen of the twenty-six fathers held high letrado positions, all but one in Spain, many were themselves "new bureaucrats" from outside the traditional service elite.[147] Five served in the courts in Seville, Zaragoza, and Barcelona, and only three, two of

146. Archivo Municipal (Lima), Libro de Cabildo 39, fols. 139–146b.
147. See Appendix IX. Bataller y Vasco went to Mexico as asesor general in 1777. At that time his son Miguel Antonio Bataller y Ros, born in the province of Granada, was already in his twenties.

Figure 6. New Appointments to the American Audiencias, 1751–1821

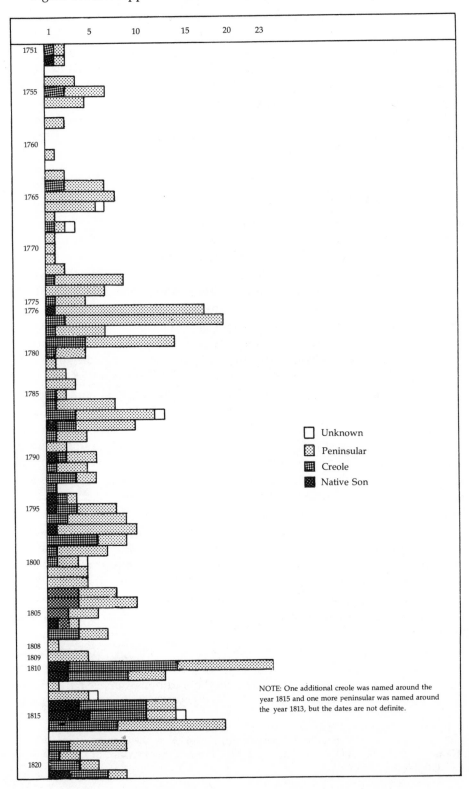

NOTE: One additional creole was named around the
year 1815 and one more peninsular was named around
the year 1813, but the dates are not definite.

whose sons received appointments in the mid-1750s, were on the Council of Castile.[148] The elevation of the Council of the Indies and the visible promotions to it of men with American service seems to have upgraded appointment to the Indies and made it respectable for sons who previously would have been loath to leave Spain.[149] Twelve of the fourteen sons of ministers in Spanish tribunals received appointments from 1776 to 1808.[150] Indeed, by the end of the period the "new bureaucrats" were themselves beginning to establish a tradition of American service. Juan Hernández de Alva and José de Alvarez de Acevedo, the final two sons named, had fathers who had inaugurated their careers in American tribunals and reached the Council of the Indies after years of service.[151]

Men whose ancestors had no record of government service benefited from the demise of the six colegios mayores and the emergence of universities outside the Castilian heartland as important sources for ministers. Educational information shows a distinct change in ministers' backgrounds from the Age of Impotence, with the 1770s serving as the time of transition. While the crown had once regularly courted colegiales, giving to many first appointments on viceregal tribunals, the deterioration of their position apparent in the 1730s and 1740s continued after midcentury. Although they received twenty-four appointments (20 percent) from 1751 to 1779, by the latter year their institution had crumbled before the crown's attack and their eminence was gone. The only colegial named directly to a major tribunal after midcentury was Bartolomé de Bruna, whose father was on the Council of Castile. The majority had dropped into the mainstream of appointees and contented themselves with beginning posts in Santo Domingo, Quito, and Manila.[152]

The end of the colegios' importance accompanied the eclipse of the universities of Salamanca, Alcalá, and Valladolid, traditionally the principal schools spawning peninsular appointees. While from 1751 to 1775 over half of the men named attended one of these universities, in the transitional years of 1776 and 1777 the margin dropped and appointees from the University of Granada increased. The emergence of Granada reflected, in part at least, José de Gálvez's

148. Seville: Fernando Márquez de la Plata y Orozco and José Márquez de la Plata y Soto. Zaragoza: Fuertes y Amar and Villalba. Barcelona: Cerdán Council of Castille: Rojas Almansa (1754), Bruna (1755), and Mata Linares (1776).

149. Further research might show that an expansion of the number of letrados in Spain analogous to that experienced in the Indies further limited employment opportunities in Spain and thus increased the attractiveness of American service.

150. The exceptions were Rojas and Bruna.

151. Lorenzo Hernández de Alba received his initial audiencia appointment as fiscal de lo civil in Santo Domingo in 1777. In 1802 he was named fiscal for New Spain in the Council of the Indies. Tomás Antonio Alvarez de Acevedo was named fiscal of Charcas in 1766; twenty years later he was named a ministro togado of the council.

152. See Appendix IX. The attack on the colegios is well known. See, for example, George M. Addy, *The Enlightenment in the University of Salamanca* (Durham, N.C., 1966), chapter 10; Vicente Rodríguez Casado, *La política y los políticos en el reinado de Carlos III* (Madrid, 1962), pp. 112–13; and, for a detailed examination of the reform of the colegios at Salamanca, Luis Sala Balust, *Visita y reforma de los colegios mayores de Salamanca en el reinado de Carlos III* (Valladolid, 1958).

notorious predilection for men from the old Moorish kingdom, but the school's increased prominence outlived the secretary. After 1778 Granada alone claimed more alumni appointed than any of the three traditional sources; indeed, more men attended only Granada (seventeen) than Salamanca (eight) and Valladolid (three) combined. Other schools as well benefited from the changing pattern of appointment. Universities like those in Toledo and Osuna that had not seen an alumnus named for decades now sent men to the American audiencias. After 1751, in fact, more peninsulares were associated with other Spanish universities than the traditional three leaders combined.[153] Since students generally attended schools in their home regions, new men were clearly entering the high courts.[154]

Final evidence that the peninsulares named after 1751 came from "new" and less prestigious families than before was their exclusion from military orders. While the prestige of the institution was deteriorating, men of requisite background still prized the sword of Santiago or cross of Calatrava or Alcántara. Only three peninsulares who received their first audiencia appointment after 1750 gained hábitos.[155] This paltry number suggests that the "new bureaucrats" generally could not boast the lineage of their predecessors and consequently either did not solicit admittance out of a premonition of failure or in fact were rejected.

In 1771 Charles III established the civil order bearing his name precisely to reward meritorious government service and to provide added luster to worthy royal servants whose antecedents were not of the traditional service elite or aristocracy. Membership quickly became the principal honor high bureaucrats sought. The thirty-two peninsular ministers named from 1751 to 1808 who were admitted were among the most distinguished men in the high American bureaucracy. Nineteen regents, twelve of whom went on to the Council of the Indies, held the cross. In addition, five other ministers of the council with audiencia experience in America and one of the Council of Castile were caballeros.[156] Thus, over three-quarters of the ministers honored had backgrounds of exceptional service in the most important letrado posts for America; they were the cream of the American tribunals and fitting representatives of the new men in high office. That only two of their fathers had belonged to military orders further reveals their distance from the old service elite.[157]

Most peninsulares named to the American courts after 1750 were "new" not only in their lack of family and educational backgrounds traditionally associated with the service elite. More frequently than their predecessors these appointees had previous university service or practical experience as a legal

---

153. See Appendix IV. There is a slight resurgence of Salamanca and Alcalá evident after 1790, a consequence perhaps of the reform in the curriculum.

154. Richard L. Kagan, *Students and Society in Early Modern Spain* (Baltimore, 1974), pp. 202–3.

155. Mosquera y Villarino (1751), Bruna (1755), and Joaquín Basco y Vargas (1776).

156. See Appendixes IX and X.

157. The fathers of Mata Linares and Arredondo.

adviser or official. While frequent movement from an academic chair into a Spanish court or council had brought repeated complaints during the heyday of the colegios, only a small number of peninsular professors had taken posts in American tribunals. After midcentury more began to appear; forty-seven were named from 1751 to 1808, twenty-seven of these after 1777.[158] Complementing this increase was the greater number of peninsulares with previous service in America. From 1751 to 1808 thirty-three held posts of protector of the Indians, asesor general, or teniente asesor, and five more served in other official capacities (two on the visita of Areche in Peru).[159] In addition, seventeen peninsulares gained audiencia posts after prior service in Spain. In sum, ninety-seven (49 percent) of the two hundred peninsular appointees had practical experience in government before joining an audiencia, a substantial increase over the thirty-two (20 percent) of the Age of Impotence.[160]

American appointees after 1750 matched peninsulares in often displaying backgrounds different from their predecessors. In sharp contrast to the peninsulares, over half of the creoles named (thirty-four out of sixty-two) had fathers with recognized government service, nine on American audiencias. The total extent of the fathers' services after midcentury was less than in the Age of Impotence, although the percentage of audiencia ministers among their number had increased.

Within the colonial world, the relative eclipse of the University of San Marcos's dominance in training future ministers paralleled the shift from the traditional centers visible in Spain. While as before nearly all future creole appointees attended American schools, they matriculated in greater proportions at institutions outside of Lima after 1750. The universities in Mexico City and Santa Fe de Bogotá in particular were well attended. Although San Marcos remained the single greatest supplier, it could now claim as alumni less than one-third rather than over two-thirds of the creole ministers.[161]

The change in educational backgrounds of Americans represented an important divergence from the previous pattern and suggests that many new families were seeing sons enter the high magistracy. Further evidence for this contention comes from examination of the places of birth for creole appointees. From 1687 to 1750 letrados from the Audiencia of Lima comprised over half of the Americans named. While Mexico added nearly another fifth, no other district sent over eight men, a scant 6 percent of the total. In sharp contrast, after midcentury Santa Fe jumped to first rank while Santo Domingo equaled Lima. Even Chile had moved ahead of Mexico. With the two original viceregal centers together providing only a quarter of the creoles named, the triumph of letrados

---

158. Two of these, Bruna and Díez Quijada, were colegiales. Five were also teniente asesores, two, protectors of the Indians, one an asesor general, two had experience in Spain, and one had experience in America. Thus, thirty-four men had professorial experience as their leading service.

159. These thirty-three men were not colegiales or professors in addition.

160. See Appendix IX.

161. See Appendix IV.

from the lesser districts seems evident.[162] Most new creoles named represented different families from different regions than had been involved in the courts or any government service before 1750.

Few American ministers entered orders, probably a consequence of the removal of hábitos from the marketplace. The sole knight was the Conde de Torre Velarde, and he gained his habit of Calatrava while a colonel in Peru, more than a decade before donning judicial robes.[163] Although six more ministers were caballeros of Charles III, two entered before joining a tribunal.[164] In entering an order, as in obtaining an audiencia position, Americans suffered discrimination.

Even more than peninsulares, Americans needed previous service to gain a plaza. Twenty creole professors joined the courts during the Age of Authority. Unlike most of their peninsular brethren, however, many of the American academicians also had experience in a royal or local office to their credit. Twenty-five other American appointees had prior service on their records. Seven had been teniente asesores, two asesores generales, and fourteen had held other positions. Two creoles had even served in Spain before gaining an audiencia appointment. Together 73 percent of the Americans (forty-five) had previous service before joining the courts, a dramatic increase over the 39 percent (fifty-four) of the Age of Impotence.[165] The increase in appointees with previous experience indicates the crown's greater control over appointments in the absence of financial considerations. The change in educational and family backgrounds for both Spaniards and Americans and the crown's ability to demand men of experience for posts in the Indies reveal the "new" and more professional nature of the high letrado bureaucracy after 1750.

The New Bureaucracy: Control

New men were but one part of the American audiencias' transformation into a "new bureaucracy" after 1750. To ensure its mastery over the courts, the crown had to end existing ties between ministers and their districts and then prevent the carefully chosen new men from similarly becoming radicado. For achieving these ends it relied upon the ascenso, which almost automatically limited the length of time ministers spent in a district to a few years; disciplinary actions; and enforcement of the marriage restrictions. Examining the composition of each tribunal for native sons and long-tenured ministers who

---

162. See Appendix II.

163. Guillermo Lohmann Villena, *Los americanos en las órdenes nobiliarias (1529–1900)*, 2 vols. (Madrid, 1947), 2:112.

164. Arias de Villafañe and Baquíjano were caballeros before obtaining audiencia appointments. The other four creoles were Urriola, José Berrio y Guzmán, Campo y Rivas, and Roa y Alarcón.

165. See Appendix IX.

served between 1751 and 1808 suggests the initial magnitude of local influence in the courts and the crown's success in limiting it.

The timing of the crown's reassertion of authority varied for the secretariats of New Spain and Peru (see Appendix VII).[166] In the north the crown recovered control over the ministers before the expansion of 1776. Connections between long-tenured ministers and local society were extensive during the 1750s in the viceregal tribunal of Mexico, but death and promotion had obviated the problem by the early 1770s. An excess of judges and occasional native sons generally posed no difficulty, since except in Guadalajara few sales had occurred in the northern tribunals. Even in the New Galician court, however, the removal of two purchasers for cause in the early 1750s and the subsequent return to numero strength meant that only two native sons (both purchasers) remained; they departed in the mid-1760s.[167] At the end of 1775, Guadalajara and Guatemala had no ministers with five years' service, Santo Domingo had but one, and Mexico only six of its fourteen. Distant Manila had the greatest proportion of long-tenured members with three of six present. In each tribunal the radicados were a smaller proportion of the total ministers than in 1750. The great expansion of 1776 and the change of secretaries for the Indies merely punctuated the extent of royal direction over the northern courts. Judicious replacements and increasing concern for the marriage laws had already alleviated the problem of radicados.

The control indicated by the low tenure figures for 1775 generally continued until 1808. For most of these years Guatemala and Guadalajara had clear majorities of ministers with less than five years' service. In contrast, a majority of newcomers was unusual in Manila and Santo Domingo. This breach in control was only nominal, for by the 1780s the crown's overall mastery meant that it could afford to relax its attention in these minor courts. In the key tribunal of Mexico, most ministers serving between 1778 and 1808 remained for over five years and a few for over a decade. The impact of such tenure, however, was far less than the experiences of the 1687–1750 period would suggest. Stringent enforcement of marriage laws prevented the widespread establishment of local ties that had taken place in the earlier period. Moreover, while many ministers were present for over five years, almost none stayed for over fifteen. By 1808 ministers who had remained for decades and founded influential families in Mexico were but memories.

In the Secretariat of Peru the crown faced heavy direct representation at midcentury as a result of the numerous sales made in the 1740s. Native sons still sat on all tribunals but Santa Fe through 1770 and remained in Chile until 1776 and then again from the mid-1790s to independence. Lima began the period with thirteen native sons serving but had only one in 1800, a hardy soul who maintained the unbroken string of direct representation begun in the late

---

166. This and the following three paragraphs are drawn from Appendix VII.

167. Aparicio del Manzano was deprived of his post in 1752; Calvo de la Puerta had been suspended in 1743 and lost his post in 1752; Garza Falcón died circa 1763; and López Portilla advanced to oidor in Mexico in 1764.

1680s and lasting until 1821. While Santa Fe had several native sons briefly in the 1770s and 1790s, Lima and Chile were the only southern tribunals to enjoy significant direct local representation after 1771. It was probably no accident that the transfers of Juan Romualdo Navarro and José Giráldes y Pino in 1771 removed the only native sons serving in Quito and Charcas.

Tenure figures indicate that the crown had nearly ended indirect representation in the southern courts by 1780. Charcas and Chile had no radicado ministers, Santa Fe had one, and Quito claimed two. Lima, although it still boasted five native sons, had not a single radicado, a rare occurrence. By 1808 the picture was quite different. Lima had nine radicado ministers, all of whom had been present a decade or more, in addition to one native son. Excepting Chile, the percentage of long-tenured ministers in the other tribunals varied from forty to sixty. Local influence in Chile was perhaps greater than anywhere else, for two native sons named in the 1790s sat beside two long-serving outsiders. As in the case of the tribunals of New Spain, however, the long-tenured ministers of the Peruvian Secretariat had far fewer proven local ties than their counterparts before 1750. The crown's routine transfer of ministers who married locally had removed potential problems almost as soon as they had arisen.

Beyond question royal control over the audiencias in 1808 far exceeded that of 1750. In many ways the revitalized ascenso was the core of the total effort to increase the crown's authority. The ascenso's expansion to include regents and the Council of the Indies at the top and asesores generales and teniente asesores at the bottom enabled more frequent movement and hence fewer radicado ministers on the one hand and a larger pool of proven officials from whom the crown could select ministers on the other. Through the ascenso the monarch could move troublesome or radicado ministers with a minimum of disturbance. Thus the ladder of promotion aided in both the selection and management of personnel.

The king's decision to place intendants throughout most of his American possessions, while restricting the power of audiencias slightly, expanded the number of letrado positions in the colonies. As intendants were not trained in the law, each received a legal adviser (teniente asesor) as a few governors had before them.[168] After an initial five-year term of office, tenientes could receive reappointment, transfer, dismissal, or, if fortunate, advancement to an audiencia position. Enjoying no guaranteed ascenso or even assurance of reemployment, their future career depended heavily upon proven ability. The Council of the Indies, however, willingly considered worthy tenientes for promotion. While individually they enjoyed less favorable chances for joining a tribunal than did asesores generales or protectors of the Indians, as a group tenientes became more important as a source of audiencia ministers. From 1751 to 1808 twenty-seven tenientes received audiencia appointments as opposed to twelve

---

168. Navarro García, *Intendencias*, p. 84. An example of an earlier analogous appointment is that of José Ferrer de la Puente as teniente de gobierno and auditor de guerra for Venezuela. AGS, XXIII, 2–39–122 (Ferrer, Buen Retiro, 22 August 1752).

asesores generales and nine protectors of the Indians.[169] After the abolishment of the office of protector in 1776, the importance of the teniente position for advancement became more apparent; its prominence increased further with the growth of the intendant system in the 1780s. Twenty-two of the tenientes entered audiencias from 1778 to 1808, sixteen of these after 1790 when a quantity of experienced tenientes was available. From 1791 to 1808 tenientes were the largest group of new men with previous important positions and accounted for about 17 percent of all audiencia appointees (see Figure 7). Despite their maturity and experience, however, not one of them went initially to Lima or Mexico and only two started in Santa Fe. The smaller, more select group of asesores generales gained the direct appointments to the old viceregal audiencias, while tenientes often went to Guatemala, Guadalajara, and Quito, audiencias of primary entrance.

As a group, ministers who had been tenientes displayed distinct characteristics. A disproportionately large number (50 percent) were Americans, although only one was a native son. In addition, the typical former teniente was older and more experienced than other appointees. Often in their mid-forties when named, the former tenientes provided a partial answer to the ongoing problem of marriages by ministers. Men of this age almost certainly would have already married if they intended to, and many would have children at least partly grown and not needing godparents. As former tenientes accounted for a larger share of new ministers, the problem of local marriages for ministers already serving would gradually decrease. Had the Wars of Independence not intervened and the upward trend favoring tenientes continued, the eventual outcome of the new, extended ascenso would have been ministers that as a group were more mature, experienced, and above all reliable and steady in their service than their predecessors had been. The unknown and potentially unsatisfactory young appointee of earlier years could be weeded out at the teniente position. Although about a quarter of the tenientes who entered audiencies qualified as "radicado" on arrival, most received appointments after 1778 when royal control over the audiencias and regulation of ministers' conduct was reaching its peak.

The ascenso, clogged by a lack of openings in Lima and Mexico from the early eighteenth century, was variously affected by the sales made between 1740 and 1750. The few sales to Mexico allowed promotions to begin at once, and from 1751 to 1775 nineteen men from other courts joined the viceregal tribunal. The return to normal advancement was evident, with seven men coming from Guadalajara, six from Guatemala, three from Santo Domingo, and three from Manila. In contrast, Lima was flush with supernumeraries and still had a surplus of ministers assigned at the end of 1765. The five men promoted to Lima by 1775 came from Charcas (three), Quito (one), and Santa Fe (one).[170]

Promotions from the viceregal tribunals were slow but underway again

---

169. See Appendix IX for the figures in this and the following paragraph.
170. See Appendix X.

Figure 7. *Teniente* and *Asesor* Backgrounds of New Appointees, 1778–1821

Year	TA	AG	Total new appointees	Year	TA	AG	Total new appointees	Year	TA	AG	Total new appointees
1778	-	-	6	1793	-	-	1	1808	-	-	1
1779	2	-	13	1794	1	-	3	1809	1	1	4
1780	-	-	4	1795	-	2	7	1810	2	-	23
1781	-	-	1	1796	3	1	8	1811	3	2	12
1782	-	-	2	1797	-	1	9	1812	-	-	1
1783	-	-	3	1798	1	-	8	1813	-	-	5
1784	-	1	2	1799	-	-	6	1814	2	-	13
1785	-	2	7	1800	-	-	4	1815	2	-	14
1786	1	1	12	1801	1	-	4	1816	4	1	18
1787	1	1	9	1802	-	-	4	1817	-	-	0
1788	1	1	4	1803	4	-	7	1818	2	1	8
1789	-	-	2	1804	1	-	9	1819	-	-	3
1790	1	-	5	1805	-	-	5	1820	1	-	5
1791	2	1	4	1806	-	-	3	1821	3	-	8
1792	-	-	5	1807	2	-	6				

NOTE: One additional *teniente* was named, probably in 1813.

after a hiatus of roughly two decades. Mexico from 1751 to 1775 sent one minister to a Spanish audiencia and three to the Council of the Indies. Lima sent only one man to the council, but with eight promotions from other tribunals, a total of thirteen positions were opened for new appointees.[171] The eight from the lesser tribunals, however, allowed less overall movement than the other five. It took the expansion of the tribunals in 1776 and the almost simultaneous promotion of two ministers in Mexico to the House of Trade and two to the Council of the Indies to inaugurate a renewal of orderly advancement throughout the empire.

An important stimulus to the ascenso was the new office of regent. From 1776 to 1808, eighteen ministers of Lima were selected regents of other tribunals. During the same years fourteen from Mexico obtained regencies, two in that tribunal. Excluding Manuel de Arredondo, who moved from Lima to Mexico and back only on paper, this new position created thirty openings. The men chosen from Lima went to each of the six other South American tribunals as well as to Manila and Guatemala. Mexico sent regents to each of the four tribunals under its sway and to Santa Fe as well. The twelve other regents selected came from a variety of tribunals in both secretariats with none providing more than three.[172]

While a regent of a lesser tribunal might be promoted to the regency in Mexico or Lima, advancement to the Council of the Indies was both more fre-

171. Ibid.
172. Ibid.

quent and prestigious. After the 1773 decree that declared the Council of the Indies equal to that of Castile, Spanish letrados without service in America rarely appeared among its new appointees.[173] After the decree, twenty-five men went directly to the council from American audiencias and two more did so after serving as visitors-general. Eighteen of the men were regents, thus providing for a chain of advancement in the American tribunals.[174] In addition, eight other men who had previously served on American audiencias moved to the council from the House of Trade or other Spanish tribunals.[175]

The advancement of men of American experience to the council not only helped to maintain the ascenso and thus restrain the growth of radicado ministers in America but also meant that the councillors displayed unprecedented personal knowledge of the Indies. While from 1687 to the decree of 1773 the council never had more than five letrados with American experience serving simultaneously and frequently had only two or three, by the end of 1775 the situation had changed dramatically. Eight letrados with American service served then, and until 1808 no fewer than eight and at times as many as twelve served. The extent of personal knowledge of America present on the council was probably never greater than from the mid-1770s until 1808.[176]

Part of the smooth working of the ascenso system after midcentury was the result of an absence of direct appointments to the viceregal tribunals of Mexico and Lima. Figure 8 demonstrates the reversal from the pattern present in the Age of Impotence. The end of sales in 1750 and the subsequent decision to employ direct appointments to the major tribunals only with great restraint, plus the expansion of the ascenso to include regents and the Council of the Indies combined to make regular advancement a reality instead of an idle fantasy for letrados whether they began their careers as teniente asesores or as ministers in Manila or Santo Domingo.

The career of the peninsular José Antonio de Urízar y Bolívar demonstrates that movement from teniente to councillor was possible. Urízar entered as a teniente asesor and auditor de guerra in Venezuela in the pre-intendant days of 1766 and rose through the ranks of oidor of Santo Domingo, alcalde del crimen and oidor in Mexico, and then regent in Santo Domingo before winning

---

173. See pp. 99–100.

174. The visitors-general were Areche and Escobedo. The following men were regents previously: García León y Pizarro, Herrera y Rivero, Jacot, Tomás Alvarez de Acevedo, Villalengua, Urízar, Saavedra y Carvajal, López Quintana, Mata Linares, Portilla, Cortines, Uruñuela, Castillo y Negrete, Cerdán, Gorvea Vadillo, Fernando Márquez de la Plata, and Mon y Velarde. Gutiérrez de Piñeres, who was also a visitor-general, is counted as a regent.

175. Agüero, González Bustillo, Villarrasa, Acedo, and Rivera y Peña joined the council after appointments to the House of Trade. Díaz and Cerda went from the Chancellery of Granada, and Huerta from the Audiencia of Barcelona. In addition, Manuel Romero had been asesor general in New Granada before going to the House of Trade and then receiving an appointment to the council.

176. These figures are based upon titles of office examined in the AGS and Bernard, *Le secrétariat*, pp. 221–29.

Figure 8. Appointments to Lima and Mexico, 1751–1808

	1751-1775	1776-1777	1778-1808	1751-1808 Totals
Lima:				
Direct appointment	2	2*	8	12*
Promotion	5	7	30*	42*
Mexico:				
Direct appointment	3	2*	3	8*
Promotion	19	5	40**	64**

* includes 1 regent   **includes 4 regents

promotion to the Council of the Indies in 1795. He spent no more than eight years in one assignment and averaged but six.[177] Although war and independence prevented the three decades necessary for this achievement for most tenientes, Urízar's career stands as a blueprint of the kind of minister the crown was trying to provide for its American audiencias: a professional who had proven himself in five years' service at a lesser post before entering the audiencias and who had little time to spend in any location establishing local ties if he were to master the many-runged ladder of promotion. The ascenso after 1750 brought the old Hapsburg concept of the "Platonic guardian" nearer to reality than at any time in the past.

Regular use of the ascenso enabled the crown not only to reward worthy ministers and prevent local ties but also to enforce discipline. By the late eighteenth century use of the ascenso joined transfer to a tribunal of equal or lower rank, loss of promotion, or the more mundane forced retirement, suspension, fines, or criminal prosecution as a means for enforcing royal control over ministers. The crown standardized these procedures and began to apply them rationally only after midcentury and the restoration of order. Previously the absence of prompt, detailed information about conditions on tribunals often had allowed scandals to become public spectacles before the crown resolved the problem. Although at times the crown had employed the ultimate weapon of the visita, more commonly it failed to provide firm and timely prosecution or meted out only haphazard punishments for offenses that at a later date would merit prompt dismissal from office. Undoubtedly financial recovery facilitated tighter discipline, for it was more expensive to retire and replace an errant letrado than to fine or send him out of an area on a prolonged inspection tour.

Ministers with love affairs and marital disorders provided the crown with endless grief because of consequent public disapproval and official embarrassment. In the early period the crown often shunted these transgressors from one tribunal to another as it avoided rather than dealt with the problems. Cristóbal de Ceballos y Borja, oidor in Quito in the late seventeenth century, was sent to Guayaquil on a commission because of a celebrated love affair; several

177. AGS, XXIII, 2–50–91 (Urízar, Aranjuez, 20 June 1766); 2–56–59 (Urízar, Aranjuez, 11 May 1771); 2–62–97 (Urízar, 10 June 1778); 2–65–55 (Urízar, San Ildefonso, 27 September 1781); 2–71–264 (Urízar, San Lorenzo, 17 November 1787); 13–8–35 (Urízar, Aranjuez, 21 April 1795).

years later he was "en depósito" in Panama.[178] Another minister in Quito, Juan de Ricuarte, allegedly twice attempted to murder his wife, but that and other questionable activities brought him only transfer "en depósito" to another court.[179] Numerous judges married local women without first procuring a license and suffered only fines.[180] By contrast, in the late eighteenth century, timely information and prompt, decisive action prevented such scandals from disrupting entire districts. Juan Romualdo Navarro, oidor in Guadalajara, created a stir by his *ilicita amistad* with a woman there in 1782. Quickly reported to the crown, Navarro was retired in 1783.[181] Another minister serving in New Galicia committed a similar offense later and in 1800 suffered forced retirement with only one-third salary and exile from Spain and his audiencia district.[182] Also, by 1800 ministers who married without the royal permit were more likely to be removed than fined.[183]

Demotion from the ranking tribunals of Lima and Mexico was a weapon occasionally employed. The checkered career of Sebastián Calvo de la Puerta of Havana illustrates its use. Calvo purchased an appointment as oidor supernumerario of Guadalajara in 1740 but was later suspended. He apparently fought the decision personally, for he was in Spain when "restored" to Guadalajara as oidor in 1755. The restoration must have been only to clear his record, for two days later the council named him a supernumerary alcalde del crimen in Mexico but with only the salary of Guadalajara. Nine years later, instead of advancing routinely to the civil chamber, Calvo found himself named to Guatemala, the only such move decreed from 1687 to 1808.[184] In the south, too, ministers always regarded appointment to a lesser-ranking tribunal as a demotion before the regency came into existence. As part of restaffing the Audiencia of Chile in 1776, Charles III named the limeño purchaser and longtime alcalde del crimen Juan José de la Puente y Ibáñez the new senior oidor. Puente successfully protested the move on the grounds that it was not in the ascenso and would be interpreted as a sign of royal displeasure. The crown conceded and, rather than force his transfer, promoted him to oidor in Lima.[185]

---

178. Manuel Moreyra y Paz-Soldán and Guillermo Céspedes del Castillo, eds., *Virreinato peruano: documentos para su historia. Colección de cartas de virreyes—Conde de la Monclova*, 3 vols. (Lima, 1954–1955), 2:52; AGI, Panama, legajo 124.

179. Restrepo Sáenz, *Biografías*, pp. 337–8; AGI, Panama, legajo 124; *AGI*, Indiferente General, legajo 1293.

180. For example, Francisco Merlo de la Fuente and Salazar y Castejón. See Restrepo, *Biografías*, p. 22, and AGI, Indiferente General, legajo 525, Relación de los empleos.

181. AGN, Historia, Vol. 120, exp. 16, consulta . . . sre habersele denunciado la ilicita amistad q tenía aquel Sr. Oydor decano Dn Juan Romualdo Navarro, . . . , 1782; AGS, XXIII, 2–67–32 (title of retirement for Navarro at half-salary, Aranjuez, 3 May 1783).

182. AGN, Historia, Vol. 120, exp. 3, expediente sobre juvilación del Oidor de la Rl Audiencia de Guadalajara D José Santos Domínguez; AGS, XXIII, 2–84–122 (title of retirement for Santos, San Lorenzo, 7 October 1800).

183. AGS, XXIII, 2–88–59 (Bataller y Ros, Aranjuez, 16 April 1804); 2–93–228 (Díaz de Rivera, Cádiz, 11 December 1811). Both Manuel Antonio de la Bodega y Mollinedo and Miguel Díaz de Rivera were removed, although later restored.

184. AGS, XXIII, 2–48–163 (Calvo de la Puerta, Aranjuez, 7 June 1764).

185. AGI, Lima, legajo 617; AGS, XXIII, 2–61–102 (Puente Ibáñez, San Ildefonso, 21 August 1777).

The complete turnover of the Audiencia of Chile in 1776 dramatically illustrates that even "advancement" could be punitive. While following the ascenso pattern of selecting judges from the lower-ranking Chile for Lima, the crown acted upon complaints that the court was preventing fiscal reform to name the four oidores to the Lima tribunal and the fiscal to the House of Trade.[186] Two of the men protested their "promotions," were subsequently retired at half pay, and died in Santiago.[187] Another, the Chilean Domingo de Martínez de Aldunate, died in Santiago in 1778 having never left, or wanted to leave, for the City of Kings.[188] The punitive nature of the fiscal's appointment to the House of Trade was evident in the peremptory demand that he leave Santiago immediately.[189] José Perfecto de Salas complied but never reached Spain, dying in Buenos Aires on Christmas Day, 1778.[190] The only one of the five "promoted" purchasers to assume his new post was Melchor de Santiago Concha, a limeño and son of the former dean of the Audiencia of Lima.[191] He was willing to go home regardless of the terms.

Even transfer between the viceregal tribunals could bear an onus in the eighteenth century. The appointments of Pedro Antonio de Echeverz and Cristóbal Mesía y Munive to Mexico were a direct result of complaints by regent Melchor Jacot Ortiz Rojano and Visitor-General José Antonio de Areche's investigation of the Audiencia of Lima.[192] Mesía, much as several of the men who had been so recently "promoted" from Chile, obtained retirement rather than move, while Echeverz stalled until his death in Lima.[193] Indeed the only minister serving in Lima who moved to Mexico without stigma after 1687 was Tomás González Calderón, a native Mexican whose slowness in moving from Guatemala to Lima earlier had suggested his dismay at leaving the ascenso into his home tribunal.[194]

For most of the twelve serving audiencia ministers named to the House of

---

186. Jacques Armand Barbier, "Imperial Reform and Colonial Politics: A Secret History of Late Bourbon Chile" (Ph.D. dissertation, University of Connecticut, 1972), pp. 74–75, 80, 141 and 164; Jacques Barbier, "Elites and Cadres in Bourbon Chile," *HAHR*, 52:3 (August 1972): 432–33.

187. Juan Antonio Verdugo and Traslaviña.

188. See AGI, Chile, legajo 191, letter 305 (dup.) from Agustín de Jáuregui to Gálvez, Santiago, 27 January 1778.

189. Barbier, "Imperial Reform and Colonial Politics," p. 165.

190. José Toribio Medina, *Diccionario biográfico colonial de Chile* (Santiago, Chile, 1906), p. 793.

191. Son of José de Santiago Concha, Marqués de Casa Concha, Melchor took possession as alcalde del crimen in Lima on 23 November 1778. He was retired in 1792 and died in 1794.

192. Burkholder, "From Creole to *Peninsular*," pp. 404–5.

193. Mesía was retired at half salary on 8 October 1778. AGI, Indiferente General, legajo 1519. Echeverz died in Peru on 30 April 1784. AGI, Lima, legajo 666, letter 11, Viceroy Croix to Gálvez, Lima, 10 May 1784.

194. Pleading ill health, González Calderón asked to be transferred to Mexico. AGI, Lima, legajo 1006, letter by Ramon Theodoro Moreno (in name of Tomás González Calderón) to king, Madrid, 16 July 1796. In February 1790, Viceroy Croix was writing about González Calderón's delay in arriving in Lima. AGI, Lima, legajo 647, index of letters by Viceroy Croix, Lima, 15 February 1790.

Trade from 1751 to its demise in 1790, the move to Spain was a desired promotion. The appointment of Francisco Ignacio González Maldonado, however, provides another glimpse at the crown's use of advancement for political purposes. González Maldonado, who joined Antonio Villaurrutia y Salcedo as the only native sons serving on the Audiencia of Mexico in 1786, was moved to the House of Trade in November of that year.[195] Four months later Villaurrutia was named regent of Guadalajara and the Mexico tribunal was swept of its direct local influence.[196] González Maldonado, however, was unahppy with his "promotion" and within four years had arranged to exchange posts with Modesto de Salcedo y Somodevilla, a Spanish colegial who was probably as delighted to end his days on the peninsula as was González Maldonado in Mexico.[197] Salas and González Maldonado were the only creole ministers to receive appointment to the House of Trade. Both had intimate connections in the districts they were serving and neither wanted to move. While Salas died before he could get the sentence lifted, González Maldonado succeeded in returning to Mexico. His actions indicate both opposition to what most of his peers would have viewed as advancement in their careers and the strength of native-son feelings.

Given the care with which the crown selected the initial regents and the subsequent promotions many obtained to the Council of the Indies, one might presume that ministers would be pleased to become the ranking judicial official in a district. Examining the appointments made from 1776 to 1808 generally confirms this. Only for Manila and Cuzco did men refuse regencies. In none of the three cases, however, was the reluctant minister's refusal detrimental to his career. Shortly after rejecting the regency of Manila, Francisco de Saavedra y Carvajal accepted the one for Guadalajara and then was named to the Council of the Indies.[198] José Gorbea Vadillo was similarly soon named to the regency of Buenos Aires and then to the Council.[199] José de Pareja, who had been absent from Lima for only two years since he first reached the city as asesor general in the mid-1780s, chose to remain there as fiscal civil rather than move to Cuzco.[200]

The crown's use of the ascenso after 1750, and most noticeably from the 1770s, underlines the new nature of the high letrado bureaucracy in the Age of

195. AGS, XXIII, 2–70–260 (González Maldonado, San Lorenzo, 29 November 1786).
196. Ibid., 2–71–95 (Villaurrutia, El Pardo, 28 March 1787).
197. Ibid., 2–74–74 (González Maldonado, 17 April 1790).
198. Ibid., 2–73–260 (Saavedra, San Lorenzo, 11 November 1789); 2–78–182 (Saavedra, San Lorenzo, 14 December 1794); 13–9–122 (Saavedra, Aranjuez, 5 March 1803).
199. Ibid., 2–86–106 (Gorbea, Aranjuez, 3 May 1802) (Gorbea, 2–87–95, Aranjuez, 13 May 1803); 13–9–217 (Gorbea, March, 1804).
200. Pareja had been named oidor in Buenos Aires in 1787 and fiscal del crimen in Lima in 1789. He turned down the move to Cuzco in 1804 and remained in Lima until 1821 when he departed for Spain. AGS, XXIII, 2–71–176 (Pareja, San Ildefonso, 23 July 1787); 2–73–139 (Pareja, Aranjuez, 19 May 1789); 2–89–204 (Pareja, San Lorenzo, 31 December 1805); Guillermo Durand Flórez, "Alta cámara de justicia," in *Quinto congreso internacional de historia de América*, 5 vols. (Lima, 1972), 5:268.

Authority. In contrast to the 1687–1750 period, after midcentury regular advancement was routine. Men could expect promotions consonant with their proven ability and, consequently, anticipate serving in two, three, or more locations. The result of their movement was a decline in local influence on the tribunals. New men, invigorated enforcement of statutes that prohibited ministers from developing local ties, and the regular use of the ascenso—this was the new bureaucracy.

The state of the audiencias in 1808 was a tribute to the success of the tenaciously followed policy of control initiated at mid-eighteenth century. Only six native sons and nineteen "outsider" creoles were among the ninety-nine men serving when Charles IV and Ferdinand VII abdicated in May 1808. On the other hand, every tribunal but Manila and Quito had at least one American present, a token representative of the crown's willingness to reward a moderate number of qualified creoles.[201] Only in the relatively unimportant tribunal of Chile had the crown allowed significant direct representation. Radicado ministers plus native sons were a slight majority of the men serving in the empire in 1808, but their number was less than in 1785, 1795, or 1800, to say nothing of 1750.[202] Moreover, the implications of radicados' tenure were not as grave as earlier for, in addition to tighter enforcement of the marriage laws, the crown demanded routine reports on the ministers from the president of each tribunal and knew their local ties, length of service, capabilities, and vices. Reprimands were forthcoming for men who abused their positions or conducted themselves in a manner inappropriate to their station.

The control over the audiencias present at the time of the abdications stands in contrast to the disruption and the relative lack of prompt information that characterized much of the Age of Impotence. The continued smooth functioning of the audiencias is all the more impressive in light of the almost continual state of war since 1793. The "crisis of administration" perceived in other spheres had not affected the audiencias significantly.[203]

It is impossible to explain with certainty why a breakdown in the audiencias did not occur between 1793 and 1808. Several important differences from the last lengthy period of war (that of Jenkins' Ear), however, are apparent. The colonies at the close of the eighteenth century were far more valuable sources of revenue than they had been earlier. Mexico, the principal source of bullion, was minting roughly three times as much silver and gold in the 1790s as it had in the 1740s. Taxable trade, too, had increased greatly during the intervening years, and the Spanish economy itself enjoyed unprecedented prosperity in the late eighteenth century. The crown had no desire to alienate any part of the vast sums at stake. Moreover, the great increase in overall royal rev-

---

201. See Appendix V.
202. See Appendix VII.
203. See R. A. Humphreys and John Lynch, eds., *The Origins of the Latin American Revolutions, 1808–1826* (New York, 1966), pp. 14–15 for the "crisis of administration" thesis.

enue meant that selling appointments would provide a far smaller percentage of the total than previously. When pressed to secure new funds the crown turned to bonds, loans, "voluntary contributions" and eventually *consolidación*.[204] Unlike the sale of appointments, which always brought distasteful results that extended for decades, the crown conceived consolidación (erroneously for America) as both of immediate financial benefit and lasting social value. Finally, throughout these years, the Council of the Indies had more ministros togados with personal experience in America than ever before. Some of these men, a majority of the council, had personally witnessed the abuses and thwarting of the royal will that the previous sales had brought and showed no interest in relaxing the grip the crown had finally achieved over the audiencias. When one anachronistic limeño sought to purchase an appointment in 1798, he quickly learned how much had changed since 1750.[205]

The Age of Authority ended with local influence on the courts far less than in 1750. The crown had successfully reestablished its control by appointing new men, almost uniformly "outsiders," and limiting their co-optation by local families. Yet the cost of success was high. The visible decline in native-son strength on the courts gave substance to the creoles' belief that they faced systematic discrimination. Of equal and perhaps greater importance, the attack on local indirect influence on the tribunals had removed an important safety valve. Even without native sons serving, local families traditionally had enjoyed social relationships with the ministers and found them receptive to their concerns. In 1808 the ministers' few local ties underscored that they were tools of Spain's will rather than representatives of local interests. As the Age of Authority yielded to the Crisis of Independence, the courts often became the focus for attack by supporters of de facto if not de jure home rule. Rather than leaders or mirrors of local opinion, ministers became its victims.

---

204. The *cédula de consolidación de vales reales* issued in late December 1804 demanded that all borrowers from charitable funds *(obras pías)* repay their principal within a short period of time. The obras pías would then turn over their liquid capital to the crown in return for low-yield government bonds.

205. The limeño was Diego Miguel Bravo de Rivero. AGI, Lima, legajo 1008, *mesa* report, 26 August 1800.

Epilog
The Crisis of Independence
(1809–1821)

Crisis and collapse succeeded the Age of Authority in May, 1808. Within two years, representatives of the right of self rule were fighting agents loyal to any symbol of the authority of Spain in several colonies. The audiencias, composed at this time almost exclusively of outsiders with few local ties, were early casualties of the conflicts. By the time the last appointee to a mainland audiencia received his title of office in 1821, royal authority was little more than a dream in the minds of officials in Madrid.

The economic and financial difficulties that Spain encountered soon after her entry into the Wars of the French Revolution in 1793 expanded into political crisis in 1808. Napoleon's success in removing both Ferdinand VII and Charles IV loosed a crisis of authority for both Spain and her colonies. While widespread opposition to the French was soon apparent in much of Spain, there was no immediate agreement on control and direction of the resistance. The rapid establishment of juntas in late May demonstrated that, whatever theory might be invoked, authority had devolved to the local level. Victory at Bailén provided a breathing space, however, and gave persons seeking to unify the resistance time to lobby for a central government. From their efforts came the Junta Central, established in late September.[1]

Invasion and the abdications at Bayonne convinced some Spaniards that the former royal favorite Manuel Godoy, Prince of the Peace, had been the real cause of Spain's grief. A desire to prevent repetition of the abuse of royal power that he represented moved many to advocate a written constitution.[2] Thus the Napoleonic invasion provoked an examination of power and political life in Spain and a reexamination of the nature of authority. The consequences of this introspection touched the empire deeply.

The telescoped news that Americas received heightened their astonishment at the the abdications and imposition of Joseph Bonaparte as king. Inspired by the patriotic reaction in Spain, creoles in every region swore fealty to Ferdinand and supported the Spanish resistance with donations. This first wave of emotion quickly gave way to a new view of politics. In imitation of the response in Spain, some Americans called for local juntas to rule until Ferdinand returned. Even as efforts to establish these were beginning, however, the newly formed Junta Central asked each viceroyalty and captaincy general to send a deputy to join it. In this unprecedented call for American representation was a request that each deputy bring instructions from the cabildo of the

1. Angel Martínez de Velasco, *La formación de la junta central* (Pamplona, 1972), pp. 121ff.
2. Gabriel H. Lovett, *Napoleon and the Birth of Modern Spain*, 2 vols. (New York, 1965), 2, chapter 10.

region's capital.³ Discussion of regional grievances followed in every part of the empire.

The propositions presented by the American representatives to the cortes on 16 December 1810 reflected the fruit of two years of continued discussion. Taking as a text successive general statements of equality and union issued by the Junta Central and Regency, the representatives made clear that the key American demand was for "equality"—equality in representation to the cortes and equality in the pursuit of civil, ecclesiastical, and military positions, among other rights. Pointedly, the propositions called for native sons serving in half of all positions.⁴ This demand for local control through native-son officials was one that Americans from every region could support.

The demand for both guaranteed native-son appointments and equality in the pursuit of posts elsewhere was a marked change from earlier creole calls for office. While fulfillment would place more Americans in high offices, the willingness to settle for native sons receiving only half of the positions indicates the extent to which the patrimonial concept of justice that Bolívar y de la Redonda had emphasized had been abandoned.⁵ Moreover, the call for equality with peninsulares in pursuit of posts outside one's home district represented the extent to which efforts to integrate the empire in the Age of Authority had succeeded. In December 1810, however, the lingering patrimonial view was the crucial part of the requests, for "modern" equality between Spaniards and Americans had been implicit in earlier royal decrees. While the cortes approved "equality" between Spaniards and Americans, it never gave native-son appointments explicit consideration.⁶ The frustration felt by native sons, and growing since the 1770s at seeing their tribunals regularly staffed by "outsiders," went unabated.

Both contemporaries and many later historians have argued that Spain's virtual exclusion of creoles from high positions in the colonies was an important, perhaps the most important, "cause" of the Wars of Independence. Although the demand for more native-son appointments clearly occupied a prominent place in Americans' lists of grievances, caution is required to avoid

3. José María Queipo de Llano Ruíz de Saravia, Conde de Toreno, *Historia del levantamiento, guerra y revolución de España* (vol. LXIV of *Biblioteca de Autores Españoles*, Madrid, 1953), pp. 174–75, *n*.3.

4. "Proposiciones que hacen al Congreso Nacional los Diputados de América y Asia," Isla de León, 16 December 1810. Lilly Library, Indiana University, Latin American Mss.—Peru Manuscripts Department. See also Nettie Lee Benson (ed.), *Mexico and the Spanish Cortes, 1810–1822: Eight Essays* (Austin and London, 1966), particularly W. Woodrow Anderson, "Reform as a Means to Quell Revolution," pp. 185–207.

5. Obviously not everyone agreed that native sons should have only half of the positions. For example, Mariano Alejo Alvarez argued in a discourse written in 1811 but not published until 1820 that native sons should hold all posts. A number of his arguments are reminiscent of those presented by Bolívar y de la Redonda. *Discurso sobre la preferencia que deben tener los americanos en los empleos de América* (Lima, 1820).

6. A decree issued in February 1811 granted equality in competition for all posts in Spain and the empire. AGI, Indiferente General, legajo 668, circular, Cadiz, 24 March 1811. The tortured efforts to define "equality" are best seen in the important article by James F. King, "The Colored Castes and American Representation in the Cortes of Cadiz," *HAHR*, 33:1 (February 1953): 33–64.

overestimating its significance. The leading families in each region sought continued or expanded access to political and economic power. The placement of native sons in office provided the most obvious and direct way in which this desire could be realized; this was only one route, however, and historically its importance had varied widely by region. From an empire-wide viewpoint, the reduction and restraints placed on radicado ministers were more important than the reduction in native sons serving on the tribunals.

Seen from the American perspective of 1750, the Hispanic-American world in 1808 was "upside down."[7] To right it meant to return to the flaccid administration and extensive indirect access to power that had characterized the Age of Impotence. As most means of indirect access to the audiencias violated restrictive statutes, however, and since the courts themselves now competed with additional rival institutions, Americans found it easier to call directly for the legally justifiable appointment of native sons to a variety of posts. The events of 1808 provided an unexpected forum for American grievances, including native-son appointments; yet without the Napoleonic invasion of Spain, local frustration over limited access to political power might have simmered indefinitely. Perhaps more important than any of the celebrated background "causes" of the Wars of Independence were the events after 1808.

The crisis in Spain and America after 1808 brought a new dimension to the selection of ministers for the audiencias. Henceforth, unquestioned loyalty and "proper" political attitudes often outweighed professional qualifications as the final determinants for appointment. "Reliable" Americans and even native sons could now get posts, while suspect outsiders could not. In the kaleidoscope of Spanish politics from 1809 to 1821 and the changing conditions in America, ministers and pretendientes alike could never be certain of the correctness of their actions and expressions.

Beginning with the Junta Central, each of the five governments present until 1821 tried to win support from Americans by the appointment of creoles and, to a limited extent, native sons (see Figure 9). While Americans received only two appointments from the Junta Central, they received over half from the regency and the cortes. Under continued pressure from creole deputies and the necessity to win support in America, peninsular authorities to 1814 took seriously the decrees of equality. In native-son appointments, however, they fell far short of creole expectations (see Appendix V). Nonetheless, the eight men named directly to their home tribunals were an obvious improvement over the eleven named from 1751 to 1808. A belated although clear sign of the cortes's willingness to use native-son appointments in an effort to curry support took place in 1811, when it optimistically reestablished the Audiencia of Buenos Aires. Three of the five Americans named to the eight-man body were native sons.[8]

---

7. We have borrowed the phrase from John L. TePaske, "The Collapse of the Spanish Empire," *Lex et Scientia: The International Journal of Law and Science* 10:1–2 (January–June 1974): 34–36.

8. Manuel Mariano de Irigoyen de la Quintana, Julián de Leyba, and Manuel Ignacio de Molina.

Figure 9. New Appointments by Regimes, 1809–1821

	Native Sons	Other Creoles	Peninsulares	Unknowns
Junta Central	-	1	5	-
Regency	1	8	8	-
Cortes	6	13	14	2
Ferdinand VII	4	21	22	1
Cortes	1	6	3	-

Despite Ferdinand VII's clouded reputation as a result of abrogating the Constitution of 1812 and returning to pre-1808 institutions, he did not turn back the clock for audiencia appointments. Americans, although not native sons, did as well during his reign from 1814 to 1820 as during the previous six years. Over half of the new men he named were creoles.[9] Ferdinand's intention to provide Americans with high posts was equally clear when he reconstituted the Council of the Indies with the injunction that some of its members would always be creoles.[10] The return of constitutional government in 1820 increased the percentage of Americans named, but with appointments covering only two years no definite conclusions about an upward as opposed to a steady trend should be drawn.[11]

Appointees after 1808 were often older than they had been previously. For the first time, the average new man was in his forties, representative in part of the fact that about one-fifth of the appointees were seasoned teniente asesores.[12] The government's overriding concern to select "safe" men placed a premium on those who had demonstrated their attachment to the government in years of service, through *donativos*, and by political or military support for the peninsular policy of continued domination in America.[13] Experienced royal officials, whether absolutist or constitutional, had already given ample proof of their fidelity and were less risky choices than men with no public background. In a sense the criterion for selecting audiencia ministers had come full circle. As in periods of sales, after 1808 nonprofessional considerations replaced more traditional requirements. Now, however, one "purchased" a position by proven political reliability rather than cash.

---

9. See Figure 9.

10. AGI, Indiferente General, legajo 888, royal decree, Madrid, 2 July 1814.

11. See Figure 9.

12. Ages are drawn from Appendix IX. See Figure 7 for tenientes who received appointments in addition to Appendix IX.

13. Donativos came from serving ministers; for example, Francisco González Maldonado who with his brother gave fifty thousand pesos in the 1790s, and from pretendientes; for example, José Gutiérrez del Rivero whose relación of 1801 related his family's donativos and loans. AGI, Santa Fe, legajo 548.

As during the earlier sales periods, after 1808 the ascenso suffered, although not as much as before. Revolt and disorder disrupted several tribunals (Buenos Aires, Caracas, Quito, and Santa Fe), but the others reveal a familiar pattern. Stagnation and long tenure in the lesser audiencias in the past had been caused by the direct appointment of supernumerary purchasers to Lima and Mexico. Similarly, after 1808 the government named deputies from the cortes and "safe" or dislodged men from Spanish tribunals to American positions.[14] Above all, the crown felt an obligation to refugees from disrupted American tribunals and granted many of them appointments elsewhere in compensation for their travail. These men often served as supernumeraries until vacancies in the numero positions occurred.[15] Ministers in the normal ascenso tribunals again found difficulty in securing promotion.

Of eighteen appointments to Lima after 1808 only nine represented the normal ascenso; the others were direct or non-ascenso transfers. For Mexico the imbalance was even more obvious. Geography dictated that ministers fleeing from New Granada would go north rather than south, and consequently only seven of nineteen appointments to Mexico were within the normal ascenso. Most affected was Guadalajara, which sent no judges to Mexico after the Napoleonic intrusion. The decline in promotions raised tenure figures noticeably in most of the relatively undisturbed feeder tribunals. The crown's concern both to succor deposed ministers and to ensure reliable men on the senior tribunals contributed unavoidably to the disruption of the high bureaucracy.[16]

The ultimate test for ministers came with independence in the regions they served. Their decisions whether to remain in office, as most could have by swearing allegiance to the fledgling states, or to leave were colored by many considerations—political persuasion, local ties, and age, among others. The decisions they made also reflected in part the ambiguous nature of independence in New Spain and Peru. At least sixteen of the Americans serving when the climax came supported independence initially.[17] Eleven of these were in regions that in 1821 accepted a "conservative" independence rather than a

---

14. The deputies who received appointment were Fernández de Leiva, Morales y Duares, Noriega, Larreinaga, Navarrete, Valdivieso, Zavala, Mújica, Castillo, Rivero y Besoain, Rodríguez de Bahamonde, Flores Alatorre, Obregón, and Mariano Mendiola. Men previously in Spanish tribunals were Modet, Solís, Osés, and Villanueva.

15. An example of the difficulties faced can be seen in the saga of Antonio Caspe y Rodríguez. Exiled from his position as fiscal in Buenos Aires in 1810, he received an appointment as a supernumerary oidor in Chile. Insurrection there, however, prevented him from taking possession until 1815, by which time he held a numero appointment. Scarcely settled, he was advanced to Lima. There he served first as alcalde del crimen and then as oidor until insurrection drove him to Spain.

16. See Appendix X for the appointments.

17. Rodríguez Aldea, Rus, Moreno y Morán, O'Horan, Larreinaga, Francisco Xavier de Moreno y Escandón, Aldunate, Irigoyen y Centeno, Campo y Rivas, Yañez y Nuño, Martínez Mansilla, Odoardo, Berasueta, Peña y Peña, Chica, and Vidaurre. Moreno y Morán, at least, went back to Spain later.

"liberal" Spain.[18] Four of the sixteen men were native sons.[19] On the other hand, at least four Americans, including one native son, chose Spain rather than independence in any guise.[20] While most Spaniards, many of them without lengthy service, elected to return to their homeland, at least six supported independence, four of them radicado ministers in Lima.[21] In the subsequent chaos that ensured in both Spain and America, however, none of the men would enjoy the serenity that their offices had provided before 1808. Crisis and collapse had replaced Authority.

---

18. That is to say Guatemala, Peru, and Mexico.

19. Rodríguez Aldea (Chile), Irigoyen (Lima), Berasueta (Mexico), and Larreinaga (Guatemala). Larreinaga had lost his appointment upon Ferdinand VII's return in 1814 but apparently regained it for he was serving at independence. J. Antonio Villacorta C., *Prehistoria e historia antigua de Guatemala* (Guatemala, 1938), p. 515.

20. Navarrete, Muñoz y Plaza, Mosquera y Cabrera, Bravo de Rivero (native son).

21. Vilches and Valdés (Guatemala), Valle del Postigo, Palomeque, Osma, and Iglesia (Lima).

Appendix I

Summary: Place of Birth for New Appointees, 1687–1821, by Percentage and Number

| | Creoles | | Peninsulares | | Unknown | | |
	Number	Percentage	Number	Percentage	Number	Percentage	Total
1687-1712	77	51	62	42	11	7	150
1713-1729	8	13	49	82	3	5	60
1730-1750	53	53	46	45	2	2	101
1751-1775	9	13	57	84	2	3	68
1776-1777	3	9	31	91	-	-	34
1778-1808	50	31	112	68	2	1	164
1809-1821	61	52	53	46	2	2	116
Totals	261	38	410	59	22	3	693

The Age of Impotence

| | Creoles | | Peninsulares | | Unknown | | |
	Number	Percentage	Number	Percentage	Number	Percentage	Total
1687-1750	138	44	157	51	16	5	311

The Age of Authority

1751-1808	62	23	200	75	4	2	266
Totals	200	35	357	62	20	3	577

Appendix II

Summary: Audiencia of Birth for Creoles, 1687–1821

	1687-1750	1751-1808	Total	1809-1821	Grand Total
Buenos Aires	—	3	3	5	8
Caracas	—	4	4	4	8
Chile	5	9	14	5	19
Charcas	6	3	9	—	9
Cuzco	—	1	1	—	1
Guadalajara	5	1	6	2	8
Guatemala	1	3	4	3	7
Lima	73	10	83	17	100
Manila	—	—	—	—	—
Mexico	26	5	31	11	42
Panama	6	—	6	—	6
Quito	3	1	4	2	6
Santa Fe de Bogotá	4	11	15	3	18
Santo Domingo	8	10	18	6	24
Unknown	1	1	2	3	5
	138	62	200	61	261

Appendix III

Men Who Purchased Appointments to the American Audiencias

Post: See the note for columns 13 and 14, Appendix IX.

Birthplace: See the note for column 3, Appendix IX.

Native Son: An asterisk indicates the purchaser was to join his home tribunal.

Disp.: For the key to the dispensations granted, see the note for column 17, Appendix IX. In addition, RE means safe from reform. These dispensations are only those that accompanied the sale of the appointment. For later dispensations, see Appendix IX.

Amt. Pd.: In the amount paid column, "p." stands for pesos and "n.a." indicates that the amount paid is unknown. The figure given is the total purchase price unless otherwise noted.

Pd. in Sp.: The amount of the total purchase paid in Spain is given when known.

Pd. in Am.: The amount of the total purchase to be paid in America is given when known.

A. Confirmed Purchasers of Initial Appointments

Year	Name	Post	Birth-place	Native Son	Disp.	Amt. Pd.	Pd. in Sp.	Pd. in Am.
1687	NUÑEZ DE SANABRIA, Miguel	AC LI	LI	*	NA	17,000 p.		
1688	CEBALLOS Y BORJA, Cristóbal de	OS QU	LI			n.a.		
1688	BLANCO REJON, José	FI CH	LI			10,000 p.		
1689	DIAZ DE DURANA, Clemente	OS CS	LI			12,000 p.		
1689	GONZALEZ CARRASCO, Miguel de	OS QU				10,000 p.		
1689	RICAURTE, Juan de	OS QU	SF			n.a.		
1689	RIVAS, Fernando José de	OS QU	*S			8,000 p.		
1689	SOMOZA, Juan de	OS GD				9,000 p.		
1689	CALDERON DE LA BARCA, Miguel	OD ME	S			12,000 p.		
1690	OSORIO ESPINOSA de los MONTEROS, José	OS GD	A			8,100 p.		
1691	MIRANDA VILLAYZAN, José de	OS GD	ME			8,000 p.		
1691	DUARDO, Juan Jerónimo	OS GT	S			8,000 p.		
1692	HIDALGO DE PAREDES, Andrés de	OF CH	CS			11,000 p.		
1693	ALCEDO Y SOTOMAYOR, Carlos de	OS SF	S			10,000 p.		
1693	HIDALGO DE ESCOBAR, Diego de	OF CS	CH			13,000 p.		
1693	PEREZ DE URQUIZU, Juan de[1]	AF LI	LI	*	NA,MN	18,000 p.		
1693	SANTIAGO CONCHA, José de[2] (Marqués de Casa Concha)	AF LI	LI	*	NA,MN	16,000 p.		
1693	SANTIAGO DE CESPEDES Y CAVERO, Juan	OF CS	LI			11,000 p.		
1693	SEGURA Y LARA, Diego de	OS QU				10,000 p.		
1693	ZUÑIGA, Francisco José	OS PA	LI			8,000 p.		
1694	PAREDES Y ARMENDARIZ, Nicolás de	OF LI	LI	*	NA	n.a.		

1. Pérez de Urquizu paid an additional 4,000 pesos for the dispensations.
2. Santiago Concha paid an additional 3,000 pesos for the dispensations.

Year	Name	Post	Birth-place	Native Son	Disp.	Amt. Pd.	Pd. in Sp.	Pd. in Am.
1695	LUNA Y ARIAS, José de	OD ME	GD		MN	16,000 p.		
1695	GRILLO Y RANGEL, Bartolomé	FI PA	PA	*	NA	n.a.		
1695	CORRAL CALVO DE LA BANDA, Juan del	OF CH	CS			8,000 p.		
1699	VASQUEZ DE VELASCO, Pedro	AX LI	LI	*		n.a.		
1699	ARANBURU Y MUÑOZ, Vicente de	AC LI	LI	*	NA	14,000 p.		
1699	NUÑEZ DE ROJAS, Gregorio	OS CS	LI		MN	n.a.		
1699	ROJAS Y ACEVEDO, Francisco de	AF LI	LI	*		n.a.		
1700	VILLAVICENCIO Y CISNEROS, Pedro de	OS LI	LI	*		n.a.		
1700	ANGUITA SANDOVAL, Francisco de	OS ME	ME	*	NA,MN	10,000 p.		
1700	AYALA MARIN, Marcelo de	FF CH	LI			n.a.		
1704	CANAL, Pedro Gregorio de la	OS LI	LI	*	NA	n.a.		
1704	PERALTA Y SANABRIA, Juan	OS LI	LI	*		8,000 p.		
1706	LASTERO SALAZAR, Lorenzo	OS QU	QU	*		6,000 p.	5,000 p.	1,000 p.
1706	CASA ALVARADO, Francisco de	AX ME	S			4,000 p.		
1707	SOLIS VANGO, Juan Prospero de	OS CH	LI		MI	n.a.[3]		
1707	RECAVARREN, Martín de	OS PA	SD			4,000 p.	2,500 p.	1,500 p.
1707	PEÑA Y FLORES, Juan Francisco de la	AX ME	ME	*	NA,MN,RE	12,000 p.	8,000 p.	4,000 p.
1707	VALDES, Juan de	OS ME	ME	*	NA	6,000 p.		
1707	VILLARREAL Y FLORENCIA, Cristóbal de	OS ME	SD			8,000 p.		
1707	SANTOS Y CUENTAS, Francisco Antonio de los	AX LI	LI	*		16,000 p.	12,000 p.	4,000 p.
1707	OLIVAN REBOLLEDO, Juan Manuel de	OS GD	ME			7,000 p.	4,000 p.	3,000 p.
1707	ROBLES Y LORENZANA, Agustín de	AX ME	S		MN	9,000 p.	6,000 p.	3,000 p.
1708	CASTAÑEDA, Diego Francisco de	OS GD	ME			8,000 p.	4,000 p.	4,000 p.
1708	MENA CABALLERO, Juan Antonio de	AX LI	LI	*	NA,MN RE	16,000 p.	16,000 p.	
1708	BRAVO DE RIVERO, Juan	OS CS	LI		MN,RE	12,000 p.	10,000 p.	2,000 p.
1708	ECHAVARRIA ZULOAGA, Juan Bautista de (Marqués de Sotohermoso)	OS LI	LI	*	NA,MN, RE	16,000 p.	12,000 p.	4,000 p.
1708	SANCHEZ DE LA BARREDA, Salvador	OS CH	LI		MN,RE	10,000 p.	8,000 p.	2,000 p.
1708	ZAPATA, Manuel Antonio	FS SF	SF	*	NA,MN	8,000 p.	4,000 p.	4,000 p.
1708	MUNARRIZ, Bartolomé de	AC LI	LI	*	NA,MN	20,000 p.	16,000 p.	4,000 p.
1708	RIVADENEIRA LUNA, Tristán Manuel de	OS ME	ME	*	NA,MN	14,000 p.		
1709	OLAIS Y AROCHE, Esteban	OF QU	LI		MN	n.a.		
1709	ALZAMORA URSINO, José de	OD PA	LI		MN	5,000 p.	3,000 p.	2,000 p.
1709	GALLEGOS, Ignacio	OS CH	LI		MN,RE	10,000 p.	8,000 p.	2,000 p.
1709	ULLOA CALLEJA, Nicolás de	OS GT	ME		MN	6,000 p.		
1709	CLAVIJO Y MEDINA, Diego	FI PA	LI			4,000 p.	2,500 p.	1,500 p.
1710	ECHAVE Y ROJAS, Pedro Antonio	FF LI	LI	*	NA,MN	14,000 p.	10,000 p.	4,000 p.
1710	ARANA, Tomás Ignacio de	OS GT	ME			6,200 p.		
1710	OYANGUREN, Francisco de	FF ME	ME	*	NA	8,000 p.	8,000 p.	
1710	URRUTIA, Fernando de	OS GD	ME			4,000 p.		
1710	RODEZNO MANZOLO, José Nicolás	OS GT	ME		MN,RE	5,000 p.	5,000 p.	
1710	LUGO CORONADO, Felipe Antonio	OS GT	ME		RE	6,000 p.	5,000 p.	1,000 p.
1710	REAL Y QUESADA, Antonio	OS GD	ME		MN	7,000 p.	4,000 p.	3,000 p.

3. Solis Vango's appointment was part of a package in which his father obtained the office of president of the Audiencia of Guadalajara. The total purchase price for the two appointments was 38,000 pesos.

Year	Name	Post	Birth-place	Native Son	Disp.	Amt. Pd.	Pd. in Sp.	Pd. in Am.
1710	GOMEZ TRIGOSSO, Bernardo	FI	PA			4,000 p.	3,000 p.	1,000 p.
1710	TORQUEMADA, Leonardo Fernando de	OS	CH			2,500 p.		
1710	VILLA BARREDA, Gregorio Manuel de	FI	MA	S		2,000 p.	2,000 p.	
1710	PEREZ DELGADO, Bartolomé Patricio	OF	MA	S		2,500 p.	2,000 p.	500 p.
1710	FRANCO VELASQUEZ DE TOLEDO, Agustín	OS	ME	ME	*	NA,MN RE	8,000 p.		
1710	SANCHEZ DE LA BARREDA, Francisco	OS	CH	LI		MN	500 p.[4]		
1710	VEQUENILLA Y SANDOVAL, Juan de la	AX	ME	ME	*	NA,MN RE	8,000 p.	7,000 p.	1,000 p.
1710	MIRONES Y BENAVENTE, Manuel Isidro de	OS	PA	LI		MI	6,000 p.	4,000 p.	2,000 p.
1710	SAGARDIA Y PALENCIA, Francisco	OS	CS	LI		MN,MI	16,000 p.	10,000 p.	6,000 p.
1711	LARREA ZURBANO, Juan Dionisio	OS	QU	SF		MN,HP[5]	6,000 p.		
1711	GOMEZ DE ANDRADE, Pedro	OS	PA	LI		RE	n.a.		
1711	BARBADILLO VICTORIA, Francisco de	AX	ME	S			2,000 p.		
1711	CAVERO DE FRANCIA, Alvaro	OS	LI	LI	*	NA,MN	16,000 p.	12,000 p.	4,000 p.
1711	SANCHEZ DE ALCAZAR, Pedro	AX	ME	ME	*	NA,MN	9,000 p.		
1711	SANTAELLA Y MELGAREJO, Ambrosio Tomás de	OF	GT	SD			7,000 p.		
1711	GOMENDIO URRUTIA, Domingo de	OS	GT	S			7,000 p.		
1712	SANCHEZ DE ORELLANA, Juan Bautista	OS	QU	QU	*	NA	6,000 P.		
1733	BRAVO DE RIVERO, Pedro	OS	LI	LI	*	NA	20,000 p.		
1736	BORDA Y ECHEVARRIA, Manuel Antonio de	AX	LI	LI	*	NA	21,000 p.	21,000 p.	
1740	TRASLAVIÑA OYAGUE, José Clemente de	OF	CH	LI		MN	17,000 p.		
1740	MARTINEZ PATIÑO, Juan José	OS	GT	S			8,000 p.		
1740	TAGLE BRACHO, José de	OD	CS	LI		MI	16,000 p.		
1740	CALVO DE LA PUERTA, Sebastián	OS	GD	SD			8,000 p.		
1740	CARFANGER Y ARTIEDA, Juan Romualdo	OS	QU	LI			7,000 p.		
1740	URQUIZU Y IBAÑEZ, Gaspar	OS	LI	LI	*	NA	21,000 p.		
1740	BAHAMONDE Y TABOADA, Juan Bautista	OS	PA	LI			6,000 p.		
1741	SANTAELLA Y MELGAREJO, Ambrosio Eugenio de	AX	ME	GT		MN	17,500 p.	17,500 p.	
1741	RODRIGUEZ DE TORO, José	OD	ME	SD			15,000 p.		
1742	APARICIO DEL MANZANO, Juan	FI	GD	SD			16,000 p.		
1744	OLAVIDE, Pablo Antonio de	OS	LI	LI	*		20,000 p.		
1745	ZURBARAN Y ALLENDE, Manuel	OD	CS	LI		MN,HP	21,000 p.	21,000 p.	
1745	SANTIAGO CONCHA, Melchor de	OD	CS	LI		MN,HP	19,000 p.	19,000 p.	
1746	TAGLE BRACHO, Pedro de	OS	CS	LI		MN	40,000 p.		40,000 p.
1746	SALAS, José Perfecto de	FI	CH	CS		MN,HP	n.a.		
1746	SANTA CRUZ Y CENTENO, Luis de	OS	QU	LI		MN,HP	10,000 p.	10,000 p.	
1746	SANZ MERINO, Antonio	OF	PA	PA	*	NA	12,000 p.	8,000 p.	4,000 p.
1746	BRAVO DE CASTILLA, Pedro José	OS	LI	LI	*	NA,HP	20,000 p.		
1747	PUENTE Y IBAÑEZ, Juan José de la (Marqués de Corpa)	AX	LI	LI	*	NA,MN, HP	27,000 p.		
1747	PEREZ BUELTA, Gaspar Francisco	OS	PA	PA	*	NA,MN, HP	19,000 p.	11,000 p.	8,000 p.

4. For the nominal sum of 500 pesos, Francisco obtained the appointment originally granted to his deceased brother Salvador in 1708. This enabled the crown to retain the original payment of 10,000 pesos.

5. Larrea also received a totally unnecessary dispensation for "having been born in the Indies."

Year	Name	Post	Birth-place	Native Son	Disp.	Amt. Pd.	Pd. in Sp.	Pd. in Am.
1747	VERDUGO DEL CASTILLO, Juan Antonio	OS CH	CH	*	NA,MN, HP	20,000 p.	20,000 p.	
1747	VEGA Y BARCENA, Pablo de la	OS CS	LI		MN,HP	34,000 p.	10,000 p.	24,000 p.
1747	LOPEZ PORTILLA, Francisco de	OS GD	GD	*	NA	11,000 p.	7,000 p.	4,000 p.
1748	VEGA Y BARCENA, Manuel de la	OS QU	LI		HP	20,000 p.		20,000 p.
1748	RIVADENEIRA Y BARRIENTOS, Antonio Joaquín de	OS GD	ME		RE	13,000 p.	5,000 p.	8,000 p.
1748	NAVARRO, Juan Romualdo	OS QU	QU	*	NA,MN	20,000 p.		20,000 p.
1748	GORENA Y BEYRA, Manuel de	OS LI	CH		MN,HP	24,000 p.		
1748	PEY Y RUIS, Juan Francisco	OS SF	S		MN	24,000 p.		24,000 p.
1748	MARTINEZ DE ALDUNATE, Domingo de	OS CH	CH	*	NA,MN, HP,CM	20,000 p.		
1749	ORRANTIA, Domingo de	OS LI	LI	*	NA,MN, MI,HP, RE	47,500 p.	5,000 p.	42,500 p.
1749	GOMEZ ALGARIN, Francisco	OS GD	S		RE	13,000 p.	8,000 p.	5,000 p.
1749	LOPEZ DE LISPERGUER, José de	OS CS	CH		HP,CM RE	27,600 p.	7,000 p.	20,600 p.
1749	LLANO Y VALDES, Félix de	OS CS	LI		RE	22,000 p.	22,000 p.	
1749	ORBEA Y ARANDIA, Diego José de	AX LI	LI	*	NA,MN HP	41,400 p.	3,000 p.	never pd. bal.
1750	GARZA FALCON, José Manuel de la	OS GD	GD	*	NA,MN	14,350 p.	5,000 p.	9,350 p.
1750	ECHEVERZ, Pedro Antonio de	OS LI	PA		HP	n.a.		
1750	MANSILLA ARIAS DE SAAVEDRA, Manuel de	AX LI	LI	*	NA,HP CM	35,400 p.	15,000 p.	never pd. bal.
1750	FUENTE Y VILLALTA, Juan José de la (Conde de Fuente Roja)	OS CH	LI			22,800 p.	6,800 p.	16,000 p.
1750	HURTADO DE MENDOZA, Gregorio (Conde de Cumbres Altas)	OS QU	LI			19,810 p.	14,110 p.	5,700 p.
					TOTAL	1,399,160 p.		

B. Probable Purchasers of Initial or Later Audiencia Appointments

Year	Name	Post	Birth-place	Native Son	Disp.
1688	CALVO DOMONTE, Luis Antonio	OS CS	CS	*	MN
1688	LAYA BOLIVAR, Juan de	OD PA	PA	*	NA
1700	CASTILLO, Ignacio Antonio de	OS CS	LI		MN
1700	VALVERDE CONTRERAS Y ALARCON, José de	OF CH	LI		
1705	SORIA VELASQUEZ, Gerónimo de	OD ME	ME	*	
1706	DIEZ DE BRACAMONTE, Juan de	OS ME	ME	*	
1710	ROJAS Y ACEVEDO, Francisco de (A confirmed initial purchaser, this would be a later purchase.)	AC LI	LI	*	
1710	CERECEDA Y GIRON, Sebastián de (A judge already serving a post won by merit.)	OS ME	S		RE
1711	TERREROS OCHOA, Antonio	OS ME	ME	*	NA,MN
1730	ORTIZ DE FORONDA, Francisco	FR LI	LI	*	NA,MN
1730	CAMPO Y ZARATE, Clemente del	AC ME	CS		MN
1741	GIRALDES Y PINO, José Esteban	OS CS	CS	*	NA
1742	MALO DE VILLAVICENCIO, Félix	OF ME	GD		
1744	QUEREJAZU Y MOLLINEDO, Antonio Hermenegildo de[6]	OS LI	LI	*	NA,MN HP

6. Querejazu's brother Ignacio Antonio had purchased a futura for the presidency of Charcas in 1730 for 22,000 pesos. He died before serving, however, and Antonio filled that post.

C. Confirmed Purchases of Promotions by Audiencia Ministers Already Serving or Having Served

Year	Name	Post	Birth-place	Native Son	Disp.	Amt. Pd.	Pd. in Sp.	Pd. in Am.
1697	OSORIO ESPINOSA DE LOS MONTEROS, José	OS ME	A			10,000 p.		
1708	NUÑEZ DE ROJAS, Gregorio	OD CS	LI			7,000 p.		
1710	CHIRINO VANDEVAL, Nicolás	AX ME	SD			5,000 p.		
1710	OLIVAN REBOLLEDO, Juan Manuel de	OS ME	ME	*		6,000 p.		
1711	CASTAÑEDA, Diego Francisco de	AX ME	ME	*	NA	5,000 p.		
1711	CALDERON DE LA BARCA, Juan Fernando	OS LI	S			6,000 p.		
	(Already serving as Alcalde del Crimen, Calderón turned down a promotion to Spain and paid to remain as oidor in Lima)							
1741	TAGLE BRACHO, José de	OS LI	LI	*	MN,HP	8,000 p.		
1745	ZURBARAN Y ALLENDE, Manuel	OS LI	LI	*	MN,HP	12,000 p.		
1748	MIRONES Y BENAVENTE, Manuel Isidro de	OS LI	LI	*		8,000 p.		
						67,000 p.		

Appendix IV

Universities Attended by Audiencia Ministers, by Periods*

Period	American Schools			SA	AL	Spanish Schools			Other
	LI	ME	Other			VD	GR	SE	
1687-1712	40	26	2	22	11	5	3	1	2
			(1-SF)						(1-ON)
			(1-QU)						(1-BA)
1713-1729	7	1	0	13	16	4	3	4	2
									(1-SN)
									(1-HU)
1730-1750	35	11	4	13	10	9	3	5	3
			(1-HA)						(2-HU)
			(1-SF)						(1-SN)
			(1-CZ)						
			(1-GT)						
1751-1775	3	5	2-SF	16	11	8	6	3	10
									(4-HU)
									(3-SN)
									(1-OR)
									(1-ZA)
									(1-OV)
1776-1777	0	1	2	9	3	6	4	3	4
			(1-SF)						(2-SN)
			(1-CZ)						(1-OM)
									(1-VA)
1778-1808	15	8	20	15	20	10	27	6	22
			(9-SF)						(5-VA)
			(2-CH)						(3-SN)
			(3-CA)						(1-JA)
			(3-CS)						(4-HU)
			(3-HA)						(1-ZA)
									(2-OR)
									(3-OV)
									(1-CE)
									(1-AS)
									(1-SN)
1809-1821	21	9	19	1	9	5	8	7	12
			(8-CH)						(3-OV)
			(3-GT)						(2-VA)
			(3-SD)						(2-CE)
			(2-CS)						(1-HU)
			(2-CA)						(1-TO)
			(1-QU)						(2-SN)
									(1-HM)

*Many men attended more than one university; in such cases either the most prestigious, or that carrying colegio affiliation is shown—usually these are the same. All universities attended are listed in Appendix IX. See note 5, Appendix IX for a key to the abbreviations.

Appendix V

Composition of the Audiencias by Place of Birth, 1687–1820

	MEXICO				GUATEMALA				GUADALAJARA				SANTA DOMINGO				MANILA			
	N	C	P	U	N	C	P	U	N	C	P	U	N	C	P	U	N	C	P	U
1687	-	1	9	4	-	1	5	-	-	-	2	3	-	-	5	-	-	1	4	1
1690	-	1	11	4	-	1	5	-	-	1	2	4	-	2	3	1	-	1	4	-
1695	-	2	11	3	-	1	5	1	-	2	1	2	-	1	3	2	-	1	5	-
1700	1	4	8	2	-	1	4	1	-	1	1	2	-	1	4	-	-	-	6	-
1705	1	3	11	-	-	1	2	1	-	1	3	1	-	1	5	-	-	-	5	-
1710	9	4	13	-	-	4	2	1	-	4	2	-	-	-	5	-	-	-	5	-
1712	12	4	10	-	-	5	3	1	-	3	2	-	-	-	5	-	-	-	5	-
1713	12	3	10	-	-	5	3	1	-	3	2	-	-	-	6	-	-	-	5	-
1715	11	2	8	-	-	5	3	1	-	3	2	-	-	-	5	-	-	-	4	-
1720	3	2	5	1	-	4	2	1	-	2	2	-	-	-	4	-	-	-	5	-
1725	3	1	9	2	-	3	4	-	-	1	3	-	-	-	5	-	-	-	4	-
1729	3	1	8	1	-	3	3	-	-	1	4	-	-	-	4	-	-	-	6	-
1730	3	2	8	1	-	3	3	-	-	1	4	-	-	1	3	1	-	-	5	-
1735	3	2	9	-	-	3	3	-	-	1	4	-	-	1	4	-	-	2	5	-
1739	1	2	15	-	-	2	3	-	-	1	3	-	-	2	4	-	-	3	4	-
1740	-	2	14	-	-	2	3	1	-	1	3	-	-	2	4	-	-	3	4	-
1745	-	4	14	-	-	-	4	1	-	2	3	-	-	2	2	1	-	3	3	-
1750	-	4	11	-	-	-	6	-	2	3	2	-	-	2	3	-	-	2	4	-
1755	1	6	11	-	-	1	5	-	2	-	3	-	-	1	4	-	-	1	4	-
1760	1	6	7	-	-	1	4	-	2	-	3	-	-	1	4	-	-	1	5	-
1762	1	6	7	-	-	1	4	-	2	-	3	-	-	1	4	-	-	-	5	-
1765	2	6	6	-	-	2	3	-	-	-	5	-	-	1	4	-	-	-	6	-
1770	2	5	7	-	-	1	4	1	-	-	5	-	-	1	4	-	-	1	5	-
1775	1	2	11	-	-	1	5	-	-	1	4	-	-	-	5	-	-	-	6	-
1777	1	4	13	-	-	1	7	1	-	1	7	-	-	-	8	-	-	-	8	-
1780	1	3	14	-	-	2	6	-	-	2	6	-	-	1	7	-	-	-	8	-
1785	1	2	16	-	-	2	6	-	-	2	6	-	-	1	7	-	-	1	7	-
1790	1	2	16	-	-	2	6	-	-	3	5	-	-	2	3	-	-	1	6	-
1795	1	4	14	-	-	2	4	-	-	1	5	-	-	2	3	-	-	-	5	-
1800	2	4	13	-	-	1	6	-	-	2	4	-	-	2	3	-	-	-	5	-
1805	3	2	13	-	-	1	6	-	-	2	5	-	-	1	3	1	-	-	7	-
1808	3	2	12	-	-	1	6	-	-	3	4	-	-	1	2	2	-	-	7	-
1810	2	2	11	-	-	2	5	-	-	2	4	-	2	2	2	-	-	-	7	-
1815	-	5	12	-	-	4	2	1	-	3	4	-	1	2	3	-	-	1	5	-
1820	1	5	10	-	-	2	3	1	-	3	5	-	1	4	5	-	-	2	2	-

	LIMA				CHARCAS				CHILE				SANTA FE				QUITO			
	N	C	P	U	N	C	P	U	N	C	P	U	N	C	P	U	N	C	P	U
1687	1	2	10	2	-	2	3	-	-	4	1	-	-	1	4	-	-	3	1	1
1690	2	1	10	1	1	2	4	-	-	2	4	-	-	2	5	-	-	3	1	4
1695	5	1	8	-	1	3	3	-	-	3	4	-	-	1	5	-	-	2	1	4
1700	9	-	8	-	1	4	2	-	-	5	4	-	-	2	4	-	-	3	-	2
1705	6	1	10	-	1	2	2	-	-	4	2	-	-	4	2	-	-	3	1	2
1710	10	1	8	-	-	6	-	-	-	6	1	1	1	3	2	-	1	4	3	-
1712	10	1	7	-	-	5	1	-	-	5	-	1	1	2	2	-	2	5	3	-
1713	10	1	6	-	-	5	1	-	-	6	-	1	1	2	2	-	2	4	3	-
1715	9	1	6	-	-	5	1	-	-	5	-	-	1	2	3	-	1	4	4	-
1720	5	-	7	-	-	4	1	-	-	5	-	-	-	1	4	-	-	2	4	-

	LIMA				CHARCAS				CHILE				SANTA FE				QUITO			
	N	C	P	U	N	C	P	U	N	C	P	U	N	C	P	U	N	C	P	U
1725	7	–	8	–	–	6	–	–	–	5	1	–	–	1	4	–	–	2	4	–
1729	5	–	8	–	–	6	–	–	–	5	1	–	–	1	4	–	–	2	4	–
1730	6	–	9	–	–	6	–	–	–	5	1	–	–	1	3	–	–	1	5	–
1735	7	–	8	–	–	6	1	–	–	5	1	–	–	–	5	–	–	1	4	–
1739	8	–	8	–	–	4	2	–	–	3	2	–	–	1	5	–	–	2	3	–
1740	9	–	8	–	–	5	2	–	–	3	2	–	–	1	4	–	–	3	3	–
1745	12	–	5	–	1	3	2	–	–	2	3	–	–	2	3	–	–	3	2	–
1750	13	2	3	–	1	7	1	–	2	4	2	–	–	1	6	–	1	5	1	–
1755	12	4	3	–	1	6	2	–	2	3	2	–	–	1	7	–	1	5	1	–
1760	11	3	2	–	1	5	1	–	2	4	2	–	–	1	5	–	1	5	3	–
1762	11	3	2	–	1	5	1	–	2	4	2	–	–	1	5	–	1	4	3	–
1765	10	3	2	–	1	3	2	–	2	4	2	–	–	1	5	–	1	3	3	–
1770	7	3	3	–	1	3	2	–	2	3	2	–	–	1	5	–	1	2	3	1
1775	6	2	4	–	–	3	2	–	2	–	3	–	–	2	4	–	–	3	2	1
1777	6	1	2	–	–	2	5	–	–	1	7	–	1	1	5	–	–	2	5	1
1780	5	2	8	–	–	1	7	–	–	4	4	–	–	1	8	–	–	2	5	1
1785	4	2	9	–	–	2	6	–	–	4	2	–	–	1	8	–	–	–	4	–
1790	4	2	8	–	–	4	2	–	–	4	2	–	–	1	5	–	–	1	5	–
1795	2	3	9	–	–	3	4	–	2	3	2	–	2	1	6	–	–	2	4	–
1800	2	1	12	–	–	3	4	–	2	2	2	–	–	2	5	–	–	1	5	–
1805	1	1	13	–	–	1	5	–	2	1	3	–	–	3	5	–	–	1	5	–
1808	1	2	11	–	–	2	3	–	2	1	3	–	–	2	5	–	–	–	5	–
1810	2	3	11	–	–	3	3	–	2	1	3	–	–	3	5	–	–	4	1	–
1815	4	1	12	–	–	3	3	–	2	2	2	–	–	1	2	–	–	2	4	–
1820	2	2	13	–	–	4	3	–	1	1	2	–	–	4	3	–	–	2	6	–

	PANAMA			
	N	C	P	U
1687	–	3	2	–
1690	–	2	1	–
1695	1	2	1	1
1700	1	1	1	1
1705	–	1	1	–
1710	–	4	1	1
1712	–	5	1	1
1713	–	5	1	1
1715	–	5	1	1
1720	–	–	–	–
1725	–	2	2	–
1729	–	3	2	–
1730	–	3	2	–
1735	–	2	2	–
1739	–	1	3	1
1740	–	2	3	1
1745	–	1	3	1
1750	2	–	3	–

	BUENOS AIRES				CARACAS				CUZCO			
	N	C	P	U	N	C	P	U	N	C	P	U
1785	–	–	6	–	–	–	–	–	–	–	–	–
1790	–	–	6	–	–	–	4	1	–	–	5	–
1795	–	–	8	–	–	–	4	1	–	–	5	–
1800	–	–	8	–	–	1	4	1	–	–	5	–
1805	–	2	6	–	–	2	4	–	–	–	5	–
1808	–	2	6	–	–	2	3	–	–	1	4	–
1810	–	2	6	–	–	3	1	3	–	2	3	–
1815	–	–	–	–	1	2	3	–	–	4	3	–
1820	–	–	–	–	–	1	4	–	–	3	4	–

Key:
N: Native son.
C: Creole appointed to serve outside his home district.
P: Peninsular
U: Unknown place of birth.
Adding the figures in each of the four columns for a given year and tribunal will provide the total number of men holding appointments at the end of the year. The figures represent the "paper totals" as seen in Madrid rather than men actually serving.

Appendix VI

Overview of the Composition of the Audiencias, 1687–1820

	New Spain					Peru					Grand Total								
Year	NS	CR	PE	UN	Total	NS	CR	PE	UN	Total	NS	(%)	CR	(%)	PE	(%)	UN	(%)	Total
1687	--	3	25	7	35	1	15	21	3	40	1	1	18	24	46	62	10	13	75
1690	--	6	25	9	40	3	12	25	5	45	3	3	18	21	50	60	14	16	85
1695	--	7	25	8	40	7	12	22	5	46	7	8	19	22	47	55	13	15	86
1700	1	7	23	5	36	11	15	19	3	48	12	14	22	26	42	50	8	10	84
1705	1	6	26	2	35	7	15	18	2	42	8	10	21	27	44	57	4	6	77
1710	9	12	27	1	49	12	24	15	2	53	21	21	36	35	42	41	3	3	102
1712	12	12	25	1	50	13	23	14	2	52	25	24	35	34	39	38	3	4	102
1713	12	11	26	1	50	13	23	13	2	51	25	25	34	34	39	40	3	3	101
1715	11	10	22	1	44	11	22	15	1	49	22	24	32	35	37	40	2	2	93
1720	3	8	18	2	31	5	12	16	--	33	8	12	20	32	34	53	2	3	64
1725	3	5	25	2	35	7	16	19	--	42	10	13	21	27	44	57	2	3	77
1729	3	5	25	1	34	5	17	19	--	41	8	11	22	29	44	59	1	1	75
1730	3	7	23	2	35	6	16	20	--	42	9	11	23	30	43	56	2	3	77
1735	3	9	25	--	37	7	14	21	1	43	10	13	23	28	46	58	1	2	80
1739	1	10	29	--	40	8	11	23	1	43	9	11	21	25	52	63	1	1	83
1740	--	10	28	1	39	9	14	22	1	46	9	11	24	28	50	58	2	3	85
1745	--	11	26	2	39	13	11	18	1	43	13	16	22	27	44	53	3	4	82
1750	2	11	26	--	39	19	19	16	--	54	21	23	30	32	42	45	--	--	93
1755	3	9	27	--	39	16	19	15	--	50	19	21	28	32	42	47	--	--	89
1760	3	9	23	--	35	15	18	13	--	46	18	22	27	33	36	44	--	--	81
1762	3	8	23	--	34	15	17	13	--	45	18	23	25	32	36	46	--	--	79
1765	2	9	24	--	35	14	14	14	--	42	16	21	23	30	38	49	--	--	77
1770	2	8	25	1	36	11	12	15	1	39	13	17	20	27	40	53	2	3	75
1775	1	4	31	--	36	8	13	12	1	34	9	13	17	24	43	61	1	1	70
1777	1	6	43	--	50	7	7	24	1	39	8	9	13	15	67	75	1	1	89
1780	1	8	41	--	50	6	10	32	1	49	7	7	18	18	73	73	1	1	99
1785	1	8	42	--	51	5	9	35	--	49	6	6	17	17	77	77	--	--	100
1790	1	10	36	--	47	7	10	42	1	60	8	7	20	19	78	73	1	1	107
1795	1	9	31	--	41	6	12	42	1	61	7	6	21	21	73	72	1	1	102
1800	2	9	31	--	42	4	10	45	1	60	6	6	19	19	76	75	1	1	102
1805	3	6	34	1	44	3	11	46	--	60	6	6	17	16	80	77	1	1	104
1808	3	7	31	2	43	3	12	40	--	55	6	6	19	19	71	72	2	2	98
1810	4	8	29	--	41	4	21	33	3	61	8	8	29	28	62	61	3	3	102
1815	1	15	26	1	43	7	15	29	--	51	8	9	30	32	55	59	1	1	94
1820	2	16	25	1	44	3	17	35	--	55	5	5	33	33	60	61	1	1	99

Key:
NS: Native sons
CR: Creoles serving outside of home province
PE: Peninsulares
UN: Unknown place of birth

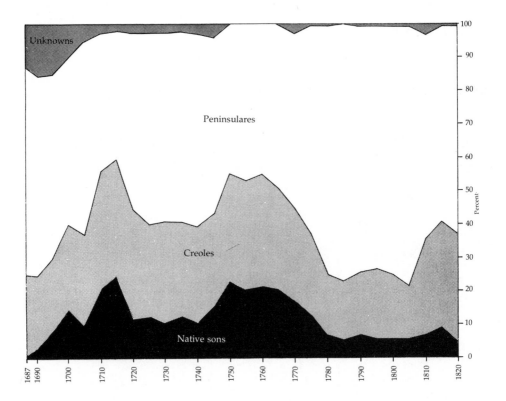

Appendix VII

Index of Local Influence in the American Audiencias[1]

Key:
N: Native son
5+: Ministers with 5 years or more residence in the district (excludes native sons)
(T): Number of ministers in column 5+ with confirmed local ties
0-4: Ministers with less than 5 years of residence in the district
(t): Number of ministers in column 0-4 with confirmed local ties

	MEXICO					MEXICO: CIVIL SALA[2]					GUATEMALA				
	N	5+	(T)	0-4	(t)	N	5+	(T)	0-4	(t)	N	5+	(T)	0-4	(t)
1687	–	7	(–)	6	(–)	–	5	(–)	2	(–)	–	2	(–)	3	(–)
1690	–	7	(–)	7	(1)	–	7	(–)	2	(–)	–	2	(–)	4	(–)
1695	–	6	(2)	4	(–)	–	3	(1)	3	(–)	–	4	(–)	4	(–)
1700	–	6	(2)	8	(2)	–	4	(1)	5	(2)	–	2	(–)	4	(–)
1705	1	9	(4)	3	(1)	1	7	(3)	1	(1)	–	4	(–)	–	(–)
1710	6	10	(5)	6	(4)	5	6	(3)	3	(2)	–	4	(–)	–	(–)
1712	12	9	(4)	5	(3)	8	6	(4)	2	(1)	–	4	(–)	5	(1)
1715	11	9	(5)	1	(–)	7	5	(3)	–	(1)	–	4	(–)	5	(1)
1720	3	2	(1)	1	(–)	2	1	(1)	–	(–)	–	7	(1)	–	(–)
1725	3	2	(1)	8	(1)	2	1	(1)	6	(–)	–	3	(1)	3	(–)
1729	3	6	(1)	4	(2)	2	5	(1)	2	(2)	–	6	(1)	–	(–)
1730	3	7	(2)	4	(2)	2	6	(2)	1	(1)	–	6	(1)	–	(–)
1735	3	7	(4)	4	(1)	2	6	(3)	1	(1)	–	5	(1)	–	(–)
1740	–	7	(2)	7	(2)	–	4	(1)	5	(2)	–	3	(1)	1	(–)
1745	–	12	(6)	6	(5)	–	8	(4)	4	(2)	–	–	(–)	3	(–)
1750	–	14	(6)	1	(–)	–	10	(5)	–	(–)	–	2	(–)	4	(–)
1755	1	14	(7)	1	(–)	–	10	(4)	–	(–)	–	4	(–)	2	(–)
1760	1	12	(7)	1	(–)	1	7	(4)	–	(–)	–	3	(–)	2	(–)
1765	2	9	(7)	3	(–)	2	6	(4)	1	(–)	–	3	(1)	2	(–)
1770	2	9	(6)	3	(1)	2	6	(3)	1	(–)	–	3	(1)	3	(–)
1775	1	6	(3)	7	(–)	1	6	(3)	2	(–)	–	–	(–)	6	(–)
1777	1	5	(4)	11	(–)	1	3	(2)	7	(–)	–	–	(–)	8	(–)
1780	1	4	(2)	13	(–)	1	2	(–)	7	(–)	–	1	(–)	7	(–)
1785	1	12	(1)	5	(1)	1	10	(–)	–	(–)	–	4	(–)	4	(–)
1790	1	11	(1)	7	(–)	1	10	(–)	2	(–)	–	4	(–)	3	(–)
1795	1	11	(1)	7	(1)	1	10	(–)	1	(–)	–	3	(–)	3	(–)
1800	2	15	(1)	2	(–)	1	11	(–)	–	(–)	–	3	(–)	4	(–)
1805	3	10	(–)	5	(–)	2	9	(–)	–	(–)	–	2	(–)	5	(–)
1808	3	7	(–)	7	(–)	3	7	(–)	1	(–)	–	1	(–)	7	(–)
1810	2	8	(–)	6	(–)	2	5	(–)	–	(–)	–	–	(–)	8	(–)
1815	–	6	(–)	11	(1)	–	6	(–)	2	(–)	–	3	(–)	4	(–)
1820	1	10	(1)	5	(–)	–	9	(–)	–	(–)	–	2	(–)	4	(–)

Notes:
1. The figures reflect men actually serving at the end of each year given. As in the table "Composition of the Audiencias by Place of Birth, 1687-1820," the figures are based on presently available data and may change slightly with further research, particularly for the early years.
2. The civil chambers for both Mexico and Lima were more important than the criminal because of their involvement with cases concerning economic interests and other high matters. Sitting with the chief executive, they also functioned as a *real acuerdo*. A civil chamber consisted of the oidores and the fiscal civil.
3. In 1687 the audiencia had been suspended for cause; five men had been assigned, but none had arrived.
4. The Audiencia of Panama was suppressed during the years 1718-1722.

GUADALAJARA · SANTO DOMINGO · MANILA

	GUADALAJARA					SANTO DOMINGO					MANILA			
	N	5+	(T)	0-4	(t)	N	5+	(T)	0-4	(t)	N	5+	(T)	0-4	(t)
1687	-	2	(-)	4	(-)	-	-	(-)	5	(-)	Note 3.				
1690	-	4	(-)	2	(-)	-	1	(-)	4	(-)	-	-	(-)	5	(-)
1695	-	4	(-)	2	(-)	-	3	(-)	1	(-)	-	4	(-)	-	(-)
1700	-	5	(-)	-	(-)	1	1	(-)	1	(-)	-	1	(-)	4	(-)
1705	-	3	(-)	-	(-)	1	1	(-)	4	(-)	-	2	(-)	-	(-)
1710	-	1	(1)	5	(1)	-	5	(-)	1	(-)	-	1	(-)	3	(-)
1712	-	3	(1)	2	(1)	-	5	(-)	1	(-)	-	3	(-)	2	(-)
1715	-	5	(2)	-	(-)	-	5	(-)	-	(-)	-	3	(-)	1	(-)
1720	-	4	(1)	-	(-)	-	2	(-)	2	(-)	-	2	(-)	-	(-)
1725	-	1	(-)	3	(-)	-	2	(-)	3	(-)	-	1	(-)	3	(-)

	GUADALAJARA					SANTO DOMINGO					MANILA			
	N	5+	(T)	0-4	(t)	N	5+	(T)	0-4	(t)	N	5+	(T)	0-4)	(t)
1729	-	3	(-)	2	(-)	-	1	(-)	3	(-)	-	4	(-)	1	(-)
1730	-	4	(-)	1	(-)	-	1	(-)	4	(-)	-	3	(-)	2	(-)
1735	-	3	(-)	2	(-)	-	4	(-)	1	(-)	-	4	(-)	1	(1)
1740	-	2	(-)	-	(-)	-	4	(-)	1	(-)	-	4	(1)	2	(1)
1745	-	2	(-)	3	(-)	-	1	(-)	4	(-)	-	2	(2)	2	(-)
1750	1	4	(-)	2	(-)	-	3	(-)	2	(-)	-	3	(2)	1	(-)
1755	2	1	(-)	2	(-)	-	3	(-)	2	(-)	-	2	(1)	2	(-)
1760	2	2	(-)	1	(1)	-	4	(-)	1	(-)	-	3	(1)	3	(-)
1765	-	2	(1)	3	(-)	-	2	(-)	3	(-)	-	4	(1)	1	(-)
1770	-	5	(2)	-	(-)	-	3	(-)	2	(-)	-	-	(-)	5	(-)
1775	-	-	(-)	5	(-)	-	1	(1)	4	(1)	-	3	(-)	5	(-)
1777	-	1	(-)	7	(-)	-	2	(2)	6	(-)	-	1	(-)	7	(-)
1780	-	3	(1)	5	(-)	-	1	(-)	7	(-)	-	1	(-)	7	(-)
1785	-	5	(1)	3	(-)	-	5	(1)	3	(-)	-	6	(1)	2	(-)
1790	-	2	(-)	6	(-)	-	3	(1)	2	(-)	-	1	(-)	5	(-)
1795	-	2	(-)	4	(-)	-	4	(1)	1	(-)	-	3	(1)	1	(-)
1800	-	2	(-)	4	(-)	-	4	(-)	1	(-)	-	1	(1)	3	(-)
1805	-	2	(-)	5	(-)	-	3	(-)	2	(-)	-	3	(-)	2	(-)
1808	-	2	(-)	5	(-)	-	2	(-)	3	(-)	-	4	(-)	3	(-)
1810	-	3	(-)	3	(-)	2	2	(-)	2	(-)	-	4	(-)	3	(-)
1815	-	4	(-)	3	(-)	1	-	(-)	4	(-)	-	4	(-)	1	(-)
1820	-	5	(-)	2	(-)	1	2	(-)	7	(-)	-	2	(-)	2	(-)

LIMA · LIMA CIVIL SALA · CHARCAS

	LIMA					LIMA CIVIL SALA					CHARCAS			
	N	5+	(T)	0-4	(t)	N	5+	(T)	0-4	(t)	N	5+	(T)	0-4	(t)
1687	-	9	(5)	4	(-)	-	7	(3)	2	(-)	-	1	(-)	3	(-)
1690	1	7	(3)	4	(1)	-	7	(3)	3	(-)	1	-	(-)	4	(-)
1695	4	6	(2)	3	(1)	2	6	(2)	-	(-)	1	3	(-)	3	(-)
1700	5	8	(2)	-	(-)	2	7	(2)	-	(-)	1	4	(-)	-	(-)
1705	6	4	(1)	4	(2)	4	3	(1)	3	(1)	-	2	( )	-	(-)
1710	9	6	(4)	2	(2)	6	4	(3)	1	(1)	-	2	(1)	3	(1)
1712	10	7	(4)	1	(1)	7	5	(3)	1	(1)	-	3	(1)	2	(2)
1715	9	7	(5)	1	(-)	6	6	(4)	-	(-)	-	4	(2)	2	(1)
1720	5	3	(3)	2	(-)	4	2	(2)	-	(-)	-	5	(3)	-	(-)
1725	7	1	(1)	7	(3)	6	1	(1)	3	(1)	-	3	(2)	3	(-)
1729	4	5	(3)	1	(-)	3	4	(2)	-	(-)	-	4	(2)	2	(-)
1730	5	6	(3)	1	(-)	4	4	(2)	1	(-)	-	5	(1)	1	(-)
1735	6	6	(3)	2	(1)	4	4	(2)	1	(-)	-	6	(1)	1	(-)
1740	8	8	(6)	-	(-)	4	5	(4)	-	(-)	-	5	(1)	1	(-)
1745	10	4	(3)	-	(-)	6	2	(2)	-	(-)	1	3	(-)	1	(-)
1750	13	2	(2)	3	(2)	9	1	(1)	1	(1)	1	3	(1)	5	(4)
1755	12	6	(4)	-	(-)	9	3	(3)	2	(-)	1	7	(4)	1	(-)
1760	11	5	(3)	-	(-)	8	3	(3)	-	(-)	1	5	(3)	1	(-)
1765	10	5	(3)	-	(-)	7	3	(3)	-	(-)	1	5	(3)	-	(-)
1770	7	4	(3)	2	(-)	3	3	(2)	1	(-)	1	3	(3)	2	(-)
1775	6	4	(3)	1	(-)	3	2	(2)	1	(-)	-	3	(2)	2	(-)
1777	6	3	(3)	1	(-)	5	3	(3)	2	(-)	-	1	(1)	7	(-)
1780	5	-	(-)	8	(-)	5	-	(-)	5	(-)	-	-	(-)	8	(-)
1785	5	5	(-)	3	(-)	5	3	(-)	-	(-)	-	6	(-)	2	(-)
1790	5	5	(-)	5	(-)	5	5	(-)	-	(-)	-	1	(-)	5	(-)
1795	3	9	(1)	3	(-)	3	6	(1)	1	(-)	-	5	(-)	2	(-)

	LIMA					LIMA CIVIL SALA					CHARCAS			
	N	5+	(T)	0-4	(t)	N	5+	(T)	0-4	(t)	N	5+	(T)	0-4	(t)
1800	1	10	(1)	2	(-)	1	7	(1)	1	(-)	-	5	(-)	2	(-)
1805	1	10	(4)	2	(-)	-	4	(4)	5	(-)	-	5	(-)	1	(-)
1808	1	9	(4)	4	(1)	1	9	(4)	-	(-)	-	2	(-)	3	(-)
1810	1	9	(4)	2	(-)	1	8	(4)	-	(-)	-	2	(-)	4	(-)
1815	2	10	(2)	1	(-)	2	8	(1)	-	(-)	-	2	(-)	4	(-)
1820	2	8	(2)	6	(-)	1	11	(2)	-	(2)	-	4	(-)	3	(-)

	CHILE					SANTA FE					QUITO			
	N	5+	(T)	0-4)	(t)	N	5+	(T)	0-4	(t)	N	5+	(T)	0-4	(t)
1687	-	2	(-)	2	(-)	-	1	(-)	4	(1)	-	3	(-)	2	(-)
1690	-	2	(-)	1	(-)	-	2	(-)	3	(-)	-	2	(-)	2	(-)
1695	-	1	(-)	5	(-)	-	4	(-)	1	(-)	-	1	(-)	5	(-)
1700	-	6	(-)	1	(-)	-	3	(-)	1	(-)	-	3	(-)	-	(-)
1705	-	4	(-)	-	(-)	-	2	(-)	3	(-)	-	3	(-)	2	(-)
1710	-	2	(-)	4	(-)	1	2	(-)	3	(-)	1	3	(-)	2	(-)
1712	-	1	(-)	5	(1)	1	2	(-)	1	(-)	1	2	(-)	4	(-)
1715	-	2	(-)	3	(2)	1	2	(-)	1	(-)	1	3	(-)	3	(-)
1720	-	5	(2)	1	(-)	-	1	(-)	2	(-)	-	2	(-)	-	(-)
1725	-	5	(2)	1	(-)	-	1	(1)	3	(-)	-	2	(-)	4	(-)
1729	-	6	(2)	-	(-)	-	4	(2)	1	(-)	-	6	(-)	-	(-)
1730	-	6	(2)	-	(-)	-	3	(1)	1	(-)	-	6	(-)	-	(-)
1735	-	6	(2)	-	(-)	-	3	(-)	1	(-)	-	3	(-)	2	(-)
1740	-	3	(-)	-	(-)	-	1	(-)	3	(1).	-	4	(2)	1	(-)
1745	-	2	(-)	2	(-)	-	3	(1)	1	(-)	-	4	(2)	1	(-)
1750	2	3	(1)	2	(1)	-	4	(1)	3	(-)	1	3	(-)	2	(2)
1755	2	5	(1)	-	(-)	-	7	(2)	1	(-)	1	5	(1)	1	(-)
1760	2	5	(2)	1	(-)	-	6	(1)	-	(-)	1	6	(2)	2	(-)
1765	2	5	(1)	-	(-)	-	6	(2)	-	(-)	1	4	(1)	1	(-)
1770	2	4	(1)	-	(-)	-	6	(2)	-	(-)	1	4	(1)	2	(-)
1775	2	3	(2)	-	(-)	-	4	(2)	1	(-)	-	3	(-)	2	(-)
1777	-	-	(-)	8	(-)	1	2	(2)	3	(-)	-	2	(-)	5	(-)
1780	-	-	(-)	8	(-)	-	1	(1)	7	(-)	-	2	(-)	6	(-)
1785	-	3	(-)	2	(-)	-	1	(1)	7	(-)	-	3	(-)	1	(-)
1790	-	3	(1)	3	(-)	2	4	(-)	-	(·)	-	3	(-)	2	(-)
1795	1	4	(1)	1	(-)	1	2	(-)	3	(-)	-	3	(-)	3	(1)
1800	2	2	(-)	1	(-)	-	3	(-)	2	(-)	-	2	(1)	4	(-)
1805	2	1	(1)	2	(-)	-	1	(-)	6	(-)	-	3	(-)	3	(-)
1808	2	2	(-)	2	(-)	-	4	(-)	3	(-)	-	3	(-)	2	(-)
1810	2	2	(-)	2	(-)	-	4	(-)	3	(-)	-	-	(-)	-	(-)
1815	1	1	(1)	1	(-)	-	1	(-)	1	(-)	-	-	(-)	2	(-)
1820	1	1	(1)	2	(-)	-	-	(-)	6	(-)	-	2	(-)	5	(-)

	PANAMA						BUENOS AIRES					CARACAS					CUZCO			
	N	5+	(T)	0-4	(t)		N	5+	(T)	0-4	(t)	N	5+	(T)	0-4	(t)	N	5+	(T)	0-4	(t)
1687	-	3	(-)	1	(-)	1785	-	-	(-)	6	(-)	-	-	(-)	-	(-)	-	-	(-)	-	(-)
1690	-	-	(-)	3	(-)	1790	-	3	(-)	5	(-)	-	-	(-)	5	(-)	-	-	(-)	5	(-)
1695	-	1	(-)	3	(-)	1795	-	7	(-)	1	(-)	-	5	(-)	-	(-)	-	4	(-)	1	(-)
1700	1	2	(-)	-	(-)	1800	-	5	(-)	3	(-)	-	3	(-)	3	(-)	-	4	(-)	1	(-)
1705	-	1	(-)	1	(-)	1805	-	3	(-)	5	(2)	-	1	(-)	5	(-)	-	3	(-)	2	(-)
1710	-	-	(-)	4	(-)	1808	-	4	(-)	4	(-)	-	3	(-)	2	(-)	-	2	(-)	3	(-)
1712	-	-	(-)	7	(-)	1810	-	7	(1)	1	(-)	-	1	(-)	5	(-)	-	2	(1)	2	(-)
1715	-	3	(-)	3	(-)	1815	-	-	(-)	-	(-)	1	-	(-)	4	(-)	-	2	(1)	1	(-)
1720	Note 4.					1820	-	-	(-)	-	(-)	-	2	(-)	3	(-)	-	2	(-)	4	(-)
1725	-	2	(-)	2	(-)																
1729	-	3	(-)	2	(-)																
1730	-	3	(-)	2	(-)																
1735	-	2	(-)	3	(-)																
1740	-	3	(-)	2	(-)																
1745	-	3	(-)	-	(-)																
1750	1	1	(-)	2	(-)																

Appendix VIII

Imperial Overview of Local Influence, 1687–1820

	New Spain				Peru					Total for Empire					
Year	NS	RAD	0-4	Total	NS	RAD	0-4	Total	Total	NS	(%)	RAD	(%)	0-4	(%)
1687	--	11	18	29	--	20	15	35	64	--	--	31	48	33	52
1690	--	15	21	36	2	14	16	32	68	2	3	29	43	37	54
1695	--	21	11	32	5	17	19	41	73	5	7	38	52	30	41
1700	1	17	15	33	7	26	2	35	68	8	12	43	63	17	25
1705	2	20	7	29	6	18	8	32	61	8	13	38	62	15	25
1710	6	26	10	42	11	18	15	44	86	17	20	44	51	25	29
1712	12	29	10	51	12	19	16	47	98	24	24	48	49	26	26
1715	11	27	6	44	11	24	10	45	89	22	25	51	57	16	18
1720	3	17	4	24	5	16	5	26	50	8	16	33	66	9	18
1725	3	10	19	32	7	17	17	41	73	10	14	27	37	36	49
1729	3	21	9	33	4	28	6	38	71	7	10	49	69	15	21
1730	3	23	9	35	5	29	5	39	74	8	11	52	70	14	19
1735	3	25	6	34	6	27	8	41	75	9	12	52	69	14	19
1740	--	23	8	31	8	25	6	39	70	8	11	48	69	14	20
1745	--	24	11	35	11	19	5	35	70	11	16	43	61	16	23
1750	1	26	10	37	18	25	8	51	88	19	22	51	58	18	20
1750	1	26	10	37	18	25	8	51	88	19	22	51	58	18	20
1755	3	24	9	36	16	30	3	49	85	19	22	54	63	12	14
1760	3	25	7	35	15	27	4	46	81	18	22	52	64	11	14
1765	2	19	13	34	14	25	1	40	74	16	22	44	59	14	19
1770	2	21	12	35	11	21	6	38	73	13	18	42	57	18	25
1775	1	10	25	36	8	17	6	31	67	9	13	27	40	31	46
1777	1	9	39	49	7	8	24	39	88	8	9	17	19	63	72
1780	1	10	39	50	5	3	36	44	94	6	6	13	14	75	80
1785	1	33	16	50	5	18	20	43	93	6	7	51	55	36	39
1790	1	20	24	45	7	19	30	56	101	8	8	39	39	54	54
1795	1	23	16	40	5	40	13	58	98	6	6	63	64	29	30
1800	2	25	14	41	3	34	18	55	96	5	5	59	62	32	33
1805	3	20	19	42	3	29	24	56	98	6	6	49	50	43	44
1808	3	16	25	44	3	30	22	55	99	6	6	46	46	47	47
1810	4	17	22	43	3	27	19	49	92	7	8	44	47	41	45
1815	1	18	22	41	4	17	13	34	75	5	7	35	47	35	47
1820	2	21	20	43	3	19	29	51	94	5	6	40	42	49	52

Key:
NS: Native Sons
RAD: Radicados
0-4: Less than five years tenure in the tribunal served

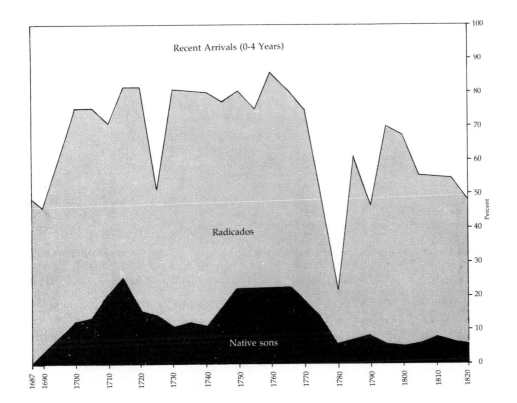

Appendix IX

New Appointees by Date: An Imperial Overview, 1687–1821

This appendix provides basic professional and family information about the 693 new men named from 1687-1821. The organization is by date of appointment.

Explanation of Categories and Abbreviations:

1. Year. Year in which the royal title (título) of office was issued for a man's first audiencia appointment. Within each year successive appointees are listed in order by month and day of title.
2. Name. Common spelling has been employed. Titles of nobility are included to facilitate identification even if not held at the date of appointment.
3. Birthplace. "S" stands for birth in Spain or the Canary Islands. An asterisk before the S (*S) indicates presumed birth in Spain. This attribution is granted only when positive information of residence in Spain before appointment is available, e.g. university attendance or government service but not abogado status, and no evidence suggesting birth in America has been found. "A" stands for birth in America, but audiencia district is unknown. Despite several cases of strong circumstantial evidence, no "A" has been granted without specific reference to American birth. For nearly all creoles, province of birth is known. The abbreviations for these audiencia districts are:

BA:	Buenos Aires	MA:	Manila
CA:	Caracas	ME:	Mexico
CH:	Chile	PA:	Panama
CS:	Charcas	QU:	Quito
CZ:	Cuzco	SD:	Santo Domingo and, after 14
GD:	Guadalajara		May 1797, Puerto Principe
GT:	Guatemala	SF:	Santa Fe de Bogotá
LI:	Lima		

4. Age. Age given should be considered approximate, particularly for men named before 1780. On the basis of checking men of known birthdate for the ages at which they received the bachelor of arts degree, entered a colegio mayor, or gained abogado status, the following formula was employed for persons without certain birthdate: Americans—bachelor's degree, 17; abogado, 22; Spaniards—bachelor's degree, 20; colegio admission, 20; abogado, 25.
5. University. University affiliation is listed regardless of whether attendance, receipt of a degree, or incorporation of a degree was involved. Abbreviations employed are:

AL:	Alcalá de Henares	CA:	Caracas
AV:	Avila	CS:	Charcas
BA:	Barcelona	CH:	Chile
CE:	Cervera	CZ:	Cuzco
GR:	Granada	GD:	Guadalajara
HI:	Hirache	GT:	Guatemala
HU:	Huesca	HA:	Havana
ON:	Oñate	HM:	Huamanga
OR:	Orihuela	LI:	San Marcos de Lima
OM:	Osma	JA:	Jaen
OS:	Osuna	ME:	Mexico
SA:	Salamanca	SF:	Santa Fe de Bogotá
SN:	Santiago de Compostela	SD:	Santo Domingo
SE:	Sevilla	BO:	Bologna
SI:	Siguenza	YU:	Yucatan
TO:	Toledo	OV:	Oviedo
VA:	Valencia	TU:	Córdoba de Tucuman
VD:	Valladolid	QU:	Quito
ZA:	Zaragoza	MA:	Manila
AS:	Asturias		
BZ:	Baeza		

6. Colegio. Membership in one of the six colegios mayores in Spain and the most important and prestigious colegios associated with the universities in Lima and Mexico City has been indicated.

AR:	Arzobispo (Salamanca)	SC:	Santa Cruz (Valladolid)
CU:	Cuenca (Salamanca)	SF:	San Felipe (Lima)
OV:	Oviedo (Salamanca)	SM:	San Martín (Lima)
SB:	San Bartolomé (Salamanca)	SI:	San Ildefonso (Mexico)
IL:	San Ildefonso (Alcalá)	TS:	Todos Santos (Mexico)

7. Degree. The degree listed is the highest for which reference has been found. We suspect inflation of degrees through honorific attribution in the same way that the use of "don" expanded in the Indies.

D: Doctorate   L: Licenciate   B: Bachelor

8. Abogado. Tribunals to which a man had been admitted to practice law.

BA:	Buenos Aires	AS:	Asturias
CA:	Caracas	CN:	Canary Islands
CS:	Charcas	CT:	Cataluña, Barcelona
CH:	Chile	EX:	Extremadura
CZ:	Cuzco	GA:	Gailicia
GD:	Guadalajara	GR:	Granada
GT:	Guatemala	BS:	Mallorca
LI:	Lima	NA:	Navarre
MA:	Manila	SE:	Seville
ME:	Mexico	VA:	Valencia
PA:	Panama	VD:	Valladolid
QU:	Quito	IN:	Abogado de Indias
SF:	Santa Fe de Bogotá	MD:	Castile
SD:	Santo Domingo	RC:	Royal councils
AR:	Aragon		

9. Previous Post. Pre-audiencia service in office is indicated.
   SP: service in Spain below the audiencias
   AS: Spanish audiencia
   X: service in America below the audiencias and in a post or posts that did not normally lead directly to an audiencia appointment, e.g. asesor to a city council, alcalde mayor. Usually "X" is followed by a province designation indicating where the services occurred, e.g. X-LI indicates services in the audiencia district of Lima.
   TA: teniente asesor
   AG: asesor general
   PI: protector of the Indians

10. University Service. Identifiable long-term employment (i.e. not serving as a substitute) in a professorial chair is indicated by CA (catedratico).

11. Relatives' Posts.
   CONQ: descended from conquerors or first settlers (usually through the maternal line).
   F: father
   P: paternal grandfather
   M: maternal grandfather
   O-Y: other important relatives, e.g. an uncle who was on a council or holding a title, a brother who was a bishop. Following the hyphen, e.g. F-, are abbreviations for the kind of position.
   XX: minor or local office in Spain or America (e.g. alcalde ordinario) or military rank below colonel.
   AB: position in the royal bureaucracy in America, e.g. contador, corregidor.
   SB: position in the royal bureaucracy in Spain, e.g. contador, corregidor.
   HM: military rank of colonel, maestre de campo, or general.
   OD: oidor in an American audiencia.
   FI: fiscal in an American audiencia.
   AC: alcalde del crimen in an American audiencia.
   PR: president of an American audiencia.
   MT: ministro togado or fiscal in a council in Spain.
   AS: minister in a Spanish audiencia, chancellery, or the House of Trade.

12. Travel: "A" indicates an American-born minister was in Spain when he received his initial audiencia appointment.

13-14. First post and first province.
Abbreviations for the initial audiencia appointments are:

AC:	alcalde del crimen	FS:	fiscal supernumerario
OD:	oidor	FH:	fiscal de hacienda
RE:	regent	OF:	oidor futurario
FI:	fiscal	OS:	oidor supernumerario
FR:	fiscal del crimen	AF:	alcalde del crimen futurario
FV:	fiscal de lo civil	AX:	alcalde del crimen
FF:	fiscal futurario		supernumerario

Provinces are:

BA:	Buenos Aires	LI:	Lima
CA:	Caracas	MA:	Manila
CH:	Chile	ME:	Mexico
CS:	Charcas	PA:	Panama
CZ:	Cuzco	QU:	Quito
GD:	Guadalajara	SD:	Santo Domingo (Puerto Principe)
GT:	Guatemala	SF:	Santa Fe de Bogotá

15. Courts Served. The number indicates the number of courts, not appointments to which a man was named. Thus a man named fiscal in Guadalajara and promoted to Mexico would have a "2" although he might have held positions of fiscal, alcalde del crimen, and oidor in Mexico.

16. Purchase. The abbreviations listed for column 13 (first post) are employed for purchased appointments. In the several cases when a man purchased two appointments, both are indicated.

17. Dispensations. Dispensations from restrictive legislation are indicated:
CP: minister's children hold property in the district
CM: minister's children marry in the district
MN: minister marries a native of the district served
NA: minister a native son
MI: minister a minor when named
HP: minister holds   property in the district served

18. Married.
Y: Yes, the minister was married at some time.
N: No, the minister was never married.
Blank: No information was available on marital status.

19. Wife's Birthplace: The same abbreviations employed in column three (birthplace) are used.

20. Honors, Order. Particularly in the Age of Authority the crown granted individuals "honors" of a minister on a given tribunal. Honors did not ensure a subsequent appointment to the tribunal, but were a source of prestige and privileged treatment for the recipient.

AM:	alcalde del crimen, Mexico	GT:	oidor, Guatemala
AS:	Spanish audiencia	OL:	oidor, Lima
CA:	Cámara of the Indies	OM:	oidor, Mexico
CI:	Council of the Indies	SD:	oidor, Santo Domingo
CL:	alcalde del crimen, Lima	SF:	oidor, Santa Fe de Bogotá
CS:	oidor, Charcas	VE:	oidor, Caracas
GD:	oidor, Guadalajara		

Orders refer to membership in a military or civil order

AL:	Alcántara	CAL:	Calatrava
CH:	Charles III	SA:	Santiago
IC:	Isabel la Católica		

21. Departure Date. The year in which the appointee ended service in an American tribunal.
N.S. refers to an appointee's failure to serve
IND. refers to independence in the last region served or 1821, whichever was first

22. Departure. The nature of a minister's termination of service in an American tribunal is indicated.

AB:	joined rebels		
AS:	Spanish audiencia, or chancellery, or the House of Trade		
CI:	Council of the Indies	RM:	removed from office
D:	death	RT:	retired (jubilado)
RC:	retired to the church	SC:	Spanish council

Year	Name	Birthplace	Age	University	Colegio	Degree	Abogado	Previous Post	University Service	Relatives' Posts	Travel	First Post	First Province	Courts Served	Purchase	Dispensations	Married	Wife's Birthplace	Honors, Order	Departure Date	Departure
1687	NUÑEZ DE SANABRIA, Miguel	LI	42	LI		D		AG LI	CA	F-XX		AC	LI	I	AC	NA	Y	LI		1729	RT
1688	RIVAS, Diego Antonio de	S		AL								OD	PA	2						N.S.	RM
1688	BERNARDO DE QUIROS, Alvaro	S		AL	IL	L				F-XX		OD	CH	2			Y	S		1734	D
1688	CEBALLOS Y BORJA, Cristóbal de	LI				L	CS	X-CS				OS	QU	I	OS		Y			1713	RM
1688	TRELLES Y VILLAMIL, Gonzalo	*S		SA	CU	L						OD	CS	I						1699	RT
1688	CALVO DOMONTE, Luis Antonio	CS	26	LI SA	SM					F-XX		OS	CS	2		MN	Y	CS		1718	RC
1688	BLANCO REJON, José	LI	33	LI SA	SM	D	LI			F-XX	A	FI	CH	I	FI					1706	RC
1688	LAYA BOLIVAR, Juan de	PA	30	LI SA		L				F-AB	A	OD	PA	I		NA				1698	D
1689	BRAVO DE ANAYA, Diego Bartolomé	*S		GR					CA	F-XX		OD	SD	I						N.S.	SC
1689	LADRON DE GUEVARA, Francisco de	LI	28	LI SA	SM	L	LI					OD	SD	I						1694	D
1689	DIAZ DE DURANA, Clemente	LI	36			L					A	OS	CS	I	OS					1716	RT
1689	GONZALEZ CARRASCO, Miguel de					L				F-XX		OS	QU	I	OS		Y			1696	D
1689	IZUNZA Y EGUILUZ, Bernardo Angel	S	29	SA	SB	L						OD	SF	I					SA	1714	RM
1689	RICAURTE, Juan de	SF	23			D				F-AB	A	OS	QU	I	OS		Y			1709	RM
1689	LANDERO, Francisco de	LI		LI		D	LI	CA				OD	PA	I						N.S.	D
1689	RON, Antonio de	S		AL	IL	B						FI	QU	I					SA	1708	
1689	RIVAS, Fernando José de	*S		GR		L	GR RC					OS	QU	I	OS					1699	D
1689	SOMOZA, Juan de											OS	GD	I	OS		Y	A			
1689	CALDERON DE LA BARCA, Miguel	S	37			L	RC					OD	ME	I	OD		Y			1702	AS
1690	REMIREZ DE BAQUEDANO, Gonzalo	S	28	ON						O-Y		FI	CH	2		MN	Y	LI	SA	1716	CI
1690	OVIEDO Y BAÑOS, Diego Antonio de	SF	25	LI	SM	L	LI	TA SD		F-OD M-AC O-Y		OS	SD	3					CI	1722	D
1690	CALDERON DE LA BARCA, Juan Fernando (Conde de las Torres)	S	28	SA AV	OV	B						AC	LI	I			Y	CS	CAL	1718	D
1690	ZUÑIGA Y TOVAR, Diego de	S	25	AV AL	IL	L						OD	CH	I					SA	1712	CI
1690	MEDINA, Francisco de	S	41	VD		L	RC					OD	PA	2			Y			1695 1710	RT D
1690	OSORIO ESPINOSA de los MONTEROS, José	A				L	ME	CA		CONQ		OS	GD	2	OS		Y				
1691	VALCARCEL, Juan de		30			L						FI	SF	2							
1691	MIRANDA VILLAYZAN, José de	ME	32	ME		D	ME	CA		F-XX		OS	GD	I	OS					1718	RT
1691	DUARDO, Juan Jerónimo	S		ME		B	ME	CA				OS	GT	I	OS		Y			1717	D
1692	ROA Y CRIALES, Alejandro de					L						OD	PA	I			Y	S		1698	D
1692	HIDALGO DE PAREDES, Andrés de	CS	30				CS			F-AB M-HM	A	OF	CH	I	OF				AL	N.S.	
1693	ALCEDO Y SOTOMAYOR, Carlos de	S	37	SN VD		L	QU	X-SF		F-XX		OS	SF	2	OS		Y		SA	1704	
1693	HIDALGO DE ESCOBAR, Diego de	CH	38	LI	SM	L	LI				A	OF	CS	I	OF						
1693	PEREZ DE URQUIZU, Juan de	LI	38			D	LI			F-XX	A	AF	LI	I	AF	NA MN	Y2	LI		1729	D

Year	Name	Birthplace	Age	University	Colegio	Degree	Abogado	Previous Post	University Service	Relatives' Posts	Travel	First Post	First Province	Courts Served	Purchase	Dispensations	Married	Wife's Birthplace	Honors, Order	Departure Date	Departure
1693	SANTIAGO CONCHA, José de (Marqués de Casa Concha)	LI	26	LI SA	SM	L	LI	X- LI		F-AB	A	\F	LI	I	AF	NA CM	Y		CS	CAL 1741	D
1693	SANTIAGO DE CESPEDES Y CAVERO, Juan	LI	40	LI	SM	L	RC LI QU			M-HM P-HM	A	OF	CS	I	OF		Y			1702	D
1693	TOVAR, Baltazar de	S				D		SP					FR	ME	I		MN	Y	ME		c1712	D
1693	SEGURA Y LARA, Diego de					D	LI						OS	QU	I	OS						
1693	ZUÑIGA, Francisco José	LI	50			L	LI					A	OS	PA	3	OS					1712	RM
1693	GUTIERREZ DE LA PEÑA, José	S											FI	GT	2			Y			1734	RC
1693	SARMIENTO y HUESTERLIN, Pedro	S	27	SA		D				F-FI P-XX			FI	SF	I			Y			1707	RM
1694	PAREDES Y ARMENDARIZ, Nicolás de	LI	20	LI SA	SM	D	LI			F-FI O-Y	A	OF	LI	I	OF					SA	1712	D
1695	ESPINOSA RIVADENEIRA, Juan de	*S	30	AL		L	RC				FF		MA	I								
1695	MARIN Y MUÑOZ, Pedro de	*S				L	RC	SP					FI	SD	I			Y			1700	D
1695	LUNA Y ARIAS, José de	GD	32	ME SA		L				F-OD	A	OD	ME	I	OD	MN					1712	RC
1695	GRILLO Y RANGEL, Bartolomé	PA	34	LI	SM	L	LI PA	X- PA		F-XX	A	FI	PA	2	FN	NA	Y			1712	D
1695	CORRAL CALVO DE LA BANDA, Juan del	CS	30	LI SA	SF	L	LI			F-OD	A	OF	CH	I	OF		Y			1737	D
1695	CERECEDA Y GIRON, Sebastián de	S		SA		L	RC						OS	SD	2						1726	D
1695	SANCHEZ DE LA BARCENA, Francisco	*S	35	VD		B	RC VD	SP					OD	MA	2					SA	1699 N.S.	
1695	PAVON, José Antonio	S		ME		B	ME RC			F-AB		OF	MA	I							1730	D
1696	LLERA Y VALDES, Manuel de	*S							CA				OD	QU	I						N.S.	REF.
1696	CARRILLO, Andrés					L	X- ME						OD	MA	I						N.S.	D
1696	AGUERO, Baltazar de					D							FI	MA	I						N.S.	D
1696	GUERUELA, Francisco	*S	28	GR		B	GR RC			F-CA		OF	MA	I								
1696	MESTRES Y BARRES, José de	S	59	BA		D	AR CT						OS	MA	I			Y			1701	D
1696	TORRALVA, José de	S	30	AL		D	RC	SP	CA	F-XX		OF	MA	I			Y			1718	RM
1699	CARRILLO ESCUDERO, Gregorio	S	35	SA		D							OD	GT	2						1727	D
1699	EGUARAS FERNANDEZ DE HIJAR, Pedro de (Marqués de Salvatierra)	S	26	SA	AR								OD	GT	2		MN	Y	ME	CI	1711	RT
1699	BLANCO DEL CASTILLO, Francisco	S		SA		D		SP					FV	ME	I			Y			1703	RT
1699	ESPINOSA OCAMPO Y CORNEJO, José Antonio	S	37	SA		D							FR	ME	I					SA	1717	RT
1699	FERNANDEZ PEREZ, Tomás	LI	25	LI	SM	L	LI					A	OD	QU	3						1723	RC
1699	VASQUEZ DE VELASCO, Pedro	LI	31	LI	SM	L				F-HM P-PR O-Y	A	AX	LI	2	AX		Y	LI	CAL	1744	D
1699	ARANBURU Y MUÑOZ, Vicente de	LI	42	LI	SM	L	RC			F-AB	A	AC	LI	2	AC	NA	Y		SA	1718	RM
1699	MARAÑON Y LARA, Marcos	*S	29	AL		B	RC	SP					OD	SD	I						N.S.	RT
1699	NUÑEZ DE ROJAS, Gregorio	LI	25	LI	SM	D				F-OD P-XX M-FI O-Y	A	OS	CS	2	OS OD	MN NA	Y			1747	D
1699	ROJAS Y ACEVEDO, Francisco de	LI	48	LI	SM			AG LI		F-FI P-HM		AF	LI	2	AF		Y		CS	1717	D
1700	CASTILLO, Ignacio Antonio de	LI	30	LI	SM	L					A	OS	CS	2		MN	Y		CS		

Year	Name	Birthplace	Age	University	Colegio	Degree	Abogado	Previous Post	University Service	Relatives' Posts	Travel	First Post	First Province	Courts Served	Purchase	Dispensations	Married	Wife's Birthplace	Honors, Order	Departure Date	Departure
1700	VALVERDE CONTRERAS Y ALARCON, José de	LI	50	LI	SM SF	L	LI			F-XX P-AB M-OD O-Y		OF	CH	I						1702	RM
1700	VILLAVICENCIO Y CISNEROS, Pedro de	LI	36	LI	SM		LI			F-HM		OS	LI	I	OS					1702	RM
1700	LOSADA SOTOMAYOR, Luis Antonio de	S		LI SA	AR	L						OD	SF	I			Y			1719	D
1700	ANGUITA SANDOVAL, Francisco de	ME				L	ME	X-ME			A	OS	ME	I	OS	NA MN	Y	ME		1703	D
1700	AYALA MARIN, Marcelo de	LI		LI	SM	L	LI				A	FF	CH	2	FF					1708	RT
1700	CASTRO Y ALDUAYN, Juan Antonio de					L						OD	PA	I						N.S.	D
1700	CHIRINO VANDEVAL, Nicolás	SD	36	ME		B	ME	TA SD		F-XX P-XX		OD	SD	2	AX		Y	ME		1722	D
1700	TORRE Y ANGULO, Mauricio de la	*S	33	AL SA		B	RC					FI	SD	I			Y			1717	RC
c1700	VALDES, Felipe de	*S										OD	SD	I						N.S.	AS
1701	FERNANDEZ MOLINILLO, Nicolás	S	30	SA		B						OD	SD	I						1702	D
1702	SIERRA OSORIO, Fernando de	*S	31	VD	SC	L		CA				OD	QU	3						1718	RT
1702	URIBE CASTEJON, José Joaquín	S	36	SA	AR	L		CA				OD	ME	I		MN	Y	ME	SA	1738	D
1703	DOMONTE Y PINTO, José	S	34	SE		D						OD	GD	I						N.S.	RT
1703	LERMA Y SALAMANCA, Baltazar José de	S	31	SA	CU	B				F-MI M-SB		FI	CH	3			Y	S			
1704	CANAL, Pedro Gregorio de la	LI	30	LI	SM	D	LI			F-XX		OS	LI	I	OS	NA MN					
1704	BARRIENTOS Y RIVERA, Agustín Miguel de	S	34	ME		L	ME					OD	MA	I						1715	D
1704	PERALTA Y SANABRIA, Juan	LI	56	LI	SM	D		PI LI	CA	F-XX		OS	LI	I	OS					1706	D
1704	ORUETA Y IRUXTA, Juan Bautista de	S		SA	AR	B						AC	LI	I		MN	Y	LI		1720	D
1704	CEPEDA, Gaspar de	*S	31	SA	AR							FR	ME	I						1715	RC
1704	LAYSEQUILLA Y PALACIOS, José de	S				L	RC			F-SB		OD	SD	3					CI SA	1723	CI
1704	FERNANDEZ DE BARCO, Francisco	S	29	AL		L						OD	SD	2			Y	S		1720	D
1705	PICADO PACHECO Y MONTERO, Juan	S	34	SA AV	CU	L						FI	GD	2					AL	1740	D
1705	HARO Y MONTERROSO, Fernando José de	S	43	ME		L	RC			F-OD M-S		OD	PA	I						1709	
1705	CASA ALVARADO, Antonio de	S	45	SA		L	RC	X-ME				FI	MA	I						1718	D
1705	LOZANO Y PERALTA, Jorge	S	50	AL		L	RC	SP				OD	SD	2			Y			1729	RT
1705	NAVIA BOLAÑOS Y MOSCOSO, Alvaro (Conde del Valle de Oselle)	S	30	SA	OV	L				F-XX		OD	CS	2		MN CM	Y	LI	SA CI	1757	D
1705	SORIA VELASQUEZ, Gerónimo de (Marqués de Villahermosa y Alfaro)	ME	45	ME	TS	D	ME GD			F-XX	A	OD	ME	I						1740	D
1706	DIEZ DE BRACAMONTE, Juan de	ME		ME	SI	D	ME					OS	ME	I						1720	RM
1706	MALO DE VILLAVICENCIO, Pedro de	S	33	SE SA		D						OD	GD	2			Y	S	CAL	1743	D
1706	LLORENTE, José de	S	31	SA		L	RC	SP				FI	PA	3						1718	RM
1706	LASTERO DE SALAZAR, Lorenzo	QU	44			B	LI			F-HM	A	OS	QU	I	OS		Y	S		1718	RM

Year	Name	Birthplace	Age	University	Colegio	Degree	Abogado	Previous Post	University Service	Relatives' Posts	Travel	First Post	First Province	Courts Served	Purchase	Dispensations	Married	Wife's Birthplace	Honors, Order	Departure Date	Departure
1706	COCO PALACIOS, Alonso	*S				L						OD	PA	I						N.S.	AS
1706	CASA ALVARADO, Francisco de	S	36	SE SA		L	SE RC	SP				AX	ME	I	AX					c1715	D
1707	GONZALEZ DE AGÜERO, Félix	S				L						OS	ME	I		MN				1720	RM
1707	SOLIS VANGO, Juan Prospero de	LI	17	LI	SM	D				F-PR M-AB		OS	CH	I	OS	MI			CAL 1743		D
1707	RECAVARREN, Martín de	SD	28	ME	TS	L	ME	X-CH		F-XX P-XX M-XX	A	OS	PA	2	OS		Y	LI		1767	D
1707	PEÑA Y FLORES, Juan Francisco de la	ME					ME					AX	ME	I	AX	NA	Y	ME		c1720	RM
1707	VALDES, Juan de	ME	56	ME		L	ME	X-ME				OS	ME	I	OS	NA				c1715	D
1707	VILLARREAL Y FLORENCIA, Cristóbal de	SD		ME	SI					F-XX	A	OS	ME	I	OS	NA				c1714	D
1707	SANTOS Y CUENTAS, Francisco de los	LI	51	LI		B		X-LI		F-XX P-CA		AX	LI	I	AX	NA MN	Y		CAL N.S.		
1707	OLIVAN REBOLLEDO, Juan Manuel de	ME	31	ME		L	ME			F-XX	A	OS	GD	2	OS OS		Y	S		1738	D
1707	ROBLES Y LORENZANA, Agustín de	S	29	LI	SF	L						AX	ME	I	AX	MN				1720	RM
1708	CASTAÑEDA, Diego Francisco de	ME		ME			ME			F-XX P-AB		OS	GD	2	OS AX	NA MN	Y	ME		1720	RM
1708	MENA CABALLERO, Juan Antonio de	LI	24	LI	SF					F-XX		AX	LI	I	AX	NA MN	Y	LI	SA	1720	RT
1708	BRAVO DE RIVERO, Juan	LI	23	LI	SM	L				F-HM P-XX M-XX		OS	CS	I	OS	MN	Y			1724	RC
1708	ECHAVARRIA ZULOAGA, Juan Bautista de (Marqués de Sotohermoso)	LI	25	LI	SM	D				P-XX M-AB	A	OS	LI	I	OS	NA MN			SA		
1708	SANCHEZ DE LA BARREDA, Salvador	LI	21	LI	SM						A	OS	CH	I	OS	MN				N.S.	D
1708	ZAPATA, Manuel Antonio	SF	30	SF		D	SF			F-AB	A	FS	SF	I	FS	MN NA	Y			1718	RM
1708	MUNARRIZ, Bartolomé de	LI	22	LI	SM					F-AB	A	AC	LI	I	AC	NA MN	Y	LI		1718	RT
1708	PEREZ BUELTA, Gaspar	*S	24	SA AV		L						OD	PA	3		CM	Y	PA		1744	D
1708	RIVADENEIRA LUNA, Tristán Manuel de	ME	28	ME	TS	L					A	OS	ME	I	OS	NA MN					RC
1709	OLAIS Y AROCHE, Esteban	LI				B		PI QU				OF	QU	2	OF	MN	Y			1750	D
1709	ALZAMORA URSINO, José de	LI		LI	SM	D						OD	PA	2	OD					1725	D
1709	GALLEGOS, Ignacio	LI	23	LI	SM	B				F-XX		OS	CH	I	OS	MN				1740	RT
1709	ULLOA CALLEJA, Nicolás de	ME		ME	SI	B	ME				A	OS	GT	I	OS	MN				N.S.	RM
1709	CLAVIJO Y MEDINA, Diego	LI	26	LI	SM SF					F-HM	A	FI	PA	I	FN					1733	D
1709	FAJARDO, Felipe Nicolás	S		AL		L				F-AS		FF	QU	2						1722	D
1710	ECHAVE Y ROJAS, Pedro Antonio	LI		LI						F-HM		FF	LI	I	FF	NA MN	Y	LI	AL	1728	D
1710	ARANA, Tomás Ignacio de	ME		ME		L	ME	CA				OS	GT	I	OS					1745	RM
1710	OYANGUREN, Francisco de	ME	52	ME		D	ME					FF	ME	I	FF	NA				1720	RM
1710	URRUTIA, Fernando de	ME										OS	GD	I	OS					1740	RT
1710	RODEZNO MANZOLO, José Nicolás	ME	23	ME		L				F-AB M-XX		OS	GT	I	OS	MN				1741	RT
1710	LUGO CORONADO, Felipe Antonio	ME	33	ME	SI	D	ME					OS	GT	2	OS		Y	ME		1724	D

Year	Name	Birthplace	Age	University	Colegio	Degree	Abogado	Previous Post	University Service	Relatives' Posts	Travel	First Post	First Province	Courts Served	Purchase	Dispensations	Married	Wife's Birthplace	Honors, Order	Departure Date	Departure
1710	REAL Y QUESADA, Antonio	ME	38	ME		B	ME RC	X-ME				OS	GD	I	OS	MN NA	Y	A		1725	D
1710	CAVERO, Pablo	*S				D		TA SD				OS	SD	I						1712	D
1710	GOMEZ TRIGOSSO, Bernardo					L		X-ME				FI	PA	I	FN					1717	D
1710	TORQUEMADA, Leonardo Fernando de											OS	CH	I	OS					1714	D
1710	VILLA BARREDA, Gregorio Manuel de	S				L						FI	MA	I	FN		Y	S		1724	
1710	PEREZ DELGADO, Bartolomé Patricio	S	37	ME		L	ME					OF	MA	I	OF					1712	D
1710	FRANCO VELASQUEZ DE TOLEDO, Agustín	ME		ME		D			CA			OS	ME	I	OS	NA MN	Y	ME		1720	RM
1710	SANCHEZ DE LA BARREDA, Francisco	LI	20	LI	SM					O-Y		OS	CH	I	OS	MN CM	Y			1738	D
1710	VEQUENILLA Y SANDOVAL, Juan de la	ME		ME		D				F-XX CONQ		AX	ME	I	AX	NA MN	Y	ME		1736	D
1710	MIRONES Y BENAVENTE, Manuel Isidro de	LI	19	LI	SM		LI			F-XX	A	OS	PA	3	OS STD OS	MI CM NA	Y	LI		1766	D
1710	SAGARDIA Y PALENCIA, Francisco	LI	19	LI	SM	D	LI			F-AB		OS	CS	2	OS	MN MI	Y	ME	CC	1736	RM
1711	LARREA ZURBANO, Juan Dionisio	SF	35			L				F-OD M-CG		OS	QU	I	OS	MN HP	Y	QU	CAL	1747	RT
1711	GOMEZ DE ANDRADE, Pedro	LI		LI	SM	B	LI					OS	PA	2	OS	MI	Y			1761	D
1711	BARBADILLO VICTORIA, Francisco de	*S	36	VD		L	RC	TA ME				AX	ME	I	AX	MN	Y	ME		1747	D
1711	CAVERO DE FRANCIA, Alvaro	LI	26	LI	SM	D	LI			F-XX	A	OS	LI	I	OS	MN	Y	LI		1739	D
1711	TERREROS OCHOA, Antonio	ME		ME		D	ME	X-ME				OS	ME	I		NA MN	Y	ME		1720	RM
1711	SANCHEZ DE ALCAZAR, Pedro	ME	27	ME		L	ME				A	AX	ME	I	AX	NA MN	Y	ME		1720	RM
1711	SANTAELLA Y MELGAREJO, Ambrosio Tomás de	SD	21	ME		B	ME				A	OF	GT	2	OF		Y			1741	D
1711	GOMENDIO URRUTIA, Domingo de	S		QU		D	QU PA					OS	GT	I	OS					1735	D
1712	SANCHEZ DE ORELLANA, Juan Bautista	QU				D				F-HM	A	OS	QU	I	OS	NA	Y			1717	RM
1712	GUTIERREZ DE ARCE, Juan	S	34	AL	IL	B	RC	SP TA SF		F-SB		OF	SF	2					SA	1747	D
1713	GOMENDIO URRUTIA, Miguel de	LI	43	SI AL		L				F-AB CONQ	A	FI	CH	2						1755	RT
1713	PALACIOS, Prudencio Antonio de	S	30	SA HU		B	RC	TA SD				OS	SD	3			Y	S	CAL	1732	SC
1714	YPES Y MIJARES DE LA QUADRA, Mateo de	*S	29	TO SA	CU	L						OD	SF	I					CAL	1718	RM
1715	COBIAN Y VALDES, Antonio de	S				L		SP				OD	SF	2			Y			1721	D
1716	SUAREZ DE FIGUEROA, Félix											OS	ME	I						1720	RM
1717	ESCOLANO, Domingo Nicolás	*S		SA								FI	SD	I						N.S.	
1718	BELENGUER, Simón	S	41	SA		B	RC					OD	SD	I			Y			1727	RT
1718	RODRIGUEZ DE CASTAÑON, Alonso	S	60	AL	IL				CA			FI	LI	I					AL	N.S.	AS
1718	FLORES Y GUZMAN, Juan de	S		SI AL	IL	L						FI	SD	I			Y			1719	D

Year	Name	Birthplace	Age	University	Colegio	Degree	Abogado	Previous Post	University Service	Relatives' Posts	Travel	First Post	First Province	Courts Served	Purchase	Dispensations	Married	Wife's Birthplace	Honors, Order	Departure Date	Departure
Pre-1719	RUIZ DE CASTRO, José	S		SE								OD	QU	I						N.S.	AS
1719	AGUIRRE NEGRO Y ESTRADA, José Francisco de	S		ON VD SA		B		TA SD	CA			OD	SD	2		MN			CI CAL	1735	RT
1719	ENRIQUEZ DE IRIARTE, Diego	*S	31	GR SA	CU	B						OD	SF	I						N.S.	D
1720	ALARCON Y VARGAS, Luis Ambrosio de	S		SE BO		B		SE AS	CA			AC	LI	I						1723	RT
1720	CASTILLA Y LISPERGUER, José Ventura de	LI	29	LI	SM	B		LI PI/SF		F-HM		FI	SF	I		MN				1734	D
1720	CEBALLOS GUERRA, José Damian (Conde de las Torres)	S	34	SA	SB	L						FI	LI	I			Y	CS		1743	D
1720	BEDOYA Y OSORIO, Pedro de	S				L						FI	MA	2					SA	1748	RT
1720	LOPEZ DE ADAN, Francisco de	S		AL		D						OD	MA	2					SA	1760	RT
1720	MARTINEZ, Francisco de	*S	27	AL		D						OD	MA	I						1731	D
1720	RIVERA AGUADO, Simón de	S	32	AL	IL	B						OD	QU	2						1742	
1720	RUBIO DE AREVALO, Manuel	S						RC				OD	QU	I		HP	Y			1765	RT
1720	MARTINEZ DE ARIZALA, Pedro	S		AL		L						OD	QU	I					CI	1738	RC
1720	CARRILLO MORENO, Juan	S		VD		L						FI	SD	3			Y			1747	AS
1720	MARTINEZ MALO, José Joaquín	S	40	VD	SC	L			CA			OD	SF	2						1741	D
1721	SALAZAR Y CASTEJON, Francisco Xavier de	S	34	VD IR	SC	B						AC	LI	I		MN CM	Y	LI		1744	D
1721	QUINTANA Y ACEVEDO, José de	S	31	TO AL SA	IL	L				F-SB		OD	SF	2			Y	S		1765	RT
1721	SALAZAR, Tomás de	LI	46	LI		D		LI X-/LI	CA			OD	SF	2		NA	N			1738	D
1721	ZARATE Y ALARCON, Diego Francisco de	LI	54	LI	SM	D		LI X-/LI	CA			FI	QU	I			Y			1731	D
1721	LOPEZ DE EZEYZA, Isidro	LI		LI	SM			PI/LI				FI	GT	I			Y	LI		1739	D
1721	JAUREGUI Y OLLO, Martín Gregorio de	S	31	SE		D			CA			FI	CH	I			Y			1746	RT
1721	DAVILA MADRID, Fernando	S	37	AL SA	AR	L						FI	GD	2			Y			1764	RT
c1721	GONZALEZ PIMENTEL, Esteban	S		GR				SE GR RC				OD	ME	I			Y		SA	N.S.	D
1722	GARZIGA, José Vicente Antonio de	*S		AL		D						OD	GD	I						1730	RC
1722	OSILIA Y RAYO, Juan Gerónimo de	*S	44	SE OS		D		SP	CA			AC	ME	I						1729	D
1722	REY VILLAR DE FRANCO, Fernando	*S	26	SN		B		RC				OD	SD	I							
1722	GARCIA CATALAN, Sebastián	S	30	SA AV AL	IL	L						OD	PA	I						1726	D
1722	FERNANDEZ DE MADRID, Luis Manuel	S	37	AL		L		ME		F-XX P-XX		OD	GT	2			Y	QU	CAL	1750	D
1723	BARCENA Y MIER, Miguel de la	S	33	OV SA	AR	B						FI	LI	I						1726	D
1723	BRUN, Tomás	S	43	HU		D		PI/LI	CA			AC	LI	I			Y	LI		1728	D
1723	ZARATE, Manuel de	S	52	SA		B		RC X-/LI				OD	PA	I						1732	D
1723	BON Y AZUZA, Sebastián	S	42			L		NA		F-SB		OD	PA	I						N.S.	D
1723	OROZCO MANRIQUE DE LARA, Francisco de	S	29	AL		L						OD	GT	2						1765	D

170

Year	Name	Birthplace	Age	University	Colegio	Degree	Abogado	Previous Post	University Service	Relatives' Posts	Travel	First Post	First Province	Courts Served	Purchase	Dispensations	Married	Wife's Birthplace	Honors, Order	Departure Date	Departure
1724	MESIA DE LA CERDA, José de la	*S	29	GR		L		ME		O-Y		OD	GD	2			Y	ME		1760	D
1724	FERNANDEZ TORIBIO, Francisco	S	34	AL	IL	L			CA			OD	GT	3			Y		MA	1742	RT
1724	VELASCO, Julián de		42						CA			AC	ME	I						1728	D
1724	GOMEZ GARCIA, José Casimiro	PA	29	LI	SM	L		LI		F-XX		FI	CS	2			Y	LI		1761	D
1724	GRANADO CATALAN, Francisco de	*S		SA	OV	L						OD	SD	I						1729	D
1725	GUERRERO Y GALVEZ, Juan Manuel	S	35	SE		D						OD	SF	I						1736	D
1725	BLANCAS Y ESPELETA, Martín de	S		SA	CU	B				F-SB		FI	SD	2			Y	ME		1754	RT
1726	RODRIGUEZ DE ALBUERNE, Juan (Marqués de Altamira)	S	30	AL		L		RC				OD	GD	2		CM CP	Y	A	SA	1753	D
1726	ARJONA, Francisco Lorenzo de	S		GR OS		D			CA			OD	MA	I						N.S.	D
1726	VELASCO, Juan Francisco de	S		AL		L		RC		F-SB		OS	MA	I						1752	D
1726	PEREZ GARCIA, Juan					L		RC				OD	SD	2			Y			1750	D
1726	ARVIZA Y UGARTE, Bernardo	LI	33	LI	SM	D		LI	CA			OD	PA	2						1746	RC
1727	GARCIA CHICANO, Juan Félix	S	56	SA TO AL		D		TA SD		F-XX P-XX		OD	SD	I						1743	RT
1727	MUÑOZ Y GUZMAN, Jaime	S	33	GR		B		GR RC		F-XX P-XX		OD	PA	I					SA	1751	RM
1727	VALCARCEL Y FORMENTO, Domingo	S	27	GR AV AL	IL	L				F-MT P-MT M-MT		AC	ME	I		MN	Y	ME	CI CA SA	1778	RT
1727	PUENTE LARREA, Lorenzo Antonio de la (Marqués de Villafuerte y Sotomayor)	S		SA	AR	B						FR	LI	I		CM CP	Y	LI		1748	RT
1728	FERNANDEZ DE VILLANUEVA VEITIA LINAJE, José	S	47	ME		B		ME	X-ME	O-Y		OD	ME	I		MN	Y	ME	SA	1743	D
1729	CARRION Y MORCILLO, Alfonso	S								O-Y		AC	LI	I		MN CM	Y	LI		1778	RT
1729	VILLALTA Y NUÑEZ, José Antonio	LI	30	LI	SM	D		LI	X-LI	F-HM M-OD O-Y		OD	CS	2		CM	Y	LI		1775	D
1730	ORTIZ AVILES Y GUZMAN, José Ignacio de	S		SE		D		SE RC	CA			OD	LI	I			Y	S		1745	D
1730	ORTIZ DE FORONDA, Francisco	LI	24	LI	SM					F-HM		FR	LI	I		CM NA MN	Y	LI	OL SA	1769	RT
1730	CAMPO Y ZARATE, Clemente del	CS	44	LI	SM	L		LI	X-LI	F-AC P-OD M-AC CONQ O-Y	A	AC	ME	I	STD	MN	Y	ME		1748	D
1730	FUENTE Y SANTA CRUZ, Francisco Xavier de la	LI	30	LI	SM	B		LI	X-LI	M-XX	A	OD	SD	I						1743	RC
1731	GARCIA DE QUESADA, Silvestre	S	41	SE		L		GR RC TA SF	SP	F-HM		OD	SF	I			Y	S		1743	D
1731	ARZADUN Y REBOLLEDO, José Ignacio	ME	31	YU ME	SI	L		RC		F-XX	A	OS	MA	I		MN				1754	D
1732	LUGO Y ARRIETA, Miguel Tomás de	S	37	SE		D			CA	F'-SB		OS	GD	I						N.S.	D
1732	VALPARADA Y LA HORMAZA, Juan de	S	25	VD SA		L						FI	QU	I			Y			1743	AS
1732	SANCHEZ SAMANIEGO, Jacobo José (Marqués de San Juan de Tassó)	S	50	SE		D		SE	SP			OD	PA	I					CAL	1739	AS

Year	Name	Birthplace	Age	University	Colegio	Degree	Abogado	Previous Post	University Service	Relatives' Posts	Travel	First Post	First Province	Courts Served	Purchase	Dispensations	Married	Wife's Birthplace	Honors, Order	Departure Date	Departure
1733	CAVALLERO, José Antonio	S	35	AL		B	RC					OD	GD	I						1752	RC
1733	BRAVO DE RIVERO, Pedro	LI	32	LI	SM SF	D	LI			F-HM P-XX M-XX O-Y	A	OS	LI	I	OSN	NA MN CM CP	Y	LI		1778	RT
1733	FEIJOO CENTELLAS, Juan Manuel	GD	29	ME	SI	B	ME RC	TA SF	CA	F-OD		FI	PA	I						1743	D
1734	PEREZ DE ARROYO, Cristóbal	*S	33	GR			GR			O-Y		FI	MA	I		MN	Y	MA		1742	D
1734	ROJAS Y ABREU, Antonio de	S	31	GR SA		L	RC	SP				FI	SD	2		CM	Y			1773	RT
1734	TINEO, Felipe	*S					RC	SP PI ME				AX	ME	I			Y			1753	D
1735	ALVAREZ, Manuel Bernardo de	S	35	SA AL		B	RC	TA SD				FI	SF	I		CM	Y			1755	RT
1735	COSTILLA BORROTO, Francisco	SD	37	HA ME	TS	L	ME			P-XX M-XX		OS	MA	I						1746	D
1735	ECHAVARRI Y UGARTE, Francisco Antonio de	S	30	VD AL	IL	B						OD	ME	I		MN	Y	ME	SA CI	1770	RT
1735	ANDREU Y FERRAZ, Antonio	S		HU		D			CA			OD	GT	2						c.1756	
1736	BORDA Y ECHEVARRIA, Manuel Antonio de	LI	25	LI	SM	D	LI				A	AX	LI	I	AX	NA	N			1776	RT
1736	SOTILLO VERDE, José Manuel					D		TA SD	CA			OD	SD	I						1739	D
1736	CALDERON ENRIQUEZ, Pedro	S	32	VD		L	VD RC					OS	MA	I			Y	MA	CAL	1765	AS
1737	CHINCHILLA Y HENESTROSA, Manuel	S	31	GR SA	CU	B						AC	ME	I					CAL	c.1747	D
1738	TRESPALACIOS Y ESCANDON, Domingo de	S	33	SA		B	RC			O-Y		OD	SF	3		MN	Y	ME	SA	1764	CI
1738	VERDUGO Y OQUENDO, Andrés	S	33	SI VD AL		B			CA			OD	SF	I						1758	D
1739	ALVAREZ DE CASTRO, Fernando	S	43	GR			GR RC	SP				OD	GT	I							
1739	JIMENEZ CARO, Agustín	*S	28	VD AV		L	RC		CA			FI	GD	I						N.S.	D
1739	CAMPUZANO Y SALAMANCA, Damaso José de	*S	30	VD	SC	B						OD	PA	I						c1741	D
1739	PADILLA Y CORDOBA, Pedro de	S	40	ME	SI	D	ME					OD	ME	I						1763	D
1739	BALMASEDA CENTANO, Juan de	S	46	VD		B	RC	SP	F-XX P-XX O-Y		OD	CH	I				Y	S		1773	RT
1739	PALACIOS, Francisco Xavier de	S	35	AL		D		SP				OD	CS	I							
1739	AROSTEGUI Y ESCOTO, Joaquín de	S	42	HU		D			CA	F-XX P-XX		OD	SF	I			Y			1775	D
1739	LEAEGUI, José Gonzalo	ME	48	ME AV	SI	D	ME RC	X-ME				OS	MA	I							
1739	VELARDE Y CIENFUEGOS, Juan Antonio	S	29	SA VD	SC	B						FI	SD	3					MO	1772	AS
1739	VERDUGO Y RIVERA, Alonso	ME	30	ME SA	SI	D	ME		F-XX	A	OD	SD	I				Y			1751	D
1740	HOLGADO DE GUZMAN, Diego de	S	27	OM SA		L						FI	GT	2						1767	RT

Year	Name	Birthplace	Age	University	Colegio	Degree	Abogado	Previous Post	University Service	Relatives' Posts	Travel	First Post	First Province	Courts Served	Purchase	Dispensations	Married	Wife's Birthplace	Honors, Order	Departure Date	Departure
1740	TRASLAVIÑA Y OYAGUE, José Clemente de	LI	26	LI	SM	D	LI			F-XX		OF	CH	2	OF	MN				1778	RT
1740	MARTINEZ PATIÑO, Juan José	S	35	CU AL		L	RC GT			O-Y		OS	GT	I	OS					1745	RM
1740	TAGLE BRACHO, José de	LI	23	LI	SM	D				F-AB M-AB		OD	CS	2	OD OS	MN HP MI	N			1795	D
1740	CALVO DE LA PUERTA, Sebastián	SD	23	HA		D		CA		F-XX P-XX O-Y	A	OS	GD	3	OS		Y			1767	D
1740	CARFANGER Y ARTIEDA, Juan Romualdo	LI	25	LI	SM	D	LI	X-LI		F-AB M-AB		OS	QU	I	OS						
1740	URQUIZU IBAÑEZ, Gasper	LI	27	LI	SM	D	LI	PI CS		F-OD	A	OS	LI	I	OS	NA MN	Y			1783	D
1740	BAHAMONDE Y TABOADA, Juan Bautista	LI	39	CZ		D	GT	TA SF				OS	PA	I	OS					1750	RC
1741	SANTAELLA Y MELGAREJO, Ambrosio Eugenio de	GT	27	ME		L	ME			F-OD CONQ	A	AX	ME	I	AX	MN	Y	ME		1774	D
1741	GIRALDES Y PINO, José Esteban	CS	32			D				F-AB		OS	CS	2		NA	Y	A		1771	
1741	RODRIGUEZ DE TORO, José	SD	26			L				F-XX	A	OD	ME	I	OD	MN CM	Y	ME	CAL	1773	D
1742	HUERTA Y CIGALA, Jacobo Andrés de	S	30	GR		D	RC			F-SB		OD	GT	I			Y	S		1756	AS
1742	APARICIO DEL MANZANO, Juan	SD					ME			F-XX	A	FI	GD	I	FN					1752	RM
1742	VERASTEGUI Y SARACHO, Antonio de	LI	42	LI SF	SM SF	D	SF	AG SF	CA			OS	SF	I			Y			1776	D
1742	VILLAURRUTIA Y SALCEDO, Antonio Bernardino	ME	30	ME	SI	L	ME		CA	F-AB	A	OD	SD	3			Y	S	CI	1792	RT
1742	CORREA VIGIL Y QUIÑONES, Ramón											OD	SD	I						1747	D
1742	AGÜERO RIVA, José Pablo	S	29	OM VD		B						FI	SD	I					CH	1765	AS
1742	MALO DE VILLAVICENCIO, Félix	GD	22	ME SE	SI		ME		CA	F-OD		OF	ME	I	STD		Y	ME	CAL	1775	RC
1743	LUJAN Y BEDIA, Juan de	LI	56	LI	SM	D	LI	PI QU				FI	QU	I						1755	D
1743	AGUIRRE Y CELAA, Pedro Antonio	S	32	TO AL		L						OD	GT	I						1757	RC
1743	PEREZ DE URIONDO Y MURGUIA, Joaquín de	S	29	SI SA	SB	L						OD	CS	I			Y	CS		1759	D
1744	ALAS CIENFUEGOS, Esteban Fernando	S		AV AL	IL	L			CA			FI	PA	I						1751	RT
1744	PINEDA Y TABARES, José de	S		AL	IL	L				F-MT		OS	GT	I			Y	S	SA	1754	AS
1744	OLAVIDE, Pablo Antonio de	LI	19	LI	SM	D	LI	X-LI	CA	F-AB O-Y		OS	LI	I	OS	MI			SA	1750	RT
1744	QUEREJAZU Y MOLLINEDO, Antonio Hermenegildo de	LI	33	LI	SM	D				F-HM M-HM O-Y		OS	LI	I		MN HP CM	Y	LI	CI SA	1791	RT
1744	BLANCO LAYSSEQUILLA, Gregorio	S	34	OM SA		B				O-Y		OD	CH	I		MN	Y	CH		1772	D
1744	MERINO Y RIVERA, José Joaquín de	S		SA TO	CU	L						FI	MA	I						1755	AS
1745	ZURBARAN Y ALLENDE, Manuel	LI	29	LI	SM	D	LI		CA	M-SB	A	OD	CS	2	OD OS	MN HP NA	Y	LI		1769	D
1745	SANTIAGO CONCHA, Melchor de	LI	29	LI	SM	L	LI	X-LI		F-OD P-AB M-AB		OD	CS	3	OD	MN HP	Y	CS		1794	RT

Year	Name	Birthplace	Age	University	Colegio	Degree	Abogado	Previous Post	University Service	Relatives' Posts	Travel	First Post	First Province	Courts Served	Purchase	Dispensations	Married	Wife's Birthplace	Honors, Order	Departure Date	Departure
1745	LOPEZ DE URRELO, Domingo	S	40	AL SI VD		L		SP TA SF				OD	GT	I						1765	RT
1746	TAGLE BRACHO, Pedro de	LI	24	LI		SM	D	LI		F-AB M-AB	A	OS	CS	3	OS	MN	Y		CI CAL	1792	RT
1746	LACUNZA, Andrés de	*S	40	SA SI		D						OD	SD	I						N.S.	D
1746	SALAS, José Perfecto de	CS	32	LI		SM	D	LI	CA	F-XX		FI	CH	I	FN	MN HP	Y	CS		1776	AS
1746	CARRILLO DE MENDOZA, Luis de	S	41	SI VD AL		L						OD	PA	3			N			1772	D
1746	SANTA CRUZ Y CENTENO, Luis de	LI	30	LI		SF	D	LI		F-AB P-HM M-HM CONQ	A	OS	QU	3	OS	MN HP			CAL	1785	D
1746	SANZ MERINO, Antonio	PA	35	LI		SM	B					OF	PA	2	OF	NA CM	Y	LI		1778	RT
1746	BRAVO DE CASTILLA, Pedro José	LI	44	LI		SM SF	D	LI AG LI	CA	F-AB		OS	LI	I	OS	NA HP			CI	1756	RT
1746	CASAL Y MONTENEGRO, Benito de	S	31	AV SN		D		GA SP				OD	SF	2		HP	Y	SF		1779	RT
1747	PUENTE Y IBAÑEZ, Juan José de la (Marqués de Corpa)	LI	23	LI		SM SF	D	LI		F-HM M-HM		AX	LI	I	AX	MN HP NA	Y	LI	CI CAL	1796	D
1747	PEREZ BUELTA, Gaspar Francisco	PA	28	LI		SM SF	D	LI X-LI		F-OD		OS	PA	I	OS	MN HP NA	Y			1751	RT
1747	VERDUGO DEL CASTILLO, Juan Antonio	CH	45	LI		SM SF	D	LI X-LI				OS	CH	2	OS	MN HP NA	Y	CS		1777	RT
1747	VEGA Y BARCENA, Pablo de la	LI	36	LI		SF	D	LI X-LI			A	OS	CS	I	OS	MN HP				1763	
1747	ENRIQUEZ DE VILLACORTA, Francisco de	S	38	AL		L						OS	MA	2						1774	D
1747	GOMEZ DE LA TORRE, Jacinto Antonio	S	25	VD OM		B		RC	CA			OD	SF	I						1757	D
1747	LOPEZ PORTILLA, Francisco de	GD	34	GT		B		X-GT		CONQ O-Y		OS	GD	2	OS	NA	Y	GT		1766	D
1748	VEGA Y BARCENA, Manuel de la	LI	32	LI		SM	D	LI		O-Y	A	OS	QU	I	OS	HP					
1748	RIVADENEIRA Y BARRIENTOS, Antonio Joaquín de	ME	38	ME		TS	B	ME		P-AB	A	OS	GD	2	OS		Y			1772	D
1748	MOSQUERA Y PIMENTEL, Luis Francisco (Marqués de Aranda)	S		AV SA	OV	B				F-XX		FR	ME	I			Y		CH	1761	CI
1748	GALINDO QUIÑONES, Francisco de	S	34	SE		D				O-Y		OD	SD	3		MN	Y	GD	SA	1779	D
1748	NAVARRO, Juan Romualdo	QU	33	SF		D				F-XX		OS	QU	3	OS	MN	Y			1783	RT
1748	GORENA Y BEYRA, Manuel de	CH	28	LI		SM SF	D	LI X-LI		F-AB		OS	LI	I	OS	MN HP	N			1774	D
1748	GOMEZ BUELTA, José	S	34	VD		B						OD	SD	I						1763	
1748	PEY Y RUIS, Juan Francisco	S	28	AL		L		RC				OS	SF	I	OS	MN CM	Y	SF		1790	D
1748	MARTINEZ DE ALDUNATE, Domingo de	CH	41	CH LI		SM SF	D	LI X-LI	CA	M-HM		OS	CH	2	OS	NA MN CM HP	Y	CH	LI	1778	D

Year	Name	Birthplace	Age	University	Colegio	Degree	Abogado	Previous Post	University Service	Relatives' Posts	Travel	First Post	First Province	Courts Served	Purchase	Dispensations	Married	Wife's Birthplace	Honors, Order	Departure Date	Departure
1748	DAVILA, Fernando	ME								F-OD		OS	MA	I						1762	D
1749	BECERRA Y GUTIERREZ, Sebastián de	*S		SA		B	RC		CA			FI	GT	I						1754	D
1749	ORRANTIA, Domingo de	LI	20	LI	SM	D	LI			F-XX M-XX	A	OS	LI	I	OS	NA MN HP MI				1774	CI
1749	GOMEZ ALGARIN, Francisco	S					ME					OS	GD	3	OS		Y			1785	D
1749	LOPEZ DE LISPERGUER, José de	CH	41	CH LI	SM	D	LI	PI CS		F-HM M-AB O-Y		OS	CS	2	OS	HP CM MN	Y	CS		1777	RT
1749	LLANO Y VALDES, Félix de	LI		LI	SM	D	LI		CA	F-XX		OS	CS	I	OS					1766	D
1749	ORBEA Y ARANDIA, Diego José de	LI	37	LI	SM	D	LI			F-HM	A	AX	LI	I	AX	MN HP NA	Y	LI	SA	N.S.	SA
1750	GARZA FALCON, José Manuel de la	GD	34	ME	TS	L	ME GD				A	OS	GD	I	OS	NA MN	Y	GD		1763	D
1750	ECHEVERZ, Pedro Antonio de	PA	25	LI	SM SF	D	LI	X-LI		F-AB P-CG	A	OS	LI	2	OS	HP	Y	PA		1784	D
1750	MANSILLA ARIAS DE SAAVEDRA, Manuel de	LI	24	LI	SM SF	D	LI		CA	F-AB		AX	LI	I	AX	HP CM MN MI	Y	LI	CI	1804	RT
1750	FUENTE Y VILLALTA, Juan José de la (Conde de Fuente Roja)	LI	24	LI	SM					F-AB M-OD O-Y		OS	CH	I	OS	MN				N.S.	D
1750	HURTADO DE MENDOZA, Gregorio Ignacio (Conde de Cumbres Altas)	LI	28	LI	SM			X-LI		CONQ		OS	QU	2	OS		Y		A	1789	
1751	MOSQUERA Y VILLARINO, Rosendo de	S										FI	CS	I					SA	1753	D
1751	FERNANDEZ DE MADRID, Diego Antonio	GT	25	ME		B	ME			F-OD P-XX M-CG		AC	ME	I		MN	Y	ME		1784	D
1752	URRUTIA, Bernardo de	SD	47			D	SD	X-SD	CA	F-HM		OD	SD	I			Y	SD	SD	1752	D
1752	DIAZ, Manuel	S	40	AL		D						OD	GT	I			Y	S		1767	AS
1754	ROJAS ALMANSA, Miguel José de	*S	39	GR VD		B	RC			F-CC		FI	GD	2			Y			1767	D
1754	PUERTA Y PEROSIO, Torquato Manuel de la	S	39	GR		L			CA			FI	CS	I						1765	D
1754	CERDA Y SOTO, José Antonio de la	S	37	AL	IL							OD	SD	I					CH	1766	AS
1755	ROMANA Y HERRERA, Felipe	SF	33	SF		D	SF		CA	F-HM P-HM M-XX CONQ	A	FI	GT	I						1772	D
1755	BRUNA Y AHUMADA, Bartolomé de	S	53	AV VD	SC	B			CA	F-MT		AX	ME	I					CAL	1757	RT
1755	GALVAN Y VENTURA, Manuel	S	35	HU		L			CA			OS	MA	I						1769	RT
1755	ANDA Y SALAZAR, Simón de	S	46	SI AL		D						OS	MA	I			Y	S	CH	1765	SC
1755	PUEYO Y URRIES, Andrés de	S	34	HU		D		SP	CA	P-XX		OD	SD	I		CM	Y	S		1780	RT
1755	MESIA Y MUNIVE, Cristóbal (Conde de Sierra bella)	CH	38	LI	SM SF	D	LI	X-LI	CA	F-AB P-HM O-Y	A	OS	LI	2		CM	Y	LI		1778	RT
1756	VIANA, Francisco Leandro de (Conde de Tepa)	S	26	SA	SB	L						FI	MA	2			Y		CH	1776	CI
1756	PEÑALVER VEQUE, José de	S	58	SI AL		D		PI SF				FI	SF	I			Y			1771	RT

Year	Name	Birthplace	Age	University	Colegio	Degree	Abogado	Previous Post	University Service	Relatives' Posts	Travel	First Post	First Province	Courts Served	Purchase	Dispensations	Married	Wife's Birthplace	Honors, Order	Departure Date	Departure
1756	MORALES ARCE Y REYNOSO, Andrés de	S	30	SA AL	IL	D						FI	QU	I		MN				1757	RT
1756	GONZALEZ BUSTILLO, Juan Manuel	S	30	SA		B	RC			O-Y		OD	GT	2						1776	AS
1758	VILLARRASA VENEGAS, Basilio	S	34	GR		D			CA			OD	GT	2						1779	AS
1758	CISTUE Y COLL, José de (Barón de la Menglana)	S	33	HU		B			CA			FI	QU	3			Y	S	CH	1777	CI
1761	ULLOA Y SOUSA, Martín de	S	47	SE AV		D		TA SD		F-XX P-XX O-Y		FI	SD	I					SD N.S.		AS
1763	ACEDO, Miguel Calixto de	S	33	SA	SB	L						OD	SD	2						1786	AS
1763	ARANGOYTI, Domingo de	S		AL		L						FI	GD	2		MN				1781	D
1764	GAMBOA, Francisco Xavier	GD	47	ME	SI	L		ME		X-ME	A	AC	ME	I			Y			1794	D
1764	HERRERA Y RIVERO, Vicente de (Marqués de Herrera)	S		SA	SB	L						FI	SD	3					CH	1786	CI
1764	NAVIA BOLAÑOS, Nuño	LI	30	LI SA	SM OV					F-OD P-XX O-Y		OD	SD	2			Y			1774	D
1764	SANCHEZ PAREJA DE LA TORRE, Eusebio	S	48	GR		L		TA SF				OD	GD	2			Y			1787	RT
1764	GONZALEZ BECERRA, Ramón Joaquín	S		SN SA		L						OD	GD	2			Y			1777	AS
1764	FERRER DE LA PUENTE, José	S	45	OR		D	VA RC	SP TA SF				OD	QU	3					SD CI	1791	D
1765	PORLIER, Antonio de (Marqués de Bajamar)	S	43	AL SA		D	RC	PI CS		F-XX		OD	CS	2			Y	CS	CH	1775	CI
1765	VEYAN Y MOLA, Serafín	S		HU					CA			OD	QU	2			Y	LI		1778	D
1765	ARECHE Y SORNOZA, José Antonio de	S	34	AL SA		D			CA			OD	MA	2						1776	CI
1765	BASARAZ Y GARAGORTA, Domingo Blas de	S		SA		D						OD	MA	I						1773	D
1765	PARAMO Y NEYRA, José de	S	53	SN		L		GA RC				OS	MA	I						1766	D
1765	ANDRADE Y CUELLAR, Antonio Lorenzo de	*S		SE		L						FI	MA	I			Y			1775	D
1765	FERNANDEZ VILLANUEVA, Manuel	S	39	AL GR SI SN		L		TA ME		O-Y		OD	GT	2			Y	S		1776	D
1766	VASQUEZ DE ALDANA, José Antonio	S	33	SA VD	OV	B						OD	GT	I						1771	D
1766	LUYANDO, Ruperto Vicente de	S	32	ZA		D	AR	SP		O-Y		OD	SD	3			Y			1786	AS
1766	RIVERA Y PEÑA, Ramón de	S	36	SN		D	GA	SP	CA			OS	CS	2			Y	CS		1781	AS
1766	ALVEAR Y ARTUNDUAGA, Isidro Santiago de		52	LI	SF	D		X-PA				OD	QU	I			Y			1785	D
1766	URUÑUELA ARANSAY, Juan Antonio	S	37	SA AV SI	OV	L				O-Y		OS	MA	3					CH	1789	CI
1766	ALVAREZ DE ACEVEDO, Tomás Antonio	S	31	SA		B						FI	CS	3			Y	LI	CH	1788	CI
1767	RUEDAS MORALES, Gerónimo Manuel de	S		OM SA BO		D			CA			FR	LI	2			Y	LI		1785	D
1768	GONZALEZ MALDONADO, Francisco Ignacio	ME	30	ME	SI	D		ME	CA	M-XX	A	OS	MA	3		MN			CI	1799	RT
1768	CON, Benito Antonio de						RC	SP				OD	GT	I						1771	D

Year	Name	Birthplace	Age	University	Colegio	Degree	Abogado	Previous Post	University Service	Relatives' Posts	Travel	First Post	First Province	Courts Served	Purchase	Dispensations	Married	Wife's Birthplace	Honors, Order	Departure Date	Departure
1768	BONILLA XIMENO, Juan Bautista	S		VD		B	RC VD			O-Y		OD	MA	1						1784	
1769	ANDA Y SALAZAR, Juan Francisco de	S	32	GR		L	RC			O-Y		OS	MA	3						1801	D
1770	RIOS Y VELASCO, Luis de los	S	33	AL VD SA	IL							FI	SD	2			Y	S		1778	AS
1771	MIRAFUENTES, Simón Antonio de	S		HI VD		L	RC	TA SD				OD	SD	2						1790	D
1772	MARTINEZ SANCHEZ DE ARAQUE, Diego de	S	36	GR		B	GR RC					FI	SD	3						1786	
1772	URIZAR Y BOLIVAR, José Antonio de	S	35	ON VD		L	RC	TA SD				OD	SD	2		MN			CH CI	1795	CI
1773	VALERA, Juan Antonio de	*S					RC					OD	QU	1						N.S.	AS
1773	GALDEANO ALONSO Y MOTA, Joaquín de	S	33	SA HU		D		PI QU	CA			FI	QU	3			Y	LI		1786	D
1773	VELEZ DE GUEVARA, Nicolás	SF		SF		D	SF		CA	CONQ	A	OD	QU	2			Y			1795	D
1773	BELEÑA, Eusebio Ventura	S	37	SI AL		D	RC	X-GD	CA	F-SB		OD	GT	4						1794	
1773	ARREDONDO Y PELEGRIN, Manuel Antonio (Marqués de San Juan Nepomuceno)	S	35	SA		B	RC			O-Y		OD	GT	4			Y	LI	CI CA CH	1816	RT
1773	EGUIA RAMIREZ DE ARRELLANO, Antonio	*S		HI GR	SC							OD	GD	1						N.S.	D
1773	CABEZA ENRIQUEZ, Joaquín	S		SA VD	AR	B						OD	GD	1						1782	D
1773	PLAZA Y UBILLA, Joaquín de	S	29	SA VD	SB	L						OD	GT	2						1784	D
1774	MARTINEZ ESCOBAR, Miguel de	S	46	ME	SI	B	RC	PI CS		F-XX O-Y		FI	CS	1			Y	CS		1774	D
1774	CACHO CALDERON DE LA BARCA, Emeterio	S		OV			VD			F-XX O-Y		OS	MA	2						1803	D
1774	DIEZ QUIJADA Y OVEJERO, Félix	S	47	SI AL	IL	L		SP	CA			OD	MA	2			Y			1806	D
1774	MON Y VELARDE, Juan Antonio	S	27	OV SA	OV	B						OD	GD	3						1790	CI
1774	OSORIO PARDO Y LLAMAS, José Bernardo	S		SN			GA RC					OD	SD	2						1781	D
1774	POSADA Y SOTO, Ramón de	S	24	AV VD OM		L	RC					OD	GT	3		MN	Y		CH	1793	CI
1775	GONZALEZ CALDERON, Tomás	ME	35	ME	TS	D	ME				A	OD	GT	3			Y			1814	D
1775	SAAVEDRA Y CARVAJAL, Francisco de	S	37	SN VD		D	RC					FI	GT	4					CI	1803	CI
1775	SALCEDO Y SOMODEVILLA, Modesto de	S	32	VD	SC	B						OD	GD	2					SJ	1790	AS
1775	CASTILLA CAVALLERO, José	S	39	SE		D		PI CS	CA	O-Y		FI	CS	2						1783	AS
1776	CABEZA ENRIQUEZ, José	S		VD SA	SB	L	RC					OD,	QU	3			N			1798	D
1776	MARQUEZ DE LA PLATA, Fernando	S	36	SE		D		PI CS		F-AS P-AS O-Y		FR	CS	4			Y	CH	CH	1806	RT
1776	MIER Y TRESPALACIOS, Cosme Antonio de	S	31	OM VD		D	VD	PI LI		O-Y		AC	LI	2			Y		CH CI	1805	D
1776	MORENO Y ESCANDON, Francisco Antonio de	SF	40	SF		D	SF	PI	CA	F-XX		FR	SF	3		CM MN	Y	S		1792	D
1776	VILLALENGUA Y MARFIL, Juan José de	S	28	AL TO		B	RC	PI QU		O-Y		FR	QU	3			Y		CI	1794	CI

Year	Name	Birthplace	Age	University	Colegio	Degree	Abogado	Previous Post	University Service	Relatives' Posts	Travel	First Post	First Province	Courts Served	Purchase	Dispensations	Married	Wife's Birthplace	Honors, Order	Departure Date	Departure
1776	BASCO Y VARGAS, Joaquín	S	47	GR SA	CU	B	GR			O-Y		OD	SF	2					↓ SA	1796	RT
1776	ESCOBEDO ALARCON, Jorge	S	34	GR SA	CU	B				F-HM		OD	CS	2			Y	S	CI CH	1781	VG
1776	MATA LINARES, Benito María de la	S	27	AL SA	SB	B				F-CA		OD	CH	3					CI CH	1803	CI
1776	ALVAREZ VALCARCEL, Juan	S	45	OM AV		L	RC		CA			FV	MA	1					CH	1785	AS
1776	BLANCO CICERON, Lorenzo	S	33	SN		L	GA	SP		F-XX O-Y		FV	CH	2			Y	CH		1791	D
1776	CERDAN Y PONTERO, Ambrosio	S		SI AL		L	RC			F-OD P-MT O-Y		FR	CH	3			Y	CH	CH	1803	CI
1776	GACITUA GOMEZ DE LA TORRE, Joaquín de	S	26	VD SA	SB	L						OD	QU	1						1778	D
1776	ROMA ROSSELL, Francisco	S				CT	AS					RE	ME	1			Y	S	CI	1782	RT
1776	JACOT ORTIZ ROJANO, Melchor (Conde de Pozos Dulces)	S	45	GR		L	GR RC	AS		P-XX		RE	LI	1			Y	LI	AS CA CH	1788	CI
1776	GARCIA LEON Y PIZARRO, José	S		GR		D		AS		F-HM		RE	QU	1			Y		CH	1783	CI
1776	GUTIERREZ DE PIÑERES, Juan Francisco	S	44	SE			SE	AS				RE	SF	1			Y	S	CH	1784	CI
1777	LADRON DE GUEVARA, Baltazar	GT		ME		L	ME	AG ME				FV	ME	1					AM CI	1804	D
1777	GORVEA VADILLO, José	S	31	VD TO		B	RC		CA			OD	CH	4			Y	CH	CH	1804	CI
1777	MERIDA Y SEGURA, Nicolás de	S				D		SP		F-AS		OD	CH	1						1781	D
1777	REZABAL Y UGARTE, José de	S	30	GR SA	AR	B						OD	CH	3			Y	LI	CH OL CI	1800	D
1777	MARTIN MERINO, Manuel de	S	45	OM VD		B	VD					FR	GD	2			Y			1783	D
1777	CALVO ANTEQUERA, Juan de Dios	CZ	36	CZ CS		D	CS			P-OD M-OD CONQ O-Y		OD	CS	1						1801	D
1777	CERNADAS BERMUDEZ, Pedro Antonio de	S	37	SN		L	GA	SP				OD	CS	3					CH	1806	CI
1777	ANDINO, Estanislao Joaquín de	S		TO VD		B	RC		CA			OD	GD	3			Y	S		1795	D
1777	CHAVES Y MENDOZA, Luis de	S		SA		L	RC			O-Y		OD	SD	3			Y	CI CH		1815	RT
1777	EMPARAN Y ORBE, Agustín Ignacio	S		VD SA	SB	L				P-HM O-Y		OD	SD	3					CI CH	1801	
1777	HERNANDEZ DE ALVA Y ALONSO, Lorenzo	S	37	VD		B	RC	SP				FV	SD	2			Y	S		1802	CI
1777	IRISARRI Y DOMINGUEZ, Miguel Cristóbal de	S	36	SE GR		B	RC		CA			FR	SD	2						1808	D
1777	JOVER Y FERNANDEZ, Ramón	*S		VA RC		D	VA	SP				OD	SD	1	CM		Y	S		1789	
1777	CASTILLO Y NEGRETE, Manuel del	S	27	SI AL		L	RC	SP				OS	MA	5			Y	GD		1807	CI
1777	GONZALEZ CARBAJAL, Ciriaco	S	42	GR		L	GR RC					OD	MA	2	MN		Y	MA	CI CH	c.1809	CI
1777	TOSTA Y HIERRO, Pedro José	S		SE		L	SE RC					FR	GT	1			Y			1788	D
1777	ORTIZ DE LA PEÑA, José	*S		SA		D	RC		CA			OD	GT	1			Y	S		1792	RC

Year	Name	Birthplace	Age	University	Colegio	Degree	Abogado	Previous Post	University Service	Relatives' Posts	Travel	First Post	First Province	Courts Served	Purchase	Dispensations	Married	Wife's Birthplace	Honors, Order	Departure Date	Departure
1777	REVENGA Y ALVAREZ, Gerónimo	S	44	VD		R	RC					FR	MA	1						1786	D
1778	GUZMAN PERALTA, Alonso de	CH	72	LI	SM	D	CH	PI CH	CA			OD	SF	1			Y	CH		N.S.	RT
1778	GONZALEZ PEREZ, Alonso	S	35	SA	OV	L						OD	CS	3						1798	RT
1778	GARCIA DE LA PLATA, Manuel	S	28	GR		L	RC			F-SB		OD	CS	4		CM	Y	S		1816	RT
1778	RODRIGUEZ DE QUIROGA, José Benito	S	40	AS CS		B	CS	X-CS				FR	QU	1			Y			1782	
1778	PINO MANRIQUE DE LARA, Juan del	S	31	GR				X-LI				FR	CS	2		CM	Y	CH		1815	D
1778	CATANI, Pedro	S		BA		D	CT RC	SP				OD	SF	4			Y			1810	
1779	INCLAN Y ARANGO, Joaquín José	S	37	OV		L	AS RC					OD	SD	2			Y	S		1797	RT
1779	MUÑOZ Y CUBERO, Lucas	S	45	GR		D	GR		CA			OD	QU	4			N		CH	1810	
1779	URRUTIA, Manuel José de	SD	47	ME HA	SI	D	SD	X-SD	CA		A	OD	QU	3					SD OM	1802	D
1779	LOPEZ QUINTANA, Antonio	S	38	SA		L	RC CN	SP	CA			FR	GD	3			Y		CH CI	1805	CI
1779	MOYA, José de	S	54	HU		B	AR					OD	GD	2						1796	D
1779	BRAVO Y BERMUDEZ, Manuel	S	40	SA AV	OV	L	RC	SP				OD	SD	2			Y	S	OM CH	1799	D
1779	ZUBIRIA, Juan José de	S		SA		D	RC					OD	GT	2						1786	D
1779	DIEZ DE MEDINA, Francisco Tadeo	CS	41	CS		D	CS	X		F-XX		OD	CH	1			N			1803	D
1779	MARQUEZ DE LA PLATA Y SOTO, José	S	38	SE			SE RC			F-AS P-AS		FV	CH	2			Y	CH		1810	
1779	MARTINEZ, Manuel Silvestre	S	46	AL		L	RC	SP	CA			FR	SF	2			Y	S		1803	RT
1779	PEREZ DE URIONDO Y MARTIERENA, Joaquín de (Marqués del Valle del Tojo)	CS	27	CS VD		D	VD			F-OD		FR	CH	1			Y	S	OL CH	1797	D
1779	QUADRADO Y VALDENEBRO, Fernando	S	49	VD SA		B		TA SF				OD	QU	2			N		CH	Ind.	
1779	REY Y BOZA, Félix del	SD				L	ME SD	TA SD				OD	GT	2						1787	D
1780	MERCHANTE DE CONTRERAS, José	S	36	HU		B	RC					FR	SF	2	MN					1810	
1780	URRIOLA Y ECHEVERZ, Luis de	SF	32	SI AL		B			CA	F-XX P-AB		OD	CH	1			Y	CH	CH	1798	D
1780	DIAZ DE SARAVIA, Julián	S	49	OM VD		L	VD RC	SP				FR	SD	2						1797	D
1780	ARNAIZ DE LAS REVILLAS, Domingo	S	30	OM VD		D	VD	CA				FR	CS	2			Y	S		1817	RM
1781	YAÑEZ, Antonio Vicente de	S		GR			RC	CA				FR	QU	2					AS	1789	AS
1782	MESIA Y CAICEDO, José de	S	29	GR		D		CA		P-SB		OD	SF	2			Y	SF		1819	
1782	VALIENTE Y BRAVO, José Pablo Antonio de	S	34	SE		D	SE RC	CA				OD	GT	2					CI IC	1804	CI
1783	AGUIRRE Y VIANA, Guillermo de	S	31	ZA AL		D				F-SB O-Y		OD	GD	2						1810	D
1783	PALOMEQUE, Tomás Ignacio	S	27	AL BO		B		CA	O-Y			OD	BA	3			Y	BA		Ind.	
1783	VELASCO Y MUNGUIA, Sebastián	S	59	UM VD		B	RC	X-CS				OD	BA	1			Y	S		1804	RT
1784	MORENO Y ESCANDON, Francisco Xavier de	SF	33	SF OM SA VD		D	RC			F-XX O-Y	A	OD	MA	3						Ind.	

Year	Name	Birthplace	Age	University	Colegio	Degree	Abogado	Previous Post	University Service	Relatives' Posts	Travel	First Post	First Province	Courts Served	Purchase	Dispensations	Married	Wife's Birthplace	Honors, Order	Departure Date	Departure
1784	BATALLER Y VASCO, Miguel Antonio	S	63					GR RC		AG ME		AC	ME	1			Y	S	AM	1795	D
1785	ROBLEDO DE ALBUQUERQUE, Francisco de	S	42	GR		B		SE RC		AG SF		OD	GT	2			Y	SF		1811	CI
1785	SALAMANCA, Ramón José de	S		OM VD		B			SP		CA	OD	CH	1						N.S.	
1785	BODEGA Y MOLLINEDO, Manuel Antonio de la	LI	37	LI AL		D		LI RC			CA	OD	GT	2			Y	ME		1804	RM
1785	PASTOR, Julián Hilarión	S		AL		D			SP		O-Y	FR	MA	1						1794	D
1785	BOETO, Antonio	S								X- LI		AC	LI	2			Y	BA	CL	1808	D
1785	PORTILLA Y GALVEZ, José de la	S		GR		D		GR		AG LI		OD	LI	2						1804	CI
1785	VIDERIQUE, Rafael Antonio	S										FR	LI	3			Y			1800	D
1786	CISNEROS DE LA OLIVA, Felipe	S	49	OR		B		RC GR				OD	MA	2	MN				CI	1804	D
1786	GONZALEZ SALAZAR, Pedro Celestino	LI	45	LI	SM			SE RC	SP	F-AB	A	OD	QU	1						1790	D
1786	RODRIGUEZ BALLESTEROS, Juan	S	48	GR SE		B		SE RC	SP			OD	CH	2	CM		Y	S	CI	1817	RT
1786	SUAREZ TRESPALACIOS, Juan Hipólito de	S	41	OV		L		RC				OD	CH	1			N			1788	D
1786	SANCHEZ MOSCOSO, Miguel	S	45	GR		L		GR		AG BA		OD	BA	2			L		CI	1803	**RT**
1786	CORTINES, Francisco Ignacio	S		SE		D		RC SE	SP	TA CA	CA	OD	CA	2					CH	1806	CI
1786	PEDROSA, Juan Nepomuceno de					L		RC				OD	CA	1						1798	D
1786	RIVERA, José Patricio de	SD	50	HA		D		ME SD		X- SD	CA P-XX	OD	CA	1			Y		SD	1788	D
1786	BORBON Y TORRIJOS, Francisco Xavier	S	34	VA		B		RC		SP		FR	GD	2					CH	c.1810	
1786	SANTOS DOMINGUEZ HOYOS, Martín	S	31	GR SA		L		RC			CA	OD	GD	1			Y	A		1800	RT
1786	SAGARZURIETA, Ambrosio de	S	36	AL ZA		D		RC		SP		FV	GD	2			Y		CH	Ind.	
1786	TALAVERA Y MEDINA, Sebastián de	CA		CA		D		RC		F-XX	CONQ	OD	GT	1						1792	RT
1787	MOSQUERA Y FIGUEROA, Joaquín de	SF	39	SF		D		SF		TA SF	CA CONQ	OD	SF	3					IC	1810	CI
1787	HERRERA, Francisco Manuel	S	45	GR				GR		P-MT O-Y		FR	BA	4			Y			1810	D
1787	ALVAREZ DE MENDIETA, Francisco Xavier	S	32	VA		B		VA				OD	MA	2	MN					1810	D
1787	SUAREZ RODRIGUEZ, Antonio	S	49	AL		B		RC	SP			FI	CZ	2			Y			1810	RM
1787	FONCERRADA Y ULIBARRI, Melchor José de	ME	38	ME	SI TS	L		ME		X- LI		OD	SD	2			Y			1814	
1787	PAREJA Y CORTES, José de	S	33	GR		D				AG LI	CA O-Y	OD	BA	3			Y	S	CH	Ind.	
1787	VILLAURRUTIA Y LOPEZ OSORIO, Antonio de	SD	32	ME		B		ME RC		F-RE	A	OD	CS	2			Y	S		1819	AS
1787	INQUANZO DIAZ, Marcos	S	31	ME	SI			ME RC				OD	MA	1						1795	D
1787	ALONSO DE TEJADA, Joaquín José	S	31	VD				RC				FV	MA	1						1800	D

Year	Name	Birthplace	Age	University	Colegio	Degree	Abogado	Previous Post	University Service	Relatives' Posts	Travel	First Post	First Province	Courts Served	Purchase	Dispensations	Married	Wife's Birthplace	Honors, Order	Departure Date	Departure
1788	ASTEGUITA Y SARRALDE, José Bernardo	S	39	GR OR		D							OD	MA	3			Y		CH	1810	RT
1788	BATALLER Y ROS, Miguel Antonio	S	32	GR		L	GR			F-OD			FR	GT	2						Ind.	
1788	MONSERRATE Y URBINA, Francisco Rafael de	CA	44	CA HA		D	SD RC	TA SD		M-HM			OD	GD	I						1795	RC
1788	MORENO AVENDAÑO, Juan de	S	45	OS GR		B	SE RC	AG SF					OD	QU	2			Y	QU	SF	1806	D
1789	VILLALBA, Victoriano de	S		HU					CA	F-AS O-Y			FI	CS	I			Y			1800	RT
1789	ANSOTEGUI Y BARROETA, Francisco Tomás de	S	32	SN		D	RC						OD	BA	3						Ind.	
1790	IGLESIA Y HUGUES, José de la	S	51	SE		D	SE RC	TA LI					OD	CS	2			Y			Ind.	
1790	ESTERRIPA, Francisco Xavier	S	27	AL		D				F-MT			OD	SF	3			Y	SF	CI	1819	D
1790	ALVAREZ CALDERON, Andrés	LI		LI		B	VD					A	FI	SD	I						1810	RT
1790	BERRIO Y GUZMAN, José Antonio	SF	55	SF		D	SF			CONQ			FV	SF	I			Y		SD CH	1800	D
1790	HERNANDEZ DE ALVA Y ALONSO, Juan	S	40	AL		B	RC			O-Y			OD	SF	3			Y	S	OM IC	Ind.	
1791	PRIETO Y DAVILA, Nicolás	SF	42	SF		D		TA QU	CA	F-AB CONQ			OD	QU	I						1796	D
1791	VALENZUELA Y AGUILAR, Pedro Jacinto de	S	53	JA			GR	AG ME					AC	ME	I					AM CI	1798	CI
1791	GARASA JIMENEZ DE BAQUES, Francisco	S	40	ZA		D	AR						OD	BA	I						1803	D
1791	MUZQUIZ Y ALDUNATE, Luis Antonio de	S		AL				TA ME		O-Y			OD	GD	I					CH	1794	AS
1792	PONCE DE LEON Y MAROTO, Ignacio	SD						X-SD					FR	GD	I			Y	SD	SD	N.S.	
1792	VILLAURRUTIA Y LOPEZ OSORIO, Jacobo de	SD	35	AL TO		D	RC	SP		F-RE P-XX M-HM	A		OD	GT	2			Y	S		1810	AS
1792	CAMPO Y RIVAS, Manuel del	SF	42	SF		D	SF RC			F-XX M-HM	A		OD	GT	3					CH	Ind.	
1792	PARDO RIVADENEYRA, Manuel	S	33										AC	LI	2		MN	Y	LI	CI IC	Ind.	
1792	FUENTES GONZALEZ BUSTILLO, José	S	30	SA		L	RC			F-XX O-Y			OD	CZ	2					CI	1810	RT
1793	RUBIANES, Manuel Antonio	A	45	SF		D	SF QU	X-QU	CA				FI	QU	2			Y	QU		1796	D
1794	CAMACHO CANOVAS, Francisco	S		AL TO		B			CA				OD	GD	2						1810	RT
1794	SANTIAGO CONCHA JIMENEZ LOBATON, José	CH	34	LI			LI			F-OD P-OD M-PR			OD	CH	2		MN	Y	CH		1818	D
1794	CONTI, José Pablo	BA		CS		D	CS	TA CS					OD	CS	I			Y			1802	D
1795	MOYA Y COLON, Diego Miguel de	SD	57	ME		D	ME	AG SD				A	FI	GD	I					GT	1799	D
1795	QUEIPO DE LLANO, Fernando	S											OD	MA	I						N.S.	AS
1795	QUIJANO VELARDE, José (Conde de Torre Velarde)	LI	56	LI	SF	D	LI	X-LI		F-XX M-XX	A		OD	SF	I			Y	S	CAL	1801	D
1795	RIQUELME, Rodrigo	S	34	AL OR GR		B	RC			F-SB			FH	MA	I						N.S.	

Year	Name	Birthplace	Age	University	Colegio	Degree	Abogado	Previous Post	University Service	Relatives' Posts	Travel	First Post	First Province	Courts Served	Purchase	Dispensations	Married	Wife's Birthplace	Honors, Order	Departure Date	Departure
1795	ALDUNATE, José Santiago	CH	39	CH		D	CH			F-AC O-Y	A	OS	CH	2			Y			Ind.	
1795	NAVA GRIMON, Francisco de	S	25	AL		B	RC			O-Y		OD	GD	1					CH	1804	RT
1795	BACHILLER DE MENA, Rafael	S						AG ME				AC	ME	1					AM	1796	D
1796	MESIA Y CAICEDO, Nicolás de	S	32	SF		D	SF		CA	P-SB		OD	MA	2							
1796	COLLADO, Juan	S	48	AL	SE	B	RC	TA ME	CA	F-SB		OD	GT	4							
1796	RIO Y VIAL, Luis Gonzalo del	S	36	VD		B	RC		CA			FI	CZ	3						1816	
1796	ROCHA Y LANDECHE, Domingo de la	SD	71	ME		B	ME SD	TA ME		F-AB P-OD M-HM		FI	GT	1			Y		GD	1797	D
1796	CAMPUZANO Y SALAZAR, Joaquín Bernardo de	S	28	VD	OR	D	RC					OD	BA	3						Ind.	
1796	GUTIERREZ DE PIÑERES, Fernando Antonio	S	34	VD		B	VD	TA ME		O-Y		FH	MA	2					CH	1813	D
1796	ROA Y ALARCON, Bernardo de (Marqués de Piedra Blanca de Huana)	CH	30	LI		D	LI	X-LI	CA	F-AB P-AB M-AB CONQ O-Y	A	OD	QU	2					CH	1798	AS
1796	VALLE DEL POSTIGO, Manuel María de	S	42	BZ	GR	B	SE RC	AG LI		O-Y		AC	LI	1			Y	LI		Ind.	
1797	BLAYA Y BLAYA, Manuel Mariano de	S	38	OR		B	GR RC					FR	SF	3			Y			Ind.	
1797	BAQUIJANO Y CARRILLO, José Xavier (Conde de Vistaflorida)	LI	46	LI		D	LI	X-LI	CA	M-AB CONQ O-Y	A	AC	LI	1			N		CL CH	1812	SC
1797	USOZ Y MOCI, José Agustín	S	34	AL		B				F-SB		OD	CS	1			Y	S		1809	
1797	VILLOTA, Manuel Genaro de	S	30	GR		D			CA			FI	QU	4						Ind.	
1797	CASAS Y ALCALDE, Anacleto Ventura de las	S	37	AL	VD	B	RC	AG QU				OD	QU	2			Y			Ind.	
1797	LLAVE Y MARQUELI, Rafael de la	S	42	AL			RC					FI	SD	3						1811	
1797	GARRIDO DURAN, Pedro	*S					SP	X-GD				OD	SF	1						N.S.	
1797	CASTAÑO Y RUIZ, Pasqual	S	27	SA		B	RC			F-MT		OD	MA	2						1815	D
1797	INCLAN Y ARANGO, Romualdo	S		SA			RC			O-Y		OD	SF	1						1809	RT
1798	IRIARTE, Andrés José de	SF	43	SF			SF	X-SF		F-AB CONQ		FR	BA	2						1809	D
1798	PILONA Y AYALA, Diego Francisco	S	44	OV		B	IN RC AS	TA GT	CA			FR	GT	2			Y	GT	GD	1808	D
1798	BERRIO Y GUZMAN, Francisco de	SF	52	SF		D	SF	X-SF		CONQ	A	FH	CA	1						1810	RB
1798	MORALES Y GABALDON, Francisco Ignacio	S	34	GR		B	GR		CA			FI	CA	1						N.S.	D
1798	IBARRA Y GALINDO, José Francisco	CA	45	CA		D			CA	F-XX P-HM M-HM CONQ	A	OD	SF	1					CH	N.S.	D
1798	FERNANDEZ MUNILLA, Juan Ignacio	ME	32	ME	SI	B	RC		CA	F-XX	A	FR	GD	1						1810	D
1798	ARIAS DE VILLAFAÑE, José Joaquín de	ME	60	ME	SI	L	ME GT	X		CONQ	A	OD	QU	2					CH	1810	RT
1798	CIFUENTES, Roque Jacinto	S	33	AL		B	RC		CA			FR	GT	1						1806	D

Year	Name	Birthplace	Age	University	Colegio	Degree	Abogado	Previous Post	University Service	Relatives' Posts	Travel	First Post	First Province	Courts Served	Purchase	Dispensations	Married	Wife's Birthplace	Honors	Order	Departure Date	Departure
1799	AURIOLES DE LA TORRE, Miguel	S	38	OS SE		B	RC					OD	CA	1							1809	D
1799	CASTRILLO EZEYZA, Antonio	*S		GR		D						OD	CH	1							N.S.	D
1799	CORTAZAR LABAYEN, Francisco	QU	42	LI		D	QU			F-AB CONQ	A	OS	SF	2				Y	QU		1813	D
1799	RIVA, Juan Antonio de la	S	41	SA TO		D	RC		CA			OD	BA	3							Ind.	
1799	MIÑANO Y LAS CASAS, Baltazar	S				D						OD	QU	1			Y				1810	RT
1799	AGUADO Y OQUENDO, Manuel	S					RC					FR	GD	1							1809	D
1800	IRIGOYEN DE LA QUINTANA, Manuel Mariano de	BA	37				BA	X-BA			A	OD	GD	4			Y				1819	D
1800	ROMERO Y MONTERO, Diego						RC					FI	CA	1							1801	D
1800	AYALA VARONA, José de	S	35	SA SE		B	SE RC					OD	MA	2							1818	RT
1800	LOPEZ DE ANDREU, Miguel	S										FI	CS	2							Ind.	
1801	MARTINEZ DE ARAGON, Felipe de	S	27	HU ZA		D				F-XX		OD	CS	2		MN					Ind.	
1801	BAZO Y BERRI, Juan	S	45	LI		B	LI	TA LI				OD	BA	2	CM		Y				Ind.	
1801	DIAZ DE RIVERA, Miguel	S	40	AL		D	RC		CA			FV	MA	1			Y	MA			1811	D
1801	GARCIA DE FRIAS, Diego	S	51	AL		B	RC	SP				FR	SF	3			Y	S			Ind.	
1802	GUTIERREZ DEL RIVERO, José	S	33	VA ON		B	RC	SP				FI	CA	1							1810	RT
1802	BAZO Y BERRI, José	S	33	GR OR		D	GR RC					OD	SF	1			N				1809	D
1802	VASQUEZ BALLESTEROS, José	S	29	SN		B	RC					OD	CS	1							1809	
1802	FUERTES Y AMAR, Félipe	S				D				F-ASO-Y		OD	QU	1							1810	D
1803	DURAN Y FERNANDEZ, Onesimo Antonio	S	53	GR		B	GR	SP TA GD				OD	GT	1					GD		1809	D
1803	RODRIGUEZ DE CARDENAS, Antonio	S	51	GR OR		D	GR RC	TA ME	CA			OD	MA	2					GT		1809	D
1803	ODOARDO Y PALMA, Cecilio	SD	61	HA SD		D	SD	TA CA				OD	GD	2			Y		CI		1819	RT
1803	RAMOS, José Antonio (Marqués de Casa Ramos de la Fidelidad)	*S										OD	SD	1			Y				1812	RT
1803	MORALES Y UGALDE, Andrés José	LI	34	LI		B	LI			F-AB		FR	GT	1							1804	D
1803	MOJO DE FRANCOLI, José Antonio de (Barón de Juras Reales)	S	52	CE		D			CA			FI	CH	1			Y	S			1810	D
1803	MARTINEZ MANSILLA, Manuel	BA	24	SN		B	RC	TA CA	CA			FR	SF	3			Y				Ind.	
1804	BERRIOZABAL, Manuel Plácido (Conde de Valle Hermoso)	S	30	OR GR			RC		CA			OD	CZ	3			Y	CZ	CI CH		Ind.	
1804	VELASCO Y CAMBEROS, Manuel Dionisio de	CS		CS			BA CS			F-OD	A	OD	MA	2							1810	
1804	CASPE Y RODRIGUEZ, Antonio	S	44	GR		L	GR RC		CA	F-XX P-XX		FR	BA	3			Y		CI		Ind.	
1804	BAZO Y BERRI, Félix Francisco	S	39	GR OR		D	GR					OD	CH	1			Y				Ind.	
1804	PORTOCARRERO Y OJEDA, Andrés	LI	58	LI	SM		LI	X-LI		F-AB M-AB	A	OD	SF	1							1808	D

Year	Name	Birthplace	Age	University	Colegio	Degree	Abogado	Previous Post	University Service	Relatives' Posts	Travel	First Post	First Province	Courts Served	Purchase	Dispensations	Married	Wife's Birthplace	Honors, Order	Departure Date	Departure
1804	REYES Y BORDA, Manuel Jose de	CH		CH		D		CH CZ	TA CZ		A	OD	MA	3					CI	Ind.	
1804	RECACHO, Juan José	S	31	SA		L		RC				OD	GD	2						Ind.	
1804	HERNANDEZ DE ALVA, Juan	S	28	VA TO		B		RC		F-FN O-Y		OD	GD	I						Ind.	
1804	FAES DE MIRANDA, Matías	S	41	OV SA		D		RC	CA			OD	MA	I						1816	
1805	MATA RAMOS, Juan de	S	34	GR		B		GR RC				FI	MA	2						Ind.	
1805	RUIZ RAMIREZ, Alfonso	S	56	OS GR SE		B		SE	SP			OD	MA	I						1817	D
1805	YAÑEZ Y NUÑO, José Isidro	CA	35	CA		D		CA	X- SF			FR	GT	2						Ind.	
1805	EYZAGUIRRE Y ARECHAVALA, Miguel de	CH	35	CH		D		CH	CA	F-AB M-HM	A	FR	LI	I			N			1815	RM
1805	OSMA Y TRICIO, Gaspar Antonio de	S	31	VD AL		B		RC		O-Y		AC	LI	I			Y	LI		Ind.	
1806	ALVAREZ NAVARRO, Antonio Julián	S	29	SA		B		RC				OD	CA	2					IC	Ind.	
1806	ALVAREZ DE ACEVEDO Y SALAZAR, José de	CH	28	VA		D				F-MT	A	OD	CH	3						Ind.	
1806	GOYENECHE Y BARREDA, Pedro Mariano	LI	34	LI		D		LI	X- LI	F-XX M-HM O-Y		OD	CZ	2					CI IC	1819	RT
1807	REMIREZ DE LAREDO, Gaspar (Conde de San Javier y Casa Laredo)	CH	60	LI	SM SF	D		LI	X- LI	F-HM P-AB M-AB		OD	CS	2			Y	LI		1811	CI
1807	SEDANO, Diego José de	S	46	SE OS		B		ME IN	TA SD			FV	GT	I					AS	N.S.	RT
1807	CAMPOBLANCO Y CORDERO, José Félix de	LI	30	LI				LI		M-XX	A	OD	CS	I					CI	Ind.	
1807	SOUSA VIANA, Juan de	S										OD	GD	I						Ind.	
1807	CELAYA, José Tomás de	GT							X- SD			FI	SD	I						1812	
1807	SERRANO POLO, Antonio Norberto	S	51	SA AL		B		RC	TA GT			OS	GT	I			Y	S			
1808	CARRION Y MORENO, Joaquín	S	30	GR		D		RC		F-XX		OD	SF	2			Y	XX	IC	1814	RT
1809	BIERNA Y MAZO, Anselmo de	S	44	HU ZA				RC	AG SF			OD	CS	3					CS	Ind.	
1809	ALONSO DE ANDRADE, Vicente	S	52	VD		B		RC				FR	GD	I						Ind.	
1809	CEA VILLARROEL, Juan de	S	40					GR				OD	BA	I						N.S.	
1809	JURADO DE LAINEZ, Juan	S	52	SE		B		RC	TA CA			OD	SF	2			Y	S	VE	Ind.	
1810	HEREDIA Y MIESES, José Francisco	SD	34	SD		D		SD RC	X- SD	F-XX	CA	OD	CA	2			Y	CA		1820	D
1810	MOJO, Luis (Barón de Juras Reales)	S	34	CE		D			X- CS	F-FI O-Y		FI	CH	I			Y	BA		N.S.	AS
1810	GONZALEZ BRAVO, Juan Gualberto	S	33	SE		D		SE RC				OD	GT	I						1814	CI
1810	LASTARRIA, Miguel José	LI	51	LI CH		D			X- BA			FI	QU	2			Y			N.S.	
1810	ARECHAGA, Tomás de	A				D						OD	QU	3						1813	D
1810	GARCIA, Manuel	SD	57	SD		D		SD SD	X- SD		A	OD	SF	2			Y			Ind.	
1810	MUÑOZ Y PLAZA, Juan Nepomuceno	CH	34	LI				LI	X- CH			OD	QU	I						Ind.	

Year	Name	Birthplace	Age	University	Colegio	Degree	Abogado	Previous Post	University Service	Relatives' Posts	Travel	First Post	First Province	Courts Served	Purchase	Dispensations	Married	Wife's Birthplace	Honors, Order	Departure Date	Departure
1810	BERASUETA, José Ignacio	ME	39	VD AL		D	RC	TA ME			A	OD	GT	2						Ind.	
1810	ORTIZ DE SALINAS, José Ignacio	ME	55	ME		B	ME	TA GD					OD	GT	2						Ind.	
1810	MENDIOLA, Ramón de	SD					RC					A	OD	SD	1						Ind.	
1810	ROBLEDO Y ALVAREZ, Luis de	SF	31	AL			RC			F-MT M-FI			OD	SD	1						Ind.	
1810	BENITO Y VIDAL, Pedro	*S				D		SP					OD	CA	1						1813	D
1810	SEOANE, José	*S					RC						OD	CA	1						N.S.	
1810	MODET, Ramón de	*S						AS					OD	ME	1						1814	
1810	PUENTE, Pedro Lucio de la	S		ON VD				SP					AC	ME	1					VE CH	1814	SD
1810	VIDAURRE Y ENCALADA, Manuel Lorenzo	LI	36	LI		D	LI			F-HM	A	OD	CZ	2			Y				Ind.	
1810	COSTA Y GALI, José	*S				D	RC	SP					FI	CA	1						1813	AS
1810	SOLIS, Sebastián de	*S						AS					OD	CA	1						N.S.	D
1810	CAVALLERO Y RIVAS, Andrés	S	36	AL				SP					FV	GT	1						1812	
1810	OSES, Juan Ramón de	S	40	HI SA		D	EX RC	AS	CA				FR	ME	2						Ind.	
1810	VILLANUEVA Y AREVALO, José	SF				D		AS					AC	LI	1						N.S.	
1810	FERNANDEZ DE LEIVA, Joaquín	CH	35	CH		D	CH	DP		O-Y			AX	LI	1			Y			1814	D
1810	MORALES Y DUARES, Vicente	LI	55	LI		D	LI	DP X-LI	CA	F-XX CONQ			AC	LI	1						N.S.	D
1811	RODRIGUEZ, Victoriano de	BA	51	CS		D	BA	TA BA	CA				FI	CS	1					BA	N.S.	D
1811	BACHILLER Y MENA, Miguel	S	50	VA		D	RC	AG ME					AC	ME	1			Y	A	AM	Ind.	
1811	FIGUERA DE VARGAS, Francisco	CA	56			D	SD RC IN			P-XX M-XX	A		AC	ME	1			Y	SD	SD VE	1811	D
1811	MOLINA, Manuel Ignacio de	BA	53	CH		D				F-HM			FI	BA	1						N.S.	RB
1811	LEYBA, Julián de	BA	62	CH		D		X-BA					OD	BA	1			Y			N.S.	
1811	VILCHES, Francisco de Paula	S	34	SE OS		D	SE RC	SP					OD	CA	2						Ind.	
1811	MAROTO, José Joaquín	S	49	GR OR		D	GR RC	TA CA					FI	QU	2					VE	Ind.	
1811	BEDOYA, Bartolomé de	LI	52	LI		B	LI	TA LI					FI	CZ	1						Ind.	
1811	MANZANOS, Francisco Xavier	S	49	GR		B	GR RC	AG QU					OD	QU	2						Ind.	
1811	POSADA FERNANDEZ DE CORDOBA, Vicente de	ME	31	AL VA		D	IN RC			F-MT	A		OD	MA	1						1821	
1811	OSTOLAZA Y RIOS, José Ramón de	LI	39	LI		D	LI		CA	F-XX O-Y			OD	QU	2			N			1815	D
1811	RODRIGUEZ ZORRILLA, José Joaquín	CH	41	CH		L	CH		CA				OD	QU	1			Y	CH		N.S.	
1812	BADILLO, José Manuel de	S					RC			F-SB			FR	SF	1						N.S.	
1813	PARDO OSORIO, Francisco Bernardo	S	57	SN GR		D	RC						OD	CA	1						N.S.	

Year	Name	Birthplace	Age	University	Colegio	Degree	Abogado	Previous Post	University Service	Relatives' Posts	Travel	First Post	First Province	Courts Served	Purchase	Dispensations	Married	Wife's Birthplace	Honors, Order	Departure Date	Departure
1813	GONZALEZ DE LA PORTILLA, Bruno	S	34	VD		B	RC	SP				OD	CA	1					CH	Ind.	
1813	MEDINA, Ildefonso José de	S	36	SE		L	SE RC	SP				OD	CA	2						Ind.	
1813	UCELAY, Francisco Xavier	S				L	RC	X-CA				OD	CA	1						Ind.	
1813	ZALVIDEA, José Antonio					D						OD	CA	1						1815	D
1813	PINILLA Y PEREZ, Angel	S		AL		B	RC	TA GD				FV	SF	2					IC		
1814	MORENO Y MORAN, Miguel	QU	32	LI		D				F-XX	A	OD	GT	1			Y	S		Ind.	
1814	CORBALAN, Santiago	A	42	CH		B						OD	QU	2						Ind.	
1814	IZQUIERDO DE LA TORRE, Antonio María	S	51	SE ME		D	ME	TA ME				OD	QU	1						Ind.	
1814	LOPEZ DE SEGOVIA, Pedro	S	40	TO				TA CZ		F-SB		OD	QU	2					IC	Ind.	
1814	NORIEGA DOMINGUEZ, Manuel Antonio	LI	56	LI	SM	D	LI	DP	CA	CONQ	A	FI	QU	1						N.S.	D
1814	BRAVO DE RIVERO, Diego Miguel (Marqués del Castel-Bravo de Rivero)	LI	58	LI		B	LI	X-LI		F-OD P-HM M-AB CONQ O-Y		OD	LI	1			Y	LI	CL SA	Ind.	
1814	GALEANO, Manuel	A				D		X-CZ				OD	QU	2					CZ	1816	
1814	OTERMIN, Miguel de	ME	40	LI		D			CA	F-AB	A	OD	QU	2						1819	D
1814	BARRIO Y VALLE, José	S	51	GT		D	GT	X-GT		F-AB		OD	GT	2			Y			Ind.	
1814	LARREINAGA, Miguel de	GT	37	GT		B		DP X-GT				OD	GT	1						Ind.	
1814	PALOMO, José Ignacio	GT					GT	X-GT				OD	GT	1						N.S.	
1814	RUS, José Domingo	CA	38	CA SD		D	CA	X-CA			A	OD	GD	1						Ind.	
1814	MOSQUERA Y CABRERA, Francisco de	SD	42				SD RC	DP X-SD				OD	SF	1						Ind.	
1815	VERGES Y LOSTAU, Juan	S	50	VA		D	RC		CA			FR	MA	1						N.S.	
1815	LEVEL DE GODA, Andrés	CA				L	CA	X-CA			A	FH	CA	1			Y		VE	Ind.	
1815	NAVARRETE, José Antonio de	LI		LI		D	LI	DP X-LI			A	FR	CH	1						Ind.	
1815	VALDIVIESO Y PRADAS, Francisco	LI	47	LI		D	LI	DP	CA		A	OD	CH	1						1821	D
1815	VELASCO DE LA VARA, Francisco Antonio de	GD	67	GD ME	SI	D	GD ME	DP X-GD	CA		A	AC	ME	1			Y			Ind.	
1815	ZAVALA, Juan Antonio	CA	38	CA		D	CA	DP X-CA			A	FR	CS	1						Ind.	
1815	RODRIGUEZ ALDEA, José Antonio	CH				D		X-CH				OS	CH	1						Ind.	
1815	IRIGOYEN Y CENTENO, José de	LI	62	LI		D	LI	X-LI		M-HM		FR	LI	1			Y	LI	OS	Ind.	
1815	CEBALLOS Y CALDERON, Gaspar (Marqués de Casa Calderón)	LI	48	LI		D	LI	X-LI	CA			AC	LI	1			Y	LI	CL	1820	D
1815	ODOARDO, José Hipólito	SD				B	RC	SP		F-RE	A	FR	ME	1						Ind.	
1815	RODRIGUEZ ROMANO, Vicente de	S	61	VD AL		L	VD RC	TA CS				FR	QU	2						Ind.	

Year	Name	Birthplace	Age	University	Colegio	Degree	Abogado	Previous Post	University Service	Relatives' Posts	Travel	First Post	First Province	Courts Served	Purchase	Dispensations	Married	Wife's Birthplace	Honors, Order	Departure Date	Departure
1815	BUSTAMANTE Y CASTRO, Juan						RC	TA GT				OD	GT	I			Y	GT		Ind.	
1815	MUJICA, Martín José de	S	41	CZ HM		B	LI	DP				FR	CZ	I						Ind.	
1815	VILLAFAÑE, José	ME		ME		B	ME	X-SD		CONQ		FR	GT	I						1817	
c1815	MENDIOLA VELARDE, Mariano	ME		GD		D	GD ME	DP				OD	GD	2						Ind.	
1816	BERNALDEZ Y PIZARRO, Manuel	S						AG MA				OD	MA	I			Y			Ind.	
1816	PEREIRA, Antonio Luis	S	41	VD		B	RC	TA LI		F-AS		OD	CH	I			Y			Ind.	
1816	VILLASANTE, Teodoro Andrés de	S	40									OD	CS	I						Ind.	
1816	BASTUS Y FAYA, Juan	S	43	CE		L	CT	X-SF				OD	QU	2						Ind.	
1816	GARCIA VALERO, José Mariano	S	·55	GR		B	RC IN	TA GT				FR	SD	I						N.S.	D
1816	CAÑETE Y DOMINGUEZ, Pedro Vicente	BA	65	TU CH		D	CH CS	TA CS	CA	M-XX CONQ		OD	QU	2			Y	CS		N.S.	D
1816	GOMEZ ECHAGAVIA, Agustín	BA	32	AL VA		D		TA SD	CA			OD	GT	2						Ind.	
1816	VALDES Y POSADA, José Francisco	S	43	OV		B	RC	X-SF				OD	GT	I						Ind.	
1816	AGUILA YCAZA, Pedro Antonio del	SF		LI ME	SM SI			LI ME			A	FR	MA	I						Ind.	
1816	LOPEZ DE LA LINERA, José Cleto	S	35	OV		B	AS					OD	CA	I						Ind.	
1816	POMAR E HIDALGO, Ramón	S	39	SE		B	SE					FV	MA	I						N.S.	
1816	PORTILLA Y QUADRA, Mateo José de la	LI	42	LI		B	LI RC	X-BA			A	OD	MA	I						Ind.	
1816	CASTILLO Y TALLEDO, José Miguel del	LI	43	LI		D	LI	DP			A	OD	SF	I						Ind.	
1816	CHICA Y ASTUDILLO, Pablo Mario	QU	53	QU				QU		F-XX		OD	SF	I			Y	QU		Ind.	
1816	GARCIA VALLECILLOS, Gabriel Antonio	S	40	SE		D	RC	X-GT				OD	SF	I						Ind.	
1816	O'HORAN, Tomás Antonio	ME	40	ME	SI	L	ME		CA		A	FR	SF	2						Ind.	
1816	DARICOURT Y CARTA, José	S	66	LI		B	LI			F-XX		OD	CZ	I						Ind.	
1816	NOVAS, Miguel Agustín	S	34	SN		L	RC					OD	SF	I			N			1818	D
1818	LOPETEDI Y GARCIARENA, Agustín de	S	44	GR OR		D	RC	TA ME				FV	SF	I						Ind.	
1818	MIOTA Y MATURANA, Eugenio de	LI	34	LI		D	LI	X-LI			A	FR	SF	I			Y			Ind.	
1818	ELIZALDE, Juan Manuel de	CH	27	CH		B	CH	X-CH				OD	MA	I					IC	N.S.	
1818	LOPEZ TORMALEO, Juan	S	62				RC	TA LI				OD	QU	I						Ind.	
1818	IBAÑEZ RAMOS, Joaquín	S	41	SI AL		D	RC	AG GT				OD	GT	I						Ind.	
1818	MOSQUERA Y PUGA, Bartolomé	S	31	GR		B	CS CH	X-BA				OD	CZ	I						Ind.	
1818	MONTENEGRO, Manuel Asencio	S	40									OD	QU	I						Ind.	
1818	MARTIN DE VILLODRES, Diego	S	43	GR		D	GR RC					FV	QU	I						Ind.	

Year	Name	Birthplace	Age	University	Colegio	Degree	Abogado	Previous Post	University Service	Relatives' Posts	Travel	First Post	First Province	Courts Served	Purchase	Dispensations	Married	Wife's Birthplace	Honors, Order	Departure Date	Departure
1819	MAGARIÑOS, Mateo	S	54	CS		D	BA RC					OD	CS	I				Y		Ind.	
1819	BASTANERO CARRILLO, Eugenio	S		AL			RC					FR	QU	I						Ind.	
1819	QUIÑONES, José María	SD	34	CA			SD					OD	CA	I						N.S.	
1820	ARANCE Y CALVACHE, Nicolás	S	32	GR		B	GR					OD	CS	I						N.S.	
1820	MOYA Y AMEZQUETA, Antonio Xavier de	LI	43	LI		B	LI			F-HM		OD	CZ	I						Ind.	
1820	PEÑA Y PEÑA, Manuel	ME	31	ME			ME					OD	QU	I						N.S.	
1820	RIVERO Y BESOAIN, Mariano de	LI	39	LI		L	LI	DP TA LI				OD	SD	I						Ind.	
1820	RODRIGUEZ DE BAHAMONDE, Agustín	S	50	SN		B	RC	DP				OD	SD	I						Ind.	
1821	BELTRANENA Y LLANO, Manuel	GT	34	GT		B	GT	TA GT				OD	GT	I			Y	GT		Ind.	
1821	FERNANDEZ BLANCO, Simón	S	61	OV		B				O-Y		OD	MA	I							
1821	GORVEA Y CALVO ENCALADA, Manuel	LI	36	CH		D	CH	TA LI	CA	F-FI O-Y		OD	MA	I							
1821	ANSORENA Y FONCERRADA, José Ignacio	ME	36	ME	SI	B	ME	TA ME				OD	GD	I							
1821	FLORES ALATORRE, Juan José	GD	55	ME	SI	B	ME	DP				OD	GD	I					GD		
1821	MORENO, Santiago	S		AL								OD	GT	I							
1821	OLLOQUI SANCHEZ HIDALGO, Ignacio María	ME	38	ME		B	ME					FI	GD	I							
1821	OBREGON, Octaviano	ME	39	GD ME		B	ME	DP				OD	GD	I							

Appendix X

New Appointees by Tribunal, Office, and Date, 1687–1821

1-2. Post and Audiencia. See abbreviations for columns 13-14 (first post and first province) in Appendix IX.

3. Year. Year in which the title of office was issued for the appointment indicated in columns 1-2. Within each year successive appointees are listed in order by month and day of title.

4. Native son. An asterisk indicates the appointee is a native son.

5. Name: See notes for column 2, Appendix IX.

6. Place of birth. See notes for column 3, Appendix IX.

7. Age: See notes for column 4, Appendix IX.

8. University: See notes for column 5, Appendix IX.

9. Colegio: See notes for column 6, Appendix IX.

10. Degree. See notes for column 7, Appendix IX.

11. Abogado: See notes for column 8, Appendix IX.

12. Previous Post. For second and later audiencia appointments, previous post will be an audiencia appointment. Abbreviations are the same as for first post and first province (columns 13 and 14, Appendix IX) and previous post (column 9, Appendix IX).

13. University service: Service indicated here includes:
    CA: professor (catedrático)
    OP: seeking a university chair (opositor)
    SU: interim service in a chair as a substitute
    RE: service as regent in a chair

14. Relatives' post. See column 11, Appendix IX.

15. Total appointments. This number is the total of audiencia appointments in a minister's career. Often it exceeds the number of courts served found in column 15, Appendix IX.

16. Purchase: Purchase of the appointment indicated in columns 1 and 2 are noted. See column 16, Appendix IX for abbreviations.

17. Date. This is the year in which the appointment was purchased.

18. Dispensations: Only dispensations relevant to the audiencia position indicated in column one are listed. See column 17, Appendix IX for abbreviations.

19. Married. See column 18, Appendix IX.

20. Wife's Birthplace. See column 19, Appendix IX.

21. Honors, Order. See column 20, Appendix IX.

22. Departure.
    AS: Spanish audiencia or chancellery, or the House of Trade
    CI: Council of the Indies
    C: Council other than that for the Indies
    D: Death
    Ind.: Independence in the region served
    RC: Retired to the church
    Ref.: Refused appointment
    RM: Removed from office
    RT: Retired (jubilado)
    For transfers to other American positions, see the abbreviations in columns 13-14, Appendix IX.

23. Years of service. This is an approximate figure for the length of time a minister served in the audiencia listed in column 2. The figure is based on the time between successive appointments to different audiencias when date of possession and departure from office are unknown.   N.S. refers to an appointee's failure to serve. Ind. refers to service until independence.

Post	Audiencia	Year	Native Son	Name	Birthplace	Age	University	Colegio	Degree	Abogado	Previous Post	University Service	Relatives' Posts	Total Appts.	Purchase	Date	Dispensations	Married	Wife's Birthplace	Honors, Order	Departure	Years of Service
AUDIENCIA OF BUENOS AIRES																						
RE	BA	1783		ARREDONDO y PELEGRIN, Manuel Antonio (Marqués de San Juan Nepomuceno)	S	45	SA		B	RC	OD LI		O-Y	6				Y		CI RE CA LI CH		4
RE	BA	1787		MATA LINARES, Benito María de la	S	38	AL SA	SB	B		OD LI	OP	F-CA	3						CI MT CH CI		16
RE	BA	1803		GORVEA VADILLO, José	S	57	VD TO		B	RC	RE MA	CA		5				Y	CH	CH FI CI		I
RE	BA	1804		MUÑOZ y CUBERO, Lucas	S	70	GR		D	GR	RE SF	CA		4				N		Ind.		
RE	BA	1811		GARCIA de la PLATA, Manuel	S	61	GR		L	RC	OD LI		F-SB	5				Y	S	Ind.	N.S.	
OD	BA	1783		CABEZA ENRIQUEZ, José	S		VD SA	SB	L	RC	AC LI	OP		3				N		D	14	
OD	BA	1783		GONZALEZ PEREZ, Alonso	S	40	SA	OV	L		OD CS	OP		3						OD CH	6	
OD	BA	1783		PALOMEQUE, Tomás Ignacio	S	27	AL BO					CA	O-Y	4				Y	BA	OD CS	4	
OD	BA	1783		VELASCO y MUNGUIA, Sebastián de	S	59	OM VD		B	RC	X- CS	OP		I				Y	S	RT	21	
OD	BA	1786		SANCHEZ MOSCOSO, Miguel	S	45	GR		L	GR	AG BA			2						CI OD CZ	I	
OD	BA	1786		BLANCO CICERON, Lorenzo	S	43	SN		L	GA	OD CS		F-XX O-Y	3				Y	CH	D	3	
OD	BA	1787		PAREJA y CORTES, José de	S	33	GR		D		AG LI	CA	O-Y	4				Y	S	FR LI	2	
OD	BA	1789		VIDERIQUE, Rafael Antonio	S						FR LI			3				Y		OD ME	11	
OD	BA	1789		ANSOTEGUI y BARROETA, Francisco Tomás de	S	32	SN		D	RC		SU		3						RE CS	20	
OD	BA	1791		GARASA JIMENEZ de BAQUES, Francisco	S	40	ZA		D	AR				I						D	11	
OD	BA	1796		CAMPUZANO y SALAZAR, Joaquín Bernardo de	S	28	VD OR		D	RC		SU		3						OD GT	10	
OD	BA	1799		RIVA, Juan Antonio de la	S	41	SA TO		D	RC		CA		4						OD GD	N.S.	
OD	BA	1801		BAZO y BERRI, Juan	S	45	LI		B	LI	TA LI			2				CM Y		OD LI	8	
OD	BA	1804		MARQUEZ de la PLATA, José	S	63	SE			SE RC	FI BA		F-AS P-AS	3				Y	CH	Ind.	16	
OD	BA	1804		VELASCO y CAMBEROS, Manuel Dionisio de	CS	29	CS			BA CS	OD MA		F-OD	2						Ind.	5	
OD	BA	1804		REYES y BORDA, Manuel José de	CH		CH		D	CH CZ	OD MA			4						CI OD CS	5	
OD	BA	1809		CEA VILLARROEL, Juan de	S	40				GR				I						Ind.	N.S.	
OD	BA	1811		ALVAREZ de ACEVEDO y Salazar, José de	CH	33	VA				OS CH		F-MT	4						FV CS	N.S.	
OD	BA	1811	*	IRIGOYEN de la QUINTANA, Manuel Mariano de	BA	48				BA	OD CH			4				Y		AC	N.S.	
OD	BA	1811	*	LEYBA, Julián de	BA	62	CH		D		AB BA			I				Y		Ind.	N.S.	
OD	BA	1811		RIO y VIAL, Luis Gonzalo del	S	51	VD			RC	FI CZ	CA		3						Ind.	N.S.	
FI	BA	1783		MARQUEZ de la PLATA, José	S	42	SE			SE RC	FV CH		F-AS P-AS	3				Y	CH	OD BA	16	
FI	BA	1811	*	MOLINA, Manuel Ignacio de	BA	53	CH		D				F-HM	I						Ind.	N.S.	
FI	BA	1813		LASTARRIA, Miguel José	LI	54	LI CH		D		FH BA	OP		3				Y		Ind.	N.S.	
FR	BA	1787		HERRERA, Francisco Manuel	S	45	GR			GR			P-MT O-Y	4				Y		FI CH	11	
FR	BA	1798		IRIARTE, Andrés José de	SF	43	SF			SF	X- SF		F-AB CONQ	2						FI QU	N.S.	
FR	BA	1799		VILLOTA, Manuel Genaro de	S	32	GR		D		FI QU	CA		6						FV BA	10	
FR	BA	1804		CASPE y RODRIGUEZ, Antonio	S	44	GR		L	GR RC			F-XX P-XX	5				Y		OS CH	5	
FV	BA	1804		VILLOTA, Manuel Genaro de	S	37	GR		D		FR BA	CA		6						OS LI	10	

Post	Audiencia	Year	Native Son	Name	Birthplace	Age	University	Colegio	Degree	Abogado	Previous Post	University Service	Relatives' Posts	Total Appts.	Purchase	Date	Dispensations	Married	Wife's Birthplace	Honors, Order	Departure	Years of Service
FH	BA	1811		LASTARRIA, Miguel José	LI	52	LI CH		D		FI QU	OP		3				Y		FI BA		N.S.

AUDIENCIA OF CARACAS

Post	Audiencia	Year	Native Son	Name	Birthplace	Age	University	Colegio	Degree	Abogado	Previous Post	University Service	Relatives' Posts	Total Appts.	Purchase	Date	Dispensations	Married	Wife's Birthplace	Honors, Order	Departure	Years of Service
RE	CA	1786		LOPEZ QUINTANA, Antonio	S	45	SA		L	RC CN	FR GD	CA		3				Y		CH MT CI CI		21
RE	CA	1804		COLLADO, Juan	S	62	AL SE		B	RC	AC ME	CA	F-SB	4						RE SF		N.S.
RE	CA	1809		ODOARDO y PALMA, Cecilio	SD	67	HA SD		D	SD	OD GD			3				Y		RE CA		N.S.
RE	CA	c1810		MOSQUERA y FIGUEROA, Joaquín de	SF	56	SF		D	SF	OD ME	CA	CONQ	4						IC MT CI		4
RE	CA	1811		ROA y ALARCON, Bernardo de (Marqués de Piedra Blanca de Huana)	CH	45	LI		D		OD QU	CA	F-AB M-AB CONQ O-Y	2						CH C		N.S.
RE	CA	1813		ODOARDO y PALMA, Cecilio	SD	71	HA SD		D	SD	RE CA			3				Y		X RT		4
RE	CA	1819		UCELAY, Francisco Xavier	S				L	RC	OD CA			2						Ind.		
OD	CA	1786		CORTINES, Francisco Ignacio	S		SE		D	SE RC	TA CA			2						CH RE QU		15
OD	CA	1786		PEDROSA, Juan Nepomuceno de					L	RC				I						D		11
OD	CA	1786		RIVERA, José Patricio de	SD	50	HA		D	ME SD	X- SD	CA	P-XX	I				Y		SD D		1
OD	CA	1788		ASTEGUITA y SARRALDE, José Bernardo	S	39	GR OR				OD MA			3				Y		CH RE GT		18
OD	CA	1799		AURIOLES de la TORRE, Miguel	S	28	OS SE		B	RC				I						D		7
OD	CA	1801		MARTINEZ de ARAGON, Felipe de	S	27	HU ZA		D				F-XX	3						AC ME		8
OD	CA	1806		ALVAREZ NAVARRO, Antonio Julián	S	29	SA		B	RC				2						OD SD		3
OD	CA	1810		HEREDIA y MIESES, José Francisco	SD	34	SD		D	SD RC	X- SD	CA	F-XX	2				Y	CA	AC ME		5
OD	CA	1810		BENITO y VIDAL, Pedro	S				D		SP			I						D		1
OD	CA	1810		SOLIS, Sebastián de	S						AS			I						D		N.S.
OD	CA	1810		SEOANE, José	S						RC			I								N.S.
OD	CA	1811		VILCHES, Francisco de Paula	S	34	SE OS		D	SE RC	SP			2						RE GT		6
OD	CA	1813		BIERNA y MAZO, Anselmo de	S	48	HU ZA			RC	OD CS			3						CS OD SD		N.S.
OD	CA	1813		GARCIA, Manuel	SD	60	SD		D	SD	OD SF			2				Y		D		4
OD	CA	1813		PARDO OSORIO, Francisco Bernardo	S	57	SN GR		D	RC				I								N.S.
OD	CA	1813		GONZALEZ de la PORTILLA, Bruno	S	34	VD		B	RC	SP	SU		I						Ind.		8
OD	CA	1813		MEDINA, Ildefonso José de	S	36	SE		B	SE RC	SP			2						AC ME		2
OD	CA	1813		UCELAY, Francisco Xavier	S				L	RC				2						RE CA		6
OD	CA	1813		ZALVIDEA, José Antonio					D					I						D		0
OD	CA	1816		LOPEZ de la LINERA, José Cleto	S	35	OV		B	AS				I						Ind.		
OD	CA	1819		QUIÑONES, José María	SD	34	CA		B	SD				I						Ind.		N.S.
OD	CA	1820		BASTUS y FAYA, Juan	S	47	CE		L	CT	OD QU			2						Ind.		N.S.
FH	CA	1798		BERRIO y GUZMAN, Francisco de	SF	52	SF		D	SF	X- SF		CONQ	I						RB		8
FH	CA	1815	*	LEVEL de GODA, Andres	CA				L	CA	X- CA			I				Y		VE Ind.		
FI	CA	1786		DIAZ de SARAVIA, Julián	S	49	OM VD		L	VD RC	FR SD	OP		2						D		10
FI	CA	1798		MORALES y GABALDON, Francisco Ignacio	S	34	GR		B	GR		CA		I						D		N.S.
FI	CA	1800		ROMERO y MONTERO, Diego						RC				I						D		N.S.
FI	CA	1802		GUTIERREZ del RIVERO, José	S	33	VA ON			RC	SP			I								7

Post	Audiencia	Year	Native Son	Name	Birthplace	Age	University	Colegio	Degree	Abogado	Previous Post	University Service	Relatives' Posts	Total Appts.	Purchase	Date	Dispensations	Married	Wife's Birthplace	Honors, Order	Departure	Years of Service
FI	CA	1810		COSTA y GALI, José	S				D	RC	SP			1								1
FI	CA	1813		MAROTO, José Joaquín	S	51	GR OR		D	GR RC	FI QU		O-Y	2								

AUDIENCIA OF CHARCAS

Post	Audiencia	Year	Native Son	Name	Birthplace	Age	University	Colegio	Degree	Abogado	Previous Post	University Service	Relatives' Posts	Total Appts.	Purchase	Date	Dispensations	Married	Wife's Birthplace	Honors, Order	Departure	Years of Service
RE	CS	1776		RUEDAS MORALES, Gerónimo Manuel de	S		OM SA		D		OD LI	CA		4				Y	LI	D		8
RE	CS	1786		BOETO, Antonio	S						AC LI			2				Y	BA	CL D		21
RE	CS	1809		REMIREZ de LAREDO, Gaspar (Conde de San Javier y Casa Laredo)	CH	62	LI	SM SF	D	LI	OD		F-HM P-AB M-AB	3				Y Y	LI LI	MT CI		3
RE	CS	1811		ANSOTEGUI y BARROETA, Francisco Tomás de	S	54	SN		D	RC	OD CS	SU		3						RE LI		5
RE	CS	1816		VILLOTA, Manuel Genaro de	S	49	GR		D		OD LI	CA		6								N.S.
RE	CS	1818		REYES y BORDA, Manuel José de	CH		CH		D	CH CZ	OD CS			3						CI Ind.		
OD	CS	1688		TRELLES y VILLAMIL, Gonzalo	S		SA	CU	L					1						RT		11
OS	CS	1688	*	CALVO DOMONTE, Luis Antonio	CS	26	LI SA	SM					F-XX	2			MN	Y	CS	FR LI		16
OS	CS	1689		DIAZ de DURANA, Clemente	LI	31			L					1	OS 1689					RT		27
OF	CS	1693		HIDALGO de ESCOBAR, Diego de	CH	38	LI	SM	L	LI				1	OF 1689							
OF	CS	1693		SANTIAGO de CESPEDES y CAVERO, Juan	LI	40	LI	SM	L	RC LI QU			P-HM M-HM	1	OF 1693					RM		1
OS	CS	1699		NUÑEZ de ROJAS, Gregorio	LI	25	LI	SM	D				F-OD P-XX M-FI O-Y	3	OS 1699		MN NA	Y		RM OD CS		23
OS	CS	1700		CASTILLO, Ignacio Antonio de	LI	27	LI	SM	L					3				Y	CS	RM OD CH		
OD	CS	1705		NAVIA BOLAÑOS Y MOSCOSO, Alvaro (Conde del Valle de Oselle)	S	30	SA	OV	L				F-XX	1				Y	LI	CI OS SA LI		4
OD	CS	1707		ZUÑIGA, Francisco José	LI	64			L	LI	OD SF			3						RM		5
OS	CS	1708		BRAVO de RIVERO, Juan	LI	23	LI	SM	L			OP	F-HM P-XX M-XX	1	OS 1708		MN	Y		RC		15
OD	CS	1708		NUÑEZ de ROJAS, Gregorio [3]LI		34	LI	SM			OS CS		F-OD P-XX M-FI O-Y	3	OD 1708		MN NA	Y		OD LI		23
OS	CS	1710		SAGARDIA y PALENCIA, Francisco	LI	19	LI	SM	D	LI			F-AB	2	OS 1710		MN MI	Y	ME	OS LI		22
OD	CS	1712		LERMA y SALAMANCA, Baltazar José de	S	40	SA	CU	B	FI CH			F-MT M-SB	3				Y	S	OD LI		11
OD	CS	1723		CASTILLO, Ignacio Antonio de	LI	50	LI	SM	L		OD CH			3				Y	CS	RM		
OD	CS	1723		MIRONES y BENAVENTE, Manuel Isidro de	LI	32	LI	SM		LI	OD PA		F-XX	4				Y	LI	OS LI		23
OD	CS	1724		VASQUEZ de VELASCO, Pedro	LI	56	LI	SM	D		FI CS		F-HM P-PR O-Y	3				Y	LI	CAL D		37
OD	CS	1729		VILLALTA y NUÑEZ, José Antonio	LI	30	LI	SM	D	LI	X- LI		F-HM M-OD O-Y	2				Y	LI	AX LI		9
OS	CS	1731		RIVERA AGUADO, Simón de	S	43	AL	IL	B	OD QU		OP		2						D		10
OD	CS	1739		PALACIOS, Francisco Xavier de	S	35	AL		D	SP		OP		1								
OD	CS	1740		TAGLE BRACHO, José de	LI	23	LI	SM	D				F-AB M-AB	1	OD 1740		MN HP MI			OS LI		N.S.
OS	CS	1741	*	GIRALDES y PINO, José Esteban	CS	32			D				F-AB	2			NA	Y	CS	OD SF		30.
OD	CS	1743		PEREZ de URIONDO y MURGUIA, Joaquín de	S	29	SI SA	SB	L				F-XX	1				Y	CS	D		15
OD	CS	1745		ZURBARAN y ALLENDE, Manuel	LI	29	LI	SM	D	LI		CA		2	OD 1745		MN HP			OS LI		N.S.

192

Post	Audiencia	Year	Native Son	Name	Birthplace	Age	University	Colegio	Degree	Abogado	Previous Post	University Service	Relatives' Posts	Total Appts.	Purchase	Date	Dispensations	Married	Wife's Birthplace	Honors, Order	Departure	Years of Service
OD	CS	1745		SANTIAGO CONCHA, Melchor de	LI	29	LI	SM		LI	X-LI		F-OD P-AB M-AB	4	OD	1745	MN HP	Y	CS	OD CH		12
OS	CS	1746		TAGLE BRACHO, Pedro de	LI	24	LI	SM	D	LI			F-AB M-AB	1	OS	1746	MN			CI AC CAL LI		26
OS	CS	1747		VEGA y BARCENA, Pablo de la	LI	36	LI	SF	D	LI	X-LI			1	OS	1747	MN HP				D	
OS	CS	1749		LOPEZ de LISPERGUER, José de	CH	41	CH LI	SM	D	LI	PI CS		F-HM M-AB O-Y	1	OS	1749	MN HP CM	Y	CS	OD QU		22
OS	CS	1749		LLANO y VALDES, Félix de	LI		LI	SM	D	LI		CA	F-XX	1	OS	1749					D	16
OD	CS	1760		SANZ MERINO, Antonio	PA	49	LI	SM	B		OF PA			2				Y	LI	RT		18
OD	CS	1765		PORLIER, Antonio de (Marqués de Bajamar)	S	43	AL SA		D	RC	PI CS		F-SB	2				Y	CS	CH FR LI		I
OS	CS	1766		RIVERA y PEÑA, Ramón de	S	36	SN		D	GA	SP	CA		5				Y	CS	AC LI		10
OD	CS	1771		CARRILLO de MENDOZA, Luis de	S	66	SI VD AL		L		OD SF	OP		3						D		N.S.
OD	CS	1771		SANTA CRUZ y CENTENO, Luis de	LI	55	LI	SF	D	LI	OS QU		F-AB P-HM M-HM CONQ	3						CAL OD CH		N.S.
OD	CS	1776		ESCOBEDO ALARCON, Jorge	S	34	GR SA	CU	B			OP	F-XX	3				Y	S	CI AC CH LI		2
OD	CS	1777		CALVO ANTEQUERA, Juan de Dios	CZ	36	CZ CS		D	CS			F-OD M-OD CONQ O-Y	1							D	23
OD	CS	1777		CERNADAS BERMUDEZ, Pedro Antonio de	S	37	SN		L	GA	SP			3						CH OD CZ		10
OD	CS	1778		GONZALEZ PEREZ, Alonso	S	35	SA	OV	L			OP		3						OD BA		5
OD	CS	1778		GARCIA de la PLATA, Manuel	S	28	GR		L	RC			F-SB	5				Y	S	AC LI		9
OD	CS	1779		BLANCO CICERON, Lorenzo	S	36	SN		L	GA	FV CH		F-XX M-XX O-Y	3				Y	CH	OD BA		7
OD	CS	1785		HURTADO de MENDOZA, Gregorio Ignacio (Conde de Cumbres Altas)	LI	63	LI	SM	D		OD QU		CONQ	2				Y	A		D	4
OD	CS	1787		PALOMEQUE, Tomás Ignacio	S	31	AL BO		B		OD BA	CA	O-Y	4				Y	BA	AC LI		10
OD	CS	1787	SD	VILLAURRUTIA y LOPEZ OSORIO, Antonio de	S	32	ME		B	ME	ME	SU	F-RE	2				Y	S	RE GD		19
OD	CS	1790		IGLESIA y HUGUES, José de la	S	51	SE		D		SE RC	TA LI		3				Y		AC LI		17
OS	CS	1794		CONTI, José Pablo	BA		CS			CS	CS	TA CS		1				Y		D		8
OD	CS	1797		USOZ y MOCI, José Agustín	S	34	AL					SU	F-SB	1				Y	S			12
OD	CS	1802		VASQUEZ BALLESTEROS, José	S	29	SN		B	RC				1								7
OD	CS	1807		REMIREZ de LAREDO, Gaspar (Conde de San Javier y Casa Laredo)	CH	60	LI	SM SF	D	LI	X-LI		F-HM P-AB M-AB	3				Y Y	LI LI	RE CS		3
OD	CS	1807		CAMPOBLANCO y CORDERO, José Félix de	LI	30	LI			LI			M-XX O-Y	1						CI	Ind.	
OD	CS	1809		BIERNA y MAZO, Anselmo de	S	44	HU ZA			RC	AG SF			3						OD CA		N.S.
OD	CS	1810		BERRIOZABAL, Manuel Plácido (Conde de Valle Hermoso)	S	36	OR GR			RC	OD CZ	CA		3				Y	CZ	CI AC CH LI		5
OD	CS	1810		REYES y BORDA, Manuel José de	CH		CH		D	CH	OD CZ BA			4						CI RE CS		10
OD	CS	1813		CARRION y MORENO, Joaquín	S	35	GR		D	RC	OD SF		F-XX	2				Y	XX	CI IC		N.S.
OD	CS	1815		MANZANOS, Francisco Xavier	S	53	GR		B	GR RC	OD QU			3						RE QU		4
OD	CS	1816		VILLASANTE, Teodoro Andrés de	S	40								1							Ind.	
OD	CS	1819		MAGARIÑOS, Mateo	S	54	CS		D	BA RC				1				Y			Ind.	

Post	Audiencia	Year	Native Son	Name	Birthplace	Age	University	Colegio	Degree	Abogado	Previous Post	University Service	Relatives' Posts	Total Appts.	Purchase	Date	Dispensations	Married	Wife's Birthplace	Honors, Order Departure	Years of Service
OD	CS	1820		ARANCE y CALVACHE, Nicolás	S	32	GR		B	GR				I							N.S.
FI	CS	1703		VASQUEZ de VELASCO, Pedro	LI	35	LI	SM	L		AX LI		F-HM P-PR O-Y	3				Y	LI	CAL OD CS	37
FI	CS	1724		GOMEZ CARCIA, José Casimiro	PA	29	LI	SM	L				F-XX	2				Y	LI	OD LI	27
FI	CS	1751		MOSQUERA y VILLARINO, Rosendo de	S								O-Y	I						SA D	I
FI	CS	1754		PUERTA y PEROSIO, Torquato Manuel de la	S	39	GR		L			CA		I						D	10
FI	CS	1766		ALVAREZ de ACEVEDO, Tomás Antonio	S	31	SA		B		OP			3				Y	LI	CH FR LI	8
FI	CS	1774		MARTINEZ ESCOBAR y CORONADO, Miguel de	S	46	ME	SI	B	RC	PI CS		F-XX O-Y	I				Y	CS	D	0
FI	CS	1775		CASTILLA CAVALLERO, José	S	39	SE		D		PI CS	SU	O-Y	I						FR LI	3
FI	CS	1788		ARNAIZ de las REVILLAS, Domingo	S	38	OM VD		D		FR CS	CA		3				Y	S	AC LI	9
FI	CS	1789		VILLALBA, Victoriano de	S		HU					CA	F-AS O-Y	I				Y		RT	10
FI	CS	1800		LOPEZ de ANDREU, Miguel	S					RC				2						FR GD	13
FI	CS	1811		RODRIGUEZ, Victoriano de	BA	51	CS		D	BA	TA BA	CA	O-Y	I						BA D	
FV	CS	1778		MARQUEZ de la PLATA, Fernando	S	38	SE		D		FR CS		F-AS P-AS O-Y	6				Y	CH	CH AC LI	5
FV	CS	1780		PINO MANRIQUE, Juan del	S	33·					FR CS			4				Y	CH	AC LI	10
FV	CS	1815		CAÑETE y DOMINGUEZ, Pedro Vicente	BA	64	TU CH		D		TA CS		M-XX	2				Y		CS OD QU	0
FV	CS	1816		ALVAREZ de ACEVEDO y SALAZAR, José de	CH	38	VA		D		OD BA		F-MT	4						Ind.	
FR	CS	1776		MARQUEZ de la PLATA, Fernando	S	36	SE		D		PI CS		F-AS P-AS O-Y	6				Y	CH	CH FV CS	5
FR	CS	1778		PINO MANRIQUE de LARA, Juan del	S	31	GR				X-			4				Y	CH	FV CS	
FR	CS	1780		ARNAIZ de las REVILLAS, Domingo	S	30	OM VD		D	VD		CA		3				Y	S	FI CS	9
FR	CS	1815		ZAVALA, Juan Antonio	CA	38	CA		D	CA	X- CA			I						Ind.	
AUDIENCIA OF CHILE																					
RE	CH	1776		ALVAREZ de ACEVEDO, Tomás Antonio	S	41	SA		B		FR LI	OP		3				Y	LI	CH MT CI	12
RE	CH	1788		MORENO y ESCANDON, Francisco Antonio de	SF	52	SF		D	SF	OD LI	CA	F-XX	6				Y	S	D	3
RE	CH	1792		REZABAL y UGARTE, Jose de	S	45	GR SA	AR	B		OD CZ	SU		4				Y	LI	OL D CI CH	5
RE	CH	1801		MARQUEZ de la PLATA, Fernando	S	61.	SE		D		RE QU		F-AS P-AS O-Y	5				Y	CH	CH MT CI	4
RE	CH	1806		RODRIGUEZ BALLESTEROS, Juan	S	68	GR SE		B	SE RC	OD LI			3				Y	S	CI RT	11
OD	CH	1688		BLANCO REJON, José	LI	33	LI SA	SM	D	LI	FI CH		F-XX	I						RC	9
OD	CH	1688		BERNARDO de QUIROS, Alvaro	S		AL	IL	L				F-XX	I				Y Y	MD LI	AC LI	21
OD	CH	1690		ZUÑIGA y TOVAR, Diego de	S	25	AV AL	IL	L					I						SA MT CI	16
OF	CH	1692		HIDALGO de PAREDES y ESPINOSA, Andrés de	CS	30				CS			F-AB M-HM	I	OF 1692					AL		N.S.
OF	CH	1695		CORRAL CALVO de la BANDA, Juan del	CS	30	LI SA	SF	L	LI		OP	F-OD	I	OF 1695			Y		D	23
OF	CH	1700		VALVERDE CONTRERAS y ALARCON, José de	LI	50	LI	SM SF	L	LI			F-XX P-AB M-OD O-Y	I						RM	0
OD	CH	1703		CASTILLO, Ignacio Antonio del	LI	30	LI	SM	L		OS CS			3				Y	CS	OD CS	15

194

Post	Audiencia	Year	NS	Name	Birthplace	Age	University	Colegio	Degree	Abogado	Previous Post	Univ. Service	Relatives' Posts	Total Appts.	Purchase	Date	Dispensations	Married	Honors, Order, Departure	Years of Service
OD	CH	1703		ROJAS y ACEVEDO, Francisco de	LI	52	LI	SM			AF LI		F-FI	2				Y	CS AC LI	N.S.
OS	CH	1707		SOLIS VANGO, Juan Prospero de	LI	17	LI	SM					F-PR	1	OS	1707	MI		CAL D	29
OS	CH	1708		SANCHEZ de la BARREDA, Salvador	LI	21	LI	SM						1	OS	1708	MN		D	N.S.
OS	CH	1709		GALLEGOS, Ignacio	LI	23	LI	SM	B				F-XX	1	OS	1709	MN		RT	27
OS	CH	1710		TORQUEMADA, Leonardo Fernando de										1	OS	1710			D	1
OS	CH	1710		SANCHEZ de la BARREDA, Francisco	LI	20	LI	SM					O-Y	1			MN CM	Y	D	27
OD	CH	1723		RECAVARREN, Martín de	SD	44	ME	TS	B		ME OS PA	OP	F-XX P-XX M-XX	2				Y	LI D	51
OD	CH	1739		BALMASEDA CENTANO, Juan de	S	46	VD		B	RC	SP	SU	F-XX P-XX O-Y	1				Y	S RT	33
OF	CH	1740		TRASLAVIÑA y OYAGUE, José Clemente de	LI	26	LI	SM	D	LI			F-XX	2	OF	1740	MN		RT	33
OD	CH	1744		BLANCO LAYSSEQUILLA, Gregorio	S	34	OM SA		B			OP	O-Y	1			MN	Y	CH D	26
OS	CH	1747	*	VERDUGO, Juan Antonio	CH	45	LI	SM		LI	X-LI	SU		2	OS	1747	NA MN HP CM	Y	CS AC LI	29
OS	CH	1748	*	MARTINEZ de ALDUNATE, Domingo de	CH	41	CH LI	SM SF	D	LI	X-LI	CA		3	OS	1748	MN CM	Y	LI CH AC LI	28
OS	CH	1750		FUENTE y VILLALTA, Juan José de la (Conde de Fuente Roja)	LI	24	LI	SM					F-AB M-OD O-Y	1	OS	1750	MN		D	N.S.
OD	CH	1758		SANTIAGO CONCHA, Melchor de	LI	42	LI	SM	L	LI	OD CS		F-OD P-AB M-AB	4				Y	CS AC LI	20
OD	CH	1776		PUENTE y IBAÑEZ, Juan José de la (Marqués de Corpa)	LI	52	LI	SM SF	D	LI	AC LI		F-HM M-HM	3				Y	LI CI OD CAL LI	N.S.
OD	CH	1776		MATA LINARES, Benito María de la	S	27	AL SA	SB	B			OP	F-CA	3					CI OD CH LI	2
OD	CH	1777		GORVEA VADILLO, José	S	31	VD TO		B	RC		RE		5				Y	CH CH FR LI	7
OD	CH	1777		MERIDA y SEGURA, Nicolás de	S				D		SP		F-AS	1				N	D	4
OD	CH	1777		REZABAL y UGARTE, José de	S	30	GR SA		B			SU		4				Y	LI CH AC LI	3
OD	CH	1777		SANTA CRUZ y CENTENO, Luis de	LI	61	LI	SF	D	LI	OD CS		F-AB P-HM M-HM CONQ	3					CAL D	7
OD	CH	1779		DIEZ de MEDINA, Francisco Tadeo	CS	41	CS		D	CS	X-CS		F-XX	1				N	D	20
OD	CH	1780		URRIOLA y ECHEVERZ, Luis de	PA	32	SI AL		B			CA	F-XX P-AB	1			MN	Y	CH CH D	16
OD	CH	1785		SALAMANCA, Ramón José de	S		OM VD		B		SP		CA	1					D	N.S.
OD	CH	1786		RODRIGUEZ BALLESTEROS, Juan	S	48	GR SE		B	SE RC	SP			3				Y	S OD LI	8
OD	CH	1786		SUAREZ TRESPALACIOS, Juan Hipólito de	S	41	OV		L	RC				1				N	D	2
OD	CH	1789		GONZALEZ PEREZ, Alonso	S	46	SA	OV	L		OD BA	OP		3					RT	9
OD	CH	1794	*	SANTIAGO CONCHA JIMENEZ LOBATON, José	CH	34	LI		B	LI			F-OD P-OD M-PR	1				Y	CH D	23
OS	CH	1795	*	ALDUNATE, José Santiago	CH	39	CH		D	CH			F-AC O-Y	1				Y	CH AC LI	19
OD	CH	1799		CASTRILLO EZEYZA, Antonio	S		GR		D					1					D	N.S.
OD	CH	1800		IRIGOYEN de la QUINTANA, Manuel Mariano de	BA	37				BA	OD GD			2				Y	OD BA	8
OD	CH	1804		BAZO y BERRI, Félix Francisco	S	39	GR OR		D	GR				1				Y		Ind.
OD	CH	1806	*	ALVAREZ de ACEVEDO y SALAZAR, José de	CH	28	VA		D				F-MT	1					OD BA	N.S.

Post	Audiencia	Year	Native Son	Name	Birthplace	Age	University	Colegio	Degree	Abogado	Previous Post	University Service	Relatives' Posts	Total Appts.	Purchase	Date	Dispensations	Married	Wife's Birthplace	Honors, Order	Departure	Years of Service
OS	CH	1810		CASPE y RODRIGUEZ, Antonio	S	50	GR		L	GR RC	FR BA		F-XX P-XX	4				Y		CI LI	AC	1
OD	CH	1815		VALDIVIESO y PRADAS, Francisco	LI	47	LI		D	LI	DP	CA		1							Ind.	
OS	CH	1815	*	RODRIGUEZ ALDEA, José Antonio	CH				D		X-CH			1							Ind.	
OD	CH	1816		PEREIRA, Antonio Luis	S	41	VD		B	RC	TA LI		F-AS	1				Y			Ind.	
FI	CH	1688		BLANCO REJON, José	LI	33	LI SA	SM	D	LI			F-XX	2	FI 1688						OD CH	N.S.
FI	CH	1690		REMIREZ de BAQUEDANO, Gonzalo	S	28	ON						O-Y	2				Y	LI		OD LI	12
FF	CH	1700		AYALA MARIN, Marcelo de	LI		LI	SM	L	LI				2	FF 1700						RM OD PA	N.S.
FI	CH	1703		LERMA y SALAMANCA, Baltazar José de	S	31	SA	CU	B				F-MT M-SB	3				Y	S		OD CS	6
FI	CH	1713		GOMENDIO URRUTIA, Miguel de	LI	43	SI AL		L			SU	F-AB CONQ	2							AC LI	7
FI	CH	1721		JAUREGUI y OLLO, Martín Gregorio de	S	31	SE		D				CA	1				Y			RT	23
FI	CH	1746		SALAS, José Perfecto de	BA	32	LI	SM	D	LI AG LI	CA		F-XX	2	FN 1746	MN HP	Y	CH		OD AS	29
FI	CH	1798		HERRERA, Francisco Manuel	S	56	GR			GR	FR BA		P-MT O-Y	4				Y			FR LI	5
FI	CH	1803		MOJO de FRANCOLI, José Antonio de (Barón de Juras Reales)	S	52	CE		D				CA	1				Y	AR		D	6
FI	CH	1810		MOJO, Luis (Barón de Juras Reales)	S	34	CE		D		X-CS		F-FI O-Y	1				Y	BA		OD AS	N.S.
FV	CH	1776		BLANCO CICERON, Lorenzo	S	33	SN		L	GA	SP		F-XX O-Y	3				Y	CH		OD CS	3
FV	CH	1779		MARQUEZ de la PLATA, José	S	38	SE			SE RC			F-AS P-AS	3				Y	CH		FI BA	4
FR	CH	1776		CERDAN y PONTERO, Ambrosio	S		SI AL		L	RC			F-OD P-MT O-Y	4				Y	CH	CH	AC LI	3
FR	CH	1779		PEREZ de URIONDO y MARTIERENA, Joaquín de (Marqués del Valle del Tojo)	CS	27	CS VD		D	VD		SU	F-OD	1				Y	S		OL CH	D	17
FR	CH	1815		NAVARRETE, José Antonio de	LI		LI		D	LI	DP X-LI			1							Ind.	

AUDIENCIA OF CUZCO

Post	Audiencia	Year	Native Son	Name	Birthplace	Age	University	Colegio	Degree	Abogado	Previous Post	University Service	Relatives' Posts	Total Appts.	Purchase	Date	Dispensations	Married	Wife's Birthplace	Honors, Order	Departure	Years of Service
RE	CZ	1787		PORTILLA y GALVEZ, José de la	S		GR		D	GR	OD LI			2				N			MT CI	17
RE	CZ	1803		PAREJA y CORTES, José de	S	46	GR		D		FV LI	CA	O-Y	4				Y	S	CH LI	FV	N.S.
RE	CZ	1805		PARDO RIVADENEYRA, Manuel	S	46					OD LI			2				Y	LI	CI IC	Ind.	
OD	CZ	1787		CERNADAS BERMUDEZ, Pedro Antonio de	S	47	SN		L	GA	OD CS			3						CH QU	RE	19
OD	CZ	1787		REZABAL y UGARTE, José de	S	40	GR SA	AR	B		AC LI	SU		4				Y	LI	CH CH	RE	5
OD	CZ	1787		SANCHEZ MOSCOSO, Miguel	S	46	GR		L	GR	OD BA			2				L		CI	RT	16
OD	CZ	1792		FUENTES GONZALEZ BUSTILLO, José	S	30	SA		L	RC			F-XX O-Y	2						CI	RT	14
OD	CZ	1804		BERRIOZABAL, Manuel Plácido (Conde de Valle Hermoso)	S	30	OR GR			RC		CA		3				Y	CZ	CI CH	OD CS	6
OD	CZ	1806		GOYENECHE y BARREDA, Pedro Mariano	LI	34	LI		D	LI	X-LI		F-XX M-HM O-Y	1						CI IC	OD LI	7
OD	CZ	1810		VIDAURRE y ENCALADA, Manuel Lorenzo	LI	36	LI		D	LI			F-HM M-XX	1				Y			OD SD	10
OD	CZ	1815		CORBALAN, Santiago	A	43	CH		B	OD QU				2							Ind.	
OD	CZ	1815		GALEANO, Manuel	A				D	OD QU				2						CZ		1
OD	CZ	1815		OTERMIN, Miguel	ME	41	LI		D	OD QU		CA	F-AB	3							D	3

Post	Audiencia	Year	Native Son	Name	Birthplace	Age	University	Colegio	Degree	Abogado	Previous Post	University Service	Relatives' Posts	Total Appts.	Purchase	Date	Dispensations	Married	Wife's Birthplace	Honors, Order	Departure	Years of Service
OD	CZ	1816		DARICOURT y CARTA, José	S	66	LI		B	LI			F-XX	1							Ind.	
OD	CZ	1818		MOSQUERA y PUGA, Bartolomé	S	31	GR		B	CS CH	X- BA			1							Ind.	
OD	CZ	1820		MOYA y AMEZQUETA, Antonio Xavier de	LI	43	LI		B	LI			F-HM	1							Ind.	
FI	CZ	1787		SUAREZ RODRIGUEZ de YABAR, Antonio	S	49	AL		L	RC	SP			2							OD QU	10
FI	CZ	1796		RIO y VIAL, Luis Gonzalo del	S	36	VD		B	RC		CA		1							OD BA	15
FI	CZ	1811		BEDOYA, Bartolomé de	LI	52	LI		B	LI	TA LI			1							Ind.	
FR	CZ	1815		MUJICA, Martín José de	S	41	CZ HM		B	LI	DP			1							Ind.	

AUDIENCIA OF GUADALAJARA

Post	Audiencia	Year	Native Son	Name	Birthplace	Age	University	Colegio	Degree	Abogado	Previous Post	University Service	Relatives' Posts	Total Appts.	Purchase	Date	Dispensations	Married	Wife's Birthplace	Honors, Order	Departure	Years of Service
RE	GD	1776		SANCHEZ PAREJA, Eusebio	S	60	GR		L		OD ME			5				Y			RE ME	10
RE	GD	1786		MARTINEZ SANCHEZ de ARAQUE, Diego de	S	50	GR		B	GR RC	RE MA			3							D	N.S.
RE	GD	1787		VILLAURRUTIA y SALCEDO, Antonio Bernardino	ME	75	ME	SI	L		OD ME	CA	F-AB	3				Y	S	CI	RT	5
RE	GD	1792		BELEÑA, Eusebio Ventura	S	56	SI AL		D	RC	RE SF	CA	F-SB	5							D	1
RE	GD	1794		SAAVEDRA y CARVAJAL, Francisco de	S	37	SN VD		D	RC	RE MA			3						MT CI		9
RE	GD	1803		CATANI, Pedro	S		BA		D	CT RC	OD SD			4				Y			RE ME	3
RE	GD	1806		VILLAURRUTIA y LOPEZ OSORIO, Antonio	SD	51	ME		D	ME RC	OD CS		F-RE P-XX M-HM	2				Y	S	C		10
RE	GD	1820		RECACHO, Juan José	S	47	SA			RC	OD ME	OP		3							Ind.	
OS	GD	1689		SOMOZA, Juan de										1	OS	1689		Y	A			
OS	GD	1690		OSORIO ESPINOSA de los MONTEROS, José	A				L		ME	CA	CONQ	1				Y			OS ME	7
OS	GD	1691		MIRANDA VILLAYZAN, José de	ME	32	ME		D		ME	CA	F-XX	1	OS	1691					RT	17
OD	GD	1703		DOMONTE y PINTO, José	S	34	SE		D					1								N.S.
OD	GD	1706		MALO de VILLAVICENCIO, Pedro de	S	33	SE SA		D					4				Y	S	CAL	FR ME	15
OS	GD	1707		OLIVAN REBOLLEDO, Juan Manuel de	ME	31	ME		L		ME	SU		2	OS	1707		Y	S		OS ME	N.S.
OS	GD	1708		CASTAÑEDA, Diego Francisco de	ME		ME				ME		F-XX P-AB	2	OS	1708		Y	ME		AX ME	
OS	GD	1710		URRUTIA, Fernando de	ME									1	OS	1710					RT	30
OS	GD	1710		REAL y QUESADA, Antonio	ME	38	ME		B	ME RC	X- ME			1	OS	1710	MN	Y	A		D	14
OD	GD	1720		PALACIOS, Prudencio Antonio de	S	37	SA HU		B	RC	OS SD			3				Y	S		FV ME	3
OD	GD	1722		GARZIGA, José Vicente Antonio de	S		AL		D			SU		1							RC	8
OD	GD	1724		MESIA de la CERDA, José de la	S	29	GR		B			SU	O-Y	2				Y	ME		AC ME	10
OD	GD	1726		RODRIGUEZ de ALBUERNE, Juan (Marqués de Altamira)	S	30	AL		L	RC	SP			2				Y	ME	SA	OD ME	10
OS	GD	1732		LUGO y ARRIETA, Miguel Tomás de	S	37	SE		D			CA		1							D	N.S.
OD	GD	1733		CAVALLERO, José Antonio	S	35	AL		B	RC				1							RC	18
OD	GD	1733		CARRILLO MORENO, Juan	S		VD		L		AC ME			3				Y			OD AS	14
OS	GD	1740		BLANCAS y ESPELETA, Martín de	S		SA	CU	B		FI SD	OP	F-SB	2				Y	ME		RT	14
OS	GD	1740		CALVO de la PUERTA, Sebastián	SD	23	HA		D			CA	F-XX P-XX O-Y	3	OS	1740		Y		RM	AX ME	
OS	GD	1747	*	LOPEZ PORTILLA, Francisco de	GD	34	GT		B		X- GT		CONQ O-Y	2	OS	1747	NA	Y	GT		OD ME	17
OS	GD	1748		RIVADENEIRA y BARRIENTOS, Antonio Joaquín de	ME	38	ME	TS	B		ME		P-AB	4	OS	1748		Y			FR ME	5

Post	Audiencia	Year	Native Son	Name	Birthplace	Age	University	Colegio	Degree	Abogado	Previous Post	University Service	Relatives' Posts	Total Appts.	Purchase	Date	Dispensations	Married	Wife's Birthplace	Honors, Order	Departure	Years of Service
OS	GD	1749		GOMEZ ALGARIN, Francisco	S						ME			3	OS	1749		Y			OD GT	23
OS	GD	1750	*	GARZA FALCON, José Manuel de la	GD	34	ME	TS	L		ME GD			1	OS	1750	NA MN	Y	GD		D	11
OD	GD	1755		GALINDO QUIÑONES y BARRIENTOS, Francisco de	S	41	SE		D		OD SD	O-Y		3	MN	MN		Y	GD	SA	FR ME	21
OD	GD	1764		SANCHEZ PAREJA, Eusebio	S	48	GR		L		TA SF			5				Y			AC ME	8
OD	GD	1764		GONZALEZ BECERRA, Ramón Joaquín	S		SN SA		L					3							AC ME	11
OD	GD	1772		LUYANDO, Ruperto Vicente de	S		ZA		D	AR	OD SD	O-Y		4				Y			AC ME	4
OD	GD	1773		EGUIA RAMIREZ de ARRELLANO, Antonio	S		HI GR	SC					SU	1							D	N.S.
OD	GD	1773		CABEZA ENRIQUEZ, Joaquín	S		SA VD	AR	B				SU	1							D	8
OD	GD	1774		MON y VELARDE, Juan Antonio	S	27	OV SA	OV	B					3							OD SF	4
OD	GD	1775		SALCEDO y SOMODEVILLA, Modesto de	S	32	VD	SC	B					3						SJ	AC ME	10
OD	GD	1777		ANDA y SALAZAR, Juan Francisco de	S	40	GR		L	RC	OD MA	O-Y		5							AC ME	1
OD	GD	1777		ANDINO, Estanislao Joaquín de	S		TO VD		B	RC		CA		3				Y			FV SF	6
OD	GD	1778		NAVARRO, Juan Romualdo	QU	63	SF		D		OD SF		F-XX	3				Y	QU		RT	5
OD	GD	1779		MOYA, José de	S	54	HU		B	AR				2							OD ME	8
OD	GD	1783		AGUIRRE y VIANA, Guillermo de	S	31	ZA AL		D			O-Y	F-SB	4							AC ME	4
OD	GD	1783		MARTINEZ, Manuel Silvestre	S	50	AL		L	RC	FV SF	CA		3				Y	S		RT	20
OD	GD	1783		URRUTIA, Manuel José de	SD	51	ME HA	SI	D	SD	OD QU	CA		4						SD OM	AC ME	8
OD	GD	1786		SANTOS DOMINGUEZ, Martín	S	31	GR SA		L	RC			F-CA	1				Y	A		RT	14
OD	GD	1787		CASTILLO y NEGRETE, Manuel del	S	37	SI AL		L	RC	OS MA	OP		6				Y	GD		OD SF	7
OD	GD	1788		MONSERRATE y URBINA, Francisco Rafael de	CA	44	CA HA		D	SD RC	TA SD		M-HM	1							RC	7
OD	GD	1791		MUZQUIZ y ALDUNATE, Luis Antonio de	S		AL				TA ME	O-Y		1							CH AS	3
OD	GD	1794		CAMACHO CANOVAS, Francisco	S		AL TO		B			CA		2							OD GT	6
OD	GD	1795		NAVA GRIMON, Francisco de	S	25	AL		B	RC		O-Y		1							CH RT	9
OD	GD	1796-1805		MESIA y CAICEDO, Nicolás de	S		SF		D	SF	OD MA	CA		2							RE MA	N.S.
OD	GD	1800		IRIGOYEN de la QUINTANA, Manuel Mariano de	BA	37				BA	X- BA			4				Y			OD CH	N.S.
OD	GD	1800		CAMPO y RIVAS, Manuel del	SF	50	SF		D	SF RC	OD GT	F-XX M-HM		4						CH	AC ME	4
OD	GD	1801		RIVA, Juan Antonio de la	S	43	SA TO		D	RC	OD BA	CA		4							AC ME	6
OD	GD	1803		ODOARDO y PALMA, Cecilio	SD	61	HA SD		D	SD	TA CA			2				Y			RE CA	6
OD	GD	1804		RECACHO, Juan José	S	31	SA		L	RC		OP		3							OD ME	
OD	GD	1804		HERNANDEZ de ALVA, Juan	S	28	VA TO		B	RC			F-FN O-Y	1							Ind.	
OD	GD	1807		SOUSA VIANA, Juan de	S									1							Ind.	
OD	GD	1814		RUS, José Domingo	CA	38	CA SD		D	CA	X- CA			1							Ind.	
OD	GD	c1815		MENDIOLA, Mariano	ME	46	GD		D	GD ME	DP			2							Ind.	N.S.
OD	GD	1816		ORTIZ de SALINAS, José Ignacio	ME	61	ME		B	ME	OD GT			2							Ind.	
OD	GD	1821		ANSORENA y FONCERRADA, José Ignacio	ME	36	ME	SI	B	ME	TA ME			1								

Post	Audiencia	Year	Native Son	Name	Birthplace	Age	University	Colegio	Degree	Abogado	Previous Post	University Service	Relatives' Posts	Total Appts.	Purchase	Date	Dispensations	Married	Wife's Birthplace	Honors, Order	Departure	Years of Service
OD	GD	1821	*	FLORES ALATORRE, Juan Jose	GD	55	ME	SI	B		ME	DP		1						GD		
OD	GD	1821		OBREGON, Octaviano	ME	39	GD ME		B		ME	DP		1						OM		
OD	GD	1821		PINILLA y PEREZ, Angel	S	46	AL		B	RC	FV SF			2						IC		
FI	GD	1705		PICADO PACHECO y MONTERO, Juan	S	34	SA AV	CU	L					2						AL	OD ME	15
FI	GD	1721		DAVILA MADRID, Fernando	S	37	AL SA	AR	L			SU		2				Y			OD ME	17
FI	GD	1739		JIMENEZ CARO, Agustín	S	28	VD AV		L	RC		CA		1							D	N.S.
FI	GD	1742		APARICIO del MANZANO, Juan	SD						ME			1	FN	1742				RM		9
FI	GD	1754		ROJAS ALMANSA, Miguel José de	S	39	GR VD		B	RC		OP	F-CC	2							FR ME	9
FI	GD	1763		ARANGOYTI, Domingo de	S		AL		L			OP		4			MN				FR ME	11
FI	GD	1774		GONZALEZ MALDONADO, Francisco Ignacio	ME	36	ME	SI	D		ME OS MA	CA	F-XX	5			MN			CI	OD ME	12
FI	GD	1795		MOYA y COLON, Diego Miguel de	SD	57	ME		D		ME AG SD			1						GT	D	4
FI	GD	1813		LOPEZ de ANDREU, Miguel	S						FI CS			2							Ind.	
FI	GD	1821		OLLOQUI SANCHEZ HIDALGO, Ignacio María	ME	38	ME		B		ME		F-ME	1								
FV	GD	1786		SAGARZURIETA, Ambrosio de	S	36	AL ZA		D	RC	SP			3				Y		CH	FR ME	9
FV	GD	1799		FERNANDEZ MUNILLA, Juan Ignacio	ME	33	ME	SI	B	RC		CA	F-XX	2							D	11
FV	GD	1811		ALONSO de ANDRADE, Vicente	S	54	VD		B	RC	FR GD			2							Ind.	
FR	GD	1777		MARTIN MERINO, Manuel de	S	45	OM VD		B		VD			2				Y			FV ME	1
FR	GD	1779		LOPEZ QUINTANA, Antonio	S	38	SA		L	RC CN	SP	CA		3				Y		CH	RE CA	7
FR	GD	1786		BORBON y TORRIJOS, Francisco Xavier	S	34	VA		B	RC	SP			4						CH	FR ME	5
FR	GD	1792		PONCE de LEON y MAROTO, Ignacio	SD						X-SD			1				Y	SD		SD	N.S.
FR	GD	1798		FERNANDEZ MUNILLA, Juan Ignacio	ME	32	ME	SI	B	RC		CA	F-XX	2							FV GD	11
FR	GD	1799		AGUADO y OQUENDO, Manuel	S					RC				1							D	8
FR	GD	1809		ALONSO de ANDRADE, Vicente	S	52	VD		B	RC				2							Ind.	
AUDIENCIA OF GUATEMALA																						
RE	GT	1776		HERRERA y RIVERO, Vicente de (Marqués de Herrera)	S		SA	SB	L		OD ME			5			MN	Y	ME	CH	RE ME	6
RE	GT	1782		URUNUELA ARANSAY, Juan Antonio	S	53	SA AV	OV	L		OD ME	CA	O-Y	4						CH	FN CI	7
RE	GT	1789		VILLALENGUA y MARFIL, Juan José de	S	41	AL TO		B	RC	RE QU		O-Y	4				Y		CI	MT CI	5
RE	GT	1794		CERDAN y PONTERO, Ambrosio	S		SI AL		L	RC	OD LI		F-AS P-MT O-Y	4				Y	CH	CH	FP CI	9
RE	GT	1803		CASTILLO y NEGRETE, Manuel del	S	53	SI AL		L	RC	AC ME	OP		6				Y	GD		RE ME	2
RE	GT	1806		ASTEGUITA y SARRALDE, José Bernardo	S	47	GR OR		D		OD CA			3				Y		CH	RT	4
RE	GT	1810		BLAYA y BLAYA, Manuel Mariano de	S	58	OR		B	GR RC	AC ME			5				Y			OD ME	7
RE	GT	1818		VILCHES, Francisco de Paula	S	41	SE OS		D	SE RC	OD CA			2							Ind.	
OS	GT	1691		DUARDO, Juan Jerónimo	S		ME		B		ME	CA		1	OS	1691		Y			D	26
OD	GT	1699		CARRILLO ESCUDERO, Gregorio	S	35	SA		D			SU		2							OD ME	21
OD	GT	1699		EGUARAS FERNANDEZ de HIJAR, Pedro de (Marqués de Salvatierra)	S	26	SA	AR						1				Y	ME	CI	AC ME	5

Post	Audiencia	Year	Native Son	Name	Birthplace	Age	University	Colegio	Degree	Abogado	Previous Post	University Service	Relatives' Posts	Total Appts.	Purchase	Date	Dispensations	Married	Wife's Birthplace	Honors, Order	Departure	Years of Service
OD	GT	1699		OVIEDO y BAÑOS, Diego Antonio de	SF	34	LI	SM	B	LI	OD SD		F-OD M-AC O-Y	3						MT CI		9
OS	GT	1709		ULLOA CALLEJA, Nicolás de	ME		ME	SI	B	ME				1	OS	1709	MN				RM	N.S.
OS	GT	1710		ARANA, Tomás Ignacio de	ME		ME		L	ME		CA		1	OS	1710					RM	35
OS	GT	1710		RODEZNO MANZALO y REBOLLEDO, José Nicolás	ME	23	ME		L				F-AB M-XX	1	OS	1710	MN				RT	31
OS	GT	1710		LUGO CORONADO y HIERRO, Felipe Antonio de	ME	33	ME		D	ME		OP		2	OS	1710		Y	ME	OD	ME	12
OF	GT	1711		SANTAELLA y MELGAREJO, Ambrosio Tomás de	SD	21	ME		B	ME		SU		4	OF	1711		Y		FR	ME	12
OS	GT	1711		GOMENDIO URRUTIA, Domingo de	S		QU		D	QU PA				2	OS	1711					D	23
OD	GT	1722		FERNANDEZ de MADRID, Luis Manuel	S	37	AL		L	ME		OP	F-XX P-XX	3				Y	QU	CAL AC	ME	16
OD	GT	1723		OROZCO MANRIQUE de LARA, Francisco de	S	29	AL		L			SU		2						RM AX	ME	21
OD	GT	1724		FERNANDEZ TORIBIO, Francisco	S	34	AL	IL	L			CA		3				Y		MA OS	MA	N.S.
OD	GT	1735		ANDREU FERRAZ, Antonio	S		HU		D			CA		4						FR	ME	3
OD	GT	1738		TRESPALACIOS y ESCANDON, Domingo de	S	33	SA		B	RC	OD SF	O-Y		3				Y	ME	SA OD	ME	N.S.
OD	GT	1739		ALVAREZ de CASTRO, Fernando	S	43	GR			GR RC		SP		1								
OS	GT	1740		MARTINEZ PATINO, Juan José	S	35	CU AL		L	RC GT			O-Y	1	OS	1740					RM	4
OD	GT	1742		HUERTA y CIGALA, Jacobo Andrés de	S	30	GR			RC			F-SB	2				Y	S	OD	AS	14
OS	GT	1744		PINEDA y TABARES, José de	S		AL	IL	L				F-MT	1				Y	S	SA OD	AS	8
OD	GT	1745		AGUIRRE y CELAA, Pedro Antonio	S	44	TO AL		L	OD PA		OP		2						RC		12
OD	GT	1745		LOPEZ de URRELO, Domingo	S	40	AL SI		L	TA SF		SU		1							RT	20
OD	GT	1746		VELARDE y CIENFUEGOS, Juan Antonio	S	36	SA VD	SC	B	OD SD		SU		5						MO FR	ME	14
OD	GT	1752		DIAZ, Manuel	S	40	AL		D			OP		1				Y	S	OD	AS	12
OD	GT	1756		GONZALEZ BUSTILLO, Juan Manuel	S	30	SA		B	RC		OP	O-Y	2						AC	ME	18
OD	GT	1758		VILLARRASA VENEGAS, Basilio	S	34	GR		D			CA		3						AC	ME	15
OD	GT	1764		CALVO de la PUERTA, Sebastián	SD	47	HA		D	AX ME	CA	F-XX P-XX O-Y		3				Y			D	2
OD	GT	1764		FERNANDEZ VILLANUEVA, Manuel	S	39	AL GR SI		L	TA ME		O-Y		2				Y		AC	ME	9
OD	GT	1766		VASQUEZ de ALDANA, José Antonio	S	33	SA VD	OV	B			OP		1							D	4
OD	GT	1768		CON, Benito Antonio de						RC	SP			1							D	2
OD	GT	1771		NAVIA BOLAÑOS, Nuño	LI	37	LI SA	SM OV			OD SD	F-OD P-XX O-Y		2				Y			D	N.S.
OD	GT	1772		GOMEZ ALGARIN, Francisco	S					ME	OS GD			3				Y		RT OS	ME	N.S.
OD	GT	1773		BELEÑA, Eusebio Ventura	S	37	SI AL		D	RC	X- GD	CA	F-SB	5						AC	ME	4
OD	GT	1773		ARREDONDO y PELEGRIN, Manuel Antonio (Marqués de San Juan Nepomuceno)	S	35	SA		B	RC		O-Y		5				Y	LI	CI CA CH	OD LI	6
OD	GT	1773		PLAZA y UBILLA, Joaquín	S	29	SA VD	SB	L					2						AC	ME	8
OD	GT	1774		POSADA y SOTO, Ramón de	S	24	AV VD		L	RC		OP		3			MN	Y		CH AC	LI	5
OD	GT	1775		GONZALEZ CALDERON, Tomás	ME	36	ME	TS	D	ME		SU		5				Y		AC	LI	13
OD	GT	1777		ORTIZ de la PEÑA, José	S		SA		D	RC				1				Y	S	RC		15

Post	Audiencia	Year	Native Son	Name	Birthplace	Age	University	Colegio	Degree	Abogado	Previous Post	University Service	Relatives' Posts	Total Appts.	Purchase	Date	Dispensations	Married	Wife's Birthplace	Honors, Order	Departure	Years of Service
OD	GT	1779		ZUBIRIA, Juan José de	S		SA		D	RC		OP		2							OD SF	6
OD	GT	1779		REY y BOZA, Félix del	SD				L	ME SD	TA SD			3						AC ME		5
OD	GT	1782		VALIENTE y BRAVO, José Pablo	S	34	SE		D	SE RC		CA		2						CI IC	FR ME	2
OD	GT	1783		BASCO y VARGAS, Joaquín	S	54	GR SA	CU	B	GR	OD SF		O-Y	2						SA	RT	13
OD	GT	1785		ROBLEDO de ALBUQUERQUE, Francisco de	S	42	GR		B	SE RC	AG SF			3				Y	SF	FR ME		17
OD	GT	1785		BODEGA y MOLLINEDO, Manuel Antonio de la	LI	37	LI AL		D	LI RC		CA		3				Y	ME	AC ME		7
OD	GT	1786		TALAVERA y MEDINA, Sebastián de	CA		CA		D	RC		OP	F-XX CONQ	1							RT	6
OD	GT	1792		VILLAURRUTIA y LOPEZ OSORIO, Jacobo de	SD	35	AL TO		D	RC		SP	F-RE P-XX M-HM	2				Y	S	AC ME		12
OD	GT	1792		CAMPO y RIVAS, Manuel del	SF	42	SF		D	SF RC			F-XX M-HM	4						CH	OD GD	8
OD	GT	1796		COLLADO, Juan	S	48	AL SE		B	RC	TA ME	CA	F-SB	4						AC ME		8
OD	GT	1800		CAMACHO CANOVAS, Francisco	S		AL TO		B		OD GD	CA		2							RT	10
OD	GT	1803		DURAN y FERNANDEZ, Onesimo Antonio	S	53	GR		B	GR	TA GD			1						GD	D	5
OD	GT	1804		RODRIGUEZ de CARDENAS, Antonio	S	52	GR OR		D	GR RC	OD MA	CA		2							D	4
OD	GT	1806		CAMPUZANO y SALAZAR, Joaquín Bernardo de	S	38	VD OR		D	RC	OD BA	SU		3							RE SD	9
OD	GT	1807		LLAVE y MARQUELI, Rafael de la	S	52	AL			RC	FI SD			3						AC ME		2
OS	GT	1807		SERRANO POLO, Antonio Norberto	S	51	SA AL		B	RC	TA GT			1				Y	VD	Y		
OD	GT	1810		GONZALEZ BRAVO, Juan Gualberto	S	33	SE		D	SE RC				1						FN CI		4
OD	GT	1810		BERASUETA, José Ignacio	ME	39	VD AL				TA ME			2						FR ME		6
OD	GT	1810		ORTIZ de SALINAS, José Ignacio	ME	55	ME		B	ME	TA GD			2							OD GD	6
OD	GT	1814		MORENO y MORAN, Miguel	QU	32	LI		D				F-XX	3				Y	S		Ind.	
OD	GT	1814		BARRIO y VALLE, José	S	51	GT		D	GT	X- GT	SU	F-AB	2				Y			OD SF	5
OD	GT	1814	*	LARREINAGA, Miguel de	GT	37	GT		B		X- GT			1							Ind.	
OD	GT	1814	*	PALOMO, José Ignacio	GT					GT	X- GT			1								N.S.
OD	GT	1815		BUSTAMANTE Y CASTRO, Juan Manuel						RC	TA GT			1				Y	GT		Ind.	
OD	GT	1816		GOMEZ ECHAGAVIA, Agustín	BA	32	AL VA		D		TA SD	CA		2							OD SD	N.S.
OD	GT	1816		VALDES y POSADA, José Francisco	S	43	OV		B	RC	X- SF			1							Ind.	
OD	GT	1818		IBAÑEZ RAMOS, Joaquín	S	41	SI AL		D	RC	AG GT	OP		1							Ind.	
OD	GT	1821	*	BELTRANENA y LLANO, Manuel	GT	34	GT		B	GT	TA GT			1				Y	GT		Ind.	
OD	GT	1821		MORENO, Santiago	S		AL							1								
FI	GT	1693		GUTIERREZ de la PEÑA, José	S									2							OD ME	27
FI	GT	1721		LOPEZ de EZEYZA, Isidro	LI		LI	SM			PI LI			1				Y	LI		D	18
FI	GT	1740		HOLGADO de GUZMAN, Diego de	S	27	OM SA		L			SU		2						FR LI		8
FI	GT	1749		BECERRA y GUTIERREZ, Sebastián de	S		SA		B	RC		CA		1							D	5
FI	GT	1755		ROMANA y HERRERA, Felipe	SF	33	SF		D	SF	X- SF	CA	F-HM P-HM M-XX CONQ	1							D	16
FI	GT	1773		CISTUE y COLL, José de (Barón de la Menglana)	S	48	HU		D		FI QU	CA		4				Y	S	CH AC ME		2

201

Post	Audiencia	Year	Native Son	Name	Birthplace	Age	University	Colegio	Degree	Abogado	Previous Post	University Service	Relatives' Posts	Total Appts.	Purchase	Date	Dispensations	Married	Wife's Birthplace	Honors, Order	Departure	Years of Service
FI	GT	1775		SAAVEDRA y CARVAJAL Francisco de	S	37	SN VD		D	RC				4						AC ME		12
FI	GT	1796		ROCHA y LANDECHE, Domingo de la	SD	71	ME		B	ME SD	TA ME		F-AB P-OD M-HM	I				Y	GD	D		I
FI	GT	1798		PILOÑA y AYALA, Diego Francisco	S	44	OV		B	IN RC AS	TA GT	CA		2				Y	GT	GD OD SD		5
FI	GT	1812		OSES, Juan Ramón de	S	42	HI SA		D	EX RC	FV ME	CA		4				Y		AC ME		N.S.
FV	GT	1788		TOSTA y HIERRO, Pedro José	S		SE		L	SE RC	FR GT			2				Y		D		10
FV	GT	1803		CIFUENTES, Roque Jacinto	S	38	AL			RC	FR GT	CA		2						D		7
FV	GT	1807		SEDANO, Diego José de	S	46	SE OS			MD IN	TA SD			I						AS Ref.		N.S.
FV	GT	1810		CAVALLERO y RIVAS, Andrés	S	36	AL			SP				I								
FR	GT	1777		TOSTA y HIERRO, Pedro José	S		SE		L	SE RC				2				Y		FV GT		10
FR	GT	1788		BATALLER y ROS, Miguel Antonio	S	32	GR		L	GR			F-OD	4						AC ME		8
FR	GT	1798		CIFUENTES, Roque Jacinto	S	33	AL			RC		CA		2						FV GT		7
FR	GT	1803		MORALES y UGALDE, Andrés José	LI	34	LI		B	LI			F-AB	I						D		
FR	GT	1805		YAÑEZ y NUÑO, José Isidro	CA	35	CA		D	CA	X- CA			3						AC ME		5
FR	GT	1815		VILLAFAÑE, José	ME		ME		B	ME	X- SD		CONQ	I								
FR	GT	1817		O'HORAN, Tomás Antonio	ME	41	ME	SI	L	ME	FR SF	CA		2						Ind.		

AUDIENCIA OF LIMA

Post	Audiencia	Year	Native Son	Name	Birthplace	Age	University	Colegio	Degree	Abogado	Previous Post	University Service	Relatives' Posts	Total Appts.	Purchase	Date	Dispensations	Married	Wife's Birthplace	Honors, Order	Departure	Years of Service
RE	LI	1776		JACOT ORTIZ ROJANO, Melchor (Conde de Pozos Dulces)	S	45	GR		L	GR RC AS	OD AS	SU	P-XX	I				Y Y	S LI	AS MT CA CI CH		12
RE	LI	1787		ARREDONDO y PELEGRIN, Manuel Antonio (Marqués de San Juan de Nepomuceno)	S	49	SA		B	RC	RE BA		O-Y	6				Y	LI	CI RE CA ME CH		33
RE	LI	1813		REMIREZ de LAREDO, Gaspar (Conde de San Javier y Casa Laredo)	CH	66	LI SM SF		D	LI	MT CI		F-HM P-AB M-AB	3				Y Y	LI LI	MT CI		N.S.
RE	LI	1813		ARREDONDO y PELEGRIN, Manuel Antonio (Marqués de San Juan de Nepomuceno)	S	75	SA		B	RC	RE ME		O-Y	6				Y	LI	CI RT CA CH		33
RE	LI	1816		ANSOTEGUI y BARROETA, Francisco Tomás de	S	59	SN		D	RC	RE CS	SU		3						Ind.		
OF	LI	1694	*	PAREDES y ARMENDARIZ, Nicolás de	LI	20	LI SA	SM	D		OP		F-FI O-Y	I	OF	1694	NA N			SA D		16
OD	LI	1694		NUÑEZ de SANABRIA, Miguel	LI	49	LI	SM	D		AC LI	CA	F-XX	2	AC	1687	NA Y		LI	RT		41
OS	LI	1700	*	VILLAVICENCIO y CISNEROS, Pedro de	LI	36	LI	SM		LI			F-HM	I	OS	1700				RM		0
OD	LI	1702		REMIREZ de BAQUEDANO, Gonzalo	S	40	ON			FI CH			↗O-Y	2			MN	Y	LI	SA FI CI		9
OD	LI	1703		RIVAS, Diego Antonio de	S		AL			OD PA				2						Ref.		N.S.
OS	LI	1704	*	CANAL, Pedro Gregorio de la	LI	30	LI	SM	D	LI			F-XX	I	OS	1704	NA MN					c.10
OS	LI	1704	*	PERALTA y SANABRIA, Juan	LI	56	LI	SM	D	PI LI		CA	F-XX	I	OS	1704				D		I
OS	LI	1708	*	ECHAVARRIA ZULOAGA, Juan Bautista de (Marqués de Soto Hermoso)	LI	25	LI	SM	D				M-AB P-XX	2	OS	1708	NA MN			SA		14
OF	LI	1709	*	SANTIAGO CONCHA, José de (Marqués de Casa Concha)	LI	42	LI SA	SM	L	LI	AC LI	SU	F-AB	2	AF	1693	NA MN CM CP	Y	CS	CAL D		47
OS	LI	1709		NAVIA BOLAÑOS y MOSCOSO, Alvaro (Conde del Valle de Oselle)	S	34	SA	OV	L		OD CS		F-XX	2			MN CM	Y	LI	CI D SA		48
OS	LI	1710	*	ECHAVE y ROJAS, Pedro Antonio	LI								F-HM	2			NA MN	Y	LI	AL D		13

Post	Audiencia	Year	Native Son	Name	Birthplace	Age	University	Colegio	Degree	Abogado	Previous Post	University Service	Relatives' Posts	Total Appts.	Purchase	Date	Dispensations	Married	Wife's Birthplace	Honors, Order	Departure	Years of Service
OD	LI	1711		CALDERON de la BARCA, Juan Fernando (Conde de las Torres)	S	49	SA AV	OV	B		AC LI			2				Y	CS	CAL	D	27
OS	LI	1711	*	CAVERO de FRANCIA, Alvaro	LI	26	LI	SM	D	LI		SU	F-XX	1	OS	1711	MN	Y	LI		D	28
OD	LI	1720		COBIAN y VALDES, Antonio de	S				L		OD SF			2				Y			D	
OD	LI	1721		ORUETA y IRUXTA, Juan Bautista de	S	47	SA	AR	B		AC LI	SU		2			MN	Y	LI		D	11+
OD	LI	1721	*	PEREZ de URQUIZU, Juan de	LI	66			D	LI	AC LI		F-XX	2	AF	1693	NA MN	Y	LI		D	35
OD	LI	1721		BERNARDO de QUIROS, Alvaro	S		AL	IL			AC LI		F-XX	3				Y Y	S LI		D	19
OD	LI	1723		LERMA y SALAMANCA, Baltazar José de	S	51	SA	CU	B		OD CS		F-MT M-SB	3				Y	S		N.S.	
OD	LI	1723		CEBALLOS GUERRA, José Damian de (Conde de las Torres)	S	34	SA	SB	L		FI LI		F-XX	2				Y	CS		D	
OD	LI	1725	*	ECHAVARRIA ZULOAGA, Juan Bautista de (Marqués de Soto Hermoso)	LI	42	LI	SM	D		OS LI		M-AB P-XX	2	OS	1708	NA MN			SA		14
OD	LI	1729	*	NUÑEZ de ROJAS, Gregorio	LI	55	LI	SM	D		OD CS		F-OD P-XX M-FI O-Y	3	OS	1699		Y CS			D	17
OD	LI	1729		PEREZ BUELTA, Gaspar	S	41	SA AV		L		FV LI	SU		4			CM	Y	PA		D	20
OD	LI	1730		ORTIZ AVILES, José Ignacio de	S		SE		D		SE RC	CA		1				Y			D	14
OS	LI	1733	*	BRAVO de RIVERO, Pedro	LI	32	LI	SM SF	D	LI			F-HM P-XX M-XX O-Y	1	OS	1733	NA MN CM CHP	Y	LI	RT		32
OS	LI	1735	*	SALAZAR, Tomás de	LI	60	LI		D	LI	OD SF	CA		2			NA	N			D	2
OS	LI	1736	*	SAGARDIA y PALENCIA, Francisco	LI	45	LI	SM	D	LI	OD CS		F-AB	2				Y	ME	CC RM		6
OS	LI	1740	*	URQUIZU IBAÑEZ, Gaspar	LI	27	LI	SM	D	LI	PI CS		F-OD	1	OS	1740	NA MN	Y	LI		D	39
OS	LI	1741	*	TAGLE BRACHO, José de	LI	24	LI	SM	D		OD CS		F-AB M-AB	2	OS	1741	MN HP MI	N			D	36
OS	LI	1744	*	OLAVIDE, Pablo Antonio José de	LI	19	LI	SM	D	LI	X- LI	CA	F-AB O-Y	1	OS	1744				SA	RM	6
OS	LI	1744	*	QUEREJAZU y MOLLINEDO, Antonio Hermenegildo de	LI	33	LI	SM	D		PR CS		F-HM M-HM O-Y	1			MN HP	Y	LI	CI CA SA	RT	40
OS	LI	1745	*	ZURBARAN y ALLENDE, Manuel	LI	29	LI	SM	D	LI	OD CS	CA		2	OS	1745	NA MN HP	Y	LI		D	24
OS	LI	1746	*	BRAVO de CASTILLA, Pedro José	LI	44	LI	SM SF	D	LI	X- LI	CA		1	OS	1746	NA HP			CI	RT	10
OD	LI	1748		GUTIERREZ de ARCE, Juan	S	43	AL	IL	B	RC	AC LI		F-SB	3						SA	D	N.S. 23
OS	LI	1748		GORENA y BEYRA, Manuel de	CH	34	LI	SM SF	D	LI	X- LI	OP	F-AB	1	OS	1748	MN HP	N			D	25
OS	LI	1748	*	MIRONES y BENAVENTE, Manuel Isidro de	LI	57	LI	SM		LI	OD CS		F-XX	4	OS	1748	CM NA	Y	LI		D	17
OS	LI	1749	*	ORRANTIA, Domingo de	LI	21	LI	SM	D	LI		OP	F-XX M-XX	1	OS	1749	NA MI MN HP			MT CI		24
OS	LI	1750		ECHEVERZ, Pedro Antonio de	PA	25	LI	SM SF	D	LI	X- LI		F-AB P-CG	2	OS	1750	HP	Y	PA	OD ME		27
OD	LI	1751		GOMEZ GARCIA, José Casimiro	PA	56	LI	SM	L	LI	FI CS		F-XX	2				Y	LI		D	8
OS	LI	1755		MESIA y MUNIVE, Cristóbal (Conde de Sierrabella)	CH	38	LI	SM SF	D	LI	X- LI	CA	F-AB P-HM O-Y	2			CM	Y	LI	OD ME		22
OD	LI	1763		CASAL y MONTENEGRO, Benito de	S	60	AV SN		D	GA	OD SF	OP		2			HP	Y	SF	Ref.		N.S.
OD	LI	1770	*	MANSILLA ARIAS de SAAVEDRA, Manuel de	LI	44	LI	SM SF	D	LI	AX LI	CA	F-AB	2	AX	1750		Y	LI	CI	RT	32
OD	LI	1775		CARRION y MORCILLO, Alfonso	S						AC LI		O-Y	2			MN CM	Y	LI		RT	38

Post	Audiencia	Year	Native Son	Name	Birthplace	Age	University	Colegio	Degree	Abogado	Previous Post	University Service	Relatives' Posts	Total Appts.	Purchase	Date	Dispensations	Married	Wife's Birthplace	Honors, Order	Departure	Years of Service
OD	LI	1775		RUEDAS MORALES, Gerónimo Manuel de	S		OM SA		D		FV LI	CA		4				Y	LI	RE CS		9
OD	LI	1776	*	BORDA y ECHEVARRIA, Manuel Antonio de	LI	65	LI	SM	D	LI	AX LI			2	AX	1736	NA	N		RT		N.S. 40
OD	LI	1776	*	TRASLAVIÑA y OYAGUE, José Clemente de	LI		LI	SM	D	LI	OF CH		F-XX	2	OF	1740				RT		N.S.
OD	LI	1777	*	PUENTE y IBAÑEZ, Juan José de la (Marqués de Corpa)	LI	53	LI	SM SF	D	LI	OD CH		F-HM M-HM	3	AX	1747	NA	Y	LI	CI MN HP	D CAL	48
OD	LI	1778		FERRER de la PUENTE, José	S		OR		D	VA RC	OD QU			3						SD CI	RE SF	4
OD	LI	1778		MATA LINARES, Benito María de la	S	29	AL SA	SB	B		OD CH	OP	F-CA	3						CI CH	RE BA	9
OD	LI	1778		RIVERA y PEÑA, Ramón de	S	48	SN		D	GA	AC LI	CA		3				Y	CS		OD HT	4
OD	LI	1779	*	SANTIAGO CONCHA, Melchor de	LI	63	LI	SM	L	LI	AC LI		F-OD P-AB M-AB	4	OD CS	1745	CS	Y	CS	RT		17
OD	LI	1779		ARREDONDO y PELEGRIN, Manuel Antonio (Marqués de San Juan de Nepomuceno)	S	41	SA		B	RC	OD GT		O-Y	6				Y	LI	CI CA CH	RE BA	4
OD	LI	1780		ESCOBEDO ALARCON, Jorge	S	38	GR SA	CU	B		AC LI	OP		3				Y	S	CI	VG	3
OD	LI	1784		CERDAN y PONTERO, Ambrosio	S		SI AL		L	RC	AC LI		F-OD P-MT O-Y	4				Y	CH	CH GT	RE	15
OD	LI	1785		PORTILLA y GALVEZ, José de la	S		GR LI		D	GR	AG LI			2	MN			N		RE CZ		2
OD	LI	1785		MORENO y ESCANDON, Francisco Antonio de	SF	49	SF		D	SF	FV LI	CA	F-XX	6				Y	S	RE CH		8
OD	LI	1787		VELEZ de GUEVARA, Nicolás	SF		SF		D	SF	AC LI	CA		3				Y		D		15.
OD	LI	1789		MARQUEZ de la PLATA, Fernando	S	49	SE		D		AC LI		F-AS P-AS O-Y	5				Y	CH	CH QU	RE	15
OD	LI	1792		GONZALEZ CALDERON, Tomás	ME	52	ME	TS	D	ME	AC LI	SU		5				Y		OS ME		7
OD	LI	1794		RODRIGUEZ BALLESTEROS, Juan	S	56	GR SE		B	SE RC	OD CH			3	CM			Y		RE CH		12
OD	LI	1794		GARCIA de la PLATA, Manuel	S	44	GR		L	RC	AC LI		F-SB	5	CM			Y	S	RT		29
OD	LI	1796		MUÑOZ y CUBERO, Lucas	S	62	GR		L	GR	OD QU	CA		4				N		RE SF		4
OD	LI	1796		PINO MANRIQUE de LARA, Juan del	S	49	GR				AC LI			3	CM			Y	CH		D	27
OD	LI	1796		QUADRADO y VALDENEBRO, Fernando	S	60	VD SA		B		OD QU			2				N			Ind.	
OD	LI	1797		ARNAIZ de las REVILLAS, Domingo	S	47	OM VD		D	VD	AC LI	CA		3				Y	S		D	27
OD	LI	1797		PARDO RIVADENEYRA, Manuel	S	37					AC LI			3				Y	LI	CI IC	RE CZ	13
OD	LI	1800		MORENO y ESCANDON, Francisco Xavier de	SF	49	SF OM VD SA		D	RC	AC LI	SU	F-XX O-Y	4							Ind.	
OD	LI	1804		VALLE del POSTIGO, Manuel María de	S	50	BZ GR		B	SE RC	AC LI		O-Y	2				Y	LI		Ind.	
OD	LI	1805		PALOMEQUE, Tomás Ignacio	S	49	AL BO		B		AC LI	CA	O-Y	4				Y	BA		Ind.	
OD	LI	1806	*	BAQUIJANO y CARRILLO, José Xavier (Conde de Vistaflorida)	LI	55	LI		D	LI	AC LI	CA	M-AB O-Y	2						CL CH	MT C	10
OS	LI	1810		VILLOTA, Manuel Genaro de	S	43	GR		D		FV BA	CA		6						RE C		6
OD	LI	1810		ESTERRIPA, Francisco Xavier	S	47	AL		D		AC LI		F-MT	4				Y	SF	CI QU	RE	11
OS	LI	1811		BRAVO de RIVERO, Diego Miguel (Marqués de Castel-Bravo de Rivero)	LI	58	LI		B	LI	X- LI		F-OD P-HM M-AB CONQ O-Y	1				Y	LI	AL SA	Ind.	
OD	LI	1813	*	GOYENECHE y BARREDA, Pedro Mariano	LI	41	LI		D	LI	OD CZ		F-XX M-HM O-Y	2						CI IC	RT	6

204

Post	Audiencia	Year	Native Son	Name	Birthplace	Age	University	Colegio	Degree	Abogado	Previous Post	University Service	Relatives' Posts	Total Appts.	Purchase	Date	Dispensations	Married	Wife's Birthplace	Honors, Order Departure	Years of Service
OD	LI	1815		BAZO y BERRI, Juan	S	59	LI		B	LI	OD BA			2				Y		Ind.	
OD	LI	1815		IGLESIA y HUGUES, José de la	S	76	SE		D	SE RC	AC LI			3				Y		Ind.	
OD	LI	1815		OSMA y TRICIO, Gaspar Antonio de	S	41	VD AL		B	RC	AC LI		O-Y	2				Y	LI	Ind.	
OD	LI	1816		ALDUNATE, José Santiago	CH	60	CH		D	CH	AC LI		F-AC O-Y	3				Y	CH	Ind.	
OD	LI	1819		CASPE y RODRIGUEZ, Antonio	S	60	GR		L	GR RC	AC LI		F-XX P-XX	4				Y		Ind.	
AC	LI	1687	*	NUÑEZ de SANABRIA, Miguel	LI	42	LI	SM	D		AG LI	CA		2	AC	1687	NA	Y	LI	OD LI	41
AC	LI	1690		CALDERON de la BARCA, Juan Fernando (Conde de las Torres)	S	28	SA AV	OV	B					2				Y	CS	CAL OD LI	27
AF	LI	1693	*	PEREZ de URQUIZU, Juan de	LI	38			D	LI			F-XX	2	AF	1693	NA	Y	LI	OD LI	35
AF	LI	1693	*	SANTIAGO CONCHA, José de (Marqués de Casa Concha)	LI	26	LI SA	SM	L	LI	X- LI	SU	F-AB	2	AF	1693	NA CM MN CP	Y	CS	CAL OD LI	47
AX	LI	1699	*	VASQUEZ de VELASCO, Pedro	LI	31	LI	SM	L				F-HM P-PR O-Y	3	AX	1699		Y	LI	CAL RM FI CS	N.S.
AC	LI	1699	*	ARANBURU y MUÑOZ, Vicente de	LI	42	LI	SM	L	RC		OP	F-AB	2	AX	1699	NA	Y		SA RM OD SF	N.S.
AF	LI	1699	*	ROJAS y ACEVEDO, Francisco	LI	48	LI	SM			AG LI		F-FI	3	AF	1699		Y	CS	RM OD CH	7
AC	LI	1704		ORUETA y IRUXTA, Juan Bautista de	S		SA	AR	B			SU		2			MN	Y	LI	D	
AC	LI	1704		BERNARDO de QUIROS, Alvaro	S		AL	IL			OD CH		F-XX	3				Y Y	S LI	OD LI	19
AX	LI	1707	*	SANTOS y CUENTAS, Francisco Antonio de los	LI	51	LI		B		X- LI		F-XX	1	AX	1707	NA MN	Y		CAL Ref.	N.S.
AX	LI	1708	*	MENA CABALLERO, Juan Antonio de	LI	24	LI	SF					F-XX	1	AX	1708	NA MN	Y	LI	SA RT	11
AC	LI	1708	*	MUNARRIZ, Bartolomé de	LI	22	LI	SM				OP	F-AB	1	AC	1708	NA MN	Y Y	LI LI	RT	10
AC	LI	1710	*	ROJAS y ACEVEDO, Francisco	LI	53	LI	SM			OD CH		F-FI	3				Y	CS	D	7
AC	LI	1718		FAJARDO, Felipe Nicolás	S		AL		L		FF QU		F-AS	2						D	3
AC	LI	1720		ALARCON y VARGAS, Luis Ambrosio de	S		SE BO		B	SE	AS	CA		1				Y		MT CI	3
AC	LI	1721		SALAZAR y CASTEJON, Francisco Xavier de	S	34	VD	SC	B			SU		1			MN CM	Y	LI	D	23
AC	LI	1721	*	GOMENDIO URRUTIA, Miguel de	LI	51	SI AL		L		FI CH	SU	F-AB	2						RT	34
AC	LI	1723		BRUN, Tomás	S	43	HU				PI LI	CA		1				Y	LI	D	4
AC	LI	1723		GUTIERREZ de ARCE, Juan	S	45	AL	IL	B	RC	OF SF		F-SB	3						SA OD LI	23
AC	LI	1729		CARRION y MORCILLO, Alfonso	S								O-Y	2			MN CM	Y	LI	OD LI	38
AX	LI	1736	*	BORDA y ECHEVARRIA, Manuel Antonio de	LI	25	LI	SM	D	LI				2	AX	1736	NA	N		OD LI	40
AX	LI	1738	*	VILLALTA y NUÑEZ, José Antonio	LI	39	LI	SM	D	LI	OD CS		F-HM M-OD O-Y	2			CM	Y	LI	D	36
AX	LI	1747	*	PUENTE y IBAÑEZ, Juan José de la (Marqués de Corpa)	LI	23	LI	SM SF	D	LI			F-HM M-HM	3	AX	1747	NA MN HP	Y	LI	CI OD CAL CH	48
AX	LI	1749	*	ORBEA y ARANDIA, Diego José de	LI	37	LI	SM	D	LI			F-HM	1	AX	1749	MN HP	Y	LI	SA Ref.	N.S.
AX	LI	1750	*	MANSILLA ARIAS de SAAVEDRA, Manuel de	LI	24	LI	SM SF	D	LI		CA	F-AB	2	AX	1750	NA MN	Y	LI	CI Ref. OD LI	N.S.
AC	LI	1776	*	TAGLE BRACHO, Pedro de	LI	54	LI	SM	D	LI	OS CS		F-AB M-AB	3	OS	1746	CS			CI OD CAL SF	2

Post	Audiencia	Year	Native Son	Name	Birthplace	Age	University	Colegio	Degree	Abogado	Previous Post	University Service	Relatives' Posts	Total Appts.	Purchase	Date	Dispensations	Married	Wife's Birthplace	Honors, Order	Departure	Years of Service
AC	LI	1776		MIER y TRESPALACIOS, Cosme Antonio de	S	31	OM VD		D		PI LI	SU	O-Y	4				Y		CH	AC ME	N.S.
AC	LI	1776		MARTINEZ de ALDUNATE, Domingo de	CH	69	CH LI	SM SF	D	LI	OD CH	CA	M-XX	2	OS CH	1748		Y	CH		D	N.S.
AC	LI	1776		VERDUGO del CASTILLO, Juan Antonio	CH	74	LI	SM		LI	OD CH	SU		2	OS CH	1747		Y	CS		RT	N.S.
AC	LI	1777		RIVERA y PEÑA, Ramón de	S	47	SN		D	GA	OS CS	CA		3				Y	CS		OD LI	4
AC	LI	1777	*	SANTIAGO CONCHA, Melchor de	LI	61	LI	SM	L	LI	OD CH		F-OD P-AB M-AB	4	OD CS	1745		Y	CS		OD LI	17
AC	LI	1778		CABEZA ENRIQUEZ, José	S		VD SA	SB	L	RC	OD QU	SU		3				N			OD BA	5
AC	LI	1778		ESCOBEDO ALARCON, Jorge	S	36	GR SA	CU	B		OD CS	OP		3				Y	S	CI	OD LI	3
AC	LI	1779		CERDAN y PONTERO, Ambrosio	S		SI AL		L	RC	FR CH		F-AS P-MT O-Y	4				Y	CH	CH	OD LI	15
AC	LI	1779		VELEZ de GUEVARA, Nicolás	SF		SF		D	SF	OD QU	CA		3				Y			OD LI	15
AC	LI	1779		POSADA y SOTO, Ramón de	S	29	AV VD		L	RC	OD GT	SU		3				Y		CH	FH ME	N.S.
AC	LI	1780		REZABAL y UGARTE, José de	S	33	GR SA	AR	B		OD CH	SU		4				Y	LI	CH	OD CZ	7
AC	LI	1781		MARQUEZ de la PLATA, Fernando	S	41	SE		D		FR CS		F-AS P-AS O-Y	5				Y	CH	CH	OD LI	15
AC	LI	1785		BOETO, Antonio	S						X- LI			2						CL	RE CS	1
AC	LI	1787		GARCIA de la PLATA, Manuel	S	37	GR		L	RC	OD CS		F-SB	5			CM	Y	S		OD LI	29
AC	LI	1788		GONZALEZ CALDERON, Tomás	ME	48	ME	TS	D	ME	OD GT	SU		5				Y			OD LI	7
AC	LI	1788		PINO MANRIQUE de LARA, Juan del	S	41	GR				FR CS			3			CM	Y	CH		OD LI	27
AC	LI	1789		ARNAIZ de las REVILLAS, Domingo	S	39	OM VD		D	VD	FR CS	CA		3				Y			OD LI	27
AC	LI	1792		PARDO RIVADENEYRA, Manuel	S	33								3				Y	LI	CI IC	OD LI	13
AC	LI	1794		MORENO y ESCANDON, Francisco Xavier de	SF	43	SF OM SA VD		D	RC	OD MA	SU	F-XX O-Y	4							OD LI	26
AC	LI	1796		VALLE del POSTIGO, Manuel María de	S	42	BZ GR		B	SE RC	AG LI		O-Y	2				Y	LI		OD LI	24
AC	LI	1797		PALOMEQUE, Tomás Ignacio	S	41	AL BO		B		OD CS	CA	O-Y	4				Y	BA		OD LI	23
AC	LI	1797	*	BAQUIJANO y CARRILLO, José Xavier (Conde de Vistaflorida)	LI	46	LI		D	LI	X- LI	CA	M-AB CONQ O-Y	2				N		CL CH	OD LI	10
AC	LI	1800		CISNEROS de la OLIVA, Felipe	S	63	OR		B	GR RC	OD MA			3						CI	RE MA	
AC	LI	1802		MORENO AVENDAÑO, Juan de	S	59	OS GR		B	SE RC	OD QU			2				Y	QU		D	3
AC	LI	1804		ESTERRIPA, Francisco Xavier	S	41	AL		D		OD SF		F-MT	4				Y	SF	CI	OD LI	11
AC	LI	1805		OSMA y TRICIO, Gaspar Antonio de	S	31	VD AL		B	RC			O-Y	2				Y	LI		OD LI	15
AC	LI	1806		SANTIAGO CONCHA JIMENEZ LOBATON, José	CH	46	LI		B	LI	OD CH		F-OD P-OD M-PR	2				Y	CH		Ref.	N.S.
AC	LI	1807		IGLESIA y HUGUES, José de la	S	68	SE		D	SE RC	OD CS			3				Y			OD LI	14
AC	LI	1810		VILLANUEVA y AREVALO, José	SF				D		AS			1							Ref.	N.S.
AX	LI	1810		FERNANDEZ de LEIVA, Joaquín	CH	35	CH		D	CH	DP X- CH		O-Y	1				Y			D	3
AC	LI	1810	*	MORALES y DUARES, Vicente	LI	55	LI		D	LI	DP X- LI	CA	F-XX	1							D	N.S.
AC	LI	1814	*	OSTOLAZA y RIOS, José Ramón de	LI	42	LI		D	LI	OD QU	CA	F-XX O-Y	2				N			D	N.S.

Post	Audiencia	Year	Native Son	Name	Birthplace	Age	University	Colegio	Degree	Abogado	Previous Post	University Service	Relatives' Posts	Total Appts.	Purchase	Date	Dispensations	Married	Wife's Birthplace	Honors, Order / Departure	Years of Service
AC	LI	1815		ALDUNATE, José Santiago	CH	59	CH		D	CH	OD CH		F-AC O-Y	3				Y	CH	OD LI	5
AC	LI	1815		BERRIOZABAL, Manuel Plácido (Conde de Valle Hermoso)	S	41	OR GR			RC	OD CS		CA	3				Y		CI Ind. CH	
AC	LI	1815		CASPE y RODRIGUEZ, Antonio	S	55	GR		L		GR OD RC CH		F-XX P-XX	5				Y		Ind.	
AC	LI	1815	*	CEBALLOS y CALDERON, Gaspar (Marqués de Casa Calderón)	LI	48	LI		D		LI X- LI		CA	1				Y	LI	CL D	4
AC	LI	1815		MATA RAMOS, Juan de	S	44	GR		B		GR FI RC MA			2							
AC	LI	1818		IRIGOYEN de la QUINTANA, Manuel de	BA	55				BA	OD BA			4				Y		D	1
AC	LI	1819		RODRIGUEZ ROMANO, Vicente de	S	65	VD AL		L		VD FR RC QU	SU		2						Ind.	
FV	LI	1723		PEREZ BUELTA, Gaspar	S	39	SA AV		L		OD SF		SU	4	CM	Y	PA			OD LI	20
FV	LI	1744		PUENTE LARREA, Lorenzo Antonio de la (Marqués de Villafuerte y Sotomayor)	S		SA	AR	B					2	CM CP	Y		LI	RT	20
FV	LI	1748	*	ORTIZ de FORONDA, Francisco	LI	42	LI	SM			FR LI		F-HM	2	NA MN CM	Y		LI	OL SA RT	39
FV	LI	1767		HOLGADO de GUZMAN, Diego de	S	54	OM SA		L		FR LI		SU	3						RT	20
FV	LI	1774		RUEDAS MORALES, Gerónimo Manuel de	S		OM SA		D		FR LI		CA	4				Y	LI	OD LI	9
FV	LI	1778		VEYAN y MOLA, Serafín	S		HU				FR LI		CA	3				Y	LI	D	1
FV	LI	1778		GALDEANO, Joaquín de	S	38	SA HU		D		FR LI		CA	4				Y	LI	OD ME	2
FV	LI	1780		MORENO y ESCANDON, Francisco Antonio de	SF	44	SF		D	SF	FR LI		CA F-XX	6				Y	S	OD LI	8
FV	LI	1785		GORVEA VADILLO, José	S	39	VD TO		B	RC	FR LI			5				Y	CH	CH RE MA	17
FV	LI	1803		PAREJA y CORTES, José de	S	46	GR		D		FR LI	CA	O-Y	4				Y	S	RE CZ Ind.	32
FR	LI	1704		CALVO DOMONTE, Luis Antonio	CS	42	LI SA	SM			OD CS		F-XX	2				Y	CS	RC	14
FF	LI	1710	*	ECHAVE y ROJAS, Pedro Antonio	LI		LI						F-HM	2	FF 1710 NA MN	Y		LI	AL D	13
FR	LI	1718		RODRIGUEZ de CASTAÑON, A.	S	60	AL	IL	L				CA	1						AL Ref.	N.S.
FR	LI	1720		CEBALLOS GUERRA, José Damián de (Conde de las Torres)	S	34	SA	SB	L				F-XX	2				Y	CS	OD LI	23
FR	LI	1721		SIERRA OSORIO, Fernando de	S		VD	SC	B		OS SF		SU	3						Ref.	N.S.
FR	LI	1723		BARCENA y MIER, Miguel de la	S	33	OV SA	AR	B				SU	1						D	3
FR	LI	1727		PUENTE LARREA, Lorenzo Antonio de la (Marqués de Villafuerte y Sotomayor)	S		SA	AR	B					2	CM CP	Y		LI	FV LI	20
FR	LI	1730	*	ORTIZ de FORONDA, Francisco	LI	24	LI	SM					F-HM	2	NA MN CM	Y		LI	OL SA FV LI	39
FR	LI	1748		HOLGADO de GUZMAN, Diego de	S	35	OM SA		L		OS GT		SU	3						FV LI	20
FR	LI	1766		PORLIER, Antonio de (Marqués de Bajamar)	S	44	AL SA		D	RC	OD CS			2				Y	CS	CH FN CI	9
FR	LI	1767		RUEDAS MORALES, Gerónimo Manuel de	S		OM SA		D				CA	4				Y	LI	FV LI	9
FR	LI	1774		ALVAREZ de ACEVEDO, Tomás Antonio	S	39	SA		B		FI CS	OP		3				Y	LI	CH RE CH	2
FR	LI	1775		VEYAN y MOLA, Serafín	S		HU				OD QU		CA	3				Y	LI	FV LI	1
FR	LI	1778		GALDEANO, Joaquín de	S	38	SA HU		D		FI QU		CA	4				Y	LI	FV LI	2
FR	LI	1778		CASTILLA CAVALLERO, José	S	42	SE		D		FI CS	SU	O-Y	2						FI HT	4
FR	LI	1780		MORENO y ESCANDON, Francisco Antonio de	SF	44	SF		D	SF	FV SF		CA F-XX	6				Y		FV LI	8

Post	Audiencia	Year	Native Son	Name	Birthplace	Age	University	Colegio	Degree	Abogado	Previous Post	University Service	Relatives' Posts	Total Appts.	Purchase	Date	Dispensations	Married	Wife's Birthplace	Honors, Order	Departure	Years of Service
FR	LI	1781		VILLALENGUA y MARFIL, Juan José de	S	33	AL TO			RC	FR QU		O-⚥	4				Y			RE QU	2
FR	LI	1784		GORVEA VADILLO, José	S	38	VD TO		B	RC	OD CH			5				Y	CH		CH FV LI	17
FR	LI	1785		VIDERIQUE, Rafael Antonio	S									3				Y			OD BA	4
FR	LI	1789		PAREJA y CORTES, José de	S	32	GR		D		OD BA	CA	O-Y	4				Y	S		FV LI	32
FR	LI	1803		HERRERA, Francisco Manuel	S	61	GR			GR	FI CH		P-MT O-Y	4				Y			RE SF	2
FR	LI	1805		EYZAGUIRRE y ARECHAVALA, Miguel de	CH	35	CH		D	CH		CA	F-AB M-HM	I							RM	10
FR	LI	1815	*	IRIGOYEN y CENTENO, José de	LI	62	LI		D	LI	X- LI		M-HM	I				Y	LI		OS Ind.	

AUDIENCIA OF MANILA

Post	Audiencia	Year	Native Son	Name	Birthplace	Age	University	Colegio	Degree	Abogado	Previous Post	University Service	Relatives' Posts	Total Appts.	Purchase	Date	Dispensations	Married	Wife's Birthplace	Honors, Order	Departure	Years of Service
RE	MA	1776		MARTINEZ SANCHEZ de ARAQUE, Diego de	S	40	GR	BS	B	GR RC	FI SD			3							RE GD	10
RE	MA	1789		SAAVEDRA y CARVAJAL, Francisco de	S	51	SA SN VD AV		D	RC	AC ME			4							Ref. RE GD	N.S.
RE	MA	1790		EMPARAN y ORBE, Agustín Ignacio	S		VD SA	SB	L		AC ME	OP	P-HM O-Y	3			MN				CI CH	
RE	MA	1801		GORVEA VADILLO, José	S	55	VD TO		B	RC	FV LI			5				Y	CH		CH Ref. RE BA	N.S.
RE	MA	1802		CISNEROS de la OLIVA, Felipe	S	65	OR		B	RC	AC LI			3			MN				CI D	2
RE	MA	1805		MESIA y CAICEDO, Nicolás de	S	41	SF		D	SF	OD GD	CA		3								
OF	MA	1695		PAVON, José Antonio	S		ME		B	ME RC		OP	F-AB	I							D	33
OD	MA	1695		SANCHEZ de la BARCENA, Francisco	S	35	VD		B	RC VD	SP	SU		2					SA		OD QU	N.S.
OD	MA	1696		CARRILLO, Andrés	S				L		X- ME			I				Y			D	N.S.
OD	MA	1696		ESPINOSA RIVADENEIRA, Juan de	S	31	AL		L	RC	FF MA			2								
OD	MA	1696		PAVON, José Antonio	S		ME		B	ME RC	OF MA	OP	F-AB	I							D	33
OF	MA	1696		GUERUELA, Francisco	S	28	GR		B	GR RC		CA		I								
OF	MA	1696		AGÜERO, Baltazar de					D		FI MA			I							D	N.S.
OS	MA	1696		MESTRES y BARRES, José de	S	59	BA		D		AR CT			I				Y			D	I
OD	MA	1696		TORRALVA, José de	S	30	AL		D	RC	SP	CA	F-XX	I							RM	9
OD	MA	1704		BARRIENTOS y RIVERA, Agustín Miguel de	S	34	ME		L	ME				I							D	9
OF	MA	1710		PEREZ DELGADO, Bartolomé Patricio	S	37	ME		L	ME				I	OF 1710						D	I
OD	MA	1720		LOPEZ de ADAN, Francisco de	S		AL		D					2					SA		OS ME	17
OD	MA	1720		MARTINEZ, Francisco de	S	27	AL		D					I							D	10
OD	MA	1726		ARJONA, Francisco Lorenzo de	S		GR OS		D			CA		I							D	N.S.
OS	MA	1726		VELASCO, Juan Francisco de	S		AL		L	RC			F-SB	I							D	23
OS	MA	1728		FERNANDEZ TORIBIO, Francisco	S	38	AL	IL	L		OD GT	CA		3				Y		MA	AC ME RT	12
OS	MA	1731		ARZADUN y REBOLLEDO, José Ignacio	ME	31	YU ME	SI	L	RC			F-XX	I			MN				D	21
OD	MA	1735		COSTILLA BORROTO, Francisco	SD	37	HA ME	TS	L	ME		OP	P-XX M-XX	I							D	10
OS	MA	1736		CALDERON ENRIQUEZ, Pedro	S	32	VD		B	VD RC		SU		I				Y	MA		CAL OD AS	28
OS	MA	1739		LEAEGUI, José Gonzalo de	ME	48	ME AV	SI	D	ME RC	X- ME			I								

Post	Audiencia	Year	Native Son	Name	Birthplace	Age	University	Colegio	Degree	Abogado	Previous Post	University Service	Relatives' Posts	Total Appts.	Purchase	Date	Dispensations	Married	Wife's Birthplace	Honors, Order	Departure	Years of Service
OS	MA	1747		ENRIQUEZ de VILLACORTA, Francisco de	S	38	AL		L		OP			2							OD ME	16
OS	MA	1748		DAVILA, Fernando	ME								F-OD	1							D	12
OS	MA	1755		GALVAN y VENTURA, Manuel	S	35	HU		L	.	RE			1							RT	12
OS	MA	1755		ANDA y SALAZAR, Simón de	S	46	SI AL		D		OP			1				Y	S	CH	MT CC	9
OD	MA	1765		ARECHE y SORNOZA, José Antonio de	S	34	AL		D		CA			3							FR ME	N.S.
OD	MA	1765		BASARAZ y GARAGORTA, Domingo Blas de	S		SA		D		OP			1							D	7
OS	MA	1765		PARAMO y NEYRA, José de	S	53	SN		L		GA RC			1							D	
OS	MA	1766		URUÑUELA ARANSAY, Juan Antonio	S	37	SA AV	OV	L		CA		O-Y	4						CH	AC ME	11
OS	MA	1768		GONZALEZ MALDONADO, Francisco Ignacio	ME	30	ME	SI	D	ME	CA		F-XX M-XX	1						CI	FI GD	4
OD	MA	1768		BONILLA XIMENO, Juan Bautista	S		VD		B		RC VD		O-Y	1								
OS	MA	1769		ANDA y SALAZAR, Juan Francisco	S	32	GR		L		RC		O-Y	4							OD GD	8
OS	MA	1774		CACHO CALDERON de la BARCA, Emeterio	S		OV				VD		F-XX O-Y	3							AC ME	12
OD	MA	1774		DIEZ QUIJADA y OVEJERO, Félix	S	47	SI AL	IL	L			SP	CA	3				Y			AC ME	11
OS	MA	1777		CASTILLO y NEGRETE, Manuel de	S	27	SI AL		L		RC	SP	OP	6				Y		GD	OD ME	10
OD	MA	1777		GONZALEZ CARBAJAL, Ciriaco	S	42	GR		L		GR RC			2	MN			Y	MA	CI CH	OD ME	10
OD	MA	1784		MORENO y ESCANDON, Francisco Xavier de	SF	33	SF OM SA VD		D		RC	SU	F-XX O-Y	4	MN						AC LI	10
OD	MA	1786		CISNEROS de la OLIVA, Felipe	S	49	OR		B		GR RC			3	MN					CI	AC LI	14
OD	MA	1787		ALVAREZ de MENDIETA, Francisco Xavier	S	32	VA		B		VA			3	MN						AC ME	16
OD	MA	1787		INQUANZO DIAZ, Marcos	S	31	ME	SI			ME RC			1							D	7
OD	MA	1788		ASTEGUITA y SARRALDE, José Bernardo	S	39	GR OR		D					3				Y		CH	OD CA	N.S.
OD	MA	1795		QUEIPO de LLANO, Fernando	S									1							AS	N.S.
OD	MA	1796		MESIA y CAICEDO, Nicolás de	S	32	SF		D		SF		CA	3							OD GD	
OD	MA	1797		RUBIANES, Manuel Antonio	A	49	SF		D		SF QU	FI QU	CA	2				Y	QU		D	N.S.
OD	MA	1797		CASTAÑO y RUIZ, Pasqual	S	27	SA		B		RC		F-MT	3							AC ME	
OD	MA	1800		AYALA VARONA, José de	S	35	SA SE		B		SE RC			2							AC ME	16
OD	MA	1803		RODRIGUEZ de CARDENAS, Antonio	S	51	GR OR		D		GR RC	TA ME	CA	2						GT	OD GT	N.S.
OD	MA	1804		VELASCO y CAMBEROS, Manuel Dionisio de	CS		CS				BA CS RC		F-OD	2							OD BA	N.S.
OD	MA	1804		REYES y BORDA, Manuel José de	CH		CH		D		CH CZ	TA CZ		4						CI	OD BA	N.S.
OD	MA	1804		FAES de MIRANDA, Matías	S	41	OV SA		D		RC		CA	1								
OD	MA	1805		RUIZ RAMIREZ, Alfonso	S	56	OS GR SE		B		SE	SP		1							D	11
OD	MA	1811		POSADA FERNANDEZ de CORDOBA, Vicente de	ME	31	AL VA		D		IN RC		F-MT	1								
OD	MA	1816		BERNALDEZ y PIZARRO, Manuel	S						AG MA			1								
OD	MA	1816		PORTILLA y QUADRA, Mateo José de la	LI	42	LI		B		LI RC		X- BA	1								
OD	MA	1818		ELIZALDE, Juan Manuel de	CH	27	CH		B		CH CH		X- CH	1						IC		N.S.
OD	MA	1821		FERNANDEZ BLANCO, Simón	S	61	OV		B		.		O-Y	1								

Post	Audiencia	Year	Native Son	Name	Birthplace	Age	University	Colegio	Degree	Abogado	Previous Post	University Service	Relatives' Posts	Total Appts.	Purchase	Date	Dispensations	Married	Wife's Birthplace	Honors, Order	Departure	Years of Service
OD	MA	1821		GORVEA y CALVO ENCALADA, Manuel	LI	36	CH		D		CH	TA LI	CA F-FI O-Y	I								
FH	MA	1795		RIQUELME, Rodrigo	S	34	AL OR GR		B		RC		F-SB	I								N.S.
FH	MA	1796		GUTIERREZ de PIÑERES, Fernando Antonio	S	34	VD		B		VD	TA ME	O-Y	2						CH	D FR ME	15
FF	MA	1695		ESPINOSA RIVADENEIRA, Juan de	S	30	AL		L		RC			2							OD MA	
FI	MA	1696		AGÜERO, Baltazar de					D					2							OF MA	N.S.
FI	MA	1705		CASA ALVARADO, Antonio de	S	45	SA		L		RC		X- ME	I							D	12
FI	MA	1710		VILLA BARREDA, Gregorio Manuel de	S				L					I	FN	1710	Y	S			D	11
FI	MA	1720		BEDOYA y OSORIO, Pedro de	S				L					3						SA	FR ME	13
FI	MA	1734		PEREZ de ARROYO, Cristobal	S	33	GR		L		GR	SU	O-Y	I	MN			Y	MA		D	6
FI	MA	1744		MERINO y RIVERA, José Joaquín de	S		TO SA	CU	L			OP		I								5
FI	MA	1756		VIANA, Francisco Leandro de (Conde de Tepa)	S	26	SA	SB	L					3				Y		CH	AC ME	8
FI	MA	1765		ANDRADE y CUELLAR, Antonio Lorenzo de	S		SE		L			SU		I				Y			D	9
FI	MA	1801		DIAZ de RIVERA, Miguel	S	40	AL		D		RC	FI MA	CA	2				Y	MA		RM FH MA	3
FI	MA	1805		MATA RAMOS, Juan de	S	34	GR		B		GR RC			2							AC LI	
FH	MA	1811		DIAZ de RIVERA, Miguel	S	50	AL		D		RC	MA	CA	2				Y	MA		FI MA	
FV	MA	1776		ALVAREZ VALCARCEL, Juan	S		OM AV		L		RC		CA	I						CH	OD AS	9
FV	MA	1785		REVENGA y ALVAREZ, Gerónimo	S		VD				RC		FR MA	2							D	8
FV	MA	1787		ALONSO de TEJADA, Joaquín José	S	31	VD				RC			I							D	11
FV	MA	1816		POMAR e HIDALGO, Ramón	S	39	SE		B		SE			I								N.S.
FR	MA	1777		REVENGA y ALVAREZ, Gerónimo	S	44	VD				RC			2							FV MA	8
FR	MA	1785		PASTOR, Julián Hilarión	S		AL		D		RC	SP	OP O-Y	I							D	9
FR	MA	1815		VERGES y LOSTAU, Juan	S	50	VA		D		RC	SP	CA	I							Ref.	N.S.
FR	MA	1816		AGUILA YCAZA, Pedro Antonio del	SF		LI ME	SM SI			LI ME			I								

AUDIENCIA OF MEXICO

Post	Audiencia	Year	Native Son	Name	Birthplace	Age	University	Colegio	Degree	Abogado	Previous Post	University Service	Relatives' Posts	Total Appts.	Purchase	Date	Dispensations	Married	Wife's Birthplace	Honors, Order	Departure	Years of Service
RE	ME	1776		ROMA ROSSELL, Francisco	S						CT	AS		I				Y	S	CI	RT	6
RE	ME	1782		HERRERA y RIVERO, Vicente de (Marqués de Herrera)	S		SA	SB	L		RE	GT		5	MN			Y	ME	CH CI	MT CI	10
RE	ME	1786		SANCHEZ PAREJA, Eusebio	S	70	GR		L		RE GD			5				Y			RT	4
RE	ME	1787		GAMBOA, Francisco Xavier	GD	70	ME	SI	L		ME	RE SD		4				Y			D	17
RE	ME	1795		LADRON de GUEVARA, Baltazar	GT		ME		L		ME	OD ME		3						AM CI	D	27
RE	ME	1804		MIER y TRESPALACIOS, Cosme Antonio de	S	69	OM VD		D		OD ME	SU	O-Y	4				Y	ME	CH	D	28
RE	ME	1805		CASTILLO y NEGRETE, Manuel del	S	55	SI AL		L	RC	RE GT	OP		6				Y	GD		FN CI	8
RE	ME	1806		CATANI, Pedro	S		BA		D	CT RC	RE GD			4				Y				3
RE	ME	1810		AGUIRRE y VIANA, Guillermo de	S	58	ZA AL		D		OD ME	F-SB O-Y		4							D	22
RE	ME	1811	*	GONZALEZ CALDERON, Tomás	ME	71	ME	TS	D		ME	OS	SU	5				Y			D	14
RE	ME	1813		ARREDONDO y PELEGRIN, Manuel Antonio (Marqués de San Juan de Nepomuceno)	S	75	SA		B		RC	RE LI	O-Y	5				Y	LI	CI CA CH		N.S.
RE	ME	1815		MESIA y CAICEDO, José de	S	62	GR		D		OD ME		CA	2				Y	SF		D	24

Post	Audiencia	Year	Native Son	Name	Birthplace	Age	University	Colegio	Degree	Abogado	Previous Post	University Service	Relatives' Posts	Total Appts.	Purchase	Date	Dispensations	Married	Wife's Birthplace	Honors	Order	Departure	Years of Service
RE	ME	1820		BATALLER y ROS, Miguel Antonio	S	64	GR		L		GR / OD/ME		F-OD	2								Ind.	
OD	ME	1689		CALDERON de la BARCA, Miguel	S	37			L	RC				1	OD	1689		Y		OD	AS		11
OD	ME	1695		LUNA y ARIAS, José de	GD	32	ME/SA		L				F-OD	1	OD	1695	MN					RC	17
OS	ME	1697		OSORIO ESPINOSA de los MONTEROS, José	A				L	ME	OS/GD	CA	CONQ	2	OS	1697		Y					
OD	ME	1699		TOVAR, Baltazar de	S				D		FV/ME			3			MN	Y	ME			D	18
OS	ME	1700	*	ANGUITA ...AL y ROJAS, Francisco	ME				L	ME	X-/ME			1	OS	1700	NA/MN	Y	ME		RM	D	1
OD	ME	1702		URIBE CASTJON y MEDRANO, José Joaquín	S	36	SA	AR	L			CA		1			MN	Y	ME	SA		D	36
OD	ME	1705	*	SORIA VELASQUEZ, Gerónimo de (Marqués de Villahermosa y Alfaro)	ME	45	ME	TS	D		ME/GD		F-XX/CONQ	1								D	4
OD	ME	1705		ALCEDO y SOTOMAYOR, Carlos de	S	49	SN/VD		L	QU	OD/SF	SU		2				Y		SA		N.S.	
OS	ME	1706	*	DIEZ de BRACAMONTE, Juan de	ME		ME	SI	D	ME		OP		1								RM	13
OS	ME	1707		GONZALEZ de AGÜERO, Félix	S				L					1			MN					RM	12
OS	ME	1707	*	VALDES, Juan de	ME	56	ME		L	ME	X-/ME			1	OS	1707	NA					D	7
OS	ME	1707		VILLARREAL y FLORENCIA, Cristóbal de	SD		ME		L				F-XX	1	OS	1707	NA					D	6
OS	ME	1708	*	RIVADENEIRA LUNA, Tristán Manuel de	ME	28	ME	TS	L					1	OS	1708	NA/MN					RC	
OS	ME	1710	*	FRANCO VELASQUEZ de TOLEDO, Agustín	ME		ME		D			CA		1	OS	1710	NA/MN	Y	ME			RM	9
OS	ME	1710	*	OLIVAN REBOLLEDO, Juan Manuel de	ME	34	ME		L	ME	OS/GD	SU		2	OS	1710		Y	S			D	27
OS	ME	1710		CERECEDA y GIRON, Sebastián de	S		SA		L		OS/SD			2									
OS	ME	1711	*	TERREROS OCHOA, Antonio	ME		ME		D	ME	X-/ME	SU	F-XX	1			NA/MN	Y	ME			RM	
OS	ME	1716		SUAREZ de FIGUEROA, Félix										1								RM	3
OS	ME	1718		OVIEDO y BANOS, Diego Antonio de	SF	53	LI	SM	B	LI	OD/GT		F-OD/M-AC/O-Y	3						CI		D	3
OD	ME	1720		CARRILLO ESCUDERO, Gregorio	S	56	SA		D		OD/GT	SU		2								D	6
OD	ME	1720		GUTIERREZ de la PEÑA, José	S									2				Y				RC	13
OD	ME	1720		PICADO PACHECO y MONTERO, Juan	S	49	SA/AV	CU	L		FI/GD			2							AL	D	19
OD	ME	c1721		GONZALEZ PIMENTEL, Esteban	S		GR				SE/GR			1				Y		SA		D	N.S.
OD	ME	1722	*	LUGO CORONADO y HIERRO, Felipe Antonio de	ME	45	ME		D	ME	OS/GT	OP		2				Y	ME			D	1
OD	ME	1723		MALO de VILLAVICENCIO, Pedro de	S	50	SE/SA		D		FV/ME			4				Y	S	CAL		D	22
OD	ME	1725		AGUIRRE NEGRO, José Francisco	S		ON/VD/SA		B	AC	ME	CA		3			MN			CI/CAL	RT		12
OD	ME	1728		FERNANDEZ de VILLANUEVA VEITIA LINAJE, José	S	47	ME		B	ME	X-/ME	SU	O-Y	2			MN	Y	ME	SA		RC	10
OD	ME	1735		ECHAVARRI y UGARTE, Francisco Antonio de	S	30	VD/AL	IL	B					1				Y	ME	CI/SA/CI	RT/MT		34
OD	ME	1735		VALCARCEL y FORMENTO, Domingo	S	35	GR/AV	IL	L	AC	ME	OP	F-MT/P-MT/M-MT	2			MN	Y	ME	CI/CA/SA	RT		50
OS	ME	1736		LOPEZ de ADAN, Francisco de	S		AL		D		OD/MA			2						SA		D	21
OD	ME	1738		RODRIGUEZ de ALBUERNE, Juan (Marqués de Altamira)	S	42	AL		L	RC	OD/GD			2			CM/CP	Y	ME	SA		D	15
OD	ME	1738		SANTAELLA y MELGAREJO, Ambrosio Tomás de	SD	48	ME		B	ME	FV/ME	SU		2				Y				D	18
OD	ME	1738		DAVILA MADRID, Fernando	S	54	AL/SA	AR	L		FI/GD	SU		2				Y			RT		25

Post	Audiencia	Year	Native Son	Name	Birthplace	Age	University	Colegio	Degree	Abogado	Previous Post	University Service	Relatives' Posts	Total Appts.	Purchase	Date	Dispensations	Married	Wife's Birthplace	Honors, Order	Departure	Years of Service
OD	ME	1739		PADILLA y CORDOBA, Pedro de	S	40	ME	SI	D	ME				1							D	22
OD	ME	1739		FERNANDEZ de MADRID, Luis Manuel	S	54	AL		L	ME	AC ME	OP	F-XX P-XX	3				Y	QU	CAL	D	11
OD	ME	1741		RODRIGUEZ de TORO, José	CA	26			L			OP	F-XX	1	OS	1741	MN CM	Y	ME	CAL	D	31
OD	ME	1741		TRESPALACIOS y ESCANDON, Domingo de	S	35	SA		B	RC	OD GT		O-Y	3			MN	Y	ME	SA	MT CI	23
OD	ME	1741		CAMPO y ZARATE, Clemente del	CS	55	LI	SM	L	LI	AC ME		F-AC P-OD M-AC CONQ O-Y	1			MN	Y	ME		D	17
OS	ME	1742		FERNANDEZ de VILLANUEVA VEITIA LINAJE, José	S	61	ME		B	ME	OD ME	SU	O-Y	2			MN	Y	ME	SA	D	10
OF	ME	1742		MALO de VILLAVICENCIO, Félix	GD	22	ME SE	SI			ME		CA	F-OD	1				Y	ME	CAL	RC	29
OD	ME	1754		ANDREU y FERRAZ, Antonio	S		HU		D		FV ME	CA		4								17
OD	ME	1761	*	RIVADENEIRA y BARRIENTOS, Antonio Joaquín de	ME	51	ME	TS	B	ME	FV ME		P-AB	4			MN	Y			D	18
OD	ME	1763	*	VILLAURRUTIA y SALCEDO, Antonio Bernardino	ME	51	ME	SI			OD SD	CA	F-AB	3				Y	S	CI	RE GD	23
OD	ME	1764		SANTAELLA y MELGAREJO, Ambrosio Eugenio de	GT	50	ME		L	ME	AX ME		F-OD CONQ	2				Y	ME		D	32
OD	ME	1764		LOPEZ PORTILLA, Francisco de	GD	51	GT		B		OS GD		CONQ O-Y	2				Y	GT		D	2
OD	ME	1766		ENRIQUEZ de VILLACORTA, Francisco de	S	57	AL		L		OS MA	OP		2							D	7
OD	ME	1769		VIANA, Francisco Leandro de (Conde de Tepa)	S	39	SA	SB	L		AC ME			3				Y	ME	CH	MT CI	10
OD	ME	1773		HERRERA y RIVERO, Vicente de (Marqués de Herrera)	S		SA	SB	L		AC ME			5				Y	ME	CH	RE GT	6
OD	ME	1774		FERNANDEZ de MADRID, Diego Antonio	GT	48	ME		B	ME	AC ME		F-OD P-XX A-CG	2			MN	Y	ME		D	32
OD	ME	1774		GAMBOA, Francisco Xavier	GD	57	ME	SI	L	ME	AC ME			4							RE SD	17
OD	ME	1774		SANCHEZ PAREJA, Eusebio	S	58	GR		L		AC ME			5				Y			RE GD	4
OD	ME	1774		VILLARRASA VENEGAS, Basilio	S	50	GR		D		AC ME	CA		2							FI AS	6
OS	ME	1776		GOMEZ ALGARIN, Francisco	S					ME	OD GT			3				Y			D	9
OD	ME	1776		ACEDO, Miguel Calixto de	S	46	SA	SB	L					3						CH	OD AS	12
OD	ME	1776		CISTUE y COLL, José de (Barón de la Menglana)	S	51	HU		D		AC ME	CA		4				Y		CH	FP CI	2
OD	ME	1776		ARANGOYTI, Domingo de	S		AL		L		FV ME	OP		2							D	6
OD	ME	1776		GONZALEZ BECERRA, Ramón Joaquín	S		SN SA				AC ME			3				Y			OD AS	2
OS	ME	1777		MESIA y MUNIVE, Cristóbal (Conde de Sierrabella)	CH	60	LI	SM SF	D	LI	OS LI	CA	F-AB O-Y	2			CM	Y	LI		RT	N.S.
OD	ME	1778		LUYANDO, Ruperto Vicente de	S		ZA		D	AR	AC ME		O-Y	4				Y			FI AS	9
OD	ME	1778		LADRON de GUEVARA, Baltazar	GT		ME		L	ME	FV ME			3						AM CI	RE ME	28
OD	ME	1778		URUÑUELA ARANSAY, Juan Antonio	S	49	SA AV	OV	L		AC ME	OP		4						CH	RE GT	5
OD	ME	1778		ECHEVERZ, Pedro Antonio de	PA	53	LI	SM SF	D	LI	OS LI		F-AB P-CG	2			HP	Y	PA		D	N.S.
DD	ME	1780		GALDEANO, Joaquín de	S	40	SA HU		D		FV LI	CA		4				Y			D	
OD	ME	1781		URIZAR y BOLIVAR, José Antonio de	S	44	ON VD		L	RC	AC ME			4						CI CH	RE SD	9
OD	ME	1784		MIRAFUENTES, Simón Antonio de	S		HI VD		L	RC	AC	CA		3							D	13
OD	ME	1784		BELEÑA, Eusebio Ventura	S	48	SI AL		D	RC	AC ME	CA	F-SB	5							RE SF	15
OD	ME	1785		ANDA y SALAZAR, Juan Francisco	S	48	GR		L	RC	AC ME		O-Y	5							D	22

Post	Audiencia	Year	Native Son	Name	Birthplace	Age	University	Colegio	Degree	Abogado	Previous Post	University Service	Relatives' Posts	Total Appts.	Purchase	Date	Dispensations	Married	Wife's Birthplace	Honors, Order	Departure	Years of Service
OD	ME	1785		MIER y TRESPALACIOS, Cosme Antonio de	S	40	OM VD		D		AC ME	SU	O-Y	4				Y	ME	CI CH	RE ME	28
OD	ME	1786		BATALLER y VASCO, Miguel Antonio	S	65				GR RC	AC ME			2				Y	S	AM	D	10
OD	ME	1786	*	GONZALEZ MALDONADO, Francisco Ignacio	ME	48	ME	SI	D	ME	FI GD	CA	F-XX M-XX	5			MN			CI	FI	8
OD	ME	1787		REY y BOZA, Félix del	SD					ME SD	AC ME			3							D	3
OD	ME	1787		MOYA, José de	S	62	HU			AR	OD GD			2							D	8
OD	ME	1787		SALCEDO y SOMODEVILLA, Modesto de	S	32	VD	SC	B		AC ME			3						SJ	FI AS	5
OD	ME	1787		GONZALEZ CARBAJAL, Ciriaco	S	52	GR	*	L	GR RC	OD MA			2			MN	Y	MA	CI CH	MT CI	19
OD	ME	1788		DIEZ QUIJADA y OVEJERO, Félix	S	61	SI AL	IL	L		AC ME	CA		2				Y			D	19
OD	ME	1790	*	GONZALEZ MALDONADO, Francisco Ignacio	ME	52	ME	SI	D	ME	FI HT	CA	F-XX M-XX	5			MN			CI	RT	8
OD	ME	1791		CHAVES y MENDOZA, Luis de	S		SA		L	RC	AC ME	SU	O-Y	5				Y		CI CH	RE SF	6
OD	ME	1791		CACHO CALDERON de la BARCA, Emeterio	S		OV			VD	AC ME		F-XX O-Y	3							D	14
OD	ME	1792		AGUIRRE y VIANA, Guillermo de	S	40	ZA AL		D		AC ME		F-SB O-Y	4							RE ME	22
OD	ME	1795		IRISARRI y DOMINGUEZ, Miguel Cristóbal de	S	54	SE GR		B	RC	AC ME	CA		3							D	17
OD	ME	1796		BODEGA y MOLLINEDO, Manuel Antonio de la	LI	48	LI AL		D	LI RC	AC ME	CA		3				Y	ME		RM MT CI	12
OS	ME	1797	*	GONZALEZ CALDERON, Tomás	ME	57	ME	TS	D	ME	OD LI	SU		5				Y			RE ME	14.
OD	ME	1800		VIDERIQUE, Rafael Antonio	S						OD BA			3				Y			D	N.S.
OD	ME	1800		URRUTIA, Manuel José de	S	68	ME HA	SI	D	SD	AC ME	CA		4						OD OM	D	10
OD	ME	1802		MESIA y CAICEDO, José de	S	49	GR		D		AC ME	CA		4				Y	SF		RE ME	24
OD	ME	1803		MOSQUERA y FIGUEROA, Joaquín de	SF	55	SF		D	SF	AC ME	CA	CONQ	4						IC	RE CA	8
OD	ME	1804		BATALLER y ROS, Miguel Antonio	S	48	GR		L	GR	AC ME		F-OD	4							RE ME	Ind.
OD	ME	1804	*	ARIAS de VILLAFAÑE, José Joaquín de	ME	66	ME	SI	L	ME GT	AX		CONQ	3						CH	RT	10
OD	ME	1805		ALVAREZ de MENDIETA, Francisco Xavier	S	50	VA		B	VA	AC ME			3							D	6
OD	ME	1807	*	FONCERRADA y ULIBARRI, Melchor José de	ME	58	ME	SI TS	L	ME	AC ME			3				Y			D	10
OD	ME	1810		CAMPO y RIVAS, Manuel del	SF	60	SF		D	SF RC	AC ME		F-XX M-HM	4						CH	Ind.	
OD	ME	1810		MODET, Ramón de	S						AS			1								3
OD	ME	1810		RIVA, Juan Antonio de la	S	51	SA TO		D	RC	AC ME	CA		4							Ind.	
OD	ME	1811		PUENTE, Pedro de la	S		ON VD				AC ME			1						VE CH		3
OD	ME	1811		BACHILLER y MENA, Miguel	S	50	VA		D	RC	AC ME			2				Y	ME	AM	Ind.	
OD	ME	1815		GARCIA de FRIAS, Diego de	S	65	AL		B	RC	OD SD			3				Y			Ind.	
OD	ME	c1816		HERNANDEZ de ALVA y ALONSO, Juan	S	66	AL		B	RC	AC ME		O-Y	4				Y	S	OM IC	OD SD	N.S.
OD	ME	1816		VELASCO de la VARA, Francisco Antonio de	GD	68	GD ME	SI	D	GD ME	AC ME	CA		2							D	4
OD	ME	1816		MARTINEZ de ARAGON, Felipe de	S	42	HU ZA		L		AC ME		F-XX	3			MN				Ind.	
OD	ME	1817		BLAYA y BLAYA, Manuel Mariano de	S	65	OR		B	GR RC	RE GT			5				Y			Ind.	11
OD	ME	1817		YAÑEZ y NUÑO, José Isidro	CA	47	CA		D	CA	AC ME			3							Ind.	
OD	ME	c1820		RECACHO, Juan José	S	47	SA		L	RC	OD GD	OP		3							RE GD	N.S.

Post	Audiencia	Year	Native Son	Name	Birthplace	Age	University	Colegio	Degree	Abogado	Previous Post	University Service	Relatives' Posts	Total Appts.	Purchase	Date	Dispensations	Married	Wife's Birthplace	Honors, Order	Departure	Years of Service
OD	ME	1820		MARTINEZ MANSILLA, Manuel	BA	41	SN		B	RC	AC ME	CA		3				Y			Ind.	
AX	ME	1693		VALCARCEL, Juan de					L		FI SF			2								
AC	ME	1705		EGUARAS FERNANDEZ de HIJAR, Pedro de (Marqués de Salvatierra)	S	32	SA	AR			OD GT			2			MN	Y	ME	CI	RT	6
AX	ME	1706		CASA ALVARADO, Francisco de	S	36	SE SA		L	SE RC	SP			1	AX	1706					D	8
AX	ME	1707	*	PEÑA y FLORES, Juan Francisco de la	ME					ME				1	AX	1707	NA MN				RM	12
AX	ME	1707		ROBLES y LORENZANA, Agustín de	S	29	LI	SF	L					1	AX	1707	MN				RM	11
AC	ME	1710		CHIRINO VANDEVAL, Nicolás	SD	46	ME		B	ME	OD SD	F-XX P-XX		2	AX	1710	MN	Y			D	
AX	ME	1710	*	VEQUENILLA y SANDOVAL, Juan de la	ME		ME		D			CONQ		4	AX	1710	NA MN	Y	ME		D	25
AX	ME	1711	*	CASTAÑEDA, Diego Francisco de	ME		ME			ME	OS GD	F-XX P-AB		2	AX	1711	NA MN	Y	ME		RM	
AX	ME	1711		BARBADILLO VICTORIA, Francisco de	S	36	VD		L	RC	TA ME			1	AX	1711	MN				D	15
AX	ME	1711	*	SANCHEZ de ALCAZAR, Pedro	ME	27	ME		L	ME				2	AX	1711	NA MN	Y	ME		RM	8
AC	ME	1722		OSILIA y RAYO, Juan Gerónimo de	S	44	SE OS		D		SP	CA		1							D	6
AC	ME	1723		AGUIRRE NEGRO, José Francisco de	S		ON VD SA		B		OD SD	CA		3			MN			CI CAL	OD ME	12
AC	ME	1724		VELASCO, Julián de		42			D			CA		1							D	0
AC	ME	1725		CARRILLO MORENO, Juan	S		VD		L		FI SD			3				Y			OD GD	8
AC	ME	1727		VALCARCEL y FORMENTO, Domingo	S	27	GR AV	IL	L			OP	F-MT P-MT M-MT	2			MN	Y	ME	CI CA SA	OD ME	50
AC	ME	1730		CAMPO y ZARATE, Clemente del	CS	44	LI	SM	L	LI	X-ME		F-AC P-OD M-AC CONQ O-Y	2			MN	Y	ME		OD ME	17
AC	ME	1733		MESIA de la CERDA, José de la	S	38	GR		B		OD GD	SU	O-Y	2				Y	ME		D	25
AX	ME	1734		TINEO, Felipe	S					RC	PI ME			1				Y			D	18
AC	ME	1737		CHINCHILLA y HENESTROSA, Manuel	S	31	GR SA	CU	B			SU		1							D	9
AC	ME	1738		FERNANDEZ TORIBIO, Francisco	S	48	AL	IL	L		OS MA	CA		3				Y			RT	N.S.
AC	ME	1738		FERNANDEZ de MADRID, Luis Manuel	S	53	AL		L	ME	OD GT	OP	F-XX	3				Y	QU	CAL	OD ME	11
AX	ME	1755		CALVO de la PUERTA, Sebastián	SD	38	HA		D		OD GD	CA	F-XX P-XX O-Y	3			CM	Y			OD GT	9
AX	ME	1755		BRUNA y AHUMADA, Bartolomé de	S	53	AV VD	SC	B			CA	F-MT	1						CAL		1
AC	ME	1764		GAMBOA, Francisco Xavier	GD	47	ME	SI	L	ME	X-ME			4							OD ME	17
AC	ME	1765		VIANA, Francisco Leandro de (Conde de Tepa)	S	35	SA	SB	L		FI MA			3				Y	ME	CH	OD ME	10
AC	ME	1770		HERRERA y RIVERO, Vicente de (Marqués de Herrera)	S		SA	SB	L		FI SD			5			MN	Y	ME	CH	OD ME	6
AC	ME	1773		VILLARRASA VENEGAS, Basilio	S	49	GR		D		OD GT	CA		3							OD ME	6
AC	ME	1773		SANCHEZ PAREJA, Eusebio	S	57	GR		L		OD GD			5				Y			OD ME	4
AC	ME	1774		ACEDO, Miguel Calixto de	S	44	SA	SB	L		OD SD			3							OD ME	12
AC	ME	1774		GONZALEZ BUSTILLO, Juan Manuel	S	48	SA		B	RC	OD GT	OP	O-Y	2							FI HT	2
AC	ME	1775		CISTUE y COLL, José de (Barón de la Menglana)	S	50	HU		B		FI GT	CA		4			Y	S		CH	OD ME	2
AC	ME	1775		FERNANDEZ VILLANUEVA, Manuel	S	49	AL GR SI				OD GT		O-Y	2				Y			D	N.S.

Post	Audiencia	Year	Native Son	Name	Birthplace	Age	University	Colegio	Degree	Abogado	Previous Post	University Service	Relatives' Posts	Total Appts.	Purchase	Date	Dispensations	Married	Wife's Birthplace	Honors, Order	Departure	Years of Service
AC	ME	1775		GONZALEZ BECERRA, Ramón Joaquín	S		SN SA		L		OD GD			3							OD ME	2
AC	ME	1776		MIER y TRESPALACIOS, Cosme Antonio de	S	31	OM VD		D		AC LI	SU	O-Y	4				Y	ME	CH	OD ME	28
AC	ME	1777		LUYANDO, Ruperto Vicente de	S		ZA		D	AR	OD GD		O-Y	4				Y			OD ME	9
AC	ME	1777		MIRAFUENTES, Simón Antonio de	S		HI VD		L	RC	OD SD	CA		3							OD ME	13
AC	ME	1777		URUÑUELA ARANSAY, Juan Antonio	S	48	SA AV	OV	L		OS MA	CA		4						CH	OD ME	5
AC	ME	1777		BELEÑA, Eusebio Ventura	S	41	SI AL		D	RC	OD GT	CA	F-SB	5							OD ME	15
AC	ME	1778		URIZAR y BOLIVAR, José Antonio de	S	41	ON VD		L	RC	OD SD			4						CH	OD ME	9
AC	ME	1778		ANDA y SALAZAR, Juan Francisco de	S	41	GR		L	RC	OD GD		O-Y	5							OD ME	22
AC	ME	1781		PLAZA y UBILLA, Joaquín de	S	37	SA VD	SB	L		OD GT			2							D	2
AC	ME	1784		BATALLER y VASCO, Miguel Antonio	S	63				GR RC	AG ME			2				Y	S	AM	OD ME	10
AC	ME	1784		REY y BOZA, Félix del	SD				L		ME SD GT			3							D OD ME	3
AC	ME	1785		DIEZ QUIJADA y OVEJERO, Félix	S	58	SI AL	IL	L		OD MA	CA		3				Y			OD ME	19
AC	ME	1785		SALCEDO y SOMODEVILLA, Modesto de	S	42	VD	SC	B		OD			3							OD ME	5
AC	ME	1786		CHAVES y MENDOZA, Luis de	S		SA		L	RC	OD SD	SU	O-Y	5				Y		CI CH	OD ME	6
AC	ME	1786		CACHO CALDERON de la BARCA, Emeterio	S		OV			VD	OS MA		F-XX O-Y	3							OD ME	14
AC	ME	1787		EMPARAN y ORBE, Agustín Ignacio	S		VD SA	SB	L		OD SD	OP	P-HM O-Y	3			MN			CI CH	RE MA	3
AC	ME	1787		SAAVEDRA y CARVAJAL, Francisco de	S	49	SN VD		D	RC	FI GT			4							RE MA	
AC	ME	1788		AGUIRRE y VIANA, Guillermo de	S	36	ZA AL		D		OD GD		F-SB O-Y	4							RE ME	22
AC	ME	1790		IRISARRI y DOMINGUEZ, Miguel Cristóbal de	S	49	SE GR		B	RC	FR SD	CA		3							OD ME	17
AC	ME	1791		VALENZUELA y AGUILAR, Pedro Jacinto de	S	53	JA			GR	AG ME			1							MT CI	8
AC	ME	1791		URRUTIA, Manuel José de	SD	59	ME HA	SI	D	SD	OD GD	CA		4						SD OM	OD ME	10
AC	ME	1792		BODEGA y MOLLINEDO, Manuel Antonio de la	LI	44	LI AL		D	LI RC	OD GT	CA		3				Y	ME		OD ME	12
AC	ME	1794		MESIA y CAICEDO, José de	S	41	GR		D		OD SF	CA		4				Y	SF		OD ME	24
AC	ME	1795		MOSQUERA y FIGUEROA, Joaquín de	SF	47	SF		D	SF	OD SF	CA	CONQ	4						IC	OD ME	8
AC	ME	1795		BACHILLER de MENA, Rafael	S						AG ME			1						AM	D	0
AC	ME	1796		BATALLER y ROS, Miguel Antonio	S	40	GR		L	GR	FR GT		F-OD	4							OD ME	Ind.
AC	ME	1797		CASTILLO y NEGRETE, Manuel del	S	47	SI AL		L	RC	OD SF	OP		6				Y	GD		RE GT	8
AX	ME	1799	*	ARIAS de VILLAFAÑE, José Joaquín de	ME	61	ME	SI	L	ME GT	OD QU		CONQ	3						CH	OD ME	10
AC	ME	1803		ALVAREZ de MENDIETA, Francisco Xavier	S	48	VA		B	VA	OD MA			3							OD ME	6
AC	ME	1803	*	FONCERRADA y ULIBARRI, Melchor José de	ME	54	ME	SI TS	L	ME	OD SD			3				Y			OD ME	10
AC	ME	1803		BLAYA y BLAYA, Manuel Mariano de	S	51	OR		B	GR RC	FR SF			5				Y			RE GT	Ind. 11
AC	ME	1804		VILLAURRUTIA y LOPEZ OSORIO, Jacobo de	SD	47	AL TO		D	RC	OD GT		F-RE	2				Y	S		OD AS	6
AC	ME	1804		CAMPO y RIVAS, Manuel del	SF	54	SF		D	SF RC	OD GD		F-XX M-HM	3						CH	OD ME	Ind.
AC	ME	1804		COLLADO, Juan	S	56	AL		B	RC	OD GT	CA	F-SB	4							RE CA	5
AC	ME	1807		RIVA, Juan Antonio de la	S	49	SA TO		D	RC	OD GD	CA		4							OD ME	Ind.

Post	Audiencia	Year	Native Son	Name	Birthplace	Age	University	Colegio	Degree	Abogado	Previous Post	University Service	Relatives' Posts	Total Appts.	Purchase	Date	Dispensations	Married	Wife's Birthplace	Honors, Order	Departure	Years of Service
AC	ME	1809		LLAVE y MARQUELI, Rafael de la	S	54	AL			RC	OD GT			3								
AC	ME	1810		PUENTE, Pedro de la	S		ON VD				SP			2						VE CH	OD ME	3
AC	ME	1810		YAÑEZ y NUÑO, José Isidro	CA	40	CA		D	CA	FR GT			3							OD ME	Ind.
AC	ME	1811		BACHILLER y MENA, Miguel	S	50	VA		D	RC	AG ME			2				Y	ME	AM OD	ME	Ind.
AC	ME	1811		FIGUERA de VARGAS, Francisco José	CA	56			D	SD RC			P-XX M-XX	1				Y	SD	SD VE	D	0
AC	ME	1811		MARTINEZ de ARAGON, Felipe de	S	37	HU ZA		L		OD CA		F XX	3			MN				OD ME	Ind.
AC	ME	1811		CASTAÑO y RUIZ, Pasqual	S	41	SA		B	RC	OD MA		F-MT	3							OD MA	N.S.
AC	ME	1811		MARTINEZ MANSILLA, Manuel	BA	32	SN		B	RC	FR SF	CA		3				Y			OD ME	Ind.
AC	ME	1812		HERNANDEZ de ALVA y ALONSO, Juan	S	62	AL		B	RC	OD SF		O-Y	2				Y	S	OM IC	OD ME	N.S.
AC	ME	1815		MEDINA, Ildefonso José de	S	38	SE		L	SE RC	OD CA			2								Ind.
AC	ME	1815		VELASCO, Francisco Antonio de	GD	67	GD ME	SI	D	GD ME	X- GD	CA		2							OD ME	4
AC	ME	1816		AYALA VARONA, José de	S	51	SA SE		B	SE RC	OD MA			2							RT	
AC	ME	1816		OSES, Juan Ramón de	S	46	HI SA		D	EX RC	FI GT	CA		4								Ind.
AC	ME	1817		HEREDIA y MIESES, José Francisco	SD	41	SD		D	SD RC	OD CA	CA	F-XX	2				Y	CA		D	2
AC	ME	1818		LOPEZ de SEGOVIA, Pedro	S	44	TO				OD QU		F-SB	2						IC		Ind.
FH	ME	1779		POSADA y SOTO, Ramón de	S	29	AV VD		L	RC	AC LI	OP		3			MN	Y		CH	FN CI	14
FH	ME	1795		HERNANDEZ de ALVA y ALONSO, Lorenzo	S	55	VD		B	RC	FV ME			4				Y	S		FN CI	22
FH	ME	1802		BORBON y TORRIJOS, Francisco Xavier	S	50	VA		B	RC	FV ME			4						CH		18
FH	ME	c1810		SAGARZURIETA, Ambrosio de	S	60	AL ZA		D	RC	FV ME			4				Y		CH		Ind.
FV	ME	1694		TOVAR, Baltazar de	S				D		FR ME			3				Y			OD ME	18
FV	ME	1699		BLANCO del CASTILLO, Francisco	S		SA		D		SP	SU		1				Y			RT	4
FV	ME	1704		ESPINOSA OCAMPO y CORNEJO, José Antonio	S	42	SA		D		FR ME			2						SA		17
FV	ME	1723		MALO de VILLAVICENCIO, Pedro de	S	50	SE SA		D		FR ME			4				Y	S	CAL	OD ME	22
FV	ME	1723		PALACIOS, Prudencio Antonio de	S	40	SA HU		B	RC	OD GD			3				Y	S	CAL	C	9
FV	ME	1733		SANTAELLA y MELGAREJO, Ambrosio Tomás de	SD	43	ME		B	ME	FR ME	SU		4				Y			OD ME	18
FV	ME	1738		BEDOYA y OSORIO, Pedro de	S				L		FR ME			3						SA	RT	14
FV	ME	1748		ANDREU y FERRAZ, Antonio	S		HU		D		FR ME	CA		4							OD ME	17
FV	ME	1755		MOSQUERA y PIMENTEL QUINTANILLA, Luis Francisco (Marqués de Aranda)	S		AV SA	OV	B		FR ME	OP	F-XX	2				Y		CH	FN CI	12
FV	ME	1760	*	RIVADENEIRA y BARRIENTOS, Antonio Joaquín de	ME	50	ME	TS	B	ME	FR ME		P-AB	4				Y			OD ME	18
FV	ME	1761		VELARDE y CIENFUEGOS, Juan Antonio	S	51	SA VD	SC	B		FR ME	SU		5						MO	OD AS	11
FV	ME	1774		ARECHE y SORNOZA, José Antonio de	S	43	AL		D		FR ME	CA		3							VG	9
FV	ME	1776		ARANGOYTI, Domingo de	S		AL		L		FR ME	OP		4							OD ME	6
FV	ME	1777		LADRON de GUEVARA, Baltazar	GT		ME		L	ME	AG ME			3						AM CI	OD ME	27
FV	ME	1778		MARTIN MERINO, Manuel de	S	46	OM VD		B	VD	FR GD			2				Y			D	4
FV	ME	1784		HERNANDEZ de ALVA y ALONSO, Lorenzo	S	44	VD		B	RC	FR ME			4				Y	S		FH ME	22

Post	Audiencia	Year	Native Son	Name	Birthplace	Age	University	Colegio	Degree	Abogado	Previous Post	University Service	Relatives' Posts	Total Appts.	Purchase	Date	Dispensations	Married	Wife's Birthplace	Honors	Order	Departure	Years of Service
FV	ME	1794		BORBON y TORRIJOS, Francisco Xavier	S	42	VA		B	RC	FR ME			4						CH		FH ME	18
FV	ME	1792		SAGARZURIETA, Ambrosio de	S	52	AL ZA		D	RC	FR ME			4				Y		CH		FH ME	Ind.
FV	ME	c1810		ROBLEDO de ALBUQUERQUE, Francisco de	S	67	GR		B	SE RC	FR ME			3				Y	SF	CI			18
FV	ME	c1811		OSES, Juan Ramón de	S	41	HI SA		D	EX RC	FR ME			4								FI GT	Ind.
FV	ME	c1815		ODOARDO, Jose Hipólito	SD		AL		B	RC	SP		F-RE	1									Ind.
FR	ME	1693		TOVAR, Baltazar de	S				D		SP			3			MN	Y	ME			FV ME	18
FR	ME	1699		ESPINOSA OCAMPO y CORNEJO, José Antonio	S	37	SA		D					2						SA		FV ME	17
FR	ME	1704		CEPEDA, Gaspar de	S		SA	AR	L		SP			1								RC	10
FF	ME	1710	*	OYANGUREN, Francisco de	ME	52	ME		D	ME		SU		1	FF	1710			NA	RM			9
FR	ME	1718		FERNANDEZ de BARCO, Francisco	S	43	AL		L		OS SD	SU	F-XX	2								D	N.S.
FR	ME	1721		MALO de VILLAVICENCIO, Pedro de	S	48	SE SA		D		OD GD			4				Y	S	CAL		OD ME	22
FR	ME	1722		FERNANDEZ PEREZ, Tomás	LI	48	LI	SM	L		LI SD	OP		2								Ref	N.S.
FR	ME	1723		SANTAELLA y MELGAREJO, Ambrosio Tomás de	SD	33	ME		B	ME	OD GT	SU		4				Y				FV ME	18
FR	ME	1732		BEDOYA y OSORIO, Pedro de	S				L		FI MA			3						SA		FV ME	14
FR	ME	1738		ANDREU y FERRAZ, Antonio	S		HU		D		OD GT	CA		4								FV ME	17
FR	ME	1748		MOSQUERA y PIMENTEL QUINTANILLA, Luis Francisco (Marqués de Aranda)	S		AV SA	OV	B			OP	F-XX	2				Y		CH		FV ME	12
FR	ME	1753	*	RIVADENEIRA y BARRIENTOS, Antonio Joaquín de	ME	43	ME	TS	B	ME	OS GD		P-AB	4				Y				FV ME	18
FR	ME	1760		VELARDE y CIENFUEGOS, Juan Antonio	S	50	SA VD	SC	B		OD GT	SU		5						MO		FV ME	11
FR	ME	1763		ROJAS ALMANSA, Miguel José de	S	48	GR VD		B	RC	FI GD	OP	F-CC	2								D	3
FR	ME	1767		ARECHE y SORNOZA, José Antonio de	S	36	AL		D		OD MA	CA		3								FV ME	9
FR	ME	1774		ARANGOYTI, Domingo de	S		AL		L		FI GD	OP		4								FV ME	6
FR	ME	1776		GALINDO QUIÑONES y BARRIENTOS, Francisco de	S		SE		D		OD GD		O-Y	3				Y	GD	SA		D	2
FR	ME	1780		HERNANDEZ de ALVA y ALONSO, Lorenzo	S	40	VD		B	RC	FV SD			4				Y	S			FV ME	22
FR	ME	1784		VALIENTE y BRAVO, José Pablo	S	36	SE		D	SE RC	OD GT	CA		2						CI	IC		6
FR	ME	1791		BORBON y TORRIJOS, Francisco Xavier	S	39	VA		B	RC	FR GD			4						CH		FV ME	18
FR	ME	1795		SAGARZURIETA, Ambrosio de	S	45	AL ZA		D	RC	FV GD			4				Y		CH		FV ME	Ind.
FR	ME	1802		ROBLEDO de ALBUQUERQUE, Francisco de	S	59	GR		B	SE RC	OD GT			3				Y	SF			FV ME	8
FR	ME	1810		OSES, Juan Ramón de	S	40	HI SA		D	EX RC	AS CA			4								FV ME	Ind.
FR	ME	1811		GUTIERREZ de PIÑERES, Fernando Antonio	S	49	VD		B	BD	FH MA		O-Y	2						CH		D	N.S.
FR	ME	1815		ODOARDO, José Hipólito	SD		AL		B	RC	SP		F-RE	1								FV ME	Ind.
FR	ME	1816		BERASUETA, José Ignacio	A	45	VD AL		D	RC	OD GT			2			MN						Ind.
AUDIENCIA OF PANAMA																							
OD	PA	1688		RIVAS, Diego Antonio de	S		AL							2								Ref	N.S.
OD	PA	1688	*	LAYA BOLIVAR, Juan de	PA	30	LI SA		L				F-AB	1					NA			D	9
OD	PA	1689		LANDERO, Francisco de	LI		LI		D		LI	CA		1								D	N.S.
OD	PA	1690		MEDINA, Francisco de	S	41	VD		L	RC				2				Y	S	RT	OD	SF	3

Post	Audiencia	Year	Native Son	Name	Birthplace	Age	University	Colegio	Degree	Abogado	Previous Post	University Service	Relatives' Posts	Total Appts.	Purchase	Date	Dispensations	Married	Wife's Birthplace	Honors, Order	Departure	Years of Service
OD	PA	1692		ROA y CRIALES, Alejandro de					L					1				Y	S		D	5
OS	PA	1693		ZUNIGA, Francisco José	LI	50			L	LI				3	OS	1693					OD SF	11
OD	PA	1700		CASTRO y ALDUAYN, Juan Antonio de					L					1							D	N.S.
OD	PA	1705		HARO y MONTERROSO, Fernando José de	S	43	ME		L		X-ME		F-OD M-SB	1							D	
OD	PA	1705		AYALA MARIN, Marcelo de	LI	44	LI	SM	L		OD CH			2							RT	N.S.
OD	PA	1706		COCO PALACIOS, Alonso	S				L					1							AS	N.S.
OS	PA	1707		RECAVARREN, Martín de	.SD	28	ME	TS	L	ME	X-ME	OP	F-XX P-XX M-XX	2	OS	1707		Y	LI		OD CH	
OD	PA	1708		PEREZ BUELTA, Gaspar	S	24	SA AV		L			SU		4				Y	PA		OD SF	10
OD	PA	1709		ALZAMORA URSINO, José de	LI		LI	SM	D					5	OD	1709					OD SF	
OS	PA	1710		MIRONES y BENAVENTE, Manuel Isidro de	LI	19	LI	SM		LI			F-XX	4	OS	1710	MI	Y	LI		RM	7
OS	PA	1711		GOMEZ de ANDRADE, Pedro	LI		LI	SM	B	LI				3	OS	1711	MI	Y			OD QU	17
OD	PA	1722		ALZAMORA URSINO, José de	LI		LI	SM	D		OD SF			5				Y				
OD	PA	1722		MIRONES y BENAVENTE, Manuel Isidro de	LI	31	LI	SM		LI	OS PA		F-XX	4				Y	LI		OD CS	7
OD	PA	1722		GARCIA CATALAN, Sebastián	S	30	SA AV		L			SU		1							D	3
OD	PA	1723		GOMEZ de ANDRADE, Pedro	LI		LI	SM	B	LI	OS PA			3				Y			OD QU	17
OD	PA	1723		ZARATE, Manuel de	S	52	SA		B	RC	X-LI			1							D	8
OD	PA	1723		BON y AZUZA, Sebastián	S	42			L	NA			F-SB	1							D	N.S.
OD	PA	1725		ALZAMORA URSINO, José de	LI		LI	SM	D		OD SF			5				Y	LI		D	N.S.
OD	PA	1726		ARVIZA y UGARTE, Bernardo	LI	33	LI	SM	D	LI		CA		2							OD SF	13
OD	PA	1727		MUÑOZ y GUZMAN, Jaime	S	33	GR		B	GR RC		SU	F-XX P-XX	1						SA	RM	23
OD	PA	1732		SANCHEZ SAMANIEGO, Jacobo José (Marqués de San Juan de Tasso)	S	49	SE		D	SE	SP	SU		1							OD AS	
OD	PA	1733		PEREZ GARCIA, Juan					L	RC	OD SD			2				Y			D	16
OD	PA	1739		CAMPUZANO y SALAMANCA, Damaso José de	S	30	VD	SC	B					1							D	1
OD	PA	1739		MARTINEZ MALO, José Joaquín	S	50	VD	SC	L		OD SF	CA		2							D	N.S.
OD	PA	1740		BAHAMONDE y TABOADA, Juan Bautista	LI	39	CZ		D	GT	TA SF			1	OD	1740					RC	9
OD	PA	1743		AGUIRRE y CELAA, Pedro Antonio	S	32	TO AL		L			OP		2							OD GT	2
OD	PA	1746		CARRILLO de MENDOZA, Luis de	S	41	SI VD AL		L			OP		3			N				OD SF	4
OF	PA	1746	*	SANZ MERINO, Antonio	PA	35	LI	SM	B					2	OF	1746	NA	Y	LI		OD CS	4
OS	PA	1747	*	PEREZ BUELTA, Gaspar Francisco	PA	28	LI	SM SF	D	LI	X-LI	OP		1	OS	1747	NA MN HP	Y			RM	
FI	PA	1695	*	GRILLO y RANGEL, Bartolomé	PA	34	LI	SM	L	LI PA	X-PA	SU	F-XX		FI	1695	NA	Y			OD SF	10
FI	PA	1706		LLORENTE, José de	S	31	SA		L	RC	SP			3							OD QU	
FI	PA	1709		CLAVIJO y MEDINA, Diego	LI	26	LI	SM SF				OP	F-HM	2	FI	1709					RM FI PA	19
FI	PA	1710		GOMEZ TRIGOSSO, Bernardo					L		X-ME			1	FI	1710					D	6
FI	PA	1722		CLAVIJO y MEDINA, Diego	LI	39	LI	SM SF			FI PA	OP	F-HM	2							D	19
FI	PA	1733		FEIJOO CENTELLAS, Juan Manuel	GD	29	ME	SI	L	ME	TA SF	CA	F-OD	1							D	10
FI	PA	1744		ALAS CIENFUEGOS, Esteban Fernando	S		AV AL		L			CA		1								

Post	Audiencia	Year	Native Son	Name	Birthplace	Age	University	Colegio	Degree	Abogado	Previous Post	University Service	Relatives' Posts	Total Appts.	Purchase	Date	Dispensations	Married	Wife's Birthplace	Honors, Order	Departure	Years of Service
AUDIENCIA OF QUITO																						
RE	QU	1776		GARCIA LEON y PIZARRO, José	S		GR		D		AS			I				Y		CH	MT CI	7
RE	QU	1783		VILLALENGUA y MARFIL, Juan José de	S	36	AL TO		B	RC	FR LI		O-Y	4				Y			RE GT	6
RE	QU	1789		MON y VELARDE, Juan Antonio	S	42	OV SA	OV	B		OD SF			3							MT CI	1
RE	QU	1790		ANDINO, Estanislao Joaquín de	S		TO VD		B	RC	FV SF	CA		3				Y	S		D	4
RE	QU	1796		MARQUEZ de la PLATA, Fernando	S	56	SE		D		OD LI		F-AS P-AS O-Y	6				Y	CH	CH	RE CH	5
RE	QU	1801		CORTINES, Francisco Ignacio	S		SE		D		SE RC OD CA	RE		2						CH	MT CI	5
RE	QU	1806		FUENTES-GONZALEZ BUSTILLO, José	S	44	SA		L	RC	OD CZ		O-Y	2						CI	RT	4
RE	QU	1810		MORENO y ESCANDON, Francisco Xavier de	SF	59	SF OM		D	RC	OD LI		F-XX O-Y	4							Ref.	N.S.
RE	QU	1811	*	CORTAZAR y LABAYEN, Francisco	QU	54	LI		D		QU OD SF		F-AB CONQ	3				Y	QU		D	1
RE	QU	1815		ESTERRIPA, Francisco Xavier	S	52	AL		D		OD LI		F-MT	4				Y	SF	CI	RT	4
RE	QU	1819		MANZANOS, Francisco Xavier	S	57	GR		B		GR RC OD CS			3							Ind.	
OD	QU	1704-1719		LAYSEQUILLA y PALACIOS, José de	S				L	RC	OD SD		F-SB	3						CI SA	OD SF	
OD	QU	pre-1719		RUIZ de CASTRO, José	S		SE							I							OD AS	N.S.
OS	QU	1688		CEBALLOS y BORJA, Cristóbal de	LI				L	CS	X-CS			I	OS	1688		Y			RM	25
OS	QU	1689		GONZALEZ CARRASCO, Miguel de					L				F-XX	I	OS	1689		Y			D	6
OS	QU	1689		RICAURTE, Juan de	SF	23			D				F-AB	I	OS	1689		Y			RM	20
OS	QU	1689		RIVAS, Fernando José de	S		GR		L	GR RC				I	OS	1689					D	9
OS	QU	1693		SEGURA y LARA, Diego de					D	LI				I	OS	1693						
OS	QU	1696		LLERA y VALDES, Manuel de	S							CA		I							Ref.	N.S.
OD	QU	1696		SANCHEZ de la BARCENA, Francisco	S	36	VD		B	RC VD	OD MA	SU		2						SA		N.S.
OD	QU	1699		FERNANDEZ PEREZ, Tomás	LI	25	LI	SM	L	LI		OP		2							OD SD	9
OD	QU	1702		SIERRA OSORIO, Fernando de	S	31	VD	SC	L		CA			3							OD SF	15
OS	QU	1706	*	LASTERO de SALAZAR, Lorenzo	QU	44			B	LI			F-HM	I	OS	1706		Y	S		RM	11
OD	QU	1709		LLORENTE, José de	S	34	SA		L	RC	FI PA			3							OD SF	
OF	QU	1709		OLAIS y AROCHE, Esteban	LI				B		PI QU			2	OF	1709	MN	Y			D OS SF	40
OS	QU	1711		LARREA ZURBANO, Juan Dionisio	SF	35			L				F-OD M-CG	I	OS	1711	MN HP	Y	QU	CAL	RM OS QU	15
OS	QU	1712	*	SANCHEZ de ORELLANA, Juan Bautista	QU				D				F-HM	I	OS	1712	NA	Y			RM	5
OD	QU	1720		RIVERA AGUADO, Simón de	S	32	AL	IL	B			OP		I							OS CS	10
OD	QU	1720		RUBIO de AREVALO, Manuel	S					RC				I			HP	Y			RT	35
OD	QU	1720		MARTINEZ de ARIZALA, Pedro	S		AL		L					I						CI	RC	17
OD	QU	1734		GOMEZ de ANDRADE, Pedro	LI		LI	SM	B	LI	OD PA			3				Y			D	26
OS	QU	1738		LARREA ZURBANO, Juan Dionisio	SF	62			L		OS QU		F-OD M-CG	2			MN HP	Y	QU	CAL	RT	15
OD	QU	1739		QUINTANA y ACEVEDO, José de	S	49	TO AL	IL			OD SF	OP	F-SB	2				Y	S		RT	25
OS	QU	1740		CARFANGER y ARTIEDA, Juan Romualdo	LI	25	LI	SM	D	LI	X-LI		F-AB M-AB	I	OS	1740						
OS	QU	1746		SANTA CRUZ y CENTENO, Luis de	LI	30	LI	SF	D	LI			F-AB P-HM M-HM CONQ	3	OS	1746	MN HP			CAL	OD CS	25

Post	Audiencia	Year	Native Son	Name	Birthplace	Age	University	Colegio	Degree	Abogado	Previous Post	University Service	Relatives' Posts	Total Appts.	Purchase	Date	Dispensations	Married	Wife's Birthplace	Honors, Order	Departure	Years of Service
OS	QU	1748		VEGA y BARCENA, Manuel de la	LI	32	LI	SM	D	LI			O-Y	I	OS	1748	HP					
OS	QU	1748	*	NAVARRO, Juan Romualdo	QU	33	SF		D					I	OS	1748	MN	Y	QU	RM OD SF		15
OS	QU	1750		HURTADO de MENDOZA, Gregorio Ignacio (Conde de Cumbres Altas)	LI	28	LI	SM	D		X-LI		CONQ	2	OS	1750		Y		OD CS		35
OD	QU	1764		FERRER de la PUENTE, José	S		OR		D	VA RC	TA SF			3						SD CI	OD LI	14
OD	QU	1765		VEYAN y MOLA, Serafín	S		HU					CA		3				Y	LI	FR LI		10
OD	QU	1766		ALVEAR y ARTUNDUAGA Isidro Santiago		52	LI	SF	D		X-PA			I				Y		D RT		18
OD	QU	1771		LOPEZ de LISPERGUER, José de	CH	63	CH LI	SM	D	LI	OS CS		F-HM M-AB O-Y	2				Y	CS	RT		6
OD	QU	1773		VALERA, Juan Antonio de	S					RC				I							Ref.	N.S.
OD	QU	1773		VELEZ de GUEVARA, Nicolás	SF		SF		D	SF	CA	CONQ		3				Y		AC LI		5
OD	QU	1776		CABEZA ENRIQUEZ, José	S		VD SA	SB	L	RC	SU			I				N		CH	AC LI	2
OD	QU	1776		GACITUA GOMEZ de la TORRE, Joaquín de	S	26	VD SA	SB	L					I							D	I
OD	QU	1779		MUÑOZ y CUBERO, Lucas	S	45	GR		L	GR	CA			4				N			OD LI	17
OD	QU	1779		URRUTIA, Manuel José de	SD	47	ME HA	SI	D	SD	X-SD	CA		4						SD OM	OD GD	4
OD	QU	1779		QUADRADO y VALDENEBRO, Fernando	S	49	VD SA		B		TA SF			2				N		CH	OD LI	17
OD	QU	1786		GONZALEZ SALAZAR, Pedro Celistino	LI	45	LI	SM		SE RC	SP		F-AB	I							D	3
OD	QU	1788		MORENO AVENDAÑO, Juan de	S	45	OS GR		B	SE RC	AG SF			2			MN	Y	QU	SF	AC LI	14
OD	QU	1791		PRIETO y DAVILA, Nicolás	SF	42	SF		D		TA SF	CA	F-AB CONQ	I							D	5
OD	QU	1796		ROA y ALARCON, Bernardo de (Marqués de Piedra Blanca de Huana)	CH	30	LI		D	LI	X-LI	CA	F-AB P-AB M-AB CONQ O-Y	2						CH	OD AS	
OD	QU	1797		SUAREZ RODRIGUEZ de YABAR, Antonio	S	59	AL		L	RC	FI CZ			2				Y			RM	12
OD	QU	1797		CASAS y ALCALDE, Anacleto Ventura de las	S	37	AL VD		B	RC	AG QU			2				Y			RT	5
OD	QU	1798		ARIAS de VILLAFAÑE, José Joaquín de	ME	60	ME	SI	L	ME GT	TA CS		CONQ	I						CH	AX ME	N.S.
OD	QU	1799		MIÑANO y las CASAS, Baltazar	S				D					I				Y			RT	10
OD	QU	1802		MERCHANTE de CONTRERAS, José	S	58	HU		B	RC	FI QU			3				MN			RM	17
OD	QU	1802		FUERTES y AMAR, Felipe	S				D				F-AS O-Y	I							D	7
OD	QU	1810		ARECHAGA, Tomás de	A				D		OP			3							OD SF	N.S.
OD	QU	1810		MUÑOZ y PLAZA, Juan Nepomuceno	CH	34	LI		D	LI	X-CH			I							Ind.	
OD	QU	1811		MANZANOS, Francisco Xavier	S	49	GR		B	GR RC	AG QU			3							OD CS	Ind.
OD	QU	1811		OSTOLAZA y RIOS, José Ramón de	LI	39	LI		D	LI		CA	F-XX O-Y	2				N			AC LI	3
OD	QU	1811		RODRIGUEZ ZORRILLA, José Joaquín	CH	41	CH		L	CH		CA		I				Y	CH			N.S.
OD	QU	1814		CORBALAN, Santiago	A	42	CH		B					2							OD CZ	
OD	QU	1814		IZQUIERDO de la TORRE, Antonio María	S	51	SE ME		D	**ME**	TA ME	SU		3							FV QU	Ind.
OD	QU	1814		LOPEZ de SEGOVIA, Pedro	S	40	TO				TA CZ		F-SB	2						IC	AC ME	4
OD	QU	1814		GALEANO, Manuel	A				D		X-CZ			2						CZ	OD CZ	N.S.

220

Post	Audiencia	Year	Native Son	Name	Birthplace	Age	University	Colegio	Degree	Abogado	Previous Post	University Service	Relatives' Posts	Total Appts.	Purchase	Date	Dispensations	Married	Wife's Birthplace	Honors, Order	Departure	Years of Service
OD	QU	1814		OTERMIN, Miguel	ME	40	LI		D			CA	F-AB	3							OD AS	N.S.
OD	QU	1815		OTERMIN, Miguel	ME	41	LI		D		OD QU	CA	F-AB	3							OD CZ	N.S.
OD	QU	1816		BASTUS y FAYA, Juan	S	43	CE		L		CT	X- SF		2							OD CA	4
OD	QU	1816		CAÑETE y DOMINGUEZ, Pedro Vicente	BA	65	TU CH		D		CH CS	FV CS	CA F-XX CONQ	2				Y		CS	D	N.S.
OD	QU	1818		LOPEZ TORMALEO, Juan	S	62				RC	TA LI			1							Ind.	
OD	QU	1818		MONTENEGRO, Manuel Ascencio	S	40								1							Ind.	
OD	QU	1818		IZQUIERDO de la TORRE, Antonio María	S	55	SE ME		D		ME	FV QU	SU	3							Ind.	
OD	QU	1820		PEÑA y PEÑA, Manuel	ME	31	ME				ME			1								N.S.
FI	QU	1689		RON, Antonio de	S		AL	IL	B					1						SA		19
FF	QU	1709		FAJARDO, Felipe Nicolás	S		AL		L				F-AS	2							AC LI	**9**
FI	QU	1721		ZARATE y ALARCON, Diego	LI	54	LI	SM	D		LI	X- LI	CA	1				Y			D	9
FI	QU	1732		VALPARADA y la HORMAZA, Juan de	S	25	VD SA		L			OP		1							OD AS	10
FI	QU	1743		LUJAN y BEDIA, Juan de	LI	56	LI	SM	D		LI	PI QU	OP	1							D	11
FI	QU	1756		MORALES ARCE y REYNOSO, Andrés de	S	30	SA AL	IL	D					1			MN				RT	1
FI	QU	1758		CISTUE y COLL, José de (Barón de la Menglana)	S	33	HU		D			CA		4				Y	S	CH	FI GT	15
FI	QU	1773		GALDEANO ALONSO y MOTA, Joaquín de	S	33	SA HU		D		PI QU	CA		4				Y			FR LI	5
FI	QU	1793		RUBIANES, Manuel Antonio	A	45	SF		D		SF QU	X- QU	CA	2				Y	QU		OD MA FR BA	3 N.S.
FI	QU	1797		VILLOTA, Manuel Genaro de	S	30	GR		D			CA		6							FR BA	N.S.
FI	QU	1799		IRIARTE, Andrés José de	SF	44	SF				SF BA	FR CONQ	F-AB	2							D	10
FI	QU	1810		LASTARRIA, Miguel José	LI	51	LI CH		D			OP		3				Y			FH BA	N.S.
FI	QU	1811		MAROTO, José Joaquín	S	49	GR OR		D		GR RC	TA CA		2						VE	FI CA	2
FI	QU	1814		NORIEGA DOMINGUEZ, Manuel Antonio	LI	56	LI	SM	D		LI	X- LI	CA	1							D	N.S.
FR	QU	1776		VILLALENGUA y MARFIL, Juan José de	S	28	AL TO		B	RC	PI QU	O-Y		1				Y		CI	FR LI	5
FR	QU	1778		RODRIGUEZ de QUIROGA, José Benito	S	40	AS CS		B	CS	X- CS			1				Y				
FR	QU	1781		YAÑEZ, Antonio Vicente de	S		GR			RC		CA		2				Y	S	AS	FR SF	2
FR	QU	1783		MERCHANTE de CONTRERAS, José	S	39	HU		B	RC	FR SF			3							RT	9
FR	QU	1815		RODRIGUEZ ROMANO, Vicente de	S	61	VD AL		L	VD RC	TA CS			2							AC LI	4
FR	QU	1819		BASTANERO CARRILLO, Eugenio	S		AL			RC				1							Ind.	
FV	QU	1815		IZQUIERDO de la TORRE, Antonio María	S	52	SE ME		D		ME	OD QU	SU	3							OD QU	Ind.
FV	QU	1818		MARTIN de VILLODRES, Diego	S	43	GR		D		GR RC	RE		1							Ind.	

AUDIENCIA OF SANTA FE de BOGOTA

Post	Audiencia	Year	Native Son	Name	Birthplace	Age	University	Colegio	Degree	Abogado	Previous Post	University Service	Relatives' Posts	Total Appts.	Purchase	Date	Dispensations	Married	Wife's Birthplace	Honors, Order	Departure	Years of Service
RE	SF	1776		GUTIERREZ de PIÑERES, Juan Francisco	S	44	SE				SE	AS		1				Y		CH	MT CI	7
RE	SF	1783		FERRER de la PUENTE, José	S		OR		D		VA RC	OD LI		**3**						SD CI	D	7
RE	SF	1792		BELEÑA, Eusebio Ventura	S	56	SI AL		D	RC	OD ME	CA	F-SB	5							RE GD	N.S.
RE	SF	1792		CHAVES y MENDOZA, Luis de	S		SA		L	RC	OD ME	SU	O-Y	5						CI CH	RE SD	5
RE	SF	1797		BRAVO y BERMUDEZ, Manuel	S	58	SA AV	OV	L	RC	OD SD			2				Y		OM CH	D	2

Post	Audiencia	Year	Native Son	Name	Birthplace	Age	University	Colegio	Degree	Abogado	Previous Post	University Service	Relatives' Posts	Total Appts.	Purchase	Date	Dispensations	Married	Wife's Birthplace	Honors, Order	Departure	Years of Service
RE	SF	1800		MUÑOZ y CUBERO, Lucas	S	66	GR		L		GR	OD LI	CA	4				N		CH	RE BA	N.S.
RE	SF	1804		LOPEZ QUINTANA, Antonio	S	63	SA		L	RC	CN	RE CA	CA	3				Y		CI CH	MT CI	N.S.
RE	SF	1805		HERRERA, Francisco Manuel	S	63	GR				GR	FR LI	P-MT O-Y	4				Y			D	I
RE	SF	1811		COLLADO, Juan	S	63	AL SE		B	RC		RE CA	CA F-SB	4								N.S.
OD	SF			ALZAMORA URSINO, José de	LI		LI	SM	D		OD PA			2				Y	LI		OD PA	N.S.
OD	SF	1689		IZUNZA y EGUILUZ, Bernardo Angel	S	29	SA	SB	L					1						SA	RM	10
OS	SF	1693		ALCEDO y SOTOMAYOR, Carlos de	S	37	SN VD		L		QU	X- SF	SU	2	OS	1693		Y		SA	OD ME	8
OD	SF	1700		LOSADA SOTOMAYOR, Luis Antonio de	S		LI SA	AR	L					1				Y			D	18
OD	SF	1703		ARANBURU y MUÑOZ, Vicente de	LI	46	LI	SM	L	RC	AC LI	OP	F-AB	2				Y		SA	D	10
OD	SF	1704		ZUÑIGA, Francisco José	LI	61			L	LI	OS PA			3							•OD CS	N.S.
OD	SF	1706		GRILLO y RANGEL, Bartolomé	PA	45	LI	SM	L		LI PA FI PA	SU	F-XX	2				Y			D	6
OD	SF	1707		MEDINA, Francisco de	S	58	VD		L	RC	OD PA			2				Y	S		D	3
OF	SF	1712		GUTIERREZ de ARCE, Juan	S	34	AL	IL	B	RC	TA SF		F-SB	3						SA	AC LI	
OD	SF	1714		YPES y MIJARES de la QUADRA, Mateo de	S	29	TO SA	CU	L					1						CAL	RM	3
OD	SF	1715		COBIAN y VALDES, Antonio de	S				L		SP			2				Y			OD LI	5
OD	SF	1718		LLORENTE, José de	S	43	SA		L	RC	OD QU			3							RM	N.S.
OD	SF	1718		PEREZ BUELTA, Gaspar	S	34	SA AV		L		OD PA	SU		4				Y	PA		FV LI	N.S.
OD	SF	1719		LOZANO y PERALTA, Jorge	S	64	AL		L	RC	OD SD			2				Y			RT	7
OD	SF	1719		LAYSEQUILLA y PALACIOS, José de	S				L	RC	OD QU		F-SB	3						CI SA	FP CI	2
OD	SF	1719		ENRIQUEZ de IRIARTE, Diego	S	31	GR SA	CU	B					1							D	N.S.
OD	SF	1719		SIERRA OSORIO, Fernando	S	48	VD	SC	B		OD QU		CA	3							FR LI	N.S
OD	SF	1720		MARTINEZ MALO, José Joaquín	S	40	VD	SC	L				CA	2							OD PA	19
OD	SF	1721		QUINTANA y ACEVEDO, José de	S	31	TO AL	IL	L			OP	F-SB	2				Y	S		OD QU	19
OD	SF	1721		SALAZAR, Tomás de	LI	46	LI		D	LI	X- LI		CA	2				N			Ref. OS LI	N.S
OD	SF	1723		ALZAMORA URSINO, José de	LI		LI	SM	D		OD PA			5				Y			OD PA	N.S.
OD	SF	1725		GUERRERO y GALVEZ, Juan Manuel	S	35	SE		D			OP		1							D	8
OD	SF	1731		GARCIA de QUESADA, Silvestre	S	41	SE		L	GR RC	TA SF		F-XX	1				Y	S		D	11
OS	SF	1733		OLAIS y AROCHE, Esteban	LI				B		OF QU			2				Y			D	N.S.
OD	SF	1738		TRESPALACIOS y ESCANDON, Domingo de	S	33	SA		B	RC			O-Y	3			MN	Y	ME	SA	OD ME	N.S.
OD	SF	1738		VERDUGO y OQUENDO, Andrés	S	33	SI VD AL		B				CA	1							D	20
OD	SF	1739		ARVIZA y UGARTE, Bernardo	LI	46	LI	SM	D	LI	OD PA		CA	2							RC	N.S.
OD	SF	1739		AROSTEGUI y ESCOTO, Joaquín de	S	42	HU		D			CA	F-XX P-XX	1				Y			D	35
OS	SF	1742		VERASTEGUI y SARACHO, Antonio de	LI	42	LI SF	SM SF	D	SF	AG SF		CA	1				Y	A		D	33
OD	SF	1746		CASAL y MONTENEGRO, Benito de	S	31	AV SN		D	GA	SP	OP		2	HP			Y	SF		RT	34

Post	Audiencia	Year	Native Son	Name	Birthplace	Age	University	Colegio	Degree	Abogado	Previous Post	University Service	Relatives' Posts	Total Appts.	Purchase	Date	Dispensations	Married	Wife's Birthplace	Honors, Order	Departure	Years of Service
OD	SF	1747		GOMEZ de la TORRE, Jacinto Antonio	S	25	OM VD		B	RC		CA		1							D	7
OS	SF	1748		PEY y RUIS, Juan Francisco	S	28	AL		L	RC				1	OS	1748	MN CM	Y	SF		D	30
OD	SF	1751		CARRILLO de MENDOZA, Luis de	S	46	SI VD AL		L		OD PA	OP		2				N			OD CS	20
OD	SF	1771		GIRALDES y PINO, José Esteban	CS	62			D		OS CS		F-AB	2				Y	CS			N.S.
OD	SF	1773		NAVARRO, Juan Romualdo	QU	58	SF		D		OS QU		F-XX	3				Y	QU		OD GD	4
OD	SF	1776		BASCO y VARGAS, Joaquín	S	47	GR SA	CU	B	GR			O-Y	1						SA	OD GT	6
OD	SF	1778		GUZMAN PERALTA, Alonso de	CH	72	LI	SM	D		CH PI CH	CA		1				Y			RT	N.S.
OD	SF	1778		TAGLE BRACHO, Pedro de	LI	56	LI	SM	D		AC LI		F-AB M-AB	3				Y		CI CA	RT	N.S.
OD	SF	1778		CATANI, Pedro	S		BA		D	CT RC	SP			4				Y			OD SD	6
OD	SF	1779		OSORIO PARDO y LLAMAS, José Bernardo	S		SN			GA RC	OD SD			2							D	1
OD	SF	1781		MON y VELARDE, Juan Antonio	S	34	OV SA	OV	B		OD GD			3							RE QU	8
OD	SF	1782		MESIA y CAICEDO, José de	S	29	GR		D			CA		4				Y	SF	AC ME		12
OD	SF	1783		INCLAN y ARANGO, Joaquín José	S	41	OV		L	AS RC	OD SD	OP		2				Y	S		RT	13
OD	SF	1785		ZUBIRIA, Juan José de	S		SA		D	RC	OD GT	OP		2							D	N.S.
OD	SF	1787	*	MOSQUERA y FIGUEROA, Joaquin de	SF	39	SF		D		SF	TA SF	CA CONQ	4						IC AC ME		8
OD	SF	1790		ESTERRIPA, Francisco Xavier	S	27	AL		D				F-MT	4				Y	SF	CI AC LI		13
OD	SF	1790		HERNANDEZ de ALVA y ALONSO, Juan	S	40	AL		B	RC			O-Y	4				Y	S	OM IC AC ME		20
OD	SF	1795		QUIJANO VELARDE, José (Conde de Torre Velarde)	LI	56	LI	SF	D	LI	X- LI	SU	F-XX M-XX	1				Y	AS	CAL	D	5
OD	SF	1795		CASTILLO y NEGRETE, Manuel del	S	45	SI AL		L	RC	OD GD	OP		6				Y	GD	AC ME		N.S.
OD	SF	1797		GARRIDO DURAN, Pedro	S						X- GD			1								N.S.
OD	SF	1797		INCLAN y ARANGO, Romualdo	S		SA			RC			O-Y	1							RT	6
OD	SF	1798		IBARRA y GALINDO, José Francisco	CA	45	CA		D			CA	F-XX P-HM M-HM CONQ	1							D	N.S.
OS	SF	1799		CORTAZAR LABAYEN, Francisco	QU	42	LI		D		QU		F-AB CONQ	2				Y	QU		RE QU	9
OD	SF	1802		BAZO y BERRI, José	S	33	GR OR		D		GR RC	SU		1				N			D	6
OD	SF	1804		PORTOCARRERO y OJEDA, Andrés	LI	58	LI	SM	D	LI	X- LI		F-AB M-SB	1							D	4
OD	SF	1808		CARRION y MORENO, Joaquín	S	30	GR		D	RC			F-XX	2				Y	XX	IC	OD CS	4
OD	SF	1809		JURADO de LAINEZ, Juan	S	52	SE		B	RC RC		TA CA		2	CM			Y	S			
OD	SF	1810		GARCIA, Manuel	SD	57	SD		D	SD	X- SD			2				Y			OD CA	2
OD	SF	1812		ARECHAGA, Tomás	A				D		OD QU	OP		3							OD SD	1
OD	SF	1813		GARCIA de la PLATA, Manuel	S	63	GR		L	RC	RE BA		F-SB	5				Y	S			N.S.
OD	SF	1814		MOSQUERA y CABRERA, Francisco de	SD	39				SD RC	X			1							Ind.	
OD	SF	1816		CASTILLO y TALLEDO, José Manuel del	LI	43	LI		D	LI	X- LI	OP		1							Ind.	
OD	SF	1816		CHICA y ASTUDILLO, Pablo Mario	QU	53	QU		B		QU		F-XX	1				Y			Ind.	
OD	SF	1816		GARCIA VALLECILLOS, Gabriel Antonio	S	40	SE		D	RC	X- GT	SU		1							Ind.	
OD	SF	1816		NOVAS, Miguel Agustín	S	34	SN		L	RC				1				N			D	1

Post	Audiencia	Year	Native Son	Name	Birthplace	Age	University	Colegio	Degree	Abogado	Previous Post	University Service	Relatives' Posts	Total Appts.	Purchase	Date	Dispensations	Married	Wife's Birthplace	Honors, Order	Departure	Years of Service
OD	SF	1819		BARRIO y VALLE, José	S	56	GT		D	GT	OD GT	SU	F-AB	2				Y			Ind.	
FI	SF	1691		VALCARCEL, Juan de					L					2							AX ME	N.S.
FI	SF	1693		SARMIENTO y HUESTERLIN, Pedro	S	27	SA		D				F-AS P-XX	1				Y	S		RM	11
FS	SF	1708	*	ZAPATA, Manuel Antonio	SF	30	SF		D	SF			F-AB	1	FS	1708	NA MN	Y				9
FI	SF	1720		CASTILLA y LISPERGUER, José Ventura de	LI		LI	SM	B	LI	PI SF		F-HM	1			MN				D	14
FI	SF	1735		ALVAREZ, Manuel Bernardo de	S	35	SA AL		B	RC	TA SD	SU		1			CM	Y			RT	20
FI	SF	1756		PEÑALVER VEQUE, José de	S	58	SI AL		D		PI SF			1				Y			RT	15
FI	SF	1772		RIOS y VELASCO, Luis de los	S		AL VD SA	IL			FI SD			2				Y	S		AS	2
FV	SF	1779	*	MORENO y ESCANDON, Francisco Antonio de	SF	43	SF		D	SF	FR SF			6			CM	Y	S		FR LI	4
FV	SF	1780		MARTINEZ, Manuel Silvestre	S		AL		B	RC	FR SF	CA		3				Y	S		OD GD	3
FV	SF	1783		ANDINO, Estanislao Joaquín de	S		TO VD		B	RC	OD GD	CA		3				Y				6
FV	SF	1790	*	BERRIO y GUZMAN, José Antonio	SF	55	SF		D	SF			CONQ	1				Y		SD CH	D	10
FV	SF	1801		BLAYA y BLAYA, Manuel Mariano de	S	42	OR		B	GR RC	FR SF			5				Y			AC ME	6
FV	SF	1803		GARCIA de FRIAS Diego de	S	53	AL		B	RC	FR SF			4				Y			OD SD	8
FV	SF	c1813		PINILLA y PEREZ, Angel	S	38	AL		B	RC	TA GD			2						IC	OD GD	N.S.
FV	SF	1818		LOPETEDI y GARCIARENA, Agustín de	S	44	GR OR		D	RC	TA ME			1								
FR	SF	1776	*	MORENO y ESCANDON, Francisco Antonio de	SF	40	SF		D	SF	PI SF	CA	F-XX	6			CM	Y	S		FV SF	5
FR	SF	1779		MARTINEZ, Manuel Silvestre	S	46	AL		B	RC	SP	CA		3				Y	S		FV SF	3
FR	SF	1780		MERCHANTE de CONTRERAS, José	S	36	HU		B	RC				3							FR QU	2
FR	SF	1783		YAÑEZ, Antonio Vicente de	S		GR			RC	FR QU	CA		2				Y		AS	RT AS	5
FR	SF	1797		BLAYA y BLAYA, Manuel Mariano de	S	38	OR		B	GR RC				5				Y			FV SF	6
FR	SF	1801		GARCIA de FRIAS, Diego de	S	51	AL		B	RC	SP			4				Y			FV SF	8
FR	SF	1803		MARTINEZ MANSILLA, Manuel	BA	24	SN		B	RC	TA CA	CA		3				Y			AC ME	7
FR	SF	1812		BADILLO, José Manuel de	S					RC			F-SB	1								N.S.
FR	SF	1816		O'HORAN, Tomás Antonio	ME	40	ME	SI		ME		CA		2								N.S.
FR	SF	1818		MIOTA y MATURANA, Eugenio de	LI	34	LI		D	LI	X- LI	OP		1				Y			Ind.	
AUDIENCIA OF SANTO DOMINGO																						
RE	SD	1776		PUEYO y URRIES, Andrés de	S	55	HU		D		OD SD	CA		2			CM	Y	S		RT	24
RE	SD	1780		GAMBOA, Francisco Xavier	GD	53	ME	SI	L	ME	OD ME			4				Y			RE ME	7
RE	SD	1787		URIZAR y BOLIVAR, José Antonio de	S	50	ON VD		L	RC	OD ME			4						CH	MT CI	14
RE	SD	1797		CHAVES y MENDOZA, Luis de	S		SA		L	RC	RE SF	SU	O-Y	5				Y		CI CH	RT	27
RE	SD	1815		CAMPUZANO y SALAZAR, Joaquín Bernardo de	S	47	VD OR		D	RC	OD GT	SU		3							Ind.	
OD	SD	1689		BRAVO de ANAYA, Diego Bartolomé	S		GR					CA	F-XX	1						SC		N.S.
OD	SD	1689		LADRON de GUEVARA, Francisco de	LI	28	LI SA	SM	L	LI		OP		1							D	4
OS	SD	1690		OVIEDO y BANOS, Diego Antonio de	SF	25	LI	SM	L	LI	TA SD		F-OD M-AC O-Y	3						CI	OD GT	9

Post	Audiencia	Year	Native Son	Name	Birthplace	Age	University	Colegio	Degree	Abogado	Previous Post	University Service	Relatives' Posts	Total Appts.	Purchase	Date	Dispensations	Married	Wife's Birthplace	Honors, Order	Departure	Years of Service
OS	SD	1695		CERECEDA y GIRON, Sebastián de	S		SA		L					2							D OS ME	30
OD	SD	1699		MARAÑON y LARA, Marcos	S	29	AL		B		RC SP			1							Ref.	N.S.
OD	SD	1700	*	CHIRINO VANDEVAL, Nicolás	SD	36	ME		B		ME TA SD		F-XX P-XX	2				Y			AC ME	9
OD	SD	c1700		VALDES, Felipe de	S									1							AS	N.S.
OD	SD	1701		FERNANDEZ MOLINILLO, Nicolás	S	30	SA		B					1							D	1
OS	SD	1704		LAYSEQUILLA y PALACIOS, José de	S				L		RC		F-SB	3						CI SA	OD QU	
OD	SD	1704		FERNANDEZ de BARCO, Francisco	S	29	AL		L			SU	F-XX	2				Y	S		FR ME	14
OS	SD	1705		LOZANO y PERALTA, Jorge	S	50	AL		L		RC SP			2				Y	S		OD SF	14
OS	SD	1708		FERNANDEZ PEREZ, Tomás	LI	34	LI	SM	L		LI OD QU	OP		3							FR ME	14
OS	SD	1710		CAVERO, Pablo	S				D		TA SD			1							D	1
OS	SD	1713		PALACIOS, Prudencio Antonio de	S	30	SA HU		B		RC TA SD			3				Y	S		OD GD	N.S.
OS	SD	1718		BELENGUER, Simón	S	41	SA		B		RC AS			1				Y			RT	8
OD	SD	1719		AGUIRRE NEGRO, José Francisco de	S		ON VD SA		B		TA SD	CA		3						CI CAL	AC ME	4
OD	SD	1722		REY VILLAR de FRANCO, Fernando	S	26	SN		B		RC			1								
OD	SD	1724		GRANADO CATALAN, Francisco de	S		SA	OV	L					1							D	4
OD	SD	1726		PEREZ GARCIA, Juan					L		RC			2				Y			OD PA	6
OD	SD	1727		GARCIA CHICANO, Juan Félix	S	56'	SA TO		D		TA SD		F-XX P-XX	1							RT	16
OD	SD	1730		FUENTE y SANTA CRUZ, Francisco Xavier de la	LI	30	LI	SM	B		LI	X-LI	M-XX	1							RC	12
OD	SD	1736		SOTILLO VERDE, José Manuel					D		TA SD	CA		1							D	3
OD	SD	1739		VERDUGO y RIVERA, Alonso	ME	30	ME SA	SI	D		ME		F-XX	1				Y			D	10
OD	SD	1742		VILLAURRUTIA y SALCEDO, Antonio Bernardino	ME	30	ME	SI	L			CA	F-AB	3				Y	S	CI	OD ME	21
OD	SD	1742		CORREA VIGIL, Ramón										1							D	4
OD	SD	1743		VELARDE y CIENFUEGOS, Juan Antonio	S	33	SA VD	SC	B		FI SD	SU		5						MO	OD GT	6
OD	SD	1746		LACUNZA, Andrés de	S	40	SA SI		D			SU		1							D	N.S.
OD	SD	1748		GALINDO QUIÑONES y BARRIENTOS, Francisco de	S	34	SE		D				O-Y	1				Y	GD	SA	OD GD	7
OD	SD	1748		GOMEZ BUELTA, José	S	34	VD		B			CA		1								15
OD	SD	1752	*	URRUTIA, Bernardo de	SD	47			D		SD	X-SD CA	F-HM	1				Y	SD	SD	D	N.S.
OD	SD	1754		CERDA y SOTO, José Antonio de la	S	37	AL	IL	D					1						CH	OD AS	12
OD	SD	1755		PUEYO y URRIES, Andrés de	S	34	HU		D		SP	CA		2			CM	Y	S		RE SD	24
OD	SD	1763		ACEDO, Miguel Calixto de	S	33	SA	SB	L					3							AC ME	10
OD	SD	1764		NAVIA BOLAÑOS, Nuño	LI	30	LI SA	SM OV					F-OD P-XX O-Y	2			MN	Y			OD GT	7
OD	SD	1766		LUYANDO, Ruperto Vicente de	S	32	ZA		D		AR SP		O-Y	4				Y			OD GD	6
OD	SD	1771		MIRAFUENTES, Simón Antonio de	S		HI VD		L		RC TA SD	CA		3							AC ME	6
OD	SD	1772		URIZAR y BOLIVAR, José Antonio de	S	35	ON VD		L		RC TA SD			4						CI CH	AC ME	14
OD	SD	1774		OSORIO PARDO y LLAMAS, José Bernardo	S		SN				GA RC SP			2							OD SF	5
OD	SD	1777		CHAVES y MENDOZA, Luis de	S		SA		L		RC	SU	O-Y	5				Y		CI	AC ME	27

Post	Audiencia	Year	Native Son	Name	Birthplace	Age	University	Colegio	Degree	Abogado	Previous Post	University Service	Relatives' Posts	Total Appts.	Purchase	Date	Dispensations	Married	Wife's Birthplace	Honors, Order	Departure	Years of Service
OD	SD	1777		EMPARAN y ORBE, Agustín Ignacio	S		VD SA	SB	L			OP	P-HM O-Y	3			MN			CI CH	AC ME	10
OD	SD	1777		JOVER y FERNANDEZ, Ramón	S		VA		D	RC	VA	SP		1			CM	Y	S		D	11
OD	SD	1779		INCLAN y ARANGO, Joaquín José	S	37	OV		L	RC	AS	OP		2				Y	S		OD SF	4
OD	SD	1779		BRAVO y BERMUDEZ, Manuel	S	40	SA AV	OV	L	RC		SP		2				Y	S	OM CH	RE SF	18
OD	SD	c1783		CATANI, Pedro	S		BA		D	RC	CT OD SF			4							RE GD	20
OD	SD	1787		FONCERRADA y ULIBARRI, Melchor José de	ME	38	ME	SI TS		ME			X-LI	3				Y			AC ME	16
OD	SD	1797		ALVAREZ CALDERON, Andrés	LI		LI		B	VD	FI SD			1							RT	20
OD	SD	1803		PILOÑA y AYALA, Diego Francisco	S	49	OV		B	RC	IN AS FR GT	CA		2				Y	GT	GD	D	4
OD	SD	1803		RAMOS y FERNANDEZ, José Antonio (Marqués de Casa Ramos de la Fidelidad)	S									1				Y		OM	RT	9
OD	SD	1810	*	MENDIOLA, Ramón de	SD					RC				1								Ind.
OD	SD	1810		ROBLEDO y ALVAREZ, Luis de	SF	31	AL			RC			F-MT M-FI	1								Ind.
OD	SD	1812		ALVAREZ NAVARRO, Antonio Julián	S	35	SA		B	RC	OD CA			2						IC		Ind.
OD	SD	1813		ARECHAGA, Tomás de	A				D		OD SF	OP		3							D	N.S.
OD	SD	1813		GARCIA de FRIAS, Diego de	S	63	AL		B	RC	FR SF			4				Y			OD ME	2
OD	SD	1815		MENDIOLA, Mariano	ME	46	GD		D		GD ME OD GD			2								N.S.
OD	SD	1816		HERNANDEZ de ALVA y ALONSO, Juan	S	66	AL		B	RC	OD ME		O-Y	4				Y	S	OM IC		Ind.
OD	SD	1818		GOMEZ ECHAGAVIA, Agustín	BA	34	AL VA		D		OD GT	CA		2								Ind.
OD	SD	1820		RIVERO y BESOAIN, Mariano de	LI	39	LI		L	LI	TA LI			1								Ind.
OD	SD	1820		RODRIGUEZ de BAHAMONDE, Agustín	S	50	SN		B	RC	DP			1								Ind.
OD	SD	1820		VIDAURRE y ENCALADA, Manuel Lorenzo	LI	46	LI			LI	OD CZ		F-HM	2				Y				Ind.
OD	SD	1821		BIERNA y MAZO, Anselmo de	S	56	HU ZA			RC	OD CA			3								Ind.
FI	SD	1695		MARIN y MUNOZ, Pedro de	S				L			SP		1				Y			D	5
FI	SD	1700		TORRE y ANGULO, Mauricio de la	S	33	AL SA		B	RC				1				Y			RC	16
FI	SD	1717		ESCOLANO, Domingo Nicolás	S		SA							1							Ref.	N.S.
FI	SD	1718		FLORES y GUZMAN, Juan de	S		SI AL	IL	L			SU		1				Y			D	1
FI	SD	1720		CARRILLO MORENO, Juan	S		VD		L				O-Y	3				Y			AC ME	5
FI	SD	1725		BLANCAS y ESPELETA, Martín de	S		SA	CU	B			OP	F-SB	2				Y	ME		OS GD	15
FI	SD	1734		ROJAS y ABREU, Antonio de	S	31	GR SA		L	RC	SP	SU		2				Y			AC ME	5
FI	SD	1739		VELARDE y CIENFUEGOS, Juan Antonio	S	29	SA VD	SC	B			SU		5						MO	OD SD	6
FI	SD	1742		AGÜERO RIVA, José Pablo	S	29	OM VD		B			OP		1						CH	AS	22
FI	SD	1761		ULLOA y SOUSA, Martín de	S	47	SE AV		D		TA SD		F-XX O-Y	1						OD	AS	N.S.
FI	SD	1764		HERRERA y RIVERO, Vicente de (Marqués de Herrera)	S		SA	SB	L					5						CH	AC ME	6
FI	SD	1770		RIOS y VELASCO, Luis de los	S	33	AL VD SA	IL						2				Y	S		FI SF	1
FI	SD	1772		MARTINEZ SANCHEZ de ARAQUE, Diego de	S	36	GR		B	RC	GR			3							RE MA	4
FI	SD	1790		ALVAREZ CALDERON, Andrés	LI		LI		B	VD				2				Y	S		OD SD	20

Post	Audiencia	Year	Native Son	Name	Birthplace	Age	University	Colegio	Degree	Abogado	Previous Post	University Service	Relatives' Posts	Total Appts.	Purchase	Date	Dispensations	Married	Wife's Birthplace	Honors, Order	Departure	Years of Service
FI	SD	1797		LLAVE y MARQUELI, Rafael de la	S	42	AL			RC				3							OD GT	10
FI	SD	1807		CELAYA, José Tomás de	GT						X-SD			1								
FI	SD	1812		CASAS y ALCALDE, Anacleto Ventura de las	S	52	AL VD		B	RC	OD QU			2				Y			Ind.	
FV	SD	1777		HERNANDEZ de ALVA y ALONSO, Lorenzo	S	37	VD		B	RC	SP			4				Y	S		FR ME	2
FV	SD	1780		IRISARRI y DOMINGUEZ, Miguel Cristóbal de	S	39	SE GR		B	RC			CA	4							AC ME	13
FR	SD	1777		IRISARRI y DOMINGUEZ, Miguel Cristóbal de	S	36	SE GR		B	RC			CA	4							FV SD	13
FR	SD	1790		DIAZ de SARAVIA, Julián	S	49	OM VD		L	VD RC	SP	OP		2							FI CA	6
FR	SD	1816		GARCIA VALERO, José Mariano	S	55	GR		B	RC	TA GT			1							D	N.S.
FR	SD	1817		JURADO de LAINEZ, Juan	S	60	SE		B	RC RC	OD SF			2				Y	S	VE	Ind.	

Glossary of Spanish Terms Used

abogado a lawyer, attorney, or advocate

Acordada a special criminal tribunal in eighteenth-century New Spain

agente de negocios an agent or lobbyist who represented the interests of job-seeking clients at court

alcalde del crimen a criminal judge on the viceregal tribunals of New Spain and Lima and also in some of the Spanish audiencias

alcalde mayor magistrate or officer of a district government; **alcaldía mayor,** the office or jurisdiction

alternativa the system of filling a vacancy according to an agreed-upon principle of rotation

arbitrismo reference to the body of writings by sixteenth and seventeenth century Spanish economists and writers describing means of rehabilitating the economy and industry of Spain; **arbitrista,** one of these writers

ascenso the recognized ladder of career advancement through the stages of a bureaucratic hierarchy

asesor an adviser or counselor; one who renders legal opinions; **asesor general,** one who performed this function for a viceroy

audiencia high court of justice, exercising some administrative and executive functions

auditor de guerra a judge-advocate to a military command

bailío or **baylío** knight commander of the Order of San Juan

beca scholarship or fellowship for a student

beneficio here, the purchase of a position from the government

benemérito well-deserving; here, one descended from or related to a conqueror or one of the first settlers

bienes de difuntos intestate property or wealth

caballero a gentleman or knight of a military order

cabildo corporation of a town, or **cabildo eclesiástico,** the chapter of a cathedral

cámara chamber or cabinet; **camarista,** member of such a body

capa y espada literally cape and sword; distinguishes nonlawyers from **letrados** on high councils of state

cátedra academic chair or professorship; **catedrático,** the holder of such a position

cédula royal decree issued by council over the king's signature

chancellería chancellory, one of the highest class of audiencias

charqueña, charqueño native of the province of Charcas

colegio here, professional fraternity, as **colegio de abogados; colegio mayor,** prestigious residence hall and confraternity associated with certain Spanish and Spanish American universities; **colegio menor,** institutions performing same service but lacking prestige and rank

comerciante wholesale merchant, trader

comercio libre free trade within the Spanish Empire

compadrazgo godparentage

comuneros here, supporters of a popular revolt

consejo council; **consejero,** member of such a council

consolidación here, the effort by the crown to appropriate the funds of pious foundations and chantries

consulado merchant guild and tribunal of commerce

consulta a report or brief for the king in Council

contador accountant, auditor; **contador mayor,** chief accountant or head of finances

contaduría de Indias Bureau of Accounts for the Indies

contaduría de tributos Bureau of Accounts for the Indian tribute

coro choir

corregimiento administrative district; **corregidor,** the magistrate or chief officer of such a district

criollo, criolla a Spaniard born in America; a white

Cruzada (Santa) a tax, originally to support a crusade against non-Christians

decano senior member of a court or council

dependencias here, relatives and hangers-on

depósito (en) temporary but indefinite transfer or assignment of an official to another location

derecho law, justice

doblón, doblones a unit of money here valued at four pesos

donativo a contribution, forced loan, or gift

electo appended to an official's title, indicating that the individual has been designated but has not yet taken up duties of the post

encomienda grant or authority over groups of Indians, carrying obligation to Christianize and protect them in exchange for labor or tribute; **encomendero,** holder of such a grant

fiscal crown attorney to an audiencia or council

frey father, if a religious; also used for some knights of certain military orders

futura here, a promise of appointment or succession to a position at some future time; **futurario,** the grantee

garnacha judge's gown or robe

gente decente respectable folk; the upper classes

hábito here, the habit or uniform of a member of a military order

hacendado the owner of a large estate or plantation

hacienda a large estate; here, also the branch of government concerned with treasury affairs, as in **Consejo de Hacienda**

hidalgo gentry, lesser nobility

indios vacos here, a pension awarded by the crown and paid out of the tribute of certain groups of Indians

jubilación retirement, forced or voluntary, from a position; **jubilado,** the person so retired

junta a committee

letrado a university-trained lawyer or holder of legal degree

licenciado a higher degree in a Spanish or Spanish American university, and the person who has taken that degree; also a title given to lawyers

manteista here, a student or graduate from a Spanish university who was not affiliated with one of the **colegios mayores**

maravedí old Spanish coin of the smallest value; often an imaginary unit of value

mérito, méritos here, merit or worth pertaining to one because of intrinsic qualities of birth or position

mesa here, "table" or entity within an administrative unit charged with some particular function, in the sense of "the Latin American desk" of the Department of State

mexicana, mexicano native of New Spain

ministro royal official of substantial rank; here, **oidor, alcalde del crimen,** or **fiscal** of an audiencia

montepío one of many pension or charity associations or sodalities

natural, naturales a "native" of a particular place; one born in a given region; here translated "native son"

Noticias Secretas document written by Jorge Juan and Antonio de Ulloa and presented to the crown in 1749; details abuses and shortcomings of officialdom in Spanish America

número here, a "regular" or statutory position on an audiencia or other body; opposed to a **supernumerario,** which was temporary and above legal limits

oficial officer, official

oficina office, agency

oficio office, employ, function; also, **de oficio,** an "official" action

oficio vendible y renunciable a position that can legally be sold and which the occupant can resell

oidor judge on an audiencia or chancellory; on the viceregal tribunals, possessing civil functions only

oposición formal hearing by which academic chairs are filled

oriundo de indicating residence and association with an area but not necessarily birth

país country, land, region

patria fatherland, native land

peninsular in Spanish America, term denoting Spaniard born in Spain

peso unit of money, usually silver and containing 272 maravedís or eight **reales de plata** or twenty **reales de vellón** unless otherwise noted

peso escudo older unit of money herein valued at ten **reales de plata**

plata silver

plaza here, a position or post; a living

poblador "populator," a first-settler or conquistador credited with settling and developing an area

por vía de by way of

pretendiente here, a job applicant or candidate

prima term referring to the senior academic chair in a particular faculty; opposed to **vísperas,** the junior chair

protomedicato the Board of King's Physicians in a given district

radicado here, used to indicate "rooted" in the sense of having interests or connections with a locale

real acuerdo a meeting of an executive with his audiencia in an advisory or cabinet capacity; the viceroy-in-council

real, reales unit of money, either silver or **vellón,** containing 34 maravedís

recopolación a compilation; when capitalized and italicized referring to the collected laws issued for the governance of the Indies

regente regent; presiding officer over an audiencia, a position created in 1776

reglamento regulation, ordinance

relación a report, memoir, or account; in a court, a statement of the merits of a case; here, often a document attesting to personal qualities and accomplishments presented in support of an appeal for a position or favor

relator an officer of a court whose task it is to prepare the briefs stating the case at hand

repartimiento partition or division; an assessment of taxes; in colonial Spanish America, the right to use Indian labor

residencia formal inquiry conducted at the end of an official's term of office

sala chamber

servicio here, a money payment in return for appointment to office; can also refer to services performed

subdecano the second most senior member of a court or agency

supernumerario a supernumerary or official occupying a temporary or unauthorized extra position on a tribunal; may or may not be salaried

teniente asesor here, the legal adviser and assistant to an intendant or other executive; required to be a university-trained lawyer

título title of office; letter of appointment; also, a title of nobility

togado a **letrado** or judge

vales reales government bonds or notes

vellón a type of money used in Spain consisting of a mixture of silver and copper

vicios vices

visita official inspection into the conduct of officials; **visitador,** the individual conducting such an inspection

Bibliography

The most important sources for this study are located in the two great Spanish archives in Simancas and Seville. The General Archives of Simancas has copies of the titles (títulos) of office for appointees, the starting point of the investigation. In addition to routine provisions for salary, honors, and responsibilities, the typical title provides the name of the appointee, often his university degree, previous position or qualifications (for example, colegial of San Ildefonso or abogado of the royal councils), and, when applicable, membership in a military or civil order. Moreover, it gives the name of the appointee's predecessor and the reason for his replacement; for example, death, transfer or promotion to another position, or retirement. Most sales of appointments and accompanying dispensations are also recorded in the titles. On the basis of the titles, it was possible to construct an overall appointment list for the empire and individual lists for each audiencia. Relaciones de méritos y servicios, relaciones de títulos y grados, and consultas available in the General Archives of the Indies were examined at this point. These documents provided most of the personal and educational information presented in Appendixes IX and X. Limited material was also added from investigations in archives in Lima and Mexico City. In addition, three published works were of particular value: Guillermo Lohmann Villena, *Los americanos en las ordenes nobiliarias (1529–1900)*; José Maria Restrepo Sáenz, *Biografías de los mandatarios y ministros de la real audiencia—(1671 a 1819)*; and Ernesto Schäfer, *El consejo real y supremo de las Indias*.

The archival sources listed include all of the legajos examined specifically for this project; most legajos provided material presented in Appendixes IX and X. The printed sources include all of the works cited in the text and a handful of the most useful other works consulted. The list is not comprehensive and the more than one hundred other studies that yielded only a stray note are omitted.

Primary Sources

Manuscripts

Archivo General de Indias, Seville
  Audiencia de Lima. Legajos 103, 104, 337, 344, 345, 346, 347, 348, 349, 401, 402, 475, 596, 597, 599, 600, 615, 616, 617, 620, 621, 624, 639, 647, 666, 770, 791, 796, 819, 825, 829, 876, 877, 881, 890, 926, 959, 982, 983, 1001, 1006, 1008, 1082
  Audiencia de México. Legajos 10, 11, 240, 377, 378, 384, 385, 452, 521, 522, 523, 524, 525, 526, 670A, 1120, 1121, 1122, 1162, 1188, 1509, 1640, 1641, 1642, 1643, 1644, 1648, 1684, 1697, 1858, 1859, 1861, 1970
  Audiencia de Quito. Legajos 4, 15, 54, 102, 124, 125, 128, 129, 219, 224, 225, 226, 227, 231, 384
  Audiencia de Santa Fe. Legajos 5, 139, 283, 284, 285, 547, 548, 549, 555, 556, 557, 629, 747
  Audiencia de Chile. Legajos 84, 172, 173, 191, 258
  Audiencia de Guatemala. Legajos 186, 274, 408, 409, 415, 425, 504, 556, 617
  Audiencia de Guadalajara. Legajos 128, 240, 241, 242, 243, 244, 245, 304, 305
  Audiencia de Filipinas. Legajos 3, 5, 26, 94, 96, 118, 165, 273, 375, 376
  Audiencia de Santo Domingo. Legajos 3, 236, 273, 300, 921, 922, 932, 933, 1189, 1330, 1332
  Audiencia de Charcas. Legajos 195, 196, 197, 423, 424, 510
  Audiencia de Caracas. Legajos 14, 15, 16, 17, 18, 40, 165
  Audiencia de Panama. Legajos 3, 28, 105, 124, 131, 247, 251, 269.
  Audiencia de Cuzco. Legajo 4.
  Ultramar. Legajos 82, 91, 563, 798.
  Estado. Legajos 3, 88.
  Indiferente General. Legajos 9, 10, 18, 76, 111, 112, 113, 114, 115, 128–70, 190, 231, 232, 379, 499, 525, 526, 538, 668, 799, 800, 801, 802, 819, 826, 867, 869, 870A, 888, 901A, 1284, 1285, 1293, 1308–13, 1322, 1323, 1506–09, 1517–19, 1626, 1627, 1628A, 1628B, 1697, 1699, 1814, 1817, 1818, 1846, 1847, 1888

Contraduría. Legajos 149, 155, 156, 172, 173, 235.
Archivo General de Simancas, Simancas
    Sección XXIII, Dirección General del Tesoro.
    Inventario 2. Legajos 1–14 and 16–100.
    Inventario 13. Legajos 8–9.
    Inventario 24. Legajos 170–189.
Archivo Histórico Nacional, Madrid
    Sección de Códices y Cartularios, legajo 727B.
Archivo General de la Nación, Mexico.
    Historia, Vol. 120
    Correspondencia de Virreyes, Vol. 2.
Centro de Estudios de Historia de México, Condumex, S.A. México
    Fondo Independencia XLI-1, Carpeta 1–24.
Archivo Municipal, Lima.
    Libro de Cabildo 39.

Printed Documents

Ahumada, Juan Antonio de. *Representación político-legal Que hace a nuestro Señor Soberano Don Felipe Quinto, [que Dios guarde] Rey poderoso de las Españas, y Emperador siempre augusto de las Indias: para que se sirva declarar, no tienen los Aspañoles [sic] Indianos óbice para obtener los empleos políticos y militares de la América; y que deben ser preferidos en todos, así eclestiásticos como seculares.* c. 1725; reprinted in Mexico, 1820.

Alejo Alvarez, Mariano. *Discurso sobre la preferencia que deben tener los americanos en los empleos de América.* Lima, 1820.

Blair, Emma Helen and James Alexander Robertson, eds. *The Philippine Islands, 1493–1898.* 55 vols. Cleveland, 1903–1909.

Bolívar y de la Redonda, Pedro de. *Memorial informe y discurso legal, histórico, y político, al Rey N ^{tro} Señor en su real consejo de cámara de las Indias, En favor de los Españoles, que en ellas nacen, estudian, y sirven, para que sean preferidos en todas las provisiones Eclesiásticas, y Seculares, que para aquellas partes se hizieren.* Madrid, 1667.

Hernández y Dávalos, J. E., ed. *Colección de documentos para la historia de la guerra de independencia de México de 1808 a 1821.* 6 vols. Mexico, 1877–1882; reprinted, 1968.

Humboldt, Alejandro de. *Ensayo político sobre el reino de la Nueva España.* Ed. by Juan A. Ortega y Medina. Mexico, 1966.

Juan, Jorge and Antonio de Ulloa. *Noticias secretas de América.* 2 vols. London, 1826.

Konetzke, Richard, ed. *Colección de documentos para la historia de la formación social de Hispanoamérica, 1493–1810.* 3 vols. Madrid, 1953–1962.

Los códigos españoles concordados y anotados. 12 vols. Madrid, 1847–1851.

Mercurio peruano de historia literatura y noticias públicas que da á luz la Sociedad Académica de Amantes de Lima. 12 vols. Lima, 1791–1795.

Moreyra y Paz-Soldán, Manuel, ed. *El tribunal del consulado de Lima.* 2 vols. Lima, 1956–1959.

―――― and Guillermo Céspedes del Castillo, eds. *Virreinato peruano: documentos para su historia. Colección de cartas de virreyes—Conde de la Monclova.* 3 vols. Lima, 1954–1955.

Muro Orejón, Antonio, ed. *Cedulario americano del siglo XVIII.* 2 vols. Seville, 1956–1969.

Recopilación de leyes de los reynos de las Indias. 4 vols. Madrid, 1681; reprinted in 3 vols., 1943.

Sahagún de Arévalo, Juan Francisco. *Gacetas de México.* 3 vols. Mexico, 1949–1950.

Sempere y Guarinos, Juan. *Ensayo de una biblioteca española de los mejores escritores del reynado de Carlos III.* 3 vols. Edición facsimil. Madrid, 1969.

Solórzano Pereira, Juan de. *Política indiana.* 5 vols. Madrid, 1647; reprinted 1930.

Toreno, José María Queipo de Llano Ruiz de Saravia, Conde de. *Historia del levantamiento, guerra y revolución de España: Biblioteca de Autores Espanoles, 64.* Madrid, 1953.

Secondary Sources

Books

Addy, George M. *The Enlightenment in the University of Salamanca.* Durham, N. C., 1966.

Aguado Bleye, Pedro and Cayetano Alcázar Molina. *Manual de historia de España.* 10th ed. 3 vols. Madrid, 1967.

Aguilar Piñal, Francisco. *La Universidad de Sevilla en el siglo XVIII. Estudio sobre la primera reforma universitaria moderna.* Seville, 1969.

Alamán, Lucas. *Historia de Méjico desde los primeros movimientos que preparon su independencia en el año de 1808 hasta la época presente.* 5 vols. Mexico, 1849–1852.

Alden, Dauril. *Royal Government in Colonial Brazil.* Berkeley, 1968.

Atienza, Julio de. *Nobiliario español. Diccionario heráldico de apellidos españoles y de títulos nobiliarios.* 2d ed. Madrid, 1954.

Benson, Nettie Lee, ed. *Mexico and the Spanish Cortes, 1810–1822: Eight Essays.* Austin, 1966.

Beristain de Souza, José Mariano. *Biblioteca hispano americana septentrional.* 3d ed. 2 vols. Mexico, 1947.

Bernard, Gildas. *Le secrétariat d'état et le conseil espagnol des Indes (1700–1808).* Geneva, 1972.

Bobb, Bernard E. *The Viceregency of Antonio Maria Bucareli in New Spain, 1771–1779.* Austin, 1962.

Borah, Woodrow. *New Spain's Century of Depression.* Berkeley, 1951.

Brading, D. A. *Miners and Merchants in Bourbon Mexico, 1763–1810.* Cambridge, England, 1971.

Cadenas y Vicent, Vicento de. *Caballeros de la órden de Santiago que efectuaron sus pruebas de ingreso durante el siglo XIX.* Madrid, 1958.

Carreño, Alberto María. *Efemérides de la Real y Pontificia Universidad de México según sus libros de claustros.* 2 vols. Mexico, 1963.

Cortés, José Domingo. *Diccionario biográfico americano.* 2d ed. Paris, 1876.

Costa, Horacio de la. *The Jesuits in the Philippines, 1581–1768.* Cambridge, Mass., 1961.

Cunningham, Charles Henry. *The Audiencia in the Spanish Colonies as Illustrated by the Audiencia of Manila (1583–1800).* Berkeley, 1919.

Defourneaux, Marcelin. *Pablo Olavide ou l'afrancesado (1725–1803).* Paris, 1959.

Diffie, Bailey W. *Latin American Civilizations: Colonial Period.* New York, 1967.

Domínguez Ortiz, Antonio. *La sociedad española en el siglo XVII.* Madrid, 1964.

———. *La sociedad española en el siglo XVIII.* Vol. 1. Madrid, 1955.

Eguiguren, Luis Antonio. *Diccionario histórico cronológico de la Real y Pontificia Universidad de San Marcos y sus colegios: Crónica e investigación.* 3 vols. Lima, 1940–1951.

Elliott, J. H. *Imperial Spain, 1469–1716.* New York, 1964.

Espejo, Juan Luis. *Nobiliario de la capitanía general de Chile.* Santiago, Chile, 1967.

Esquivel Obregón, Toribio. *Biografía de Don Francisco Javier Gamboa.* Mexico, 1941.

Eyzaguirre, Jaime, ed. *Archivo epistolar de la familia Eyzaguirre, 1747–1854.* Buenos Aires, 1960.

———. *Ideario y ruta de la emancipación chilena.* Santiago, Chile, 1957.

Farriss, N. M. *Crown and Clergy in Colonial Mexico, 1759–1821: The Crisis of Ecclesiastical Privilege.* London, 1968.

Fernández de Recas, Guillermo S. *Grados de licenciados, maestros y doctores en artes, leyes, teología y todas facultades de la Real y Pontificia Universidad de México.* Mexico, 1963.

———. *Mayorazgos de la Nueva España.* Mexico, 1965.

Fisher, J. R. *Government and Society in Colonial Peru: The Intendant System 1784–1814.* London, 1970.

García-Baquero González, Antonio. *Comercio colonial y guerras revolucionarias: la decadencia económica de Cádiz a raíz de la emancipación americana.* Seville, 1972.

García Carraffa, Alberto and Arturo. *Enciclopedia heráldica y genealógica hispano-americana.* 88 vols. Madrid, 1952–1963.

García Chuecos, Hector. *Estudios de historia colonial venezolana.* 2 vols. Caracas, 1937–1938.

García Gallo, Alfonso. *Curso de historia del derecho español.* Tomo 1. 5th ed., rev. Madrid, 1950.

Hamill, Hugh M., Jr. *The Hidalgo Revolt: Prelude to Mexican Independence.* Gainesville, 1966.

Haring, C. H. *The Spanish Empire in America.* New York, 1947.

Herr, Richard. *The Eighteenth-Century Revolution in Spain.* Princeton, 1958.

Humphreys, R. A. and John Lynch, eds. *The Origins of the Latin American Revolutions, 1808–1826.* New York, 1966.

Israel, J. I. *Race, Class and Politics in Colonial Mexico 1610–1670.* London, 1975.

Kagan, Richard L. *Students and Society in Early Modern Spain.* Baltimore, 1974.

Kamen, Henry. *The War of Succession in Spain, 1700–1715.* Bloomington, Ind., 1969.

Lafuente, Modesto. *Historia general de España desde los tiempos más remotos hasta nuestros días.* 30 vols. Madrid, 1850–1867.

Lanning, John Tate. *Academic Culture in the Spanish Colonies.* London, 1940.

———. *The University in the Kingdom of Guatemala.* Ithaca, N.Y., 1955.

Lohmann Villena, Guillermo. *Los americanos en las órdenes nobiliarias (1529–1900).* 2 vols. Madrid, 1947.

———. *Los ministros de la audiencia de Lima en el reinado de los Borbones (1700–1821).* Seville, 1974.

López Cámara, Francisco. *La génesis de la conciencia liberal en México.* Mexico, 1969.

Lovett, Gabriel H. *Napoleon and the Birth of Modern Spain.* 2 vols. New York, 1965.

Lynch, John. *Spain under the Habsburgs.* 2 vols. New York, 1964–1969.

———. *Spanish Colonial Administration, 1782–1810: The Intendant System in the Viceroyalty of the Rio de la Plata.* New York, 1969.

———. *The Spanish American Revolutions, 1808–1826.* London, 1973.

McAlister, Lyle N. *The "Fuero Militar" in New Spain, 1764–1800.* Gainesville, 1957.

MacLachlan, Colin M. *Criminal Justice in Eighteenth Century Mexico: A Study of the Tribunal of the Acordada.* Berkeley, 1974.

MacLeod, Murdo J. *Spanish Central America: A Socio-economic History, 1520–1720.* Berkeley, 1973.

Martínez de Velasco, Angel. *La formación de la junta central.* Pamplona, 1972.

Medina, José Toribio. *Biblioteca hispano-chilena (1523–1817).* 3 vols. Santiago, Chile, 1963.

———. *Diccionario biográfico colonial de Chile.* Santiago, Chile, 1906.

———. *Historia de la Real Universidad de San Felipe de Santiago de Chile.* 2 vols. Santiago, 1928.

Mendiburu, Manuel de. *Diccionario histórico-biográfico del Perú.* 8 vols. Lima, 1874–1890.

Moore, John Preston. *The Cabildo in Peru under the Bourbons: A Study in the Decline and Resurgence of Local Government in the Audiencia of Lima, 1700–1824.* Durham, 1966.

Navarro García, Luis. *Intendencias en Indias.* Seville, 1959.

Olmedo, Mauro. *El desarrollo de la sociedad mexicana.* Vol. 2. Madrid, 1969.

Ots Capdequí, J. M. *El estado español en las Indias.* 4th ed. Mexico, 1965.

Ots y Capdequí, José Mª. *Historia del derecho español en América y del derecho indiano.* Madrid, 1969.

Palacio Atard, Vicente. *Los españoles de la ilustración.* Madrid, 1964.

Parry, J. H. *The Audiencia of New Galicia in the Sixteenth Century.* Cambridge, England, 1948.

———. *The Sale of Public Office in the Spanish Indies under the Hapsburgs.* Berkeley, 1953.

Phelan, John Leddy. *The Kingdom of Quito in the Seventeenth Century.* Madison, 1967.

Pike, Ruth. *Aristocrats and Traders: Sevillian Society in the Sixteenth Century.* Ithaca, N.Y., 1972.

Priestley, Herbert Ingram. *José de Gálvez, Visitor-General of New Spain (1765–71).* Berkeley, 1916.

Restrepo Sáenz, José María. *Biografías de los mandatarios y ministros de la real audiencia — (1671 a 1819).* Bogotá, 1952.

Rezabal y Ugarte, Josef de. *Biblioteca de los escritores que han sido individuos de los seis colegios mayores.* Madrid, 1805.

Rodríguez Casado, Vicente. *La política y los políticos en el reinado de Carlos III.* Madrid, 1962.

Rosenblatt, Angel. *La población indígena y el mestizaje en América.* 2 vols. Buenos Aires, 1954.

Rubio Mañé, J. Ignacio. *Gente de España en la ciudad de México año de 1689.* Mexico, 1966.

Rújula y de Ochotorena, José de. *Indice de los colegiales del mayor de San Ildefonso y menores de Alcalá.* Madrid, 1946.

Sala Balust, Luis. *Reales reformas de los antiguos colegios de Salamanca anteriores a las del reinado de Carlos III (1628–1770).* Valladolid, 1956.

———. *Visita y reforma de los colegios mayores de Salamanca en el reinado de Carlos III.* Valladolid, 1958.

Schäfer, Ernesto. *El consejo real y supremo de las Indias.* 2 vols. Seville, 1935–1947.

Schwartz, Stuart B. *Sovereignty and Society in Colonial Brazil: The High Court of Bahia and Its Judges, 1609–1751.* Berkeley, 1973.

Silva i Molina, Abraham de. *Oidores de la real audiencia de Santiago de Chile durante el siglo XVII.* Santiago, Chile, 1903.

Tibesar, Antonine. *Franciscan Beginnings in Colonial Peru.* Washington, D.C., 1953.

Udaondo, Enrique. *Diccionario biográfico colonial argentino.* Buenos Aires, 1945.

Vargas Ugarte, Rubén. *Biblioteca peruana.* Vols. 7–12. Lima, 1953–1957.

———. *Títulos nobiliarios en el Perú.* 4th ed. Lima, 1965.

Vignau, Vicente. *Indice de pruebas de los caballeros de la real y distinguida órden española de Carlos III desde su institución hasta el año 1847.* Madrid, 1904.

——— and Francisco R. de Uhagón. *Indice de pruebas de los caballeros que han vestido el hábito de Santiago desde el año 1501 hasta la fecha.* Madrid, 1901.

Villacorta C., J. Antonio. *Prehistoria e historia antigua de Guatemala.* Guatemala, 1938.

Zimmerman, Arthur Franklin. *Francisco de Toledo, Fifth Viceroy of Peru, 1569–1581.* Caldwell, Idaho, 1938; reprinted, New York, 1968.

Articles

Artola, Miguel. "Campillo y las reformas de Carlos III." *Revista de Indias* 22:50 (October-December 1952): 685—714.

Barbier, Jacques A. "Elite and Cadres in Bourbon Chile." *The Hispanic American Historical Review* 52:3 (August 1972): 416–35.

Bertrando del Balzo, Conde. "Familias nobles y destacadas del Perú en los informes secretos de un virrey napolitano (1715–1725)." *Revista del instituto peruano de investigaciones genealógicas* (Lima) 14 (1965): 107–33.

Brading, D. A., and Harry E. Cross. "Colonial Silver Mining: Mexico and Peru." *The Hispanic American Historical Review* 52:4 (November 1972): 545–79.

Burkholder, M. A., and D. S. Chandler. "Creole Appointments and the Sale of Audiencia Positions in the Spanish Empire under the Early Bourbons, 1701–1750." *Journal of Latin American Studies* 4:2 (November 1972): 187–206.

Burkholder, Mark A. "From Creole to *Peninsular:* The Transformation of the Audiencia of Lima." *The Hispanic American Historical Review* 52:3 (August 1972): 395–415.

———. "The Council of the Indies in the Late Eighteenth Century: A New Perspective." *The Hispanic American Historical Review* 56:3 (August 1976): 404–23.

Campbell, Leon G. "A Colonial Establishment: Creole Domination of the Audiencia of Lima During the Late Eighteenth Century." *The Hispanic American Historical Review* 52:1 (February 1972): 1–25.

Cútolo, Vicente Osvaldo. "Los abogados en la revolución de mayo." *Tercer congreso internacional de historia de América* (Buenos Aires, 1961): 5: 199–212.

Domínguez Ortiz, Antonio. "Un virreinato en venta." *Mercurio peruano* (Lima), año xxxix, vol. xlix, núm. 453 (enero-febrero de 1965): 43–51.

Durand Florez, Guillermo. "Alta cámara de justicia," *Quinto congreso internacional de historia de América.* 5 vols. Lima, 1972, 5: 264–316.

Ezquerra, Ramón. "La crítica española de la situación de América en el siglo XVIII." *Estudios sobre la emancipación de hispano-américa.* Madrid, 1963. pp. 291–418.

Fisher, John. "The Intendant System and the Cabildos of Peru, 1784–1810," *The Hispanic American Historical Review* 49:3 (August 1969): 430–53.

———. "Silver Production in the Viceroyalty of Peru, 1776–1824." *The Hispanic American Historical Review* 55:1 (February 1975): 25–43.

King, James F. "The Colored Castes and American Representation in the Cortes of Cadiz." *The Hispanic American Historical Review* 33:1 (February 1953): 33–64.

Klein, Herbert S. "Structure and Profitability of Royal Finance in the Viceroyalty of the Rio de la Plata in 1790." *The Hispanic American Historical Review* 53:3 (August 1973): 440-69.

Konetzke, Richard. "La condición legal de los criollos y las causas de la independencia." *Estudios americanos* (Seville) 2:5 (January 1950): 31–54.

Phelan, John L. "El auge y la caida de los criollos en la audiencia de Nueva Granada, 1700–1781." *Boletín de historia y antigüedades* (Bogotá) 59: 697, 698 (November and December 1972): 597–618.

TePaske, John J. Review of J. R. Fisher, *Government and Society in Colonial Peru*, in *The Hispanic American Historical Review* 52:1 (February 1972): 136–37.

———. "The Collapse of the Spanish Empire." *Lex et Scientia: The International Journal of Law and Science* 10: 1–2 (January–June 1974): 34–46.

Tibesar, Antonine. "The *Alternativa*: A Study in Spanish-Creole Relations in Seventeenth-century Peru." *The Americas* 11:3 (January 1955): 229–83.

Tovar Velarde, Jorge. "La audiencia de Lima 1705–1707: Dos años de gobierno criollo en el Perú." *Revista historica* (Lima) 23 (1957–1958): 338–453.

Wright, L. P. "The Military Orders in Sixteenth- and Seventeenth-Century Spanish Society." *Past and Present* 43 (May 1969): 34–70.

Manuscripts

Barbier, Jacques Armand. "Imperial Reform and Colonial Politics: A Secret History of Late Bourbon Chile." Ph.D. dissertation, University of Connecticut, 1972.

Burkholder, Mark Alan. "José Baquíjano and the Audiencia of Lima." Ph.D. dissertation, Duke University, 1970.

Carter, Constance Ann Crowder. "Law and Society in Colonial Mexico: Audiencia judges in Mexican society from the Tello de Sandoval visita general, 1543–1547." Ph.D. dissertation, Columbia University, 1971.

Chandler, Dewitt Samuel. "Pensions and the Bureaucracy of New Spain in the Later Eighteenth Century." Ph.D. dissertation, Duke University, 1970.

Fisher, J. R. "Silver mining and silver miners in the viceroyalty of Peru, 1776–1824." Seminar Paper, University of Liverpool, 1974.

Ganster, Paul Bentley. "A Social History of the Secular Clergy of Lima During the Middle Decades of the Eighteenth Century." Ph.D. dissertation, University of California, Los Angeles, 1974.

Kagan, Richard L. "Education and the State in Habsburg Spain." Ph.D. thesis, Cambridge University, 1968.

Owens, J. B. " 'Feudal' Monarch and 'Just' Monarch: An Interpretation of Fifteenth-Century Castilian Politics." Paper delivered at the 5th annual convention of the Society for Spanish and Portuguese Historical Studies, San Diego, 1974.

Index of Audiencia Ministers

Index

for Audiencia of Mexico, 47; renews sales, 49; bypasses Council of the Indies, 49; temporarily ends sales, 50; duplicity, 50; renews sales, 51; refuses marriage request, 64

Prado y Plaza, Fernando, 23*n*

Professors, and audiencia appointments, 3, 67, 70–72, 75, 76, 123, 124

Protector of the Indians: office considered undesirable by *peninsulares*, 72; service precedes audiencia appointments, 76, 123, 126–27; position abolished, 103

Puente Ibáñez, Gaspar de la, 66

Q

Quadra, Sebastián de la (Marqués de Villarias). *See* Villadarias, Marqués de

Quintana, José de la: and renewal of sales, 49–51

Quito, Audiencia of: size, 2; composition, 30, 96, 126; removal of ministers, 38; suppressed, 39*n*; appointments to, 62; ministers listed, 219–21

R

Radicado ministers (*radicados*): defined, vi, 57; crown perceives problem, 57; important to creoles, 57–58; and sales, 57, 90; and *ascenso*, 58, 124; in New Spain, 59, 60–61, 62–64; after 1750, 125, 126, 134

Recopilación de las leyes de los reynos de las Indias, 6*n*, 8, 104

Reform of audiencias: in 1691, 23; in 1701, 24–27; dispensations sold in case of, 26, 35–36, 42; after 1712, 37–42; and Audiencia of Mexico, 46–47; in 1742, 50; after 1750, 90–92; mentioned, 80, 84–85

Regents: office established, 99, 101; first appointments, 101–2; *peninsulares* desired as, 102–3; advance to Council of the Indies, 102, 128–29; impact on *ascenso*, 128–29; refusal of appointments, 133

Relaciones de méritos: standardized, 105

Río de la Plata, Viceroyalty of, revenue, 87

Ríos, Francisco de los, 69*n*

Rocha Ferrer, Domingo de la, 21*n*

Rodríguez de Solís, Bernardo. *See* Bernardo González de Solís

Rojas y Acevedo, Gregorio de, 65

Romero, Manuel, 129*n*

Royal authority. *See* authority, royal

S

Salamanca, University of: graduates and patronage, 9, 119, 121–22; mentioned, 67, 71, 72

Sale of audiencia appointments: terms of purchase, 19; prices, 19–20, 28, 54; systematic sales begin, 20–21; and appointment standards, 20, 22, 23–24, 32, 33–34, 48, 52–53; and standards of justice, 20, 33, 89; revenue from, 20, 58; protest against, 21–22, 37, 44–45, 49–50; secret sales, 21*n*, 24–25, 45, 51, 52; in Peru, 28–29, 62, 64–66, 78–79, 89; long-term

effect, 13, 34, 35, 36, 43, 54–55, 58–62, 80, 90, 127–28; mechanism for, 32, 49; to minors, 33; causes breakdown of *ascenso*, 34–35, 57, 58; impact on morale, 35; and Philip V, 41, 49–50, 51; in militarily vulnerable areas, 49–50, 53; vary with region, 53–54; effect in New Spain, 59–61; and colegial appointments, 69; to creoles, 74, 75, 76; to native sons, 75, 76, 79–80; criticized by Juan and Ulloa, 89; end of sales, 89, 90; financial impact on purchaser, 92–93; failure to purchase, 1798, 135

Sale of dispensations. *See* Dispensations, sale of

Sale of offices (*oficios vendibles y renunciables*), 18–19. *See also* sale of audiencia appointments

San Juan de Lurigancho, Conde de, 78

San Marcos, University of: graduates favored, 75; eclipse of, 123

Sánchez de Ocampo, Andrés, 21*n*

Santaella, Francisco Marcos, 117*n*

Santa Fe de Bogotá, Audiencia of: composition, 30, 96, 125, 126; removal of ministers, 39, 42; appointments to, 62, 102, 107; ministers listed, 221–24

Santa Fe, University of, 123

Santiago Concha, Juana Rosa de, 65

Santiago de Calimaya, Condes de, 62

Santo Domingo, Audiencia of: size, 2; composition, 30, 59, 60, 61, 90, 125; appointments to, 92, 94; ministers listed, 224–27

Secretary of State for the Indies, office established, 17, 37

Servicios: returned in reform of 1701, 24–25; crown's inability to repay, 41–42

Seville, University of, 72

Spaniards. *See peninsulares*

Suárez de San Martín, Gonzalo, 21*n*

Supernumerary appointments: sale of, 21, 27, 48, 58; impact on *ascenso*, 34, 58, 59. *See also* sale of audiencia appointments

Supernumerary ministers: and reform, 23, 25; appointed, 24, 143; numbers of, 30, 96; permanent position created in Manila, 39*n*; in New Spain, 59, 60, 61

T

Tello de Meneses, José, 21*n*

Teniente asesor: position considered undesirable by *peninsulares*, 72; as background for ministers, 76, 119, 123, 124, 127; importance to *ascenso*, 126–27

Toledo, Francisco de: on moving ministers, 57

Toledo, University of, 122

Toro, Marqués del, 51

Torre Tagle, Marqués de, 66

Túpac Amaru II: revolt mentioned, 106

U

Ulloa, Antonio de, *Noticias secretas* cited, 89, 93

Universities, 9, 67, 71, 72, 75, 119, 121–22, 123. *See also* professors

University service of ministers, 67, 71, 122–23